WHO'S
POISONING
AMERICA

WHO'S POISONING AMERICA

Corporate Polluters
and their Victims
in the Chemical Age

Edited by
RALPH NADER
RONALD BROWNSTEIN
JOHN RICHARD

Sierra Club Books
SAN FRANCISCO

This book is dedicated to the victims of environmental violence who, by fighting back courageously in communities across this country, are defining a new kind of patriotism.

The Sierra Club, founded in 1892 by John Muir, has devoted itself to the study and protection of the earth's scenic and ecological resources —mountains, wetlands, woodlands, wild shores and rivers, deserts and plains. The publishing program of the Sierra Club offers books to the public as a nonprofit educational service in the hope that they may enlarge the public's understanding of the Club's basic concerns. The point of view expressed in each book, however, does not necessarily represent that of the Club. The Sierra Club has some fifty chapters coast to coast, in Canada, Hawaii, and Alaska. For information about how you may participate in its programs to preserve wilderness and the quality of life, please address inquiries to Sierra Club, 530 Bush Street, San Francisco, CA 94108.

Library of Congress Cataloging in Publication Data
Main entry under title:

Who's poisoning America.

   Bibliography: p. 458

   Includes index.
   1. Pollution—Toxicology—United States. 2. Pollution—United States. I. Nader, Ralph. II. Brownstein, Ronald. III. Richard, John, 1954–
RA566.3.T69   363.7'3'0973   80-29608
ISBN 0-87156-276-6

Jacket design by Paul Bacon

Book design by Paula Schlosser

Printed in the United States of America

10   9   8   7   6   5   4   3   2   1

Contents

Preface

CHEMICAL WASTE DUMPS number in the tens of thousands throughout this country. Additional volumes of waste have been illegally thrown into sewers, ravines and parking lots, or have been abandoned in urban warehouses. Millions of Americans are drinking water contaminated with toxic substances or finding water sources quarantined by health authorities. Residues of chemical pesticides pervade the food supply. Thousands of new chemical compounds are entering the human environment each year, and each year the evidence grows of even greater danger.

This epidemic of chemical violence spilling across the land and waters of America provokes a new patriotism: to stop the poisoning of the country. It invites a new kind of neighborhood unity: to defend the community, the children and those yet unborn. It highlights the severe deficiencies in our laws, in the flow of information and in the response of our public officials. It reflects a destruction of civilized standards by corporate executives. It is victimization without representation and, for the most part, without realization. It is a massive flood of quiet, cumulative, often invisible violence, too charitably called pollution. Although it usually avoids immediate pain it silently generates future devastation.

But the future is now, and there may be worse to come. The names "Love Canal," "Kepone," "West Valley," "Reserve Mining," "2,4,5-T," "PBB," and "PCB" will be remembered for early tragedies in America's long struggle for self-defense against callous internal chemical warfare. The names of the companies responsible for these toxic spills and toxic dumps are seen on television or in the press. However, almost no one knows the names of the managers behind the company images.

In contrast, the victims know one another's names. Ask the farmers whose land and kin were contaminated with a fire retardant called PBB that was carelessly mixed with feed grain sold in Michigan. How well the families at Love Canal came to know each other as they learned that they themselves were going to have to impose accountability.

If at the outset the liabilities of a technological choice are known to society, faustian bargains are avoidable. Information about the effects of new substances should be made available to the public before the food chain and drinking water are contaminated. People need to know that many industrial materials are not necessary for a prosperous standard of living. Alternatives to these hazardous chemicals have been found—but, as a rule, only after an environmental disaster prompted a reevaluation.

PCB, PBB and Kepone are no longer produced, and most uses of 2,4,5-T are suspended; industry has adapted, agriculture continues. Reserve Mining Company could have disposed of its daily wastes onshore as did its smaller competitors nearby. And Hooker Chemical Company certainly knew how to contain its myriad of chemicals more safely.

The economic burden on society would have been a tiny fraction of the cleanup and compensation costs had the companies introducing these products acted responsibly. The human casualties would have been avoided, along with the profound community and family disruptions. It was not lack of knowledge, but the lack of corporate interest, that resulted in the transformation of the living environment into the lethal sewers of industry. Interest in controlling the damaging aspects of technology is more likely to come from the potential victims and from parents who care for their children than from the corporate perpetrators.

The case studies in this book were chronicled by writers in the affected communities—Jo-Ann Armao from Buffalo, New York, Jim Detjen from New York's Hudson Valley, Ellen Grzech from Michigan, Brian Kelly from Virginia, Alden Lind from Minnesota, Russell Mokhiber from Niagara Falls, New York, and John David Rabinovitch from California. Having lived through these toxic dramas, the writers have a deep understanding of the injustices these communities experienced.

This volume is a description of calamities but not of despair. Lessons can be learned and resolve can be strengthened to prevent future toxic tragedies and diminish the present hazards of toxic dumping. The victims depicted in these pages are also teachers of a broad audience. They have learned much that they do not want others to learn in the same way. Their suffering is, in its own poignant language, a call to action for all Americans to save their country, protect the integrity of the air, land and water, and defend future generations. Their experiences should be appreciated as more than just a plea to arouse our conscience and assume our civic duties. They must also stimulate both a fundamental reassessment of technology in terms of human values and a commitment of our time and energy to connect our political economy to human health and happiness.

RN
JR
RB

ACKNOWLEDGMENTS

Those who researched material for this book were Judy Fox, Dave Corn, Janet Wilson, Leonard Shen, David Ambler, Larry Weintraub, Matt McCormick, and Ruth Cohen.

Delores Kocsmaros, Margret Sharkey and Marilyn Osterman each helped with the typing of the manuscript.

Those who graciously read parts of the manuscript, and who offered many helpful comments, were Mike Reich, Denny Dobbins, Erik Jansson, Walter Hang, David Lennett, Dr. Marvin Resnikoff, Bill Butler, Dr. Sidney Wolfe and Steve Howard.

Foreword

THE WOMEN WHO LIVE at Love Canal are much like myself. We are housewives and mothers. Most of us have a high school education. Our biggest investments are our homes, our most precious assets our children. By and large, we led a simple life, staying close to home and watching our gardens and families.

Since the toxic wastes were discovered escaping from Love Canal, this way of life has changed. The state Health Department warned us not to grow gardens, and to limit the amount of time we spend in the basements of our homes.

The decisions we have had to make have changed too, from the normal concerns of every day life to: where can we move that's safe? Will my baby have leukemia? Will my daughter ever have a normal pregnancy, a normal baby? The fears and uncertainty of the past two years have created many stresses and many anxieties.

They have also created a sense of determination in our neighborhood. The motherly instinct to protect a family has surfaced in many women, giving them the drive to fight for their lives, their children and their futures. This instinct to fight changed many old ideas. Women who once looked down at people picketing, being arrested and speaking up against the giant corporations in our area, are now doing those very things. These women have worked in our office, conducting health surveys by phone and going door to door in the community.

They have protested before the Governor of the state and his top aides. They have given two years of their lives to this effort to protect their families.

Although Love Canal may be the best-known, it is certainly not the only toxic disaster in the country, as this book shows. Because we have received nationwide attention—national media coverage—people from around the country call to ask us questions. They want to know what we have done, how we organized the residents, and how we managed to reach our goal: permanent evacuation of all families who wish to leave Love Canal, with the state purchasing their homes.

It was not easy. It did not come without sacrifice. Lives changed. Before we began this fight, most of the women at Love Canal were homemakers: dinner was ready at five, laundry done and children cared for. Now in many households dinner is not ready at five o'clock, laundry is not quite done and a neighbor takes the children around. *Truly* taking care of the children—and ourselves—required that these sacrifices be made.

It also required a change in attitude, an understanding of the extent of the toxics problem. From Love Canal, it is clear that the problem of toxic wastes affects us all. There are thousands of known poisonous dumps across the country, and many that, so far, are unknown. Because of the costs involved to clean and monitor each site, both government and industry would prefer to ignore them. While government delays, innocent people are being hurt. Industry, meanwhile, continues to make profits.

The only way we will avoid new Love Canals, and more disasters like those described in this book, is if people force the government to implement laws requiring industry to properly dispose of their toxic wastes, which now pollute our land, air and water. Pressuring the government and the corporations to take these steps is the responsibility of all of us: taxpayers, consumers, victims.

Lois Marie Gibbs
President, Love Canal Homeowners' Association

Chapter 1

The Toxic Tragedy

RONALD BROWNSTEIN

CLARENCE SWAEBY DIDN'T GO into the mines until he was 46. Back in Indiana he had been an auto mechanic. When he moved with his wife and two children to Colorado during World War II, he worked first as a rancher east of Pueblo.

Then, during the early 1950s, Colorado experienced a modern-day gold rush—a uranium boom catalyzed in 1948 when the federal Atomic Energy Commission said it would buy all the uranium people brought in—and Swaeby was swept along. Uranium mining in those days often was no more than two or three people in a jeep going into the hills, finding the uranium, digging it up and bringing it in.

For years, that's what Swaeby did for a living. In time, he stopped freelance mining and signed on with the Cotter Corporation. The work was about the same. Swaeby was a property investigator—the scout who searched out new sites and determined whether they were worth mining. Like other miners, he carried no radiation-monitoring equipment, and as the first one onto many sites, he often had no idea how much radiation he was being exposed to.

When Swaeby stopped working underground in 1969, he was estimated to have been exposed to approximately 8,000 working level months (WLM) of radiation. (A WLM of exposure is equivalent to 100 picocuries of radiation per liter of ambient air for 173 hours.) As evidence of the cancer-causing properties of uranium grew, the standard was lowered, and lowered again. The current lifetime maximum exposure for miners is 120 WLM. The federal government suspects this standard also may be too high and is currently reevaluating its adequacy.

In 1974 Swaeby retired. Four years later, surgeons removed his cancerous left lung. On August 29, 1979, he died of cancer. He was the victim of an epidemic: Throughout the West, uranium miners have been dying of lung cancer at a rate greatly above the national average.

"If I had known my body was going to last this long, I'd have taken better care of it," Swaeby told a reporter shortly before he died. During the interview, he was breathing pure oxygen through a tube attached to his nose. "One thing I would have done was not work in a uranium mine. . . . There's no way I would let my two boys work in a uranium mine if I could help it."[1]

The first in Suzanne Prosnier's family to become sick was her 10-month-old son. Shortly after the family's 1973 move to Scottsdale, Arizona—which borders an agricultural area where pesticides are used extensively—the boy began waking up in the middle of the night, "writhing and thrashing about in his crib, crying," Mrs. Prosnier said. "The baby began to have what seemed to be repeated respiratory infections and several times had giant hives. . . . As he learned to speak, he was able to communicate to me that he had a headache and very bad cramps in his legs."

Next was her 10-year-old son, who came down with stomach aches, fevers and chest pains. Once he waved his arms about wildly, feeling "as though the room were closing in on him."

Then Mrs. Prosnier's two teenage daughters developed skin rashes, sore throats and severe headaches. One began suffering pains in her bladder. The other stopped menstruating. Her teenage son ran a fever of 105° and developed an ulcerated throat. "He experienced several episodes of profuse salivation,"

Prosnier remembered, "such that he once had to sit for the entire day with a plastic bucket to spit and drool into."

In 1975 Prosnier was pregnant. Six weeks before the baby was due she began to hemorrhage. The baby was born two weeks premature and weighed only five and three-quarter pounds. He had an unusually large head. When he was two months old, he underwent hernia surgery.

By 1976 Prosnier's husband, too, was sick. Along with the rest of the family, he suffered stomach aches, chest pains and violent headaches. Prosnier asked the city to check the family's water; it refused, telling her the tests were too expensive. She thought she might be "poisoning everyone" so she bought a new set of pots and pans. Nothing helped. The illnesses continued.

One day in October, her one-and-a-half-year-old son went outside to play in the backyard. Soon she heard him screaming; he had collapsed, drenched in perspiration. He began to suffer from stomach spasms, which came three times an hour for the next three days. A few days later he began to cough severely and to bleed from the rectum. "In short," she testified later, "our life was a nightmare . . . I would go to bed at night, uneasy, wondering what was happening to all of us."

She remembers the day she began to understand what was happening to her family: "On the morning of September 11 [1978] my children went outside to wait for a ride to school and came back running and crying that their noses were burning. When I went outside, my nose burned also, in fact, so did my chest when I breathed in an unusually pungent odor. My 5 year old suffered an alarming bronchial spasm, asthmatic attack, the first of his life. . . ." When she took her son to be checked over, the doctor told her that the attack could have been triggered by drifting pesticides, such as those sprayed on the cotton, lettuce and sugarbeet fields across from her home.

Suzanne Prosnier soon learned that hundreds, even thousands of other families living adjacent to the farmlands were suffering from similar ailments. She began to fear the pesticides —toxaphene, bolstar, parathion and others—that drifted from spray planes flying as little as 100 feet away from homes. When she called the state's Pesticide Control Board, she was told that "what was being sprayed was no more harmful than table salt or aspirin."

But her family and her neighbors continued to contract illnesses.[2]

Clarence Swaeby and Suzanne Prosnier and dozens of other people in this book all are victims of environmental violence, of industry's disregard for the long-term implications of its negligence or callousness, and of government's failure to defend the people's health from industrial plunder. We have begun to pay the bill for that failure. Our descendants will pay for hundreds of years to come.

For the American economy, World War II was a watershed. It was more than the end to the long Depression and a sudden push forward into a new age of affluence. The war had been a vast proving ground for American industrial might, particularly for its technological ingenuity. By necessity, the war accelerated the development of new technologies in all segments of industry. Nylon, the first synthetic fiber, was used for parachutes.[3] Germany and then the United States made tires from synthetic rubber when natural supplies were cut off. (From 1942 to 1945 alone, synthetic-rubber production increased from fewer than 4,000 tons to 719,000 tons.)[4] Plastics served in bugles, gas masks, urinals and insulation for radar cables. Chemical warfare research generated, as a byproduct, new insecticides. The Manhattan Project unlocked the awesome power of the atom.

After the war, the new products made their way into the domestic marketplace. Nylon was used in hosiery and automobile upholstery. In the early 1950s, the new synthetic fibers acrylic and polyester joined nylon in the fabrics of clothing. (The synthetics' share of fiber markets then doubled every five years between 1951 and 1970.)[5] In Detroit's new cars, natural rubber increasingly was displaced by its synthetic competitor. The new pesticides began to be spread over fields and forests;

the total pounds sold tripled between 1947 and 1951.[6] Plastics appeared in great quantities in items ranging from containers and toys to paneling, toothbrush handles and record albums. And under the "Atoms for Peace" program, the development of nuclear electricity generators began.

The results were overwhelming. Production of synthetic chemicals had begun seriously in the early part of the 20th century, when the basis of the chemical industry shifted from coal-tar derivatives to compounds made from petroleum, a less expensive source. Yet not until after World War II did the industry take off. Production of synthetic organic chemicals rose from 1.3 billion pounds in 1940 to 49 billion pounds in 1950. The total reached 96.7 billion pounds in 1960 and rose again to 233.1 in 1970. By 1978, production had reached 320 billion pounds.[7]

As the chemical industry expanded, no one in government seemed to be watching. The government required only a few chemicals, such as pesticides used on food crops, to be tested for possible health problems before being put on the market. Nor did the government monitor workplace exposure. The chemical industry and the government were not oblivious to the possible product liability or workplace hazards of the new substances. But when research was done at all, it usually focused on the dangers that are acute. The chronic effects and long-range consequences of the chemicals' use and disposal in the air, water and on land often were ignored in the expansive mood accompanying untrammeled growth. In some cases, as we shall see, companies anxious to expand production of new products covered up evidence of long-term dangers.

When public awareness about the dangers of chemicals increased in the early 1970s, the business community—heavily committed now to synthetic chemicals—was obdurate. Rather than accepting responsibility for long-term dangers and taking steps to control the technology, industry mobilized politically to resist the complex and expensive remedial measures proposed by government. The battle continues today and shows no signs of easing.

EXPANDING AWARENESS

The environmental movement that questioned these chemicals began in earnest as part of the reexamination of values engendered by the war in Vietnam and the civil-rights campaign of the early 1960s. Environmentalism offered an alternative to the consumption ethos of the Depression/World War II generation. This alternative was called ecology, after the branch of study that examines the "intricate web of relationships between living organisms and their living and non-living surroundings," as one writer put it.[8] "Ecology" was, at the time, a way of life as much as a science.

In 1970 the movement bloomed. President Richard Nixon, as his first official act of the decade, signed the National Environmental Policy Act (NEPA), requiring assessments of the environmental impact of federal programs and creating the Council on Environmental Quality (CEQ).[9] Like long-pent-up water rushing through a hole in a dam, other environmental actions poured out behind the NEPA. Congress toughened legislation to clean the air and water. The Environmental Protection Agency (EPA) was established, consolidating under one roof the government's programs against pollution of air, water and land. Congress created the Occupational Safety and Health Administration (OSHA) to police the nation's workplaces.

In its first report, issued in August of that year, the CEQ summed the optimism of the time. Acknowledging that the damage was immense, the Council predicted:

> Historians may one day call 1970 the year of the environment. ... 1970 marks the beginning of a new emphasis on the environment—a turning point, a year when the quality of life has become more than a phrase; environment and pollution have become everyday words; and ecology has become almost a religion to some of the young.[10]

In those heady days of environmental optimism, few had any idea that the worst was yet to come. "We ... gained success in combatting gross threats to our air and water," said Gus Speth, chairman of the CEQ in 1980, "only to discover whole new phalanxes of subtle menaces, whose danger and obstinacy often vary in inverse proportion to their ability to be quickly and easily understood."[11]

The need for so many different laws, offering protection from such a broad range of exposures, illustrated how thoroughly dangerous chemicals had dispersed in the environment. The chemical companies had become a large and powerful industry. Consider:

—In 1979, 32 companies each had annual chemical sales of $1 billion or more. DuPont, the largest chemical company, had sales of $9.7 billion; the Dow, Exxon, Union Carbide and Monsanto companies each had sales of more than $5 billion.[12]

—Sales are increasing. Each of the top 50 chemical producers sold more chemicals in 1979 than in 1978. Each sold more in 1978 than the year before. In 1978, only DuPont had sales greater than $5 billion; in 1979 the other four companies mentioned above each passed that total.[13] Overall chemical production increased after 1968 at an annual rate of 6 percent; by comparison, all manufacturing grew at the rate of only 3 percent.[14]

Though the 1980 recession has hurt the industry, the chemical lobby has been a loud and effective voice in Washington and across the country. Its trade group, the Chemical Manufacturers Association (CMA), has undertaken an expensive, highly visible campaign to restore the industry's sagging public image. (The association not long ago raised its dues 85 percent.) In one recent poll, the chemical industry ranked the lowest among 13 industries in public image.[15] In a June 1980 "confidential" CMA poll, majorities in all but one sample category "felt the industry was . . . 'unconcerned' about the welfare of the average person."[16] "I don't need any polls to tell me that the chemical industry is not held in high esteem," Robert Roland, the head of the CMA, has said. "The public accepts the benefits of chemicals out of hand, but they do not believe the industry is doing enough to manage the risks. We believe we are acting responsibly."[17]

Whether the public even has been given a chance to balance the benefits against the risks of the industry is something we will look at later. But no doubt can exist that chemicals are ubiquitous. Some 55,000 different chemicals now are in commercial use.[18] "We are living in a time of organic chemicals," notes author Dr. Samuel S. Epstein, "not just familiar ones, but exotic ones which have never previously existed on earth and to which no living thing has previously had to adapt."[19]

This proliferation of chemicals has raised an elemental concern: Is America being poisoned? Questions about the health effects of pollution and chemicals have been raised before. Air pollution combined with atmospheric inversions caused tragedies in several cities, from London, England, to Donora, Pennsylvania, in the late 1940s and early 1950s. In 1958, the Delaney clause (named for New York Congressman James J. Delaney) prohibited the use of food additives proved to cause cancer in "man or animal."[20] Rachel Carson's epic book *Silent Spring* had questioned the use of pesticides in the early 1960s.

In the mid-1970s the questions raised in the forties, fifties and sixties were answered with chemical disasters that crowded each other off the front page. The synthetic chemicals that appeared after World War II in products of all shapes and sizes also were appearing where they never were meant to be, and often with tragic results. One of those places was the Niagara Falls community of Love Canal. Chemical wastes buried there more than 30 years ago reached into the lives of hundreds of middle-class families living in neat rows of homes. Women there have had more miscarriages than normal; an unusual number of children have been born with birth defects; serious illnesses have wracked families. Love Canal is the site of the first federal emergency declared in response to a human-made disaster.

Love Canal has brought home the threats of the new industrial era. That synthetic chemicals improperly used or disposed of can cause great harm no longer is a theoretical proposition.

The polluted lakes and streams, the fish kills and eyesores of the fifties and sixties were only the first, most visible manifestations; the real impact of the belching smokestacks and autos is being realized only many years later—in the elevated levels of lead measured in the bloodstreams of young children and in the more frequent occurrence of respiratory diseases. The true cost of dirty rivers is revealed in higher rates of cancer among the people who draw their drinking water from those waterways.

At Love Canal, these delayed effects of the new technology have become piercingly evident. And a few months after the public heard about Love Canal, the Three Mile Island nuclear accident sliced through the rhetoric of the nuclear industry. Invulnerability to accident cannot be designed into a reactor. Nor has any means of handling the long-lived nuclear wastes been found; the Three Mile Island accident followed the failure of the nuclear reprocessing plant in West Valley, New York. Evidence mounted of the menace of pesticides. DDT was removed from the market. Other pesticides, too, have been banned. But their residues remain, in the environment and in our bodies.

Workers have been exposed to toxic chemicals since their production began. Every few years, the increases in the production of chemicals are punctuated by the uncovering of occupational disease epidemics in such towns as Hopewell, Virginia. The stricken locales emerge, then vanish from the public eye, like augurs. But now the danger, no longer confined to the workplace, pervades the country. This increasing threat is reflected in the continued spread of cancer, the only cause of death to rise in the United States since 1900—and a disease with deep environmental roots.[21]

This book is a report on the victims of these new technologies. We consider seven environmental disasters of the past decade: the infiltration of Michigan's food supply by the toxic chemical PBB; the Kepone poisoning of Hopewell, Virginia; the failure of the West Valley nuclear reprocessing plant; General Electric's pollution of the Hudson River with the virtually indestructible chemical PCB; the use of the herbicide 2,4,5-T in

California; Reserve Mining's pollution of Lake Superior with asbestos-like wastes; and the contamination at Love Canal. In each case, we examine the toll on citizens and their communities exacted by these hazardous chemicals and processes.

None of these tragedies, however, has turned up in the ledgers of the giant corporations producing the chemicals or of the power plants and steel mills and other industries pouring wastes into the air and water. And this, as we shall see, is the essence of the environmental dilemma. Environmental and occupational health regulations have been a belated attempt to assess industries for the true social costs of their products. That accounts for those regulations being so fervently resisted; to want a free ride prolonged forever is natural.

But in the wake of Love Canal and Reserve Mining and Kepone and PCBs and all the other disasters of the decade, the extent of this free ride's cost began to emerge. Protecting the environment was no longer a question only of cleaning up rivers unfit for swimming or of protecting farm lands threatened by suburban sprawl, or even of saving waterfowl endangered by oil spills (though all these remained concerns).

It was a question of saving ourselves.

THE HEALTH EFFECTS OF
ENVIRONMENTAL POLLUTION

Cancer has been the disease—actually, it is a group of diseases—that has made public health an integral part of the environmental debate. Business officials and lobbyists, sensing the public concern, have begun asserting there is no major cancer problem in this country and (except for some recalcitrant supporters of the tobacco industry) attributing any increase in cancer rates to smoking. "It . . . seems that of the 'environmentally-induced' cancers by far the majority come not from occupational hazards," editorialized the *Wall Street Journal*, "but from factors outside the workplace like habits and cultural patterns, particularly cigarette smoking."[22]

These defense maneuvers cannot obscure the facts. More than 56 million Americans—one-quarter of the current population—eventually will develop some form of cancer.[23] In 1980 alone, 785,000 new cases of cancer appeared, and 405,000 deaths were caused by the disease.[24] Despite billions of dollars spent looking for a cure, between 1969 and 1976 the death rate for cancer rose .9 percent annually for white males and .2 percent for white females; the rate of new cases is increasing 1.3 percent yearly for men and 2.0 percent for women.[25] Cancer is the single greatest cause of death for children between the ages of three and fourteen,[26] and the second only to heart disease in causing deaths at all ages.[27]

Cancer did not begin in the 20th century. But cancer has thrived; it is the only major cause of death that has increased in this century—and it has increased dramatically. In 1900, cancer was only the 10th leading cause of death, accounting for about 3 percent of the total. In 1930, it accounted for 9 percent of all deaths and ranked as the sixth most frequent cause. By 1975, cancer annually caused one-fifth of the deaths in the United States.[28]

The introduction of new chemical products into the environment since World War II parallels the increased cancer rate since then. Experts now believe that is no coincidence. In 1964, the World Health Organization (WHO) determined that environmental factors cause 60 to 80 percent of all cancers. Many scientific bodies have since concurred with WHO's judgment. Recently, the president's Toxic Substances Strategy Committee (TSSC)—representing 18 federal agencies—reported that 80 to 90 percent of all cancers may be environmentally caused.[29] The Department of Health, Education and Welfare has estimated that 20 percent to 38 percent of all cancer deaths are work-related.[30] One fact pointing up the preeminence of environmental factors is the wide variation in cancer rates for different countries and even for different regions of large countries. This pattern was painted starkly in 1975 with the publication by the National Cancer Institute of the *Atlas of Cancer Mortality for U.S. Counties: 1950–1969,* which reveals cancer hotspots in various parts of this country.

Environmental factors include many kinds of exposures, from cigarette smoke to contaminated water and to chemicals in the workplace. In the regulatory system, these dangers are dealt with individually, on a chemical-by-chemical basis. Outside the laboratory, however, exposure does not work that way. We are bombarded by a swarm of carcinogens—cancer-causing substances—throughout our lives: small amounts in the food we eat and in the water we drink; other substances on the job or in the air. In 1980 the U.S. Public Health Service determined that all Americans are exposed to asbestos and other carcinogens.

Together, these substances can amplify the dangers they pose individually, creating potentially powerful synergistic effects—effects greater than those to be expected from exposure to each individually. "Many scientists now believe that most cancers result from the combined effects of long-term exposure to 'weak' carcinogens acting together rather than from sporadic exposure to a few 'potent' carcinogens," determined the president's TSSC.[31] For example, an already elevated risk of cancer, such as that for uranium miners and for asbestos workers, can be greatly increased in someone who smokes cigarettes as well. Since the explosion in synthetic chemical production did not occur until the late 1940s, and cancer can take as long as 30 years to develop, the combined effect of all these exposures only now are becoming manifest.

Cancer is only one disease associated with environmental degradation. Heart disease, the number one killer in the United States, is suffered by more people in areas of high air pollution. "Morbidity and mortality rates for heart diseases have been found to be higher in areas of high air pollution than areas of low air pollution," observed one federal interagency panel.[32] Cadmium, a metal used in rubber tires, plastics, pigments, and as a plating on metal, has firmly been linked to high blood pressure, which promotes heart disease.[33] Exposure to lead or carbon monoxide also promotes heart disease, scientists believe.[34]

Respiratory diseases, too, can also be induced by air pollutants. "A wide range of environmental agents, even apart from infections, can participate in the causation and even more markedly in the aggravation of respiratory disease," wrote Douglas H. K. Lee of the National Institute of Environmental Health Sciences.[35] For people exposed to air pollutants, especially in cities or near busy highways, this means a greater risk of emphysema, chronic bronchitis and other chronic pulmonary diseases.

And the effects of air pollution are not limited to the lungs. In the early 1970s, the exposure of inner-city children to lead, a cause of brain damage, was a national scandal. At first, the government considered lead-based paint the cause of elevated levels of lead found in inner-city youngsters. Very young children, usually living in tenement areas, were pictured eating small chips of paint that peeled off the walls of their homes. Lead in paint is a problem, but research during the decade has suggested that lead in the air contributes more to lead in the body than does peeling paint.[36] In most urban areas, the lead in the air comes primarily from automobiles, even after years of phasing out leaded gasoline. Two-thirds or more of all lead intake for adults is attributed to food, which absorbs the metal from contaminated water and soil or from pesticides. [37]

Dr. Ralph Dougherty of Florida State University has tied decreasing male fertility, too, to toxic chemical exposure. Sperm density in American males has declined steadily in the past 30 years, from an average of 100 million cells per milliliter before 1950 to averages of 50 to 80 million cells today.[38] Studies comparing measurements made during several years also suggest an apparent increase in subfertility—or "functional sterility." Twenty-three percent of the students in Dougherty's sample, for example, were functionally sterile.[39] The production of sperm, which requires eight to ten cell-division steps, is a uniquely sensitive indicator of exposure to substances that inhibit cell division. "Substances that inhibit cell division are very often mutagenic, carcinogenic or both," wrote Dougherty and five associates in a 1980 paper.[40]

In the sperm of half of 132 students studied, the researchers found "a significant contamination" of semen with trichlorophenol, a metabolite of the herbicides 2,4,5-T and Silvex. Subject to further statistical analysis, the concentrations of tri-chlorophenol were found to contribute to the declining sperm counts. The students presumably were exposed to 2,4,5-T through the food chain. "It is reasonable to infer," Dougherty concluded later, "that the exposure of the human population to 2,4,5-T and Silvex and their dioxin and predioxin contaminants has probably contributed to the dramatic decline in male fertility potential in the United States. . . ."[41]

Dougherty's analyses make clear the need for quick action: The implications of chemicals in the sperm of young men may be greater than the decline of fertility, though that certainly seems cause enough for concern. Friends of the Earth, an international environmental organization, has proposed using information about a chemical's impact on sperm density as a short-term indicator of its toxic effects. This would enable the government to gather evidence about hazards more quickly— lengthy animal carcinogenesis studies being the main research tool currently used—and to move more efficiently against dangerous substances.

Further research has indicated that men who have diminished sperm counts also may have increased numbers of chromosomal aberrations in their sperm.[42] This research raises perhaps the most serious question of the chemical age. Of all the injuries pollutants and toxic chemicals inflict on our society, the greatest—and certainly the longest lasting—may be the altering of our genetic heritage. In the homes of Love Canal and the towns of northern California is evidence of the brutal legacy of chemical dangers.

Listen to Linda van Atta, who lives in the small town of Denny, California: "I myself have had three miscarriages, my daughter-in-law had a miscarriage, and a friend of mine had a miscarriage and had cancer, and another friend just had a baby born with a harelip." Denny is surrounded by woods the U.S. Forest Service has sprayed with the herbicide 2,4,5-T. Or listen to Dr. Beverly Paigen, who has studied the residents of Love Canal, where 56 percent of the children born in certain areas between 1974 and 1979 had birth defects: "This woman, for instance, had two normal children before she moved to Love Canal. When she moved to Love Canal she had four miscarriages in a row. The last child, which was born dead at 6 months, was deformed. The distraught woman decided not to have any more children. This woman [another Love Canal resident] for instance, had three miscarriages. Then she managed to carry a baby that was born live, and it had three ears. A second child she managed to have had deformed ears."[43]

Evidence increases that most cancer-causing chemicals also induce birth defects and gene mutations. A major scientific conference on chemical mutagens in 1979 concluded: "in all likelihood, environmental mutagens contribute to a large and costly genetic health burden."[44] Current estimates indicate that "about 10% of all liveborn will manifest (either at birth or during subsequent life) a wide variety of genetic diseases."[45] Some experts, such as geneticist James V. Neel of the University of Michigan, feel that, for at least some disorders—recessively inherited traits—this is a gross underestimate.[46] And, indeed, other research has placed the observed total as high as 16 percent. The role of environmental factors in this overall pattern is suggested by preliminary evidence that birth defect rates vary considerably between, and even within, states—much as does the incidence of cancer.[47] Scientists have found more than 100 organic compounds in human umbilical cords, including "halogenated hydrocarbons, plastic components, and food preservatives. . . ." The carcinogens benzene, carbon tetrachloride and chloroform "are present [in umbilical cords] in quantities equal to, or greater than, those in maternal blood."[48]

Despite this grim evidence, the production of hazardous substances and their reckless use continue to increase. Stopping or even controlling that increase has been an exasperating and frequently futile job for the regulatory agencies charged with minding the ways of industry. The results of steady, global pollution in this generation are an epidemic of cancer and increased rates of heart and respiratory diseases. But these are not the final results. The genes mutated now will pass on through generations. The effect of pollution today will long outlive us.

THE PATHWAYS OF EXPOSURE

The links between the many forms of pollution can best be understood by briefly considering the steps of production. Mining or otherwise obtaining raw materials can pollute water and air, disrupt the landscape and expose workers to dusts and dangerous conditions. At the manufacturing stage, workers can be further exposed to dusts and to hazardous chemicals. During manufacture, wastes are produced—which are dispelled in the air or water, or dumped on the land. The final product itself may be, like pesticides, a further source of contamination. Or, if the product is not recycled, eventually it will add to the nation's immense pile of waste.

Pollution, then, is a process that parallels the industrial process. Failure to control dangerous substances—the unwillingness to expend the money necessary to minimize dangers— creates both occupational and environmental hazards. Recognizing that an unsafe plant can devastate the health not only of its workers but of nearby communities requires only a few moments' thought. Only a moment more will suggest the true reach of a single plant, whose products—such as pesticides— can threaten the health of people thousands, even tens of thousands, of miles away.

The pathways of exposure begin on the job. They continue with the disposal of byproducts—air and water pollution, chemical and nuclear wastes—and with the use of such products as pesticides. Let us consider how each of these pollutants enters our lives.

OCCUPATIONAL EXPOSURE

The workplace has been the battleground for some of the most acrimonious fighting between government and industrial management in the past decade. Two million Americans suffer from occupational disease, which has disabled one-third of them. Each year, 100,000 people die from occupational diseases and 390,000 workers first contract them, according to government estimates.[49] As mentioned earlier, between 20 percent and 38 percent of all cancer deaths are estimated to be caused by exposure to carcinogens on the job.[50] Once contracted, "Most known occupational diseases are chronic, untreatable and fatal," says Dr. John M. Peters of the Harvard School of Public Health.[51]

Consider the number of workers who, being exposed to cancer-causing substances, are candidates for such diseases. In 1978, the National Cancer Institute (NCI) and the National Institute for Occupational Safety and Health analyzed the potential risk for workers exposed to nine substances. The results are staggering:

Arsenic 1.5 million workers potentially exposed. Their risk ratio—the number of cancers expected, compared to that in a normal population—is from 3 to 8 times higher for lung cancer;

Benzene 2 million workers potentially exposed. Their risk ratio for leukemia is from 2 to 7 times higher;

Coal Tar Pitch Volatiles and Coke Oven Emissions 60,000 workers potentially exposed. Their risk ratio is from 2 to 6 times higher for lung, larynx, skin and scrotum cancer;

Vinyl Chloride 2.26 million workers potentially exposed. Their risk ratios are 200, 4, and 1.9 times higher respectively for angiosarcoma (cancer of the liver), brain and lung cancer;

Chromium about 1.5 million workers potentially exposed. Their risk ratio is from 3 to 40 times higher for nasal cavity and sinus, lung and larynx cancer;

Iron Oxide about 1.6 million workers potentially exposed. Their risk ratio is from 2 to 5 times higher for lung and larynx cancer;

Nickel about 1.37 million workers potentially exposed. Their risk ratio is from 5 to 10 times higher for lung cancer;

Petroleum Distillates about 3 million workers potentially exposed. Their risk ratio is from 2 to 6 times higher for lung and larynx cancer;

Asbestos between 8 and 11 million workers have been exposed since World War II. More than 2.15 million of them are expected to die of cancer.

Exposure to asbestos alone, wrote the NCI and NIOSH researchers, "would represent about 17 percent of all cancers detected annually in the United States."[52]

When the enormous personal tragedy of even a single cancer case is considered, the human misery in these known figures on worker exposure takes on ineffable proportions. And the figures do not reflect the true extent of the disease; data are lacking for many occupational groups, including farm workers exposed to pesticides. Other groups simply were not included in the estimates. Nor do the figures forecast the potential incidence of chronic disease that will develop in the future from exposure today.

Wrote the NIOSH-NCI committee researching occupational cancer, "If only one of the thousands of chemicals introduced into commerce in the past 30 years proves to be as hazardous as asbestos, this could suffice to maintain comparable rates of occupationally-related cancer for decades into the future. In our view, any complacency about the future characteristics of present-day exposure to uncharacterized chemicals would be unjustified."[53]

Cancer is only the beginning. Diseases of the lung also are a particular occupational concern. Such occupationally divergent workers as coal miners, textile weavers and shipbuilders have been exposed to dusts on the job that will kill many of them. Death from these diseases usually comes after a long latency period that is marked by coughing, chest pains, increasing difficulty in breathing and—in some diseases—destruction of the lung tissue.

Lung disease is a particularly painful way to die. "I have worked in the coal mines 37 years," one miner told Congress at hearings on black-lung disease; "My lungs went bad on me and I had to go into the hospital. I did not know what was the matter with me. I could get no breath. I would get tired, I would work half a day, and that is all I could stand. . . . I had to crawl to work, and with the smoke, the bad air, I then went into the hospital and they told me, they said your lungs were peeling off...."[54] Other lung diseases include asbestosis, induced by exposure to asbestos; byssinosis (or "brown lung"), which comes from exposure to cotton dust, and silicosis, which derives from exposure to silica, the most common constituent of the earth's crust.

It is a measure of how slow progress is in combatting environmental dangers that all of these diseases have been listed in accounts of occupational hazards for decades. Workplace hazards often are difficult to isolate since studies often are obstructed by corporate secrecy, the diseases take a long time to develop, and patterns are not always readily apparent in a workforce that expands and changes with time. But that is not to say new dangers have not been detected: workers in industries using diisocyanates—chemical compounds used in paints, insulation, cushioning and other products—have suffered an unexplained threefold to fourfold decrease in lung functions.[55] These newer chemical dangers have not supplanted the older dust diseases. They simply have supplemented them.

AIR POLLUTANTS

For most people, the word pollution conjures up images of smokestacks and drainpipes connected to sooty factories. The visible soiling of the nation's air and water motivated many of the federal efforts to do something about the environment at the beginning of the past decade. Congress has taken up air and water pollution again and again, amending the Clear Air Act twice and passing more than half a dozen laws or new amendments to restore the nation's waters. These efforts have met with some success. Many rivers are cleaner, as is the air over most cities. For 25 major metropolitan areas, the number of "unhealthful" days—defined as days on which "persons with existing heart or respiratory ailments should reduce physical exertion and outdoor activity"[56]—after peaking in 1975, declined 15 percent overall from 1974 to 1977.[57]

Those are impressive reductions, but only a few moments spent in downtown Los Angeles will demonstrate that air pollution still hovers over our cities. Six cities—Denver, Cleveland,

Los Angeles, Louisville, New York and Riverside—with a combined population of 18 million, had an annual average of 150 or more unhealthy days from 1975 to 1977.[58] In 1977 alone, New York's air was unhealthy more than two-thirds of the time.[59]

Another reflection of the continuing problem is the resistance of some industries to meeting the law. Many of the nation's industrial polluters are not in compliance with clean-air standards. "To make the situation even more difficult," one government analysis noted, "these offenders are often power plants, steel mills, and other large sources which have a history of reluctance to comply with the standards."[60] Privately, EPA officials estimate that as few as ten percent of the pollution sources in steel mills meet clean air requirements.

WATER POLLUTANTS

Like air pollution, water pollution was the subject of extensive federal efforts in the 1970s. One federal program alone—supplying grants for waste-water treatment facility construction—has disbursed in excess of $24 billion in more than 18,000 grants.[61] These efforts have improved or at least contained the situation. A Council on Environmental Quality analysis "suggests that there has been little or no overall change in the levels of five major water pollution indicators [from] . . . 1975 through 1978."[62] Under federal law, industrial facilities must now obtain a permit to discharge wastes. As of early 1980, 59,000 permits had been handed out.[63] For the EPA and the states to keep an eye on that many facilities is impossible; so successful cleanup of the nation's waterways depends on industries' complying with the law. But EPA investigations have revealed violations at one-third of the major industrial sites inspected.[64]

Industrial sewage creates another problem. Tens of thousands of industrial plants do not pretreat their wastes—which often contain toxic synthetics and heavy metals—but send them directly to municipal treatment plants. These plants are not built to accommodate such wastes. So dangerous substances such as cadmium or PCBs accumulate in the municipal sewage sludge, which sometimes is distributed to local farmers or gardeners, contaminating their land.

Farmers are more than victims of water pollution. They are a prime source. Runoff from agricultural lands pours three billion tons of soil each year into waterways.[65] This prodigious erosion signals not only farms stripped of land and rivers clogged with silt; the runoff contains some of the 49 million tons of commercial fertilizers[66] used each year. The fertilizers—along with the two billion tons of livestock wastes produced annually[67]—contribute to the excessive growth of algae and other plants in waterways, and thus to their aging. Pesticides in the runoff are a different kind of worry: "Volume-wise erosion and sediments are the biggest agricultural pollution problem," said one EPA official, "but the most serious problem is the toxic chemicals [in the runoff] because of the possible health hazards."[68]

In water, as on land, synthetic toxic chemicals have complicated cleanup efforts originally designed for more traditional pollutants. "Fish are returning to waters they long ago fled," says Gus Speth of the CEQ, "but we are finding their flesh often contains significant amounts of toxic chemicals."[69] One study of the Hudson River, which provides water to communities all along its length, has shown the water to be contaminated with hundreds of chemicals, as many as one-fifth of them carcinogens.[70] The Hudson is not unique. Although modern filtration has cut back the risk of disease transmitted through bacteria in water, the steady presence of highly toxic, sometimes carcinogenic, chemicals in our drinking supplies raises the possibility that we have traded one kind of epidemic for another.

CHLORINATION AND CARCINOGENS

There is perhaps no greater example of the complexity of the dangers posed by synthetic chemicals, and the frequent inadequacy of traditional defenses to deal with them, than the role of chlorination in this contamination of water with carcinogens. Chlorination long has been standard operating procedure in the water-works industry: It frees water supplies of viral and bacterial contamination and of the risk of water-borne disease. But the chlorine used as a disinfectant combines with organic wastes in drinking water to form extremely dangerous com-

pounds called trihalomethanes (THMs). One of these compounds is chloroform, a known carcinogen. Others include
brominated compounds that apparently are formed by the interaction of chlorine, the organic chemicals and bromide.

In a 1975 study, the EPA found chloroform in the water of
all 80 cities surveyed. Bromine compounds were found in most
cities. A more comprehensive analysis of 10 cities, including
New York, Philadelphia and Tucson, found 129 individual organic chemicals in the drinking water. The government acknowledges that "only 9–14 percent, by weight, of the synthetic
organic contaminants found in the water has been identified."[71]

What is the effect of this pollution on human health? "Since
1974, the EPA and other government agencies have identified
a variety of contaminants in drinking water together with a
number of studies that have looked at the relationship between
drinking water quality and cancer mortality rates," says Dr.
Robert Harris, a member of the president's CEQ. "The studies
have unmistakenly indicated that pollution contaminants in
water are linked with an increase in the cancer rate." In late
1980, CEQ published a new study of water supplies in five states
which "further strengthened the evidence for an association
between rectal, colon and bladder cancer" and chlorinated
drinking water.

The list is extensive—in Ohio, Louisiana, upstate New
York, Miami—chemically contaminated drinking water has
been linked to increased risk of cancer. In the West, radiation
contaminates the drinking water of at least 15 states. Laced
with uranium wastes, the drinking water of one Denver suburb
exposed residents to 60 times the normal yearly dose of alpha
radiation.[72]

Most carcinogenic chemicals, of course, also present other
risks. As noted in a 1977 National Academy of Sciences report:

> Interactions such as additive toxicity, synergism, and antagonism
> have not been considered in development of risk assessments
> . . . [I]n light of such uncertainties, a cautious approach must be
> adopted when dealing with potentially harmful chemicals. Even
> more uncertainty exists when one considers the possibility that
> some of these chemicals may also be mutagenic or teratogenic.[73]

The chief of the Clinical Epidemiology Branch of the National Cancer Institute, Dr. Robert Miller, has said,

> It is clear that the contamination of water has shrunk the size of newborn babies, starved others for oxygen, pustulated the skin for years in persons of all ages, caused bones to ache with every step, and addled the brains of newborns, children and adults. With this array of adverse effects on the integrity of the human organism, is there really any need to invoke the specter of cancer to achieve clean water?[74]

There should not be any such need. But not even that formidable specter—raised in study after study—has been sufficient to get the job done. "The response by both federal and state regulatory agencies," says Harris, "has not really been commensurate with the increased evidence of risk." With strong opposition from industrial firms, EPA efforts to set standards for toxics in waterways have moved painfully slowly. "Most industry officials are not encouraged by the EPA's proposals and already are complaining about the high cost," reports *Business Week*.[75] Such powerful trade groups as the American Petroleum Institute, the Chemical Manufacturers Association and the American Iron & Steel Institute "have indicated they would not be adverse to court action."[76]

Granular activated carbon (GAC) filters are available as an alternative to chlorination. But their use likewise has been delayed by heavy opposition. GAC filters are the best-known method for removing organic pollutants in water; the filters are extensively used already in European cities, including Zurich, Cologne and Amsterdam. Some 40 American cities use them to improve the taste and odor of their water, but none to filter out dangerous chemicals. Why? "You have a professional bias against disrupting the status quo, whether it's a move from coal to solar or from chlorination to carbon or whatever," says Harris. "There is a large institutional bias against doing it [switching from chlorine to carbon]. It threatens their [the American Water Works Association members] position and reputation. It threatens their position in the community and profession." Such environment groups as the Environmental Defense Fund are pushing the EPA to move faster in requiring the use of GAC filters in municipal water supplies.

HAZARDOUS WASTES

Hazardous wastes are perhaps now the greatest pollution concern of both the government and the public. The reasons are easy to see. When the federal emergency was declared there in 1978, Love Canal contained a little more than 43 million pounds of hazardous wastes, deposited during a decade by the Hooker Chemical Company.[77] In 1980 alone, America produced 125 billion pounds of hazardous wastes, or enough to fill approximately 3,000 Love Canals.[78] The EPA estimates that hazardous-waste generation is increasing at the rate of about 3 percent annually.[79] If this trend continues, the current yearly production of hazardous wastes will double by the year 2000.[80] Moreover, the EPA estimates that as much as 90 percent—112 billion pounds—of the waste is disposed of improperly.[81]

Making admittedly crude estimates, an EPA consultant posits that as many as 50,000 chemical dumps are situated throughout the country: Of these, perhaps 1,200 to several thousand pose significant dangers.[82] In May 1980 the EPA revealed that more than 1.2 million people are exposed to risks from only 214 dumps that are considered "high" or "medium" health threats—these figures include only the dumps already investigated by the agency.[83] EPA consultants have estimated that containing the hazards may cost $44 billion.[84] New York State and the federal government have spent almost $70 million at Love Canal alone—and the work isn't finished. The bill for Hooker's Montague, Michigan, site—where pesticide wastes infiltrated a scenic lake and groundwater—could amount to $100 million.[85]

GROUNDWATER CONTAMINATION

Though at Love Canal toxic chemicals escaped from the dumpsite into basements and backyards, the most pervasive concern raised by chemical dumping is groundwater contamination. Siphoned from underground water supplies known as aquifers, groundwater provides about half the country with low-cost, quality water. In many areas it is the only economical source of water available. Twenty percent of the United States population draws groundwater from domestic wells, unscreened by any community filters. (Nearly all rural Americans depend on wells for their water.) Virtually none of these wells is evaluated for water quality or potential contamination.[86]

All of this makes groundwater a resource to be treasured. Another characteristic of groundwater makes it a resource to be protected carefully. Once polluted, it stays fouled for decades or even hundreds of years. Cleaning up the damage before the natural systems clean themselves is virtually impossible.

Given these conditions, the best way to ensure safe groundwater is to keep it free of toxic contaminants in the first place. That is not what has happened. "Groundwater has been contaminated on a local basis in all parts of the nation and on a regional basis in some heavily populated and industrialized areas," was the EPA's assessment in 1977.[87]

The greatest threats to groundwater come from industrial waste water held in unlined lagoons, and solid or liquid wastes dumped into disposal sites. The EPA estimates that 100 billion gallons of industrial waste waters reach nearby aquifers every year.[88] The contaminants in the waste waters range from inorganic and chemical wastes to heavy metals.

Landfills are an even greater source of contamination. Rainfall enters insecure landfills, mixes with the wastes, then leaches through the soil. The leachate can migrate into the water table and poison the groundwater. From the nation's 18,500 municipal landfills alone, an estimated 90 billion gallons of leachate enter the groundwater annually.[89] How much leachate from industrial dumpsites has reached groundwater is not known, but with as many as 50,000 chemical dumps nationwide, the amount may be prodigious.

Municipalities and industry have dumped their wastes mostly in those areas for which they had no other productive use, or which were the cheapest available sites—such as swamps, old strip mines, and abandoned pits—according to an

EPA study.[90] "Most of these sites," observed the EPA, "have hydraulic connections with natural waters."[91]

Some members of Congress believe the temptation to dump at such sites is so great, and the risks so grave, that certain extremely hazardous wastes should not be disposed of in landfills at all, under any conditions. The House Oversight and Investigations Subcommittee, which studied hazardous wastes in 1979, backed this position: "Some wastes are so resistant to biodegradation and so persistently toxic that EPA should consider prohibiting their disposal in landfills altogether. Similarly, EPA might consider requiring certain wastes to be incinerated."[92]

NUCLEAR WASTES

In fall 1979, the nuclear industry demonstrated just how close to the margin it has been living. On October 4 then-Governor Dixie Lee Ray of Washington shut down the low-level nuclear-waste dump at Hanford because, she said, wastes arriving there were improperly packaged.[93] A little more than two weeks later, Governor Robert List of Nevada shut down the dumpsite at Beatty, Nevada, citing similar reasons.[94]

At the end of the month, Richard W. Riley, the governor of South Carolina—home of the country's only other low-level waste dumpsite—announced that he had ordered Chem-Nuclear Systems, Inc., to refuse wastes displaced from the other sites and to cut its overall dumping in half. "As long as everybody can ship it off to South Carolina and forget about it," Riley said, "then everybody is going to regard low-level waste as a South Carolina problem."[95]

Riley may have accurately gauged the mood of most of the country. But the nuclear industry and the hospitals and research centers using radioisotopes were very concerned about nuclear waste disposal—at least about their end of it. Most power plants have enough space to temporarily store their low-level junk—contaminated clothing, equipment and sludges—but researchers using radioactive material complained they did not have such storage room.

With prominent scientists issuing such warnings as: "Every large university hospital doing cancer research now faces a decision to close down,"[96] first Ray and then List reopened their states' sites, only two months after closing them.

The situation for the high-level wastes—the spent fuel rapidly accumulating in storage pools alongside commercial nuclear power plants—is no better. The spent fuel and the radioactive liquid sludges that result from reprocessing fuel rods are the most dangerous nuclear wastes of all; they contain dozens of long-lived radioactive components, including plutonium, cesium-137 and strontium-90, that remain dangerous to live organisms for hundreds or for hundreds of thousands of years.

Though no plants have shut down for lack of spent-fuel-rod storage, such shut-downs may occur in the next few years.[97] Commercial reprocessing of these wastes, as was attempted by Nuclear Fuel Services Incorporated in West Valley, New York, has proven to be economically unfeasible and environmentally hazardous. So the spent fuel rods continue to pile up. And little room for them remains.

Besides being extraordinarily persistent, these wastes are extremely hazardous: They are carcinogenic, and capable of inducing genetic damage and acute illnesses.

The nuclear cycle creates other kinds of dangerous residues, as well: In addition to the power plants' wastes, the production of fuel leaves behind uranium mill tailings. Vast piles of radioactive tailings have been left from uranium mining operations in communities across the West. In some places, such as Salt Lake City, Utah, the tailings simply were dumped, without cover or protection, in massive piles near the center of town. In other places, such as Grand Junction, Colorado, the tailings were carted away for years, and actually were used to construct hundreds of offices, schools, sidewalks and highways. Radiation escaping from these tailings, which the wind often blows across and disturbs, can increase the risk of lung cancer and leukemia as much as 100 percent for people living within a half mile of the piles.[98] Like hazardous waste dumps, many tailing piles have been abandoned by mining companies, leaving the tax-payers to foot the bill for cleaning up the health hazards.

As the nation's first-built commercial reactors reach the end of their productivity in the next quarter century, a new kind of garbage problem will face us: What can be done with the finished nuclear power plants and their radioactive residues?

The public will have to wait for an answer to that question, because no effective program has been established for disposing of nuclear wastes already produced. The nuclear industry has not forwarded any plans on how it intends to deal with closed power plants. History suggests some time will pass before the industry develops its plans. In this, more than in any other industry, future public health has been mortgaged against science's ability to catch up with and neutralize the hazards its technology has created.

PESTICIDES

> From small beginnings over farmlands and forests the scope of aerial spraying has widened and its volume has increased so that it has become what a British ecologist recently called "an amazing rain of death" upon the surface of the earth.... Although today's poisons are more dangerous than any known before, they have amazingly become something to be showered down indiscriminately from the skies.[99]

So wrote Rachel Carson nearly 20 years ago. Her description remains apt today.

More than 1.4 billion pounds of insecticides, fungicides and herbicides were produced in the United States in 1978.[100] Though exact figures are not available, about 1 billion pounds were used here in 1976.[101]

Up until World War II, inorganic pesticides dominated agricultural markets. These pesticides—based on such elements as mercury, arsenic and lead—are more than persistent in the environment: They are permanent. Eventually they accumulated to a point in the soil "which made further growing of crops unprofitable."[102] Throughout the 1940s and 1950s, new technologies provided alternatives, or so it seemed, to the unsafe inorganics. Synthetic organic pesticides were developed in a flurry of innovation. First came DDT, followed by others in the same family, known as organochlorines: aldrin, dieldrin, chlordane and toxaphene. About the same time, the phenoxy herbicides—including 2,4,5-T and 2,4-D—were developed as an outgrowth of army chemical warfare research.

With the discovery of new products came the search for new markets. "Contemporary pest control," wrote entomologist Robert Van Den Bosch in *The Pesticide Conspiracy*, has turned into "a practice in which chemical merchandising has become the name of the game."[103] If it wasn't always good science, it certainly was good business. Pesticides have been a classic chemical-industry success story. Their proliferation is also proof that what is good for the chemical industry is not necessarily good for society. Sales rose from a humble $118 million in 1953 to $1.3 billion in 1973.[104] By 1978, the industry had surpassed $3 billion in annual sales, up $600 million since 1976.[105] Forty thousand different pesticide products are in use, and the EPA has only begun the ten- or twenty-year job of reregistering them for safety.

TOXICS IN THE FOOD CHAIN

Pesticide exposure reaches far beyond the workplace and the farm. "Most people," says Steven Jellinek, EPA assistant administrator for toxic substances, "are exposed to pesticides or pesticide residues every day whether they elect to use pesticides or not."[106] The average shopper browsing through the supermarket no doubt would be surprised to learn that, as former Representative John E. Moss observed at hearings on chemical contamination of food: "A housewife who carefully checks the meat and poultry she buys to determine that it has a USDA-inspected stamp on it is merely getting a product that has been inspected for . . . cleaniness and general health—but in no way does that imply that there has been an inspection to determine whether or not it is an adulterated product because of the high residues of the [chemical] products we've been talking about."[107] In fact, though, Moss's Oversight and Investigation Subcommittee determined in a 1978 report, "despite federal programs designed to protect the public from harmful chemicals, virtually all food consumed in this country contains residues of synthetic substances that have been developed in recent decades."[108]

The possible health effects of chemical contamination of the nation's food, listed by the congressional Office of Technology Assessment (OTA), include "systemic toxicity, mutations, cancer, birth defects, and reproductive disorders."[109] Obviously not everyone biting into an apple or a peach will suffer from all or any of these problems. But the presence of these substances in our food is increasing our body load of toxics, with unknown results. "The long-term health effects and the implications of possible interactions among these residues are unknown," wrote the OTA.[110]

Already, studies have determined that Americans carry measurable residues of 94 different chemical contaminants in their bodies.[111] All of the Florida State University students tested recently by Dr. Ralph Dougherty, for example, had pentachlorophenol, one of the herbicides this nation produces in greatest quantities, in their urine. Scientists have found DDT, heptachlor, dieldrin and other pesticides in mother's milk; each of these, as well as lindane and Mirex, also have turned up in human tissue samples.[112]

Some of this contamination may be attributable to impurities in the air and water, and to work exposure, but that hardly is comforting. The food chain, though, clearly is one pathway of contamination. For agricultural pesticides, about 6,000 tolerances—legal maximum limits of residues in foods—have been established. These tolerances include 940 legal limits set for pesticides implicated as carcinogens.[113]

Many of these legal tolerances are based on shoddy or incomplete information and are not comprehensively monitored. But the tolerances have a more fundamental flaw: Scientists have not yet determined any safe level of exposure for carcinogens. And, as the president's Toxic Substances Strategy Committee has noted, many believe long-term, low-level exposure to be most hazardous.

THE PESTICIDE TREADMILL

Another long-term effect of dependence on pesticides has been the creation of a kind of addiction known as "the pesticide treadmill." When a pesticide rids a crop of pests effectively, farmers come to depend on it. But frequent pesticide use can create insect resistance. By 1976, 364 species of insects had become resistant to various kinds of pesticides.[114] Pesticide use to overcome such resistance can require applications so heavy and expensive as to drive entire industries into virtual bankruptcy. That happened to the Texas cotton industry in the late 1960s, when the tobacco budworm became so resistant to methyl parathion that the pesticide no longer could control it.

To cope with the tobacco budworm, and for environmental reasons, many Texas cotton farmers have switched to Integrated Pest Management (IPM), a balanced management program that sharply reduces or eliminates pesticide use while employing natural controls and other means to limit insect damage. As we shall see in the concluding chapter, IPM has shown Texas cotton farmers a way off the treadmill.

So far we have sketched the outlines of the overall environmental problem, a problem that remains unsolved, even after a decade of slowly growing worker and public awareness and of frequently spirited government action. We have seen how the development and use of new technologies and products without adequate concern for long-term hazards have created serious, and still nascent, public health problems.

We have looked at the pathways of exposure: on-the-job exposure; wastes dispersed into the air and water or dumped on land; and contaminants in the food chain. The sliding economy, the energy dilemma and the increasing political activism of major corporations all are contributing to a climate inimical to the passage of new—or even the enforcement of old—environmental initiatives. Still the most basic question remains: How did the situation become this bad?

THE CORPORATE ROOTS OF
ENVIRONMENTAL POLLUTION

When officials at, say, the Dow Chemical Company proceed with the production and sale of a product such as 2,4,5-T despite the serious questions raised about its safety, the company traditionally has been removed from the consequences of its officials' decisions in several ways. The officials themselves are unlikely ever to actually manufacture or be sprayed with the substance. (Some overzealous public-relations personnel have been known to eat a small sample of 2,4,5-T now and then at public debates over its safety. No one appears to be doing that anymore.) And when the product damages property or people, society and not the company bears the cost. These "external" costs figure neither in the prices of the product nor the ledger sheets of the corporation. But, for society, the costs can be immense: the degradation of the environment and the loss of its use; the expense of treating illness and compensating for disability; the shortened lives and diminished opportunities.

That these costs are real is beyond dispute. But in the calculations of the balance sheet—barring successful law suits, which are infrequent—they are nonexistent. This shifting onto the general public costs in the billions of dollars annually stands in stark contrast to the strident demands of business to keep industry free from outside control. "A business enterprise that pollutes the environment is . . . being subsidized by society," writes environmentalist Barry Commoner. "To this extent, the enterprise, though free, is not wholly private."[115]

With society bearing the costs of industry's byproducts, corporations have had little economic incentive to reduce the harmful effects of their activities. George Kush, director of chemical waste management of the National Solid Wastes Management Association, put the matter bluntly: "Without federal regulations to enforce the safe management of all hazardous wastes . . . *there has not been any real incentive, given the highly competitive nature of the business community,* for companies to adopt adequate disposal procedures at the risk of losing their competitive edge through increased costs. . . ."[116] (Emphasis added.)

It is tempting to point to the poisoned children of Love Canal as an "incentive . . . for companies to adopt adequate disposal procedures." But the chemical industry, in particular, has lately asserted that these dangers are the responsibility of all segments of society, since all society uses chemical products. Commenting on the Superfund proposal—signed into law by former president Jimmy Carter in December 1980 to pay for the cleanup of hazardous dumpsites with money provided by the chemical and related industries—Jackson B. Browning, the director of health, safety and environmental affairs at Union Carbide, capsulized this attitude: "[Hazardous wastes] are an integral by-product of our industrial society, and represent by-products of the daily life of every citizen. The problems associated with abandoned hazardous waste disposal sites reflect more than 100 years of industrial development in the Nation. . . . The problem is societal in scope and the mechanisms for coping with it should reflect its societal nature, just as the benefits of resolving the problems will extend to all elements of the country."[117]

Even Browning is unlikely, however, to convincingly argue that society as a whole benefits from chemicals as much as Union Carbide, whose chemical sales in 1979 stood at a robust $5.3 billion.[118] Nor has society had the benefit of full—or, often, any—information about the hazards associated with production or disposal of the products people use in great volume. In a more fundamental sense, in fact, the prices of products that don't reflect the "external" factors of production mislead consumers about the true costs. In sum, the costs are socialized. But the profits are kept private.

Environmental regulation, observed the CEQ, "was based on the clear recognition that existing market prices were giving incorrect signals to consumers by understating what society was giving up to have goods whose production resulted in pollution."[119] The exclusion of these costs from price has upheld the demand for products whose costs were rippling beyond the marketplace, through all segments of society: in the air we breathe, in the water we drink, in the food we eat.

Opposition to environmental regulation usually is couched in concerns about decreasing corporate productivity and competitiveness in world markets. A federal consultant, however, has projected the annual productivity decline between 1970 and 1986 owing to environmental regulations at only .1 percent annually.[120] Scholarly researchers have found evidence that regulation actually can increase overall productivity by spurring technological change. A March 1980 report commissioned by the Senate Committee on Governmental Affairs observed, "Research and development aimed at compliance with health or safety regulations can increase overall productivity because the production system becomes more tightly enclosed, reducing emissions, or because the instruments used to control it are improved."[121] Recycling resources can save voluminous amounts of energy, cutting costs as well as reducing the need for waste disposal.

A company's political effectiveness hardly would be served by acknowledging its resistance to pay for proper management of the wastes produced by new technologies. Political effectiveness is an issue quite apart from truth, however. The historic resistance is best exemplified by the dumping of hazardous wastes. Hooker Chemical could have paid $4 million, in 1979 dollars, to properly dispose of its wastes at Love Canal.[122] Hooker chose instead to dump the wastes indiscriminately— sometimes simply pouring the wastes directly into the disposal site—and to cover them so inadequately that barrels repeatedly surfaced after heavy rain or snowfall. Hooker knew as early as 1958—20 years before 240 families were forced from their homes—that wastes were surfacing from the dump and children were being injured by the substances.[123]

Another reflection of the natural propensity of businesses to minimize expenditures is a figure they regularly trot out to demonstrate how heavily harassed they are by government: the cost of compliance with federal environmental laws. From the evidence already presented it should be apparent that federal laws have entirely stanched neither the flow of toxics into the environment nor the increase of environmental disease. But the laws have provided steady, and in some cases significant, improvements in the problems they were enacted to affect. Of the $55.9 billion estimated to have been spent by industry (and municipalities) on pollution control in 1979, $36.9 billion, or 66 percent, was spent in direct response to federal directives.[124] These increased expenditures contributed only .3 percentage points to the annual rise of the consumer price index and, by stimulating the pollution-control industry, actually increased employment.[125] This money represents incremental improvements in environmental quality that by definition would not have been undertaken by industry on its own. It also represents the vast gulf in the level of environmental contamination that many corporate managers—as opposed to the general society—are willing to accept.

The inexorable drive to expand production and to find new markets for products also is a significant factor in the environmental equation, particularly as it applies to the chemical industry. Traditionally, Dow Chemical or Monsanto have not asked whether society needs a new pesticide. They have asked only whether they can develop a market for it. And since the petrochemical industry is so capital-intensive, so dependent on elaborate, expensive equipment, the economies of scale are considerable. These economic factors are further stimuli to expand production and create new markets.

Even before the current offensive against regulation, the business community had vigorously resisted attempts to make it incorporate the societal costs of its activities. To keep these costs from becoming apparent, corporations have not been adverse to covering up, downplaying or outright lying. Dr. Wilhelm C. Hueper, a prominent environmental physician, recognized this almost 40 years ago:

> Industrial concerns are in general not particularly anxious to have the occurrence of occupational cancer among their employees or of environmental cancer among the consumers of their products made a matter of public records. Such publicity might reflect unfavorably on their business activities and oblige them to undertake extensive and expensive technical and sanitary

changes. . . . It is therefore not an uncommon practice by the
parties financially interested in such matters to keep information
on the occurrence of industrial cancer well under cover.[126]

Cover-ups or misrepresentations of impending dangers
were key factors in each of the environmental disasters considered in this book. Because they were concealed, the dangers
spread far beyond their original boundaries.

—Hooker Chemical knew in 1958 that wastes were surfacing
   at the Love Canal, but did not warn local residents of the
   danger.

—The Allied Chemical Corporation determined in animal
   tests as early as 1949 that Kepone attacks the nervous system, causing the tremors that were the trademark of the
   disaster made public in the mid-1970s.

—General Electric admitted at hearings on its discharge of
   PCBs into the Hudson River that the substance was involved in the illnesses of at least 65 of its workers over a
   15-year period.

—The Nuclear Fuel Services Corporation, which operated
   the West Valley nuclear reprocessing plant now the responsibility of the state and federal governments, frequently hired temporary workers. These workers were
   given little or no instruction and no information about the
   potential hazards of radiation, yet were used to clean
   highly contaminated areas until the employees reached
   their annual dose limit of radiation—sometimes in only two
   or three days.

—Velsicol Chemical Company officials were indicted for
   falsely telling FDA investigators that PBB was not stored
   near feed additives. (The charge was dropped in October
   1980 after Velsicol pleaded no contest to misdemeanor
   charges on the same incident.) The officials' statements
   were made shortly after the contamination of Michigan
   cattle feed with the toxic chemical PBB was discovered. In
   fact, employees have revealed, feed additives not only
   were stored near PBB, but were manufactured and pro-

cessed on machinery that often contained PBB residues, spreading the contamination.

—The Reserve Mining Company, testifying at 1947 hearings on its application to dump tailings into Lake Superior, failed to reveal the results of a report it had commissioned that showed the dumping would seriously disrupt the food balance for fish near the plant. The report presaged the environmental disruption that followed. Twenty-five years later, during a trial that considered ending its lake discharges, Reserve claimed that land disposal was unfeasible and withheld a report it had commissioned on how to move the tailings onto land.

—The Dow Chemical Company knew in 1964 that 2,4,5-T was contaminated with dioxin, a highly toxic, carcinogenic and mutagenic chemical. That was six years before any action was taken on the chemical. [127]

No matter how prodigious the concealment efforts, they cannot keep all dangers out of the public eye. But the intricate regulatory system for weeding out unsafe chemicals and pesticides has ground to a virtual halt under an administrative siege from the affected industries. Only a handful of pesticides— DDT, aldrin and dieldrin and a few others—have been removed from use, and those only after the bureaucratic equivalent of war. Each ban has followed the compilation of voluminous records, the filing of countless motions by highly paid Washington law firms, and repeated trips to courthouse after courthouse for what must seem to government lawyers like Sisyphean rounds of appeal.

While these painstaking efforts drag on, the pesticides under dispute continue to be used. Of course, they are joined in the market place by new products every year. And, while the EPA has been prodded to each of its bans by environmental groups, the overall impetus is not in the direction of more spirited action. Two EPA lawyers who resigned from the agency in 1976 complained that the EPA has failed "to take effective action under existing authority [because of] . . . industry pressure brought to bear through Congressional commit-tees."[128] That pressure still is a deterrent to action, especially now that some representatives are pushing to end EPA regula-tion of pesticides altogether.

Occupational health regulation similarly has been stymied by intractable resistance. Since being formed 10 years ago, the Occupational Safety and Health Administration (OSHA) has been able to promulgate exposure standards for only 22 sub-stances. In 1979, as the political climate further cooled and congressional rhetoric about over-regulation heated up, no standards were promulgated. And those standards that have been issued have typically had to withstand suits brought by trade associations in order to become law.

Pressure against taking aggressive action on environmental problems comes not only from industry, and from Congress, but additionally from White House officials—such as officials on the Council on Wage and Price Stability—concerned about the short-run inflationary impact of new regulation. This concern also keeps down the budgets of regulatory agencies, often leav-ing them with inadequate resources. Consequently, statutes that look fine in the law books—and were passed only after monumental legislative struggles—are only spottily enforced.

Consider the monitoring of the nation's food supply, a mas-sive and complex but undeniably essential task. The program to oversee the safety of food has two components: setting stan-dards for the maximum amount of contaminants permitted and monitoring to ensure compliance with the standards. On both ends, the government's program falls short.

Setting standards for pesticide residues begins with an eval-uation of a pesticide's effects on health, usually gauged through animal studies. A General Accounting Office review of EPA files on 36 chemicals for which tolerances—maximum permissable levels of residues—had been set found that 7 lacked cancer and reproductive-effect studies, 14 lacked birth-defect studies, and 23 lacked mutation studies.[129] This random sample reflects an overall trend. "EPA files are replete with safety test data gaps," determined the Oversight Subcommittee of the House Com-merce Committee in its 1978 report on carcinogens in food.[130]

Moreover, that the chemical companies themselves supply the health-effects information casts doubts on the entire process. The oversight subcommittee concluded: "There is no federal compliance testing program to evaluate these data. As a result, EPA is forced to set many tolerances on unverified test data which may not fully assess the potential dangers of the pesticide in question."[131]

Compounding the problem of faulty data is the methodology used to derive a tolerance. Before a tolerance can be set, a "food factor" is determined that indicates how much of any single product—and its accompanying pesticide residue—an average person will eat during a year. Because averaging lumps together consumers and nonconsumers, the food factor is a consumption figure that understates the amounts that those who eat the product actually consume. "You need only to eat 7.5 ounces of avocado [per year] for instance—about the amount of avocado that is contained in a single avocado—before you begin to exceed the level that EPA assumes as the usage level [for the entire year] in setting up tolerances," said Lowell Dodge, then-counsel to the Oversight Subcommittee.[132]

The program for monitoring compliance with these standards also has been inadequate. The Food and Drug Administration (FDA) and the Department of Agriculture tests do not cover all the pesticides and animal drugs for which tolerances have been set; thus for all intents and purposes even some compounds for which tolerances have been set are unregulated.

Residue monitoring is also inadequate because, as Assistant Agriculture Secretary Carol Tucker Foreman testified in 1979, it is "not a preventative program."[133] It does not keep contaminated animals off the market. By the time the test results for a sample animal are available, even the meat in violation of the standards has been wrapped, bought and cooked. The Oversight Subcommittee estimated from the test results the FDA eventually received that 1.9 million tons of beef and 1.1 million tons of swine with illegal residues were sold to the public in 1976.[134]

The vast amounts of meat sold are another factor multiplying the inherent weaknesses in the program. According to Foreman, the cost of testing all beef and poultry marketed, with conventional technology, would be "about $100 billion" annually.[135] And, after the current testing procedure, little meat or poultry would remain to be eaten. Obviously, then, even if the EPA and FDA programs were drastically improved, no regulation could clean up the national food system after the fact— especially since many scientists believe no safe level of exposure to a carcinogen can be set. The only way to effectively eliminate the contamination is to cut it off at its source. But for all the testimonials given to selective pesticide use, pesticide sales continue to increase by leaps and bounds. This increased use confounds any efforts to reduce the level of food contamination. And the failure to prevent at the first steps in the food chain the increased pesticide use — use that is carefully nurtured by chemical and some farm groups and is protected, as the EPA has learned, by their supporters in Congress—is the crucial breakdown in the entire regulatory chain.

Shortfalls like these, failures of even the modest steps taken toward solving the vast environmental problem, illustrate the need to strengthen the oversight system. But the system is not being strengthened. Even as new environmental hazards are being identified, and the agony of their human victims understood, the regulatory system revealing them is under assault. Business lobbyists, with their mushrooming political action committees, have gone on the offensive and no longer are merely resisting regulation and tying up the process, but are taking their case to Congress and attacking the health-regulation enforcement system itself.

"The days when business people can sit back in the bushes and not participate in the public decision-making process," Dow Chemical President Paul Oreffice declared in 1978, "are over."[136] Oreffice may have understated the activity of business interests in the American political process for the past 200 years. But his assessment of the current mood was on target: If ever there were any businesses out there in the bushes, they are not there any longer.

One after another in the past two years, industries of all kinds have come to Washington, fighting what they have termed "regulatory overkill" and "excessive regulation."[137]

In advertisement after advertisement, trade associations and individual corporations have hammered home the claim that regulation is strangling business in red tape, wasting taxpayer money and aiming to create an unreachable, "zero-risk" society. "Pollution takes many forms," Mobil recently opined on the op-ed page of the *New York Times;* "In the American experience, by far the most damaging form has been stagnation. Economic stagnation."[138] And from the National Cotton Council: "OVER-REGULATION COULD COST YOU THE SHIRT OFF YOUR BACK. You might never get to wear cotton again. Not if the government has its way. . . ."[139] Accompanying this message, prominently placed in major magazines, is a picture of several muscular young businessmen with ties and vests but no shirts, presumably because government regulation has made cotton a thing of the past.

Nowhere in this picture are any of the 30,000 considerably less affluent, less vigorous men and women who have contracted byssinosis from breathing cotton dust on the job. But the omission may be fitting. The entire debate over regulation—with the demands for cost-benefit analysis of laws designed to save lives—has had a certain air of unreality to it, as though the suffering of workers in the plants or the families exposed to pesticide drift could be filed away as statistics under the category of business costs, and thereafter forgotten. The debate over regulation has subjected the lives of workers and the violent pollution of the air, water and land, perhaps more blatantly than ever before, to the calculus of short-range profit and myopic management.

A SKIRMISH IN THE WAR ON REGULATION

On the morning of Tuesday, April 1, 1980, the Senate Committee on Labor and Human Resources met in room 4232 of the Dirksen Senate Office Building to consider the future of OSHA. But they could easily have been talking about the EPA, or any other federal regulatory agency. Arrayed in front of the committee were top officials from all three sides of the debate: Ray Marshall, the Secretary of Labor, and OSHA head Eula Bingham; Lane Kirkland, president of the AFL-CIO; and Richard Lesher, president of the United States Chamber of Commerce.

Each side filled its expected role in what became, through the fall and winter of 1979, a familiar drama. Marshall, speaking first, reminded the committee why the regulatory agency had been necessary in the first place. "You are well aware, Mr. Chairman, that OSHA was created because an unconscionable number of American workers were being killed, injured or made ill due to workplace conditions." Kirkland informed the committee, for the record, that the current hearings followed in a long tradition. "The history of OSHA is replete with attempts to frustrate the law in fulfillment of its mission. These have included a weak and politicized implementation during previous administrations; attacks on the Act in Congress; persistent assaults by employers, and extensive litigation. . . . Further complicating its very early history, OSHA was picked out by right wing groups and business associations as a symbol of a big government's interference with laissez-faire business practices. . . ." Lesher, speaking later in the day, told the committee, though it was unlikely to need any refreshing, that business is unhappy with OSHA. "Business has a very negative perception of OSHA. The major barrier to acceptance of OSHA is the common business perception that the agency accomplishes little, and cannot help the particular individual, whether employer or employee, with his workplace safety and health performance. . . . It [OSHA] is increasing criminal sanctions and prosecutions, inciting worker unrest with inflammatory newsletters and conferences, and expanding its power into labor-management and equal employment areas."

Lesher spoke more pointedly and forcefully than either Kirkland and Marshall, or Eula Bingham. One might infer that, unlike any of the speakers preceding him, he felt momentum —one of the great political motivators—was on his side. After all, the hearings had less to do with oversight than with the charges of overkill, and with a bill offered by Pennsylvania Senator Richard Schweiker (who is now Secretary of Health and Human Services) and New Jersey Senator Harrison Williams (the chairman of the committee and a long-time friend to labor) to exempt from OSHA safety investigation 90 percent of all workplaces and 65 percent of the workforce. Only a few days before the hearing, then-presidential nominee Ronald Reagan had said, "I question seriously [the need for] the Occupational Safety and Health Administration."[140] And, as Lesher well knew, the hearings on OSHA, following the winter-long goring of the Federal Trade Commission, would not even consider expanding the agency's powers, but had been called to find justification for clipping its wings. Labor was fighting for a draw.

This defensive position is shared across the board by Washington's regulatory agencies. "Regulation used to be defined as a law which governed behavior," former Secretary of State Edmund Muskie remarked while still a senator. "Lately the mere mention of the word is making behavior in Washington ungovernable."[141] Part of the reason, as is usually the case in congressional matters, is money. Corporate political action committees have grown rapidly in the past half decade, pouring millions of dollars annually into congressional races. Through October 1980, chemical companies gave $2.67 million to congressional races, with the most money going to the opponent of Senator John Culver of Iowa, co-sponsor of the Superfund.[142]

Responding to these and similar stimuli, and to industrial claims of economic ruin, many representatives have practically stumbled over themselves to denounce government interference in environmental concerns. Led by Georgia Representative Dawson Mathis, several southern representatives in the House recently backed legislation to reauthorize the use of Mirex, a banned, carcinogenic pesticide. Mirex degrades into Kepone, and it can pass through the placenta to menace the unborn. Mirex has been found in the tissue of 20 percent of the people in states where it was heavily used.[143] To these charges, Mathis replies: "There is a big difference between potential and actual damage. There is a broad body of scientific evidence on this thing and the truth is that the jury is still out."[144] The House finally rejected these pleas for renewed Mirex use.

Even if the Schweiker bill and these attempts to cut back the power of the EPA do not pass Congress, they already have achieved much of their purpose. Agencies have been forced to assume a low profile, restrict their activities and avoid making any new enemies—particularly enemies with powerful friends on the Hill. "Reindustrialization" has become a code word for rolling back environmental statutes. If Washington regulators were tentative in the middle of the decade, they were downright timid at its close.

On that April afternoon of the OSHA hearings, Lesher closed his statement with a ringing recital of business-sponsored "reforms" for OSHA, including a requirement that the agency firmly determine "that the benefit to be derived from the proposed standard justifies the cost of compliance." Already the American Petroleum Institute (API) and the chemical trade association had brought suit on cost-benefit grounds against OSHA's reduction in the standard for exposure to benzene—a firmly established carcinogen—from 10 parts benzene per million parts of air to 1 ppm. In October 1978, the United States Court of Appeals for the Fifth Circuit in New Orleans upheld that benzene is a carcinogen, but agreed with the API that OSHA cannot set standards for occupational hazards without first using a "cost-benefit" analysis.

In its review of the case, the U.S. Supreme Court struck down the revised standard, but sidestepped the cost-benefit issue. In a 5-4 split on July 2, 1980, the Court ruled OSHA had failed to demonstrate that the higher standard posed a "significant risk" to workers. Dissenting, Justice Thurgood Marshall wrote, "The unfortunate consequence [of this decision] is that the Federal government's efforts to protect American workers from cancer and other crippling diseases may be substantially impaired."[145] Since it voided the standard, the Court said there was no reason to rule on the cost-benefit issue. But the Court is expected to decide that question in the current session, most likely in a case involving OSHA's standard for exposure to cotton dust.

Although it sounds precise and reasonable in the abstract, cost-benefit analysis is both cold-blooded and unreliable in practice. It is cold-blooded because it attempts to put a price on such things as clean air, a death from leukemia, or a child's birth defects; and it is unreliable because cost-benefit calculations depend on strings of hidden assumptions and sometimes are based on corporate-derived, unsubstantiated cost data, while failing to take full account of benefits. (In February 1980, the EPA found that of six surveyed industries, four had overestimated the costs of compliance with environmental regulations—by as much as 247 percent.)[146] So many varying assumptions and mathematical models are available to the risk assessor, wrote the director of the National Cancer Institute in an April 1979 memo, that one might project the risk from continued use of saccharin as less than one extra cancer case in the next 70 years—or 1.144 million extra cases during that period.[147] Similarly, when the government standard for occupational exposure to vinyl chloride—another known carcinogen—was issued, the vinyl chloride manufacturers claimed that compliance would cost $90 billion and would throw out of work 2.2 million people. The total cost of compliance actually has been between $127 million and $182 million, and no one has lost a job.[148] "The industry has managed not only to comply with the standard," says Labor Secretary Marshall, "but to devise more efficient and profitable technologies that actually increased production at the same time."[149]

Obviously, risk assessment is something less than an exact science.

"Studies by the Library of Congress, House Oversight and Investigations Committee, Senate Governmental Affairs Committee and Council on Environmental Quality have all concluded that the formal, mathematical cost-benefit analysis cannot adequately judge whether health/safety regulation is warranted or not," noted one recent study.[150] But cost-benefit analysis remains a rallying cry of big business. And in pushing such analysis of all OSHA regulations before that Senate committee in April, the Chamber's Lesher clearly was riding the crest of a wave, demanding that federal regulators nail down with scientific assurance the number of lives each of their actions will save—and prove that those lives are worth the cost of saving them. That formula invites disaster. "If public health policies in the nineteenth century had awaited full scientific confirmation," wrote David Rall, the head of the National Institute of Environmental Health Sciences, with a colleague, "we might only now be recovering from the effects of polio, diphtheria, whooping cough and tuberculosis epidemics."[151]

HAZARDS WITHOUT BORDERS

The offensive against regulation of corporation-bred diseases in America notwithstanding, many of the environmental problems require not only better government oversight, but increased international cooperation. Some of the most significant environmental threats are beyond the ability of any single country to solve alone. One of these problems is "acid rain," precipitation with a pH measurement below the normal 5.6. The acidic precipitation eats away at statues and makes the water of lakes and streams too acidic to support life. As many as 200 lakes in New York's Adirondack Mountains have been made unfit for life by acid rain.[152]

Acid rain is formed by sulfur dioxides—primarily emitted from coal-fired power plants—and nitrogen oxide—much of which comes from auto exhausts—that mix with water in the atmosphere and are returned to the earth as precipitation sometimes as acidic as vinegar. It is not a problem that respects boundaries. According to a Canadian study, the United States sends about 25 millions tons of sulfur dioxide pollution north of the border each year, which is about 20 millions tons more than Canada sends here.[153] Canadian officials estimate that, in the next 20 years, 48,000 Canadian lakes will be rendered lifeless by acid rain.[154]

Canada and the United States are not alone in having relations strained by the acid-rain problem. Some 15,000 lakes in

Sweden now are fishless because of pollution from smokestacks in England.[155] Sweden is also hit with emissions from France and Germany. On the continent, such invaluable structures as the Parthenon in Athens are being worn away by the precipitation.

The continued burning of fossil fuels, such as coal and oil, is causing another transnational problem that ultimately may have a much greater impact on the earth's environment than acid rain. Government scientists have predicted that if the historic growth of fossil fuel consumption continues, the concentration of carbon dioxide in the atmosphere could double by 2025, causing a "greenhouse effect" on the earth's climate.[156] Because in the atmosphere the compound allows the sun's rays to pass through, but absorbs the infrared energy released by the earth when it's warmed by the rays, the atmosphere would hold more heat. The increase in atmospheric carbon dioxide could increase the world's temperatures by about 3 degrees Celsius in the middle latitudes and as much as 7 to 10 degrees at the poles.[157]

The effects of this worldwide climatic shift could be devastating. Some scientists predict the warming trends could partially melt the polar ice cover, raising the level of the oceans, flooding some low-lying areas and damaging the great ocean fisheries. At the same time, the warming trend would alter weather patterns, throwing the grain states of the central United States into an extended drought. "Precipitation and growing seasons for crops could be greatly altered," according to the Council on Environmental Quality, "possibly disrupting world agriculture."[158]

Considerable scientific dispute continues over the ultimate effects of the build-up. But many scientists believe that "If we wait until there is absolute proof that the increase in CO_2 is causing a warming of the earth," as Dr. George Woodwell of the Woods Hole Marine Biological Laboratory says, "it will be 20 years too late to do anything about it."[159]

The depletion of the earth's ozone layer—caused primarily by the release of fluorocarbons used as propellants in refrigerators, auto air conditioners, aerosols and other products—may contribute another few tenths of a degree to the warming trend.[160] More important, depletion of ozone would reduce the protection from the ultraviolet radiation of the sun that the atmosphere affords. More ultraviolet rays would generate more frequent incidence of skin cancer.

The United States already has banned the use of fluorocarbons in propellants, but ozone depletion is a worldwide problem. The National Academy of Sciences (NAS) has estimated that 16.5 percent of the ozone layer will be depleted in the next 100 years if releases worldwide continue at the 1977 rate.[161]

As the problem is worldwide, solving it will require an unusual degree of international cooperation. "Whatever happens it happens worldwide," said John W. Tukey of Princeton University, the chairman of the follow-up NAS panel. "We are now at the place where no one thing, other than banning aerosol propellants [worldwide], is going to make a vital change. We have to go onto several fronts, many fronts."[162]

Of all the transnational environmental threats, undoubtedly the most deliberate is the export of hazardous products and industries. Tens of millions of dollars worth of banned pesticides have been shipped abroad through such official United States government programs as the Agency for International Development, and through private sales by individual corporations. These pesticides, including DDT, chlordane and heptachlor, return to this country in the form of residues on such imported foods as bananas, coffee and sugar. "Pesticide use patterns in foreign countries clearly indicate that a large portion of food imported into the United States may in fact contain unsafe pesticide residues," the General Accounting Office reported in 1979. "Many large quantity U.S. food imports are from countries whose laws allow food to be treated with pesticides for which U.S. tolerances have not been established. In some foreign countries pesticides known or suspected of causing cancer, birth defects, and gene mutations are carelessly or excessively used."[163]

Nations such as Taiwan, South Korea and Mexico have welcomed the asbestos industry, which is fleeing regulation in western Europe and the United States. And giant chemical companies are opening pesticide manufacturing plants abroad.

These developments complicate government attempts to deal with the export of hazards. Even if the United States prohibits the export of products that are banned here, multinational firms can simply ship the product from a factory that produces it outside the country. Or U.S. firms with overseas croplands can dispose of banned pesticides by applying them on crops there—and still import the produce to the United States.

How extensive the world trade in hazardous substances may be is unclear. In industrialized nations, firms already are using the threat of relocation as a hedge against stricter environmental and occupational health controls. This threat can be yet another step in the war against regulation, as Anthony Robbins, the director of NIOSH, observed:

> For example, when a large, dirty, and obsolete smelter is closed down in a couple of years, with production transferred to a brand new home in the Phillipines, hundreds of workers in Tacoma, Washington, will lose their jobs. Although the community there will be free of a serious environmental and occupational hazard —the acute effects of the job loss will seem dominant. I predict that the company which has known for years that the 70-odd-year-old smelter needed to be replaced—it had outlived its projected life expectancy of about 40–50 years—will blame the closing on occupational health and environmental rules. Thus the exportation of hazards swings the politics against protecting workers in the US as well.[164]

In this way, the lives of workers overseas become a commodity to bargain against the lives of workers in America.

THE MACHO OF TECHNOLOGY

Much of the optimism that characterized the nascent environmental movement of 1970 has cooled. It is not that the efforts of environmentalists have been in vain; great strides have been taken toward cleaning up the air and water and ensuring that hazardous wastes are kept out of homes and drinking wells.

But great problems remain. And it is clear as the 1980s

begin that the battle over a clean environment has settled into a war of attrition. Pointing out the problems and the steps for solution has not been enough, as many believed, or perhaps hoped, it would be. Though on paper and in the Congressional Record protection of the environment and the fostering of public health truly are "apple-pie" issues—what legislator is, after all, procancer?—in practice, protection of the environment usually runs afoul of powerful industries. After all, industries have achieved positions of wealth and power in part because they have been free to despoil natural resources and endanger public health. Every attempt to restrict those dubious privileges—from the Toxic Substances Control Act to the Clean Air and Clean Water Acts to the Resource Conservation and Recovery Act and the establishment of EPA and OSHA—has been bitterly contested and, once enacted, bitterly resisted. Now, each advance (the promulgation of occupational cotton-dust standards and of the RCRA regulations, after long battles) is measured against the erosions (the legislative threats to OSHA and the EPA, the rising industrial demand for rigged cost-benefit justification of any environmental actions).

And the advances are tempered, too, by another realization. The underlying philosophy that has sustained the repeated assaults on the environment and the health of society has not changed in any significant way. American business people and many government officials still subscribe to what might be termed the macho of technology—the determined belief that the answer to any problem is the forceful development and marketing of more sophisticated, more elaborate technology; more singleminded application of American ingenuity without full consideration of its long-term impact on public health and the environment. The government's primary projected solution to our pressing energy problems is massive development of synthetic fuels. That this development will produce vast quantities of hazardous wastes and pollutants is not reassuring. Technology is not destructive in itself. The destruction grows from the failure of industry and government to consider extended effects of new technologies.

If any real lessons have been learned from Love Canal and Kepone and PBB, they are difficult to spot. Business ever urges us to press on, promising, as it has for example with nuclear waste, that technology will catch up with its byproducts, and a solution will be available . . . someday.

Government officials often remind us that "trade-offs" must be made in a modern economy. But each of the disasters in this book says something else. Each tells of the need to understand that the economic forces behind the new, complex, high-powered technologies and behind the production and marketing of the new products have far outstripped the efforts to pinpoint, or even to control, the effects of technology on life and the environment. The action that should result from the environmental wreckages described in the succeeding chapters is not the end of all technological development, slowdown of economic growth, or even incubation of a risk-free society, as the Chamber of Commerce would characterize all environmental initiatives. But the disasters should prompt evaluation of the quality and the byproducts of our nation's growth. Are polyester ties, plastic credit cards and artificial preservatives worth an epidemic of cancer, a poisoned neighborhood, or a child born with a cleft palate?

Many people already are questioning the quality of industrial growth, and are developing alternatives to the hazardous practices considered here. Integrated Pest Management, which can reduce pesticide use greatly, is employed in several agricultural areas. Recycling efforts, which can reduce the amount of waste requiring disposal, are increasing. Federal agencies are developing plans to speed the regulation of cancer-causing chemicals. And new tests are available to quickly and inexpensively pinpoint unsafe chemicals.

Most important, more communities are actively working to fight chemical contamination. As the true nature of the health problems engendered by the chemical age unfold, public concern and resolve can only grow. Rolling back years of capricious attacks on the environment and public health will not be easy. But it will not be impossible, either.

NOTES

1. "Radon Guidelines May Be Weak," *Denver Post*, September 5, 1979. This was the third part of a five-part series written by Jack Cox. Additional information supplied by Cox, November 19, 1979.

2. Testimony of Suzanne Prosnier before the Oversight and Investigations Subcommittee of the House Interstate and Foreign Commerce Committee, June 27, 1979.

3. Christopher Flavin, *The Future of Synthetic Materials: The Petroleum Connection* (Worldwatch Institute, April 1980), p. 12.

4. J. H. Dubois, *Plastics History—U.S.A.* (Calmers Books, 1972), p. 292.

5. Flavin, *The Future of Synthetic Materials*, p. 13.

6. Personal communication with D. Lee Fowler, USDA, March 1980.

7. Figures from International Trade Commission.

8. *Environmental Quality: The First Annual Report of the Council on Environmental Quality*, 1970, p. 6.

9. Ibid., p. viii.

10. Ibid., p. 5.

11. "Environmental Regulation and the ImMOBILization of Truth," speech by Gus Speth, February 28, 1980.

12. "Rising Prices Spur Sales of Leading Chemical Producers," *Chemical & Engineering News*, May 5, 1980, pp. 39–40.

13. "Sales Rise for Top U.S. Chemical Producers," *Chemical & Engineering News*, May 7, 1979; and "Rising Prices Spur Sales of Leading Chemical Producers."

14. "Facts & Figures for the U.S. Chemical Industry," *Chemical & Engineering News*, June 11, 1979, p. 36.

15. "Cleansing the Chemical Image," *Business Week*, October 8, 1979, p. 73.

16. " 'Benchmark' Survey of Public Attitudes," internal CMA document, June 13, 1980.

17. "Cleansing the Chemical Image."

18. General Accounting Office, *EPA Is Slow to Carry Out Its Responsibility to Control Hazardous Chemicals*, October 28, 1980, p. 20.

19. Samuel Epstein, *The Politics of Cancer* (Sierra Club Books, 1978).

20. Quoted in *Cancer Prevention and the Delaney Clause*, Public Citizen Health Research Group, January 1973, p. 4.

21. *Environmental Quality: The Tenth Annual Report of the Council on Environmental Quality*, p. 188 (hereafter, *Tenth Annual Report*, CEQ).

22. "Cancer Choice," *Wall Street Journal,* April 11, 1980.

23. American Cancer Society, *Cancer Facts & Figures,* 1980, p. 3.

24. Ibid., pp. 3–4.

25. Toxic Substances Strategy Committee, *Toxic Chemicals and Public Protection,* May 1980, p. 117.

26. American Cancer Society, *Cancer Facts & Figures,* p. 3.

27. Ibid., p. 13.

28. Dorothy P. Rice and Thomas A. Hodgson, *Social and Economic Implications of Cancer in the United States* (National Center for Health Statistics, June 1978), p. 54.

29. Toxic Substances Strategy Committee, *Toxic Chemicals and Public Protection,* p. 118.

30. National Institute for Occupational Safety and Health, National Cancer Institute, *Estimates of the Fraction of Cancer Incidence in the United States Attributable to Environmental Factors,* September 1978.

31. Toxic Chemicals Strategy Committee draft report, p. VII-9.

32. *Environmental Pollution and Cancer and Heart and Lung Disease: First Annual Report to Congress by the Task Force on Environmental Cancer and Heart and Lung Disease,* August 7, 1978, p. 11.

33. Henry A. Schroder, M.D., *The Poisons Around Us: Toxic Metals in Food, Air, and Water* (Indiana University Press, 1974), pp. 81–83.

34. *Environmental Pollution and Cancer and Heart and Lung Disease,* p. 9.

35. Douglas H. K. Lee, "Conclusions and Reservations," in Douglas H. K. Lee (ed.), *Environmental Factors in Respiratory Disease* (Academic Press, 1972), pp. 250–251.

36. *Tenth Annual Report,* CEQ, pp. 226–230.

37. *Environmental Quality: The Eleventh Annual Report of the Council on Environmental Quality* (GPO: January 1981), p. 207 (hereafter, *Eleventh Annual Report,* CEQ). CEQ cites the National Academy of Sciences report, *Lead in the Human Environment* (Washington, D.C.: 1980).

38. Dougherty, et al., "Sperm Density And Toxic Substances: A Potential Key to Environmental Health Hazards" (unpublished paper), p. 3.

39. Ibid., p. 11.

40. Ibid., p. 3.

41. Dougherty testimony before Environmental Protection Agency, January 15, 1980, on FIFRA docket no. 415—the 2,4,5-T cancellation case—pp. 19–22.

42. See, for example, Robert W. Kapp, Dante J. Picciano, and Cecille B. Jacobson, "Y-Chromosomal Nondisjunction in Dibromochloropropane-Exposed Workmen," *Mutation Research* 64 (1979).

43. *Hazardous Waste Disposal,* Hearings before the Subcommittee on Oversight and Investigations, House Interstate and Foreign Commerce Committee, p. 63.

44. Victor K. McElheny, Seymour Abrahamson (eds.), *Banbury Report I, Assessing Chemical Mutagens: The Risk to Humans* (Cold Spring Harbor Laboratory, 1979), p. 320.

45. Ibid., p. 319.

46. Ibid.

47. CEQ, *Chemical Hazards to Human Reproduction,* January, 1981.

48. B. J. Dowty, J. L. Laseter and J. Storer, "The Transplacental Migration and Accumulation in Blood of Volatile Organic Constituents," *Pediatric Research,* vol. 10, no. 7 (July 1976), pp. 696–701.

49. Remarks of Joseph A. Califano, Secretary of Health, Education, and Welfare, before the AFL-CIO National Conference on Occupational Safety and Health, September 11, 1978, p. 2. *Tenth Annual Report,* CEQ, p. 222.

50. See NIOSH, *Estimates of the Fraction of Cancer Incidence in the United States Attributable to Environmental Factors.*

51. "Is Your Job Dangerous to Your Health?" p. 41.

52. NIOSH, *Estimates of the Fraction of Cancer Incidence in the United States Attributable to Occupational Factors,* draft summary, pp. 2–4.

53. This passage appears in the full *Estimates of the Fraction* report, p. 18.

54. Testimony of Houston Richardson before the Senate Committee on Labor and Public Welfare, Subcommittee on Labor, January 10, 1972.

55. Department of Labor, *An Interim Report to the Congress on Occupational Diseases,* December 1979, p. 35.

56. *Tenth Annual Report,* CEQ, p. 21.

57. Ibid., pp. 17, 39.

58. Ibid., p. 33.

59. Ibid.

60. *Environmental Quality: The Ninth Annual Report of the Council on Environmental Quality,* p. 72.

61. *Eleventh Annual Report,* CEQ, p. 123.

62. *Tenth Annual Report,* CEQ, p. 78.

63. *Eleventh Annual Report,* CEQ, p. 130.

64. *Tenth Annual Report,* CEQ, p. 138.

65. *Implementation of the Federal Water Pollution Control Act* (Nonpoint Pollution and the Areawide Waste Treatment Management Program), hearings

before the Subcommittee on Oversight and Review of the House Committee on Public Works and Transportation (GPO, 1979), p. 437. This was observed in testimony by Elmer B. Staats, head of the General Accounting Office. In all, 4 million tons of sediment waste enter waterways annually.

66. *Tenth Annual Report,* CEQ, p. 149.

67. James Risser, "Farm Chemicals Dilemma: High Yield for Low Water Quality," *Des Moines Register,* September 13, 1978. This was part of an outstanding seven-part series by Risser, of the *Register's* Washington bureau.

68. Risser, "Farm Chemicals Dilemma."

69. Speth, "The ImMOBILization of Truth."

70. The New York Public Interest Group and the Environmental Defense Fund, *Troubled Waters: Toxic Chemicals in the Hudson River,* September 28, 1977.

71. Toxic Substances Strategy Committee, *Toxic Chemicals and Public Protection,* p. 6.

72. "Radiation Found in Colorado Water Supply," *Washington Post,* July 14, 1980. Also personal communication with Dr. William L. Lappenbusch, chief of health effects, EPA Office of Drinking Water.

73. National Academy of Sciences, *Drinking Water and Health* (1977), pp. 791–792.

74. Norwood, *At Highest Risk,* p. 73.

75. "Clean Water: Industry's Job Has Just Begun," *Business Week,* February 25, 1980, p. 62F.

76. Ibid., p. 62J.

77. *United States of America v. Hooker Chemical and Plastics Corporation et al.,* p. 13. Filed December 20, 1979, U.S. District Court for Western District of New York.

78. *Everybody's Problem: Hazardous Wastes,* EPA Office of Solid Wastes, p. 1.

79. *Tenth Annual Report,* CEQ, p. 181.

80. Testimony of Stephen J. Gage, assistant administrator for research and development, EPA, before the Senate Committee on the Judiciary and the Senate Committee on Labor and Human Resources, June 6, 1980.

81. *Everybody's Problem,* p. 15.

82. *Preliminary Assessment of Cleanup Costs for National Hazardous Waste Problems,* consultant report to the EPA Office of Solid Waste, 1979, p. 24.

83. "EPA: 1.2 Million May Be Exposed to Toxic Waste," *Washington Post,* June 6, 1980.

84. *Preliminary Assessment of Cleanup Costs,* p. 37.

85. For Love Canal, personal communication, New York State Department of Transportation; for Montague, *Hazardous Waste Disposal*, report of the Subcommittee on Oversight and Investigations, House Interstate and Foreign Commerce Committee, October 1979, p. 5.

86. Environmental Protection Agency, *Waste Disposal Practices and Their Effects on Ground Water, Executive Summary*, January 1977, pp. 1, 15.

87. Ibid., p. 1.

88. Ibid., p. 18.

89. Ibid., p. 40.

90. Environmental Protection Agency, *The National Potential for Damage From Industrial Waste Disposal*, p. 15.

91. Ibid.

92. *Hazardous Waste Disposal*, p. 54.

93. "Hanford, Washington, Nuclear Dump Closed Over Packaging Incident," *Washington Post* (AP), October 5, 1979.

94. "A Dangerous Dearth of Radioactive Dump Sites," *Business Week*, November 19, 1979, p. 54G.

95. "A-Dump Closing Threatens to Halt Cancer Research," *Washington Post*, October 24, 1979.

96. Ibid. The quote is from Philip Lorio of Columbia University in New York.

97. "U.S. Official Tells Panel of Nuclear Waste Needs," *Washington Post*, February 14, 1980.

98. General Accounting Office report to the Subcommittee on Energy And Power, House Committee on Interstate and Foreign Commerce, *The Uranium Mill Tailings Cleanup: Federal Leadership At Last?*, June 20, 1978, p. 4.

99. Rachel Carson, *Silent Spring* (Fawcett-Crest, 1962), p. 141.

100. The United States Department of Agriculture, Agricultural Stabilization and Conservation Service, *The Pesticide Review*, 1978 edition, p. 1.

101. Dale R. Bottrell, *Integrated Pest Management* (Council on Environmental Quality, 1980), p. 7.

102. Epstein, *The Politics of Cancer*, p. 32.

103. Robert Van den Bosch, *The Pesticide Conspiracy* (Doubleday, 1978), p. 59.

104. Personal communication, D. Lee Fowler.

105. USDA, *The Pesticide Review*, p. 5.

106. Testimony of Steven D. Jellinek, EPA assistant administrator for toxic substances, before the House Interstate and Foreign Commerce Committee, Subcommittee on Oversight and Investigations, p. 1.

107. *Cancer-Causing Chemicals in Food,* report of the Subcommittee on Oversight and Investigations, House Interstate and Foreign Commerce Committee, December 1978, p. 25.

108. Ibid., p. 2.

109. Office of Technology Assessment, *Environmental Contaminants in Food,* December 1979, p. 59.

110. Ibid., p. 19.

111. Ibid.

112. F. Kutz, S. Strassman and A. Yobs, "Survey of Pesticide Residues and Their Metabolites in the General Population of the United States" (presented at the International Workshop on Biological Specimen Collection, Luxembourg, April 18–22, 1977), pp. 8, 10.

113. *Cancer-Causing Chemicals in Food,* p. 5.

114. CRS, *Agricultural and Environmental Relationships: Issues and Priorities,* June, 1979, p. 147.

115. Barry Commoner, *The Closing Circle* (Bantam Books, 1972), p. 267.

116. Kush made the remark at the American Chemical Society Annual Meeting in Washington, D.C., September 10, 1979; it was quoted in the *Journal of Commerce,* September 11, 1979.

117. Jackson B. Browning, "Hazardous Wastes: Action On a National Problem," *Environmental Forum,* vol. I, no. I, October 1979.

118. "Rising Prices Spur Sales of Leading Chemical Producers," p. 40.

119. *Tenth Annual Report,* CEQ, p. 643.

120. Mark Green and Norman Waitzman, *Business War on the Law* (Corporate Accountability Research Group, 1979), p. 52.

121. Center for Policy Alternatives at the Massachusetts Institute of Technology, *Benefits of Environmental, Health, and Safety Regulation,* prepared for the Senate Committee on Governmental Affairs, March 25, 1980, p. 14.

122. *Hazardous Waste Disposal,* p. 23.

123. *Hazardous Waste Disposal,* hearings, p. 665. Also see Love Canal chapter.

124. *Eleventh Annual Report,* CEQ, pp. 393–396.

125. Ibid., pp. 657–659.

126. Quoted in a statement by Representative George Miller (D-California), *Congressional Record,* July 27, 1979, pp. E 3922–3923.

127. For more discussion of each of these issues, see individual chapters. Also, "House Hearing is Told Dow Knew in 1964 That Defoliant was Toxic," *New York Times,* July 23, 1980.

128. "Effort to Assess Pesticide Safety is Bogged Down," *New York Times,* December 12, 1977.

129. *Cancer-Causing Chemicals in Food,* p. 6.

130. Ibid., p. 18.

131. Ibid., p. 19.

132. Ibid., p. 12.

133. Testimony of Carol Tucker Foreman, assistant secretary for food and consumer services, USDA, before the Oversight and Investigations Subcommittee of the House Interstate and Foreign Commerce Committee, September 28, 1979, p. 4.

134. *Cancer-Causing Chemicals in Food,* p. 26.

135. Foreman testimony, p. 4.

136. "No Time To Sit Back," *Chemical Week,* June 28, 1978.

137. Testimony of Richard L. Lesher, president of the U.S. Chamber of Commerce, before the Senate Labor and Human Resources Committee, April 1, 1980, p. 9.

138. Mobil's ad first appeared on May 4, 1972. See the *New York Times,* March 20, 1980, for a recent reprint.

139. The Cotton Council, the cotton industry trade association, took out this ad in several publications in spring 1980.

140. "Sharp Contrasts With Carter's Economics," *Business Week,* March 31, 1980.

141. "Congress Doing Battle With a Monster of Its Own Creation . . ." *Washington Post,* October 21, 1979.

142. "18 Finance Panel Members Got $300,000 From Chemical Industry," *Washington Post,* November 17, 1980.

143. Letter from Douglas M. Costle, administrator of the EPA, to Representative Thomas S. Foley, chairman of the House Committee on Agriculture, May 11, 1979.

144. "Battle Against Fire Ants Heats Up Over Pesticides," *Washington Star,* October 13, 1979.

145. Supreme Court decision, July 2, 1980 on nos. 78–911 and 78–1036; dissent by Justice Marshall, p. 1.

146. "Comparisons of Estimated and Actual Pollution Control Cost for Selected Industries," consultant report for EPA Office of Planning & Evaluation, February 1980.

147. "They Bet Your Life," *Washington Post Magazine,* November 18, 1979, pp. 42–43.

148. *Business War on the Law*, p. 54. Also Marshall testimony, April 1, 1980.

149. Ibid.

150. *Business War on The Law*, p. 21.

151. Devra Lee Davis, Environmental Law Institute, and David P. Rall, director of the National Institute of Environmental Health Sciences, "Risk Assessment for Disease Prevention," *Strategies for Public Health: Promoting Health & Preventing Disease*, Lorenz Ng and Devra Lee Davis, eds. (Van Nostrand Reinhold, 1980).

152. "Acid Rain: Push Toward Coal Makes Global Pollution Worse," *Washington Post*, December 30, 1979.

153. Ibid.

154. Ibid.

155. Norman R. Glass, Gary E. Glass, Peter J. Rennie, "Environmental Effects of Acid Precipitation" (presented June 8, 1979, Washington, D.C.).

156. Testimony of Gus Speth before the Senate Energy Committee. See "Buildup of Carbon Dioxide Risky, Hill Panel Told," *Washington Star*, April 3, 1980.

157. Ibid.

158. *Tenth Annual Report*, CEQ, p. 622.

159. Ibid.

160. "Ozone: Worldwide, Many-Faceted Problem," *Science News*, January 5, 1980.

161. "Ozone Depletion: Double the Trouble," *Science News*, November 17, 1979.

162. "Ozone: Worldwide, Many-Faceted Problem."

163. *Better Regulation of Pesticide Exports and Pesticide Residues in Imported Foods is Essential*, General Accounting Office, June 22, 1979, pp. 6–7.

164. Author's notes on speech by Anthony Robbins, director, NIOSH, before the conference on *Exportation of Hazardous Industries to Developing Countries* held at Hunter College, New York City, November 3, 1979.

Chapter 2

PBB

ELLEN E. GRZECH

THOMAS THOMPSON HAD BEEN a farmer all his life, but none of his experience had prepared him for what began happening on his farm in late 1973. Thompson raised a herd of dairy cattle, which his brother had started breeding in 1939, in the rich "thumb" of Michigan's eastern lower peninsula. He had worked hard, and it showed in his farm.

Through the end of 1973 and in early 1974, however, Thompson's herd was depleted by a plague defying explanation. His cows stopped breeding. Milk production suddenly dropped. Though he didn't know it at the time, the ailments were not limited to his herd; farmers from a handful of dairy farms noticed similar problems. Like Thompson, they had no answer. Nor did state veterinarians or the farm services company that provided their dairy feed.

Then in April 1974, a U.S. Department of Agriculture (USDA) researcher who had been contacted by one of the dairy farmers identified what was harming the cows—polybrominated biphenyl, or PBB. The toxic PBB was used as a fire retardant, increasing the resistance of plastics to heat. PBB does not belong in or anywhere near animal feed. But somehow it had contaminated the feed being used by some dairy farmers.

When news of the PBB discovery in dairy feed was reported, Thompson deduced that the chemical was causing his problems. But he and his family forgot their fears when officials incorrectly reported that only one type of feed was contaminated with PBB. The Thompsons were using another mix, although it was from the same manufacturer.

Thompson and his family continued to work their herd and eat meat from their farm animals. Then, a full year after the PBB contamination was discovered in Michigan, the Thompsons found that their herd included several animals whose milk tested at levels higher than the then-legal limit of 300 parts per billion (ppb) of PBB. The state quarantined the herd for PBB contamination in May 1975, and that July the tainted animals remaining were taken away and killed.

For more than a year, however, Thompson, his wife and four children had eaten meat and drunk milk from their herd and had sold the milk, and the meat from cows sent to slaughter, to the public. The Thompsons were only one family of the millions in Michigan that consumed meat or milk contaminated with PBB.

"That's their constant pattern, everything is a year or more behind," Thompson complained about the state officials' responses to PBB. "I think they were very lax in this respect. Had they gotten right on it, I feel the problem would have been forestalled."

Thompson's criticism is echoed by scores of Michigan's farmers bitter and worried about their health, their finances and their farms. These farmers, proud of herds they had carefully and expensively bred for years, listened to state and company officials and were told the herds' problems were mismanagement, malnutrition or incorrect feeding. Farmer after farmer tells of eating tainted food long after the chemical and feed suppliers—and later the state—had learned the dairy feed was contaminated.

"[They were] horrible times. There were days when you honestly had almost suicidal thoughts," said Hubert Zuiderveen, a farmer from one of the hardest-hit areas in Michigan.

The tragedy began in 1973 with an accident allowed to happen through careless handling of chemicals. PBB, which accumulates and is stored in the body fat of animals, was known to be toxic by its manufacturer, Michigan Chemical Company, yet often was stored near other products, including additives for dairy feed.

Michigan Chemical, in St. Louis, Michigan, was owned by the Chicago-based conglomerate Northwest Industries, and in 1976 was merged into another of Northwest's properties, the Velsicol Chemical Company. Michigan Chemical manufactured a feed additive called Nutrimaster, consisting of magnesium oxide and formulated to make cows produce more and richer milk. In 1973, some bags of the fire retardant, known by the trade name Firemaster, were mistakenly shipped from the Michigan Chemical Company to a farm feed supplier about 100 miles across the state in Battle Creek.

Employees of the feed supplier, a subsidiary of a state-wide farmers' organization called the Michigan Farm Bureau, thought the bags of PBB were part of its usual shipment of magnesium oxide, and the bags of fire retardant were stored along with feed ingredients. Both substances were in poorly marked brown bags; both sets of bags had stenciled trade names ending with "-master"; the chemicals even looked somewhat alike. There was no warning on the bags that the ones stencilled Firemaster contained poison. These similarities made the mix-up terribly easy, even though the chemicals were mixed into the feed by hand. A still-undetermined amount of PBB was mixed into the feed preparation the Farm Bureau Services sold to unsuspecting farmers.

Six years after that crucial error, more than 575 farm families had suffered through quarantines that, for varying lengths of time, prohibited either selling the PBB-tainted cows for meat, selling their milk, or both. More than 25,000 dairy animals were killed and buried by the state of Michigan because they were contaminated with PBB. Thousands were destroyed by the farmers who owned them, and many more died from exposure to the chemical. Poultry, swine, sheep, horses, goats and rabbits also were killed because their feed was poisoned with PBB, usually because their food was mixed on equipment containing PBB residues.

The state estimates the disaster has cost taxpayers $59 million for testing, destruction of PBB-poisoned animals and health surveys. Although the state of Michigan is suing Velsicol and the Farm Bureau to recover the $59 million—and for $61 million more in punitive damages—years could pass before the case is settled. The Farm Bureau, which sold the tainted feed, has settled claims with almost all the farmers whose herds were quarantined because of PBB, at an estimated cost of about $20 million. Velsicol has also paid millions of dollars in out-of-court settlements to Michigan farm families who had to destroy their livestock because of PBB, but scores of lawsuits against the company remain to be settled.

These costs are only the beginning. In 1977, a team of doctors from New York's Mount Sinai Hospital evaluated 1,029 farmers and their families who consumed meat and milk from PBB-tainted dairy herds and found evidence of damaged immunological systems, which make people more susceptible to disease and infections, and evidence of damaged livers and impaired neurological functions. The dairy farmers with high levels of PBB contamination had fewer lymphocytes, which help fight infections.

Further, the Mount Sinai doctors tested 3,000 other Michigan residents to assess how the contamination affected the general population. More than 90 percent of Michigan residents have PBB in their bodies, the Mount Sinai researchers reported in 1979. While they found no evidence of serious health problems because of PBB, they suggested it could be linked with Michigan residents' increased number of minor infections and colds. Most important, the doctors are concerned about the possibility that the PBB contamination may result in extra cancers 20 or 30 years from now. Dr. Irving Selikoff, leader of the Mount Sinai team, said no data yet exists to show that PBB definitely has caused cancer in humans, "but it would be totally unlike any other chemical if it produced [cancer] in so short a time."[1] So the concern remains.

Michigan seems to have brought under control its remaining problem with PBB in meat and milk through actions taken in 1977. In that year the state established a drastically lower (and, state officials believe, safer) level of PBB permitted in animals and created an agency to track down tainted animals before they are sold to the public as meat. That agency found contaminated animals on 560 farms between October 1977 and May 1979.

Earlier, however, officials who were supposed to protect the state failed to quickly identify contaminated farms and to keep the tainted food out of stores. When PBB contamination was discovered, in 1974, highly contaminated milk and meat were flooding the food chain. Vital information was withheld by both the Farm Bureau and Michigan Chemical. As a result, a chemical accident that began with dairy farmers became an environmental disaster that spread, unchecked, into the state's marketplaces. And its frightening legacy remains.

FIREMASTER AND NUTRIMASTER

The specific details of how the fire retardant got into dairy feed remain unknown, but Farm Bureau officials believe the mix-up in shipping occurred in May 1973 and perhaps again in Michigan Chemical's July–August shipment. Velsicol officials have refused to answer questions about the accident.

But employees of Velsicol's Michigan plant said in 1977 that PBB was stored near other chemicals, including those for animal and human consumption. Some of the bags containing PBB were ripped and torn, workers charged. They also said that machinery used to manufacture and process PBB was used to handle other products, spreading the contamination. And, inventories at Michigan Chemical were not precisely kept. A review in June 1973 showed that about ten bags of the fire retardant were missing, but company officials were not concerned because they had discontinued the sale of the substance, and it was only taking up warehouse space. The bags were listed as "in process," implying that their contents had been recycled. Had the record-keeping been kept up to date, the misshipment of May could have been checked and possibly recalled before the contamination began.[2]

Charles Szeluga, an employee who mixed feed at Farm

Bureau Services' plant near Battle Creek, has claimed that he looked at two piles of brown paper bags at the warehouse on June 29, 1973, and asked his boss to explain the difference between the pile stencilled with the name Nutrimaster and those labeled with the name Firemaster. Szeluga said in a legal deposition that his boss told him no difference existed and to put the two piles together and count them as the same chemical in the regular monthly inventory.[3] Szeluga's testimony could explain why regular inventories and his boss's twice-a-day walk through the warehouse failed to detect the presence of PBB, even though it was stored in plain sight.

Szeluga piled the Firemaster—the toxic PBB—with the Nutrimaster, or magnesium oxide. Normally these chemicals do not look alike: The magnesium oxide is a fine, white powder and the PBB comes in pinkish chunks that look somewhat like peanut brittle. But late in 1971 or 1972 Michigan Chemical had ground the PBB into a white powder as an experiment. Normally, the chemicals were packed in easily identifiable color-coded bags. But, apparently because of a bag shortage, in 1973 the two chemicals were put in the same type of brown paper bag.

As a result, the only obvious difference between the two was in the prefix of their trade names, which were stencilled on the bags. And the many trade names for magnesium oxide—of which Nutrimaster was only one—clouded even this distinction. This casual handling of dangerous chemicals was what set into motion the state-wide threat to Michigan's food chain.

In 1973 a handful of farmers had asked the Farm Bureau, the State Agriculture Department and dairy experts from Michigan State University to help determine what was making their cows sick. The state veterinarians who examined the problem herds failed to find a common factor. But several farmers who complained to Farm Bureau Services all used the same feed mix, Dairy 402, which was supposed to contain magnesium oxide. The Farm Bureau was later revealed even to have discussed the numerous complaints at staff meetings during the winter of 1973–74.[4] Farmers who called the Farm Bureau, however, were not told about the other complaints. Nor were state officials notified.[5]

Because of the many complaints, Farm Bureau Services did stop making Dairy 402 in December 1973. Although company spokesmen claimed they reported the production halt to the state's Department of Agriculture, state officials maintained they were not aware of the production stoppage.

Farm Bureau officials also said they instituted a massive recall of Dairy 402 from individual farmers and dealers in January 1974. But farmers who used 402 said later they were never contacted about their bad feed. One farmer kept feeding the PBB-laden 402 to his calves right up to the day they were quarantined. A second farmer said his feed was not recalled by the Farm Bureau even after his cows were quarantined because of PBB, and he finally buried the bad feed on his farm. In February 1974—after the accident but before PBB was discovered to be in the dairy feed—a state inspector had visited the Michigan Chemical plant and asked for information about the fire retardant. Only by chance had the state inspector learned about the PBB there, since no legal requirement existed that the company report production of new chemicals. The inspector twice requested information about the toxicity of PBB and about worker exposure, but Michigan Chemical did not provide the requested material until May 31, 1974—a month after the PBB mix-up was uncovered.

That the PBB tragedy was discovered as quickly as it was largely is owed to the persistence of Rick Halbert, the owner of a prosperous dairy herd in southern Michigan who had training in chemistry and had worked for the Dow Chemical Company. Halbert, who spent thousands of dollars of his own money to determine what was making his cows ill, pushed a frustrating search for months, contacting toxicologists and researchers around the country and persuading them to test his feed.

Halbert's efforts eventually led him to George Fries, a toxicologist at the USDA labs in Beltsville, Maryland. When Halbert reported the clues other researchers had uncovered, Fries told him in a phone conversation on April 19, 1974, that the feed probably contained PBB. Tests three days later confirmed Fries' suspicion. Fries had experimented with PBB two years earlier, and he was one of a few people in the country who knew that the only company manufacturing the fire retardant under the name Firemaster was Michigan Chemical—which also produced the Nutrimaster that Halbert was feeding to his cows. Within two weeks the Food and Drug Administration, which had never before faced this contaminant, set a maximum legal level of 1,000 parts per billion of PBB in food products. (That level would be dropped by the FDA a few months later to 300 ppb and, more than three years later, by the state of Michigan to 20 ppb, the current limit.)

After the mix-up was discovered, Farm Bureau Services claimed that in May or June of 1974 it instituted a second massive recall, to retrieve all feed that contained magnesium oxide or that had been mixed at the Battle Creek plant since shortly before the mix-up occurred in 1973. As in the earlier recall of Dairy 402, many farmers who had bought possibly contaminated feed were not contacted, despite the Farm Bureau's claims of conducting a recall. Some farmers even got letters in May 1974 from local Farm Bureau mill operators assuring that the feed they used was safe. Farm Bureau Services closed its Battle Creek plant in April in an attempt to clean out its contamination, but this was to be only the first of four tries to rid the plant of the PBB taint. The Farm Bureau told both farmers and officials of the state and federal governments that the contamination had been removed. But this was less than truthful, as company officials well knew. Minutes of an August 1974 staff meeting noted: "PBB throughout the plant at Battle Creek. Could contaminate animals."[6]

At first, company officials thought only the PBB-laced Dairy 402, straight magnesium oxide, and 10 other feeds supposed to contain magnesium oxide were contaminated. Eventually they realized that even feeds that were not supposed to contain Nutrimaster were also tainted, and that what was thought to be limited contamination had spread to virtually all feeds mixed at the Battle Creek plant since the accident. The machinery used to mix the PBB-tainted feeds was itself contaminated; the PBB was passed on to other feeds mixed with that machinery. That cross-contamination had also spread to feeds mixed at other local mills, after their machinery touched the PBB feeds. State officials were doing little to clear the confusion. B. Dale Ball, then director of the state Agriculture Department, guessed in the first days after the discovery of PBB in the feed that only 25 herds were contaminated. Nonetheless, the state launched a testing program to identify contaminated herds. This program only demonstrated, however, how difficult to deal with PBB would be. The milk tests permitted highly contaminated individual cows to go undetected because the test sample included milk from the entire herd. Milk from high-PBB-level cows was diluted with milk from low-PBB-level or "clean" cows, so that the whole sample tested contained PBB at a level lower than the maximum allowed. With the knowledge and apparent approval of state officials, some farmers managed to avoid quarantine by mixing milk from highly contaminated cows with that of other cows.[7]

Many of the herds that escaped detection because of the faulty sampling process would have been quarantined and destroyed if the state had tested individual cows, and many herds were destroyed after more conscientious farmers had the individual tests done, often at their own expense. Ball, who has since retired as state agriculture boss, defended herd milk tests as faster and simpler than the more accurate fat tests or the sampling of milk from individual cows. He claimed the state's labs were too overloaded to perform individual tests. Yet the state failed to use outside laboratories to relieve that burden during those first crucial months.

State officials not only failed to keep milk contaminated with PBB off the market, they also failed to keep tainted meat from consumers; the officials made only limited and random tests of animals sold in Michigan slaughterhouses. Dairy farmers sold their cows that no longer were productive—called "cull" cows—and those cows usually were bought by packers for hamburger. "I don't think it's the right thing to do, but what else can you do?" asked Adrian Kamphouse, who said he sold his sick but nonquarantined cows on the advice of a Farm Bureau adjustor. "I think a lot of that crap went into hamburger that should not have been meat."

When the state began regular testing in slaughterhouses in January 1975, a full eight months had passed since the contamination had been discovered. Even then, the meat that was tested was not kept out of the stores, but was sold before the tests were completed and the results known.

Besides conducting the faulty test procedures, the state also failed to communicate adequately with the growing numbers of affected farmers. "They didn't come to us. The farmer had to go to them. That's the strange part—they didn't seek it [the PBB] out," said Lee Heming, a dairy farmer in the northwest part of the state.

Ball said that he did not see the need to warn every farmer in the state about the possibility of PBB-poisoned feed, because "we assume farmers can read, and [that they] read the paper —I can't mail something to every farmer in the state. He can test the same as we can if he's concerned."[8]

That insensitivity to a difficult type of agricultural crisis led to much bitterness on the part of farmers, who felt ignored and betrayed by their government. Traditionally independent, the farmers fought their battles individually for the most part, and often blamed themselves for their troubles. But many of these normally staunch defenders of conservative principles were transformed by the PBB debacle into angry and cynical critics of the government officials who were supposed to help them.

"Those big shots can sit there like God Almighty and they don't know what it's about. By God, I wish they were sitting in this seat right now. Then they'd know what life was about," said Carolyn Young, who, with her husband, Donald, took care of their quarantined cows for six months before they finally were destroyed. William June Overman, who worked his western Michigan dairy farm from a wheelchair, anguished over a herd he was certain was sick from PBB, and he expressed the frustration and despair felt by scores of farmers. "We are Christian folks. You don't go out and kill someone, you don't go out and beat someone up. But, Lord, you feel like it some days."

Many other farmers also felt betrayed, by both the feed companies they had long worked with and the state. Lee Heming suspected PBB was the problem with his cattle when he heard about the accident in 1974. He was reassured by his local grain-elevator operator that his feed was free of PBB and, when his cows continued to abort and sicken, he blamed himself and his family for their misfortune. Six months after the PBB discovery, he called state veterinarians for help with his still-sick herd and learned that one of his cows was highly contaminated. His farm was quarantined, and his cows were destroyed a week later.

Gordon Maurer, who farms in the fertile thumb area of Michigan's eastern lower peninsula, also was reassured by his elevator operator that PBB wasn't in his feed. The state inspectors, too, told him not to worry if after his milk was tested he didn't hear from them again. He didn't hear, and he breathed easy. Then in August 1976, more than two years after PBB was first discovered, a state inspector informed Maurer that he had sold for slaughter a cow whose meat had a level of PBB higher than the legal limit. The state inspector said he didn't know exactly when or where the cow had been sold, but that it had been checked at slaughter within the previous 18 months. Maurer's farm was quarantined, and six of his cows were killed before the quarantine was lifted.

Many farmers had to rely on media news reports and on word of mouth from friends to find out what was happening and to see that their personal disasters were part of a larger, statewide crisis. And the news reports weren't offering the farmers many answers. The state's newspapers reported the initial discovery of PBB and continued to cover the subsequent major events, but the coverage focused on official statements and actions and the reactions to them. In the first years of the PBB crisis, only a few isolated attempts were made to humanize the PBB story and to report it from varying perspectives that would explain the disaster within a broader context. The most thorough early reporting was done by an independent agriculture magazine called *Michigan Farmer.*

Not until 1977 did the *Detroit Free Press,* the state's largest morning daily, commit two and sometimes three reporters virtually full-time to the PBB crisis, allowing them to devote time to investigative and more complete articles on PBB. As the disaster grew instead of disappearing, and as the health of farmers and consumers became a greater concern, media coverage increased. Occasionally, television reporters attempted to cover the stories related to PBB; a handful of broadcasts were done by the national networks. But a British television crew filmed the hour-long 1977 documentary on PBB called "The Poisoning of Michigan" that provided what many considered the best single look at PBB by broadcasters.

Only when news of the crisis began to reveal its extent did farmers realize they were not alone in their misfortune. For many, that awareness was years in coming. The bitterness and anger of some farmers eventually led to the formation of vocal organizations. One group of farmers in western Michigan began a PBB Action Committee that, with a tight budget and overflowing dedication, put out newsletters and ran phone campaigns and a road show to illustrate their problems with PBB. The committee also attempted to involve consumers in such urban areas as Detroit.

When the PBB crisis became a potential threat to the health of Michigan consumers as well as to farmers, public concern outside rural areas began to mount. Consumers demanded milk and meat that were free of PBB, and many grocery stores were forced to advertise prominently that their beef came from outside the state. Consumer reaction, although unorganized, was strong enough that the Michigan beef industry began a campaign. The industry wanted to convince consumers that the better cuts of beef, unlike cheaper cuts, were safe from the taint of PBB. (Generally speaking, the better cuts were safe.)

Thomas Thompson and the hundreds of farmers who, like him, had their farms quarantined because their animals tested at levels higher than the FDA's PBB limit were among the most evident victims of PBB. But many other farmers suffered a fate that in a way was more difficult and tragic than the Thompsons'. For example, Eugene and Virginia Prehn were forced to exist in what they called a "PBB limbo" on their well-kept farm in the northwest part of the state's lower peninsula. Prehn, who had been breeding his herd for 25 years, had had only three or four of his animals die on the farm before 1974—and PBB. In the three years after the PBB contaminations he buried about 35 animals on his land. Like many farmers, Prehn blamed himself when his cows began to go lame, to get thin and sick and even to die.

Prehn believed he didn't have a PBB problem, until he had a private laboratory run tests on fat samples he took from his cows. Those privately done tests showed that some of his cows had levels of PBB more than four times the legal limit. But tests by the state, which determined contamination officially, showed that Prehn's herd had low levels of PBB—lower than the level the state legally considered safe.

The amount of PBB measured in a contaminated cow's body-fat sample could vary, sometimes widely, depending on which part of the cow provided the fat sample. Even such factors as whether a cow was giving milk or was in a dry cycle appeared to affect fat-test results. Sixteen samples taken from a single cow showed widely varying PBB levels: On the basis of some of those samples, the cow would have been quarantined by state officials; other results would have allowed that same cow to be sold for meat.

The body fat tests were more reliable than milk tests. However, the fat tests were not sufficiently precise to distinguish accurately between cows whose samples measured slightly above or below the federal level. The experiences of many farmers illustrated that the tests of fat samples accurately measured only how much PBB was in one small area, not how much was in the entire cow.[9]

So, technically and officially, Prehn's cows were clean. He could sell their milk, and he could sell their meat for hamburger. Yet they exhibited the classic symptoms of PBB contamination: Their milk production had dropped dramatically; they were always sick, with infections that wouldn't heal; their calves were stillborn or died soon after birth; they had rough-looking coats, with overgrown horns and hooves; and they were small and thin, although Prehn insisted he fed his cows well, and his veterinarian agreed.

Prehn's dilemma was similar to that of many farmers whose animals' PBB contamination was less than the legal limit. They were not quarantined, nor could he be compensated for their loss. But Prehn and other so-called low-level farmers have claimed that their cows were sick, nonetheless, and that owners of herds should be compensated by the responsible companies for the loss of the animals, as the so-called high-level farmers had been. "Initially I think it was a mistake, I really do. But . . . [the situation] has gotten way beyond the point of being a mistake. I don't think it's a mistake anymore," says Prehn. Finally, in January 1976, Prehn sold three truckloads of his sick cows for meat that he admits "shouldn't have been put on the market. . . . I couldn't convince myself I could afford to be the conscience of Michigan," Prehn said.

Although the companies involved in the accident have settled claims with most of the farmers whose herds tested as having high levels of PBB and were quarantined by the state, the companies have been unwilling to compensate the low-level farmers. In 1978, a state circuit-court judge ruled against farmers Roy and Marilyn Tacoma, who filed suit against the Farm Bureau Services and Velsicol for $250,000 and triple damages. Wexford County Circuit Judge William Peterson decided that small amounts of PBB were not harmful to the Tacomas' cows. This suit was the first filed by a low-level farmer to go to trial. (Later Velsicol did agree to pay 70 Michigan farmers, including the Tacomas, several million dollars in an out-of-court settlement. Attorneys had filed 83 lawsuits in 22 Michigan counties asking for damages for farmers who had suffered from their herds' PBB contamination. After weeks of negotiation by a three-man team of lawyers representing the farmers, in late 1979, 70 of the farmers received cash settlements and forgiveness of feed debts.) Many farmers, and some researchers, are convinced that even low levels of PBB cause cows irreparable harm.

Part of the difficulty in judging the extent of damage is a unique—and disturbing—characteristic of PBB. Experts who studied its effects on the body determined that the chemical does not behave according to the usual dose-response relationship; that is, the doctors from Mount Sinai observed, a person contaminated with a greater amount of PBB does not necessarily exhibit more or worse symptoms than one contaminated with a lesser amount.

"UNDESIRABLE AND . . . POSSIBLY . . . DANGEROUS"

Michigan Chemical Company, which later was merged into Velsicol, began manufacturing the brominated fire retardant at its plant in St. Louis, Michigan, in 1971. That year, the company sent its PBB customers a letter warning them to protect their employees from PBB dust and fumes because the chemical accumulates in the human body and is not eliminated.[10] Exposure, they warned, is "undesirable and could possibly be dangerous."

One year later, the largest chemical company in the country decided that PBB was too dangerous to produce. In 1972, the DuPont Chemical Company tested a sample of Michigan Chemical's PBB on animals and found that it caused lethargy, weight loss and liver enlargement. Both DuPont and the Dow Chemical Company decided not to manufacture a similar kind of PBB because animals exposed to it, too, developed disturbing symptoms. (When a USDA scientist asked Michigan Chemical for a sample of PBB so he could test it for toxicity, the company refused—even though it had offered free PBB samples in a trade journal. The USDA finally got a sample from the company, after further pressure and requests, and tested it on animals, but at levels too low to produce results.)

Those first exposed to PBB outside the lab were the chemical workers who manufactured more than 12 million pounds of the fire retardant for Michigan Chemical between 1971 and

1974. Now, not only do the more than 300 workers face health problems, but most of them also are unemployed, because Velsicol closed its St. Louis plant and left the state. Following an out-of-court settlement with the state in 1976, the company agreed to leave Michigan and pay a token $20,000 fine for polluting a 30-mile stretch of the nearby Pine River with PBB and other chemicals.

Velsicol officials, under federal indictment in 1979 for lying to federal officials about their role in the PBB disaster,* have refused to discuss their activities except to deny the government's charges in court. But Velsicol workers were heavily exposed to PBB dust and fumes for more than two years. The workers had complained about their poor work conditions and, as Michigan Chemical's warning letter to customers shows, the company knew such exposure was potentially dangerous. Only after the feed mix-up did Michigan Chemical grant its workers the protective clothing, showers and other safety measures that employees had been demanding unsuccessfully.

Workers say that when they complained of PBB causing skin irritation, their bosses reassured them that it was safe. When the workers asked for protective equipment and showers, their company officials refused. The workers breathed the dust, got it on their skin and the clothes they wore home, and even were allowed to eat lunch at a desk in the building where PBB was made.

Workers at Velsicol's Michigan plant were also exposed to several other potentially dangerous chemicals, including some related to PBB. One was Tris, banned from children's sleepwear in 1977 as a suspected cancer-causing agent. Workers said they often got liquid Tris on their hands. They also were exposed to such chemicals as bromine gas (nicknamed "red death" because of its choking, blinding fumes); benzene (a carcinogen and bone-marrow poison); carbon tetrachloride (a car-

---

*A U.S. District Court dropped the criminal charges in fall 1980, noting that Velsicol had earlier pleaded no contest to four misdemeanor charges brought in response to the same incident.

cinogen that affects the liver); and toluene (a central nervous system depressant).

Some Velsicol workers tested for PBB have registered extremely high levels in their systems. Like the farmers, some workers, even those with high levels, have experienced no physical problems so far. But others have complained of fatigue, aching joints, memory loss and drastic weight loss.

One chemical worker, Tom Ostrander, became so sick in March 1977 that he was unable to continue work. Instead of paying Ostrander worker's compensation, Velsicol paid him his full salary and sent him to the Mayo Clinic at company expense. A consulting doctor hired by Velsicol reported that Ostrander was probably sick from PBB. But in September 1978, Velsicol stopped paying Ostrander and, because he was still too sick to work, he could not get another job in 1979. He now believes the company chose to pay him his salary rather than have him receive worker's compensation to keep the problem informal and out of the state's eyes.[11]

The pattern of actions by the Michigan Chemical/Velsicol plant throughout the PBB crisis was not a unique one for Velsicol. At about the same time that Michigan workers were making PBB, employees at a Velsicol plant in Houston, Texas, were being exposed to the pesticide leptophos. It was made only for export because it was considered too dangerous to use in the United States. The Houston workers developed such symptoms as chest pains, weight loss, blackouts and even paralysis, and even though an Egyptian scientist informed Velsicol in 1974 that chickens exposed to the pesticide developed severe toxic effects, the company never told its employees the chemical was potentially dangerous. Subsequent use of the pesticide in Egypt killed more than 1,000 water buffalo and an unknown number of farmers.

Velsicol claims it no longer manufactures the pesticide, but documents obtained by *Mother Jones* magazine in 1980 "reveal that the company has continued selling the chemical on world markets."[12] Velsicol officials confirm that the company continues to export three pesticides—chlordane, heptachlor and endrin—whose use is being phased out in this country. Company officials say Velsicol will continue to export chlordane and heptachlor after their use is completely banned in the United States on July 1, 1983.

Even after Velsicol learned its employees were becoming sick from leptophos, the company continued production for five months before notifying the Environmental Protection Agency (EPA) of the problem. In addition, Velsicol wastes have poisoned groundwater in the community of Toone, Tennessee. As one EPA official summed up the company's performance: "Velsicol's record of compliance with environmental statutes is one of the worst of any company."[13]

FLAWS IN THE SYSTEM

For years after the accident, Michigan's governor, legislature, and key state and federal officials ignored repeated complaints by farmers that PBB was making them and their cows sick, and the state repeatedly failed to help those farmers who fell victim to the contamination.

Governor Milliken, an immensely popular Republican who first became chief executive in 1969 in a heavily-unionized state whose legislature is controlled by Democrats, consistently defended his administration's handling of the PBB crisis. But even he conceded that he did not move quickly enough in the critical first months after the PBB was identified. In fact, Milliken said he did not begin to regard the PBB contamination as a crisis until 1976, two years after its discovery in the feeds. "I think that for a long period of time there was the feeling that state government wasn't responsive and didn't really understand the plight of the farmers," Milliken admitted.

Although PBB became one of the major issues in the 1978 campaign for governor, Milliken managed to survive handily the political assaults aimed at him by Democrats and the United Auto Workers (UAW). The UAW had been one of the strongest critics of the Milliken administration's handling of the PBB affair, and UAW leaders had called for the resignation of Agriculture Director Ball long before the gubernatorial race. Ball managed to survive until after Milliken was re-elected in 1978. He announced his "retirement" barely a month after the election.

The critics made some good points. For more than four years, the legislature and governor had voted down or vetoed legislation to reduce the amount of PBB-tainted food consumed in the state. Immediately after the accident, the maximum PBB level allowed in meat and milk had been set at 1,000 ppb by the FDA. Late in 1974, when the chemical testing procedures became more sophisticated, the legal level was dropped to 300 ppb. From then until the legal maximum was dropped by the state to 20 ppb, controversy raged over whether to lower the limit to one the experts considered safer. While the issue was debated, contaminated milk and meat were sold from grocers' shelves.

Milliken's aides conceded that the failure to lower the food contamination level was the "single biggest mistake" that the state made on the PBB issue. Milliken said he regretted relying on the higher, FDA-established standard for PBB in food until the state lowered its level in October 1977, and he called it "astounding" that the FDA still insisted its 300-ppb limit was safe.

Early efforts to lower that PBB level failed repeatedly. Milliken requested in 1976 that the State Agriculture Department lower the level in food, but Ball and the agriculture commission appointed by Milliken obstinately refused. Milliken failed to pursue the issue successfully even though he had direct political power over the agriculture commission—since its members serve at his pleasure—and indirect control over the director, Ball—who is the commission's appointee.

Milliken appointed a blue-ribbon scientific panel on PBB in January 1976 headed by Dr. Isadore A. Bernstein, a well-respected biochemist at the University of Michigan. Yet here, too, he failed. Milliken did not push vigorously any of the panel's recommendations, including the most important: that the allowable level of PBB be set as low as it accurately could be measured. The legislature also refused to lower the allowable level of PBB in food, and so the measure that might have kept PBB-tainted food off the market for several years floundered until October 1977.

Finally jolting some of the state's politicians into action required a group of outside experts. In 1977, a medical and scientific team from New York's Mount Sinai Hospital, headed by Dr. Irving Selikoff, issued a report stating that PBB probably had made some farmers sick. After a frightening preliminary report in January 1977, the Selikoff team found further evidence of health problems among farmers: damaged white blood cells, unusual enzyme levels and abnormal antigens. Some of the 1,029 farmers and their families, Selikoff concluded, had suffered immunological system damage making them more susceptible to disease and infection; they had damaged livers; and they also had impaired neurological functions. The question that could not be immediately answered by scientists is whether those contaminated with PBB may have a greater chance of developing cancer. The fact that laboratory animals exposed to PBB developed both cancer and birth defects has made that terrifying possibility a genuine threat to hundreds of Michigan farmers.

Selikoff did not get an invitation to come to Michigan until mid-1976, although he had communicated his willingness to come to the state as early as 1974. In 1974 Selikoff had told a friend, A. Thomas Corbett of the University of Michigan, that he would be glad to assist the state. Corbett then told state agriculture officials and one of Milliken's aides that Selikoff would come and bring a top-notch scientific team at no cost to the state. Agriculture officials later remembered the offer, but said it had not been up to their department to issue an invitation; the governor's staff said the aide never passed on the information to them. Selikoff was only invited to the state after Corbett informed an aide to House Speaker Bobby Crim of the offer. Crim quickly convinced the state Department of Public Health—which had earlier ignored Selikoff's offer—to issue a joint invitation.

Only after Selikoff's visit and his team's testing in 1976

were farmers' health complaints verified. They had told officials that they suffered from fatigue, skin rashes, swollen joints and stomach troubles. But two earlier studies done by the state's Department of Public Health had concluded that no evidence existed that the farmers were sick from PBB. One of the studies, in 1975, concluded, after comparing the health of PBB-exposed farmers to an unexposed control group, that the farmers were not affected by PBB. That study was later criticized, when most of the control group also were discovered to have had PBB in their bodies.

Failures and critical short-sightedness occurred with other aspects of the chemical disaster as well. In May 1974, immediately after the accident was discovered, the legislature gutted a bill that would have given the state Agriculture Department the authority to order the destruction of PBB-tainted animals and to pay farmers for their stock. Because that money wasn't made available, many farmers said they were forced to sell their sick, nonproducing animals for meat at the slaughterhouse. In 1976, both the legislature and Milliken turned down state officials who requested funding for a long-term study of PBB's effect on humans. Only much later was such a study approved.

And in January 1976 Milliken vetoed a bill to provide low-interest loans for farmers hit by PBB. Although he claimed the bill was improperly funded, he later used the amount of money it required to balance the state's budget. That left the farmers, many suffering with low levels of PBB contamination that were legal but harmful to their herds, facing tough financial battles. Some farmers were threatened with loss of their farms. Low-interest loans were not provided until July 1978—five years after farmers had begun complaining about the mysterious ailments afflicting their herds.

Structural flaws in the public health system and the laws also hampered efforts to control the PBB crisis. In 1973 the lack of any strong labeling requirement allowed workers to mistake poorly marked bags of fire retardant for bags of a feed additive. That resulted in one of the few changes made in state law because of the PBB crisis—the Agriculture Department was given expanded licensing and regulatory powers over feed companies, and feeds were required to be labeled with their chemical content.

The PBB incident also pointed out the absence of adequate pretesting of chemicals; when in 1974 the contamination was first discovered, state officials learned that little scientific research had been done on the chemical's danger to humans or animals. Such pretesting is now authorized, though not mandated, under the Toxic Substances Control Act, proposed by the late Senator Philip Hart of Michigan and passed by Congress in 1976.

Besides the lingering danger of this chemical to the state's farmers and their children and to consumers, visible, raw sores still are burning because of PBB. One of the most obvious is in the small camping and fishing resort town of Mio, Michigan, in the northern part of the state's lower peninsula. State officials ordered burial pits dug there on 2.3 acres of state forest land to bury the carcasses of cows contaminated with PBB. The state already had buried more than 23,000 cows and 6,000 other animals in a pit near Kalkaska, Michigan, northwest of Mio; when the state tried to use Oscoda County and Mio as a similar dumping ground, residents—strongly believing the dump would poison them—reacted angrily.

While officials tried unsuccessfully to soothe citizens' fears that PBB-contaminated carcasses would taint their land and their drinking water, the seething Oscoda County residents used every means to stop the burial: they appealed to local judges and the state supreme court; they held protests and continuous vigils by the pit; they even sent pleas for help to the Pope in Rome and to the Soviet Union. But although the residents—more used to farming, fishing and tourists than to politics and social activism—managed to get some concessions from the state, the burials began in mid-1978. More than 1,300 cows were killed and buried in the pit, which was lined with clay after a judge's order to protect area residents.

The struggle for safe disposal is not yet over. Officials continue to find cows with levels of PBB greater than the state's acceptable limit, and in 1979 burials had to stop until a new site could be approved. In January 1980 Michigan officials decided to ship the state's remaining PBB-tainted cattle by truck to southwestern Nevada for burial. The Nevada site relieves Michigan's need for burial grounds now, but eight landfills in Michigan are the uneasy graves for several million pounds of PBB-contaminated feed, cattle and food products.

Yet another frightening remnant of the chemical contamination in Michigan requires solution. State officials have identified 13 farms that cannot get rid of their PBB—they are victims of a so-called "residual environmental contamination." After the contaminated animals on these farms were taken away, the farms were scrubbed and new, "clean" animals were brought in. But from the farms' soil and equipment those clean animals absorbed PBB at levels higher than state guidelines allowed. In June 1980 the state passed legislation calling for the cleanup of the contaminated farms—if the funds are available. Cleanup would be a massive job: removing topsoil, pouring concrete over particularly contaminated areas, and in some cases actually dismantling buildings. Because removing acres of topsoil is enormously expensive, the state may buy some properties outright to prevent them from ever again being used as farms, says Ken Van Patten, chief of the dairy division of the state Department of Agriculture. All of these plans are contingent on money becoming available before the law expires in 1982. If the cleanup is not underway by then, says Van Patten, it probably will never be done.

Despite all the flaws exposed by the PBB disaster, few changes have been made in the system's structure or in the attitudes of many officials. The PBB contamination episode clearly showed even such formerly skeptical state officials as Milliken that federal agencies failed to protect the public from exposure to the toxic chemical. The FDA set permissible levels for PBB in food that were not based on complete scientific evidence, and the agency refused to lower that legal limit even when serious questions arose about PBB-induced dangers. In the face of mounting clinical and laboratory evidence on the danger PBB poses to people, the federal maximum level for PBB remains 15 times higher than that now allowed in Michigan.

The resolution of the crisis also was hampered by a bureaucracy unable to respond on an emergency basis to this new type of environmental disaster. Officials did not have and did not get emergency powers to ban suspect food quickly, and they did not have the authority to locate, test and destroy tainted animals as soon as the contamination was discovered. While the companies responsible for the accident were holding back important information, the government's response was also frustrated by an overlapping yet independent structure of noncommunicating agencies and officials. A central coordinating body was needed to provide expertise, direction and connections between agencies. And many believe other factors, too, kept the state from moving vigorously.

"[The Farm Bureau is] a large corporation, they had excellent public relations with the governor's office and the state legislators, and they were willing to use any means at their disposal," said Lee Heming. "They worked against the farmers in this case."

Michigan finally improved its detection of contaminated products. In October 1977 a new state law was enacted requiring tissue samples of all dairy cattle sent to slaughter. And on June 11, 1980, the law was amended to require testing of all dairy herds that had not yet been evaluated by the state. Under that law, a herd can be considered safe—and its products suitable—after the milk of 15 percent of its cows has been tested, if 95 percent of those cows test at a level lower than the legal limit for PBB. All testing was completed by October 1980.

That, incredibly, was seven years after the PBB accident occurred in Battle Creek, Michigan. The scars of Michigan's chemical juggernaut remain; they will remain for years to come. One of the most disquieting results of this environmental contamination is the realization that the system designed to deal with such emergencies failed to do so with effectiveness or speed. The decisions to produce PBB at all, to store it carelessly, and to cover up the damage in the vital early days, all were made outside the public eye, in private business enterprises. The government did not react quickly. But neither did it have the power to influence the decisions bringing on the accident —to limit the contamination at the source. Perhaps most frightening is that, in the future, if a crisis occurs similarly without predetermined answers or methodology, no guarantee exists that citizens will be any safer.

NOTES

1. "90% in Michigan Have PBB in Bodies," *Detroit Free Press*, October 10, 1979.

2. Joyce Egginton, *The Poisoning Of Michigan* (W.W. Norton & Company, 1980), uncorrected proof, p. 103.

3. "How the Feed Mill Mix-up Began," *Detroit Free Press*, March 13, 1977.

4. Egginton, *Poisoning*, p. 54.

5. "Distributor Hid Facts on PBB Peril," *Detroit Free Press*, March 13, 1977.

6. Egginton, *Poisoning*, p. 125.

7. "State Knew But Did Not Warn Farmers of PBB-Tainted Feed," *Detroit Free Press*, March 14, 1977.

8. Ibid.

9. "PBB-Laced Cows Sold as Meat on State OK," *Detroit Free Press*, February 13, 1977.

10. "PBB Risk Not Told to Workers," *Detroit Free Press*, December 11, 1977.

11. In March 1980 a jury found Velsicol not liable for damages in a lawsuit filed by Szeluga, the Farm Bureau worker who said he stacked the PBB Firemaster along with a feed nutrient, which led to the tragic mix-up. Szeluga had claimed he suffered ill health because of his exposure to PBB.

12. David Weir, Mark Shapiro and Terry Jacobs, "The Boomerang Crime," *Mother Jones*, November 1979.

13. "Small Chemical Firm Has Massive Problems With Toxic Products," *Wall Street Journal*, February 13, 1978.

Chapter 3

Kepone

C. BRIAN KELLY

Don FITZGERALD, 21-YEAR-OLD U.S. Army veteran, was a dryer operator in the small pesticide plant at Hopewell, Virginia, "Chemical Capital of the South," city of stacks, city of blue-collar workers. One day early in 1975, water dripping from an overloaded trough hit hot motor parts by Fitzgerald's side in the production area. In no time, the mild popping got to him.

"I heard the water popping," he later said. "And I had been, you know, in a varied state of shakes anyway. . . . I went ahead and corrected it, but it was all I could do to stand up." Worse yet: "When I got it corrected, I thought the tension would gradually subside, but I just kept going tighter and tighter. I started having trouble breathing; my chest was tight. . . ."[1]

Fitzgerald didn't know it yet, but already he was a victim in one of the nation's most glaring, even incredible, work-safety and environmental accidents of the 20th century. Most glaring because the danger was so great, and the harm so widespread. Incredible because the danger had been clearly marked by one trouble signal after another. And for every signal, a corresponding foul-up allowed the menace to grow—and grow.

Fitzgerald, for instance, was one of probably two dozen workers from his plant to visit doctors during a 16-month period

with similarly alarming symptoms that no one really understood. Nor, it seems, did anyone care enough to investigate
thoroughly.

The day of the popping, Fitzgerald was taken to the emergency room at Hopewell's John Randolph Hospital and given a
tranquilizer shot and, he thinks, a Valium capsule. He went
home feeling "reasonably calm." But at work the next day, he
was struck again by the same constricting pain. Only two
months into his new job at Life Science Products, Inc., the
world's only producer of the seemingly harmless pesticide Kepone, Fitzgerald already had experienced what his fellow workers called "the Kepone shakes"—tremors subsequently associated with Kepone poisoning. But this "tightness" was worse.

After his second visit to the emergency room in two days,
Fitzgerald dropped out of work for three or four days. Fitzgerald visited McGuire Veterans Administration Hospital in
Richmond, 18 miles away, for more extensive examination. He
also paid a visit to his mother's doctor. In all, the young production worker saw at least two physicians and consulted medical
personnel at two different hospitals. A third hospital, the Medical College of Virginia (MCV) at Richmond, apparently was
consulted by the VA hospital across town. Finally, he wound up
facing a VA psychiatrist at McGuire. "They thought I needed
psychiatric treatment because I shook like hell."

Somewhere along the medical line, Fitzgerald had been
told—correctly—that Kepone is "a compound, something like
DDT." He was also told, however, that "the effect I was getting
could not be caused by that compound." In fact the apparent
"general consensus was [expressed by] the psychiatrist. He said
that he had no knowledge of it himself. He did not know of
anybody else that did. He never heard of the stuff. He had not
heard of any commotion being raised about it from any of the
other employees.

"He asked me if I was the only one affected. Nobody knew
anything about it. . . ."

Actually a good deal was known about Kepone's toxic
effects—on laboratory animals, at least. A host of studies some

years earlier had established its classic neurological effects, and the most classic symptom of all was tremor—"the shakes." Moreover, the MCV itself had been among the first to investigate the toxicity of the Allied Chemical Company's chlorinated hydrocarbon; MCV researchers also had a role in an early study producing an ambivalent answer, at best, to the question whether the compound could cause cancer of the liver.

And anyone mildly curious about Fitzgerald's working place could have learned that he was not the only Life Science employee affected. Thurman Dykes also worked at the small plant, for four months. "Everyone I seen had the shakes," he later said. At first, Dykes says, he didn't believe his co-workers. "They said, 'Wait until you get the shakes.' I thought it was a joke. They ran around and said, 'You are going to get them.' What they called them was 'the shakes.' " Eventually, Dykes started shaking, too.[2]

Even supervisory personnel at Life Science were aware of the shakes. One evening in late 1974, two supervisors, Dale Gilbert and Del White, went out to have a few beers together. Gilbert had become aware of White's shaking. "I had seen Del getting to where he couldn't drink a cup of coffee," Gilbert later related. That night it was a little worse: "I laughed at him," Gilbert says, "because he couldn't hold a can of beer."[3] Soon both men were to view the shakes with far more concern.

By early 1975, White was in such bad shape, "he would put his hand on your shoulder and shake *your* body," Fitzgerald recalls. After Fitzgerald experienced his "tightness" attack, White told him, "If I was you, I would get the hell out of this stuff." White himself left Life Science in the spring of 1975, a sick but as yet undiagnosed man. Gilbert stayed on, but now he too was shaking.[4]

The health menace developing so ominously within the Kepone plant was only one of many signals that trouble was brewing at Hopewell, "Kepone Maker for the World," a blue-collar dream of good pay and round-the-clock shifts, a chemical-industry town whose older residents still recalled its lusty days as a World War I munitions boom town called "Wonder City," even "Wizard City," by flamboyant journalists of the era. In addition to the immediate health menace at Life Science Products, Inc., a host of environmental signals were begging for attention in the city of Hopewell.

They began insidiously but, like Kepone itself, the signals were persistent and cumulative. One piled on another until—in July 1975—Virginia's festering environmental illness finally burst into open view. The revelation was sadly late then—too late for the historic James River to be cleansed; too late to avoid economic disruption for an estimated 3,500 watermen relying upon river produce for their livelihoods; too late to save the river's countless pleasures for anglers and seafood gourmets. Too late to apply the lessons of animal studies conducted a decade or more before. Too late, in addition, to escape the ramifications of new studies at the National Cancer Institute warning of the DDT-like pesticide's cancer-causing potential.[5] And the news was too late by far to help production workers suffering outright Kepone poisoning; likewise too late for all those, their number undiscovered, who had been exposed to Kepone in one way or another. The extent of the danger incurred in their contamination is yet another unknown.

What is known is the river's lasting sickness. "Kepone contamination is present at all levels of the food chain in the James River," reported scientists at the Virginia Institute of Marine Science (VIMS) in 1979. Further, Assistant VIMS Director Michael E. Bender has estimated, as of 1979, 20,000 to 40,000 pounds of Kepone—about 10 to 20 tons of the toxic compound —still were buried in the river's muddy sediments. Bender's unhappy conclusion: "We estimate that the problem will remain with us for between 50 and 100 years."[6] That estimate was revised in late 1980 when VIMS researchers revealed that the natural silting process appeared to be covering up the river's Kepone deposits.

In the meantime, the James has been closed to most forms of commercial fishing since late 1975. (It was reopened for recreational fishing and some forms of commercial fishing in late 1980.) Earlier, some marine species in the lower Chesapeake Bay also were forbidden as catch destined for the dinner table. The river's seed-oyster beds, the largest in North America, escaped the quarantine, however, when scientists investigating Virginia's massive Kepone spill discovered that the baby shellfish manage to cleanse themselves of the chemical's residues.

The seed oysters therefore are eligible for removal from their original beds to Kepone-free waters, and after a two-year maturing process, they go to market. But oystermen didn't escape the tragedy unharmed. According to state sources, the Campbell Soup Company once bought all its stew oysters from the James River beds. In the aftermath of Virginia's Kepone scare, Campbell's shifted to sources on the state's eastern shore —as one Virginia official puts it, "never to return."

Virginia's Kepone disaster is a classic scenario of environmental damage. Yet it never had to happen, as almost anyone now can see. Long in coming, disaster struck only on the heels of blunder, blindness, greed, and either oversight or more deliberate sins of omission on the part of some principals of the drama. Those working in government on the city, state and federal levels; in the medical community; in company management; even the workers and their supervisors—all can assume a share of the blame.

SETTING UP SHOP

"All this could have been prevented, if people had taken the proper precautions," says Silvio L. Giolito, a former Allied Chemical Company chemist who shared development of the compound in the late 1940s with his supervisor, Everett R. Gilbert. "Chemically, it was a good insecticide," Giolito recalled. In their patent application of 1950, coinventors Giolito and Gilbert asserted their new compound would combat "a wide variety of noxious organisms," specifically flies, moths, beetles, grasshoppers and vegetable fungi.

Technically known as chlordecone, the new product was similar in its chemical properties to the chlorinated hydrocarbons of the DDT family. Chlordecone was derived from chemical reactions involving hexachlorocyclopentadiene (HCP), sulfur trioxide, sodium hydroxic, sulfuric acid and antimony pentachloride catalyst. "For me, it was a routine accomplishment," added Giolito in 1976, by then a researcher for the Stauffer Chemical Company in Dobbs Ferry, New York. "An organic chemist makes umpty-umpt chemicals. He designs them, and then they're screened. One in a thousand is an active [commercial] chemical."[7]

Kepone resists deterioration like DDT does, whatever its environment, and thus is cumulative in animal tissue. As MCV neurologist John R. Taylor reported in a professional paper, Kepone "is not biodegradable, either in humans or elsewhere in nature."[8]

At first, Allied found no great market for its new bug-killer and was content to produce its own brand, Kepone, sporadically or to farm out its production to at least two other firms, the Nease Chemical Company in Pennsylvania and the Hooker Chemical Company in upstate New York. Until the late 1960s, Kepone was used chiefly as a heavily diluted but effective ingredient of ant and roach baits produced in the United States.

By the mid- to late-1960s, however, prospects improved for Allied's greater sales of Kepone, which nevertheless remained a small sliver of the giant chemical firm's multibillion-dollar pie. Research in Europe established that pesticides "derived" from Kepone would curb the Colorado potato beetle, a company spokesman later explained.[9] Further, he said, Allied received reports from the Caribbean and Central America on the use of Kepone materials in the control of the banana rootborer. In 1966, Allied moved its Kepone operation to a structure in the company agricultural division's complex in Hopewell known as the Semi-Works.

There, Kepone was produced on an intermittent, "batch" basis, more or less as needed. In time, so were two polymer products used to sheath electrical wiring, THEIC and TAIC. The Kepone concentrate produced in Hopewell was sent to an Allied plant at Baltimore (Kepone residues have been found in the ground there, too) for shipment largely to a West German firm using Kepone as the key ingredient for its own pesticide product, Despirol. In a few years, however, batch production of the increasingly popular Kepone was competing with THEIC for production time in the Semi-Works. According to Allied, one had to give way.

The problem was resolved in late 1973 by subcontracting Kepone production to Life Science Products, a new firm formed by two former Allied engineer-executives, Virgil A. Hundtofte and William P. Moore.[10]

Significantly underbidding one or more rivals for the Kepone production contract, Life Science agreed to what the chemical industry calls a tolling arrangement. The subcontractor would produce Kepone for Allied's exclusive use; Allied would supply the raw materials. In this case, however, the agreement went a step farther than simply arranging production of a chemical product for its patent-holder and commercial marketeer. Allied was to pay higher rates if Life Science needed added capital for new environmental controls.

By one state investigator's interpretation, this actually meant Allied would "supplement" the base production rate, "if LSP [Life Science Products] were required by any governmental agency to adopt environmental modifications!"

The new arrangement also meant that the production line would be shifted to an old gas station property near the Semi-Works. Production wastes would be discharged into Hopewell's municipal sewage system instead of into a creek meandering toward the James River that long had been a production-wastes dumping ground for Allied and for all Hopewell's heavy industry. And, under the agreement, the subcontractor was expected to produce more Kepone—3,000 pounds an average day. In fact, the new Kepone makers subsequently averaged between 3,000 and 4,000 pounds, often reached 6,000, and on at least one day cited by a supervisor, produced 8,000 pounds.

Hundtofte and Moore both were chemical engineers with Allied Chemical Company backgrounds. After reaching the tolling agreement with their former employers, they set up shop in the one-time gas station. The low white structure already on the premises they used for office space; the production equipment they installed in an open space and a corrugated metal shed to the rear.

Although the tolling agreement seemed to spell out who would supply what, the observer can only speculate as to who should have supplied the expertise. Accounts differ.[11] According to G. C. Matthiesen, an executive of Allied's agricultural division, Hundtofte and Moore should have known what they were doing. "Life Science was an independent concern with all the expertise, knowledge and access to resources to process and handle Kepone as safely as Allied Chemical had itself for a quarter of a century."[12] In an appearance before the Senate Subcommittee on Agricultural Research and General Legislation, which probed the Kepone disaster, Matthiesen said that Moore, a researcher with about 50 inventions under his belt, was "in charge of Kepone" for the first three years of its production at the Semi-Works. "I believe he was familiar with . . . the safety procedures for the process," said Matthiesen. After those three years, the Allied witness also volunteered, Moore provided "technical advice" that included design modifications increasing production capacity in the Semi-Works. Hundtofte, for his part, had been Allied's plant manager at Hopewell for the agricultural division. "As plant manager he was also responsible for several years for the production of Kepone in the Semi-Works," added Matthiesen.

In sum, the Allied spokesman declared: "The principals of Life Science, Mr. Moore and Mr. Hundtofte, knew as much or more about Kepone production than anyone in Allied Chemical, or probably in the country."

But Moore and Hundtofte each deny that they were Kepone experts and complain that Allied failed to give them adequate warning of the pesticide's dangers. Before the Senate subcommittee, they claimed to have been removed from the production process in the Semi-Works. Hundtofte asserted he didn't even know the four production steps in creating Kepone until the formation of his Life Science company. Moore said information from the production line reached him at Allied only "through an organization which included general foreman, foreman, Semi-Works superintendent, pilot plant manager and so forth." By Moore's account, he was "just a simple technical man."

Moore also said he hardly ever entered the back production area at Life Science. The two entrepreneurs took different tacks with supervisor Del White's claim that he warned them of the danger back in fall 1974. White later said, "I called Mr. Hundtofte and told him: 'We got a problem. There's just too many people that are shaking.' " According to White, who also said "I trusted these two men," his complaint resulted in a meeting with Hundtofte and Moore over a black binder containing the firm's information on Kepone's toxicity. By White's account, Moore "showed me that black book. He said there was absolutely nothing out there that could hurt a human being."

Moore's response to White's account? "I say this is absolutely not true."[13]

Hundtofte, however, said on the one hand that he did become aware of "some shakiness" among Life Science workers —in June 1975. But he said, on the other hand, that he and Moore did offer White some sort of explanation. According to Hundtofte, if only Life Science had been given MCV's toxicological studies done for Allied many years earlier, "I have to feel that . . . at least we would have been able to consider some of the side effects . . . that maybe he [White] would not have accepted my explanation and Bill Moore's explanation."

Hundtofte himself had worked on the production line at the outset of the Life Science operation. Sometimes, he told the subcommittee, he stayed all night. His wife and two sons, one an infant, would visit him at the plant—and sleep on cots inside.

Hundtofte was asked during his subcommittee appearance if he could confirm that employees at Life Science actually had packed the concentrated, toxic powder into barrels with their bare hands.

"Unfortunately," he said, "I am one of those employees."[14]

LISTLESS BEHAVIOR AND BUNGLING

No matter who should shoulder the blame for what appears to have been an unorthodox operation from the outset, the foul-ups later associated with the subcontracting firm's production of Kepone began on nearly the first day of production at Life Science, in early 1974. Within three weeks, say Virginia health officials, the first symptoms of Kepone poisoning appeared among some production workers. This period also began the saga of listless behavior, sad bungling and scant apparent wakefulness on the part of the public's watchdog agencies.

For Allied Kepone workers, at least one safety precaution had been required by the state. As Dr. Samuel Epstein, author of *The Politics of Cancer* and well-known environmental activist, noted in a 1978 article on Kepone, "respirators were apparently not provided until 1970, when Allied was required to do so by the State Department of Labor." Thus at least one arm of the Virginia government apparently was aware of Kepone's occupational dangers as early as 1970.[15]

First down the broad pike of opportunity to make Life Science safer was Virginia's own Air Pollution Control Board. By a board spokesman's own account, board personnel discovered "shortly after production began" that Life Science was operating without the required discharge permit. Additionally, the new plant, situated on heavily traveled state route 10 in Hopewell, was emitting sulfur trioxide, a Kepone ingredient.

Incredibly, at that same early stage board inspectors obtained Life Science data on Kepone's "physical and chemical properties and its manufacturing process"—yet no one appears to have attached any great significance to that information. For months thereafter, the same watchdogs monitored an air-filter device placed on the Hopewell News Building, a mere block away. The air-pollution experts weren't looking for Kepone residues, however. They simply were checking the filters for floating particles of hazardous air pollutants named in federal laws and regulations. A later review of those dust catchers by the federal Environmental Protection Agency (EPA) disclosed that they had gathered heavy Kepone residues all along. The Kepone dust was traceable, in fact, on filters taken from air-monitoring stations as distant as the outskirts of Richmond.

The Air Pollution Board also acknowledged that some complaints were made about discharges from the Life Sciences plant. Testifying before the Senate subcommittee, William R.

Meyer, executive director of the Virginia Air Pollution Control Board, was asked by Subcommittee Chairman James B. Allen, a Democrat from Alabama: "Had there not been complaints from people living in the area of the noxious fumes and particles in the air?"

Meyer responded: "Very few. I think, as I testified, based on some complaints, we went out, and our observations were that the cyclone collector they had on the building was inadequate . . . we required them to put in a baghouse which would, or should, reduce the visible emissions."

The Air Pollution Board itself had observed particulate emissions at Life Science from February to August 1974, Meyer acknowledged in his appearance before the Senate subcommittee. But not until October of that year did Life Science, at the Air Board's prodding, finally install the internal dust collector, or baghouse, cited by Meyer.[16] That action ended the emission of particulates, the watchdog-agency's director also testified, so far as they were "observed or made known to us."

Later, long after Virginia's Kepone disaster burst into public view, various onlookers from the pesticide plant's immediate neighborhood readily recalled the noxious emissions that once permeated the air around them.[17] The operator of a gas station across route 10 from Life Science said the plant sometimes had emitted white clouds so thick he couldn't see the company's low structure from his garage. The dust clouds slowed traffic, he said. The operator of an ice house across another street from Life Science said the white dust left a film on his desk in a closed office. Once, he added, a noxious cloud of the choking dust drove him and a companion off the loading dock and into the freezer. And, indeed, Kepone residues later were found in old ice formations at the commercial ice facility. No one knows how many of its customers consumed contaminated ice in their drinks, nor how much of the Kepone they ingested. At a nearby firehouse, firemen said they sometimes wondered if they could see well enough to wheel out their rolling stock in response to an alarm. A later survey of neighborhood residents located 40 people with measurable Kepone levels in their blood, one of them the occupant of a building one mile from the Kepone plant.[18]

The problems at Hopewell's sewage-treatment plant also sprang up soon after Life Science began production—by one state official's account, within two weeks. The pesticide firm had arranged with the city to discharge filtered production wastes into the municipal sewage system. As trial testimony in a federal courtroom later disclosed, however, the wastes frequently bypassed the filtration unit. Thus, with the knowledge of city officials, Kepone discharges often exceeded the permissible level. Meanwhile, presumably cleaned effluent from the treatment plant was discharged into Bailey's Creek, subsequently making its way to Bailey's Bay and thence to the nearby James River. Hundtofte later testified that, under "near perfect" production conditions, about one pound of Kepone was discharged daily from the Life Science plant.[19] But near-perfection wasn't always attainable. One of Hundtofte's plant supervisors testified that eight hundred pounds of Kepone went down the sewer drain one day. Another worker said the filter unit frequently became clogged and sometimes was bypassed altogether while it was cleaned out—by hand.

By mid-March 1974 the treatment plant's solid-waste digesters were inoperative, their vital bacteria killed by Kepone. The city began pumping its fast-accumulating, Kepone-laden sewage sludge into an open field, and took no action against Life Science. According to Dr. Robert S. Jackson, Virginia's state epidemiologist at the time (and later to become Virginia's assistant state health commissioner, then commissioner of South Carolina's Department of Health and Environmental Control), Hopewell officials were dumping their solid-waste sludge into the landfill "for want of a better solution and in order to continue meeting their effluent limits into the James." Eventually, Hopewell accumulated eight hundred thousand to one million gallons of Kepone-contaminated sludge in a basin irreverently known as "Kepone Lagoon."[20]

For months the State Water Control Board wasn't even aware of the Kepone discharges; nor was the board immediately informed of the problems in Hopewell's solid-waste digesters. Despite a legal requirement to do so, Hopewell failed to inform the state agency of the growing problem in the municipal sewage plant. "We first found out about that in October 1974 when, in the course of a routine survey, we found that the digesters were not working properly," the Water Board's chief administrator, Eugene Jensen, later reported to the Senate subcommittee looking into Virginia's Kepone disaster.[21]

Meanwhile Jensen's agency, seeking advice on an allowable discharge level and information on Kepone's possible toxicity, brought the federal EPA into discussions of the Hopewell problem. That also was in fall 1974. Later still in that year, according to a memorandum submitted to the Senate,[22] state officials discussed Kepone's possible chronic effects upon humans, touched briefly upon the possibility it might be carcinogenic, and speculated that it shouldn't be allowed to creep into Hopewell's drinking water, which is drawn from a point in the Appomattox River shortly upstream from its confluence with the James at Hopewell.

No Kepone residues appeared in domestic water samples then tested for traces of the pesticide. But traces later did appear from time to time in the city's separate industrial water pipeline—servicing not only industry but also a nearby federal reformatory and the U.S. Army's Fort Lee. Those residues, state health officials later said, were considered below any danger level. But the fact remains that the water was tested only intermittently even after the first traces appeared in the industrial samples—until discovery of the illnesses among Kepone production workers forced the closure of the Kepone plant, in July 1975.[23] Thereafter, water tests were run every week.

In the winter of 1974–75, as city, state and federal officials conferred about the Kepone threat in Hopewell, the plant continued to operate. While the experts debated the appropriate discharge limits, Life Science agreed to install costly new environmental controls. The firm actually spent, by one owner's estimate, several hundred thousand dollars overall on various pollution controls.[24] But no one was looking inside the plant boundaries, where workers were eating sandwiches laden with Kepone dust and showering in a stall caked with the toxic powder.

One official with EPA's municipal permits branch later told the Senate subcommittee he didn't "see any need for any curiosity to go up and find out how they make Kepone, in relation to a problem with the sewage-treatment plant." As he also said, "perfectly clean" companies occasionally experienced "bad batch" discharges.[25] In fairness, the environmental agency should be noted to have been engaged with Life Science in the common exercise known as "negotiated compliance."

Yet the various arms of government aware of problems associated with the Life Science operations in 1974 weren't putting together the full picture of the threat Kepone posed to Life Science workers and the environment. And at this point they had no idea that Allied Chemical itself had dumped enormous amounts of Kepone production wastes into a tributary of the James for many years beforehand.

An inspector from the EPA's Philadelphia Regional Office actually did visit the Life Science plant in March 1975.[26] His interest was the registration process, however; Allied was describing its compound as a pesticide ingredient, a technicality raising the question of whether Kepone itself need be registered as a pesticide. The visitor from EPA saw only the front office at Life Science, whose officials referred him to an Allied attorney. "Unbelievably," commented state epidemiologist Jackson, "his conclusion was that Kepone need not be registered—only its final commercial product."

Finally alerted by a municipal sewer worker's strange collapse at the city treatment plant, two miles from the Life Science operation, Virginia's state industrial hygienists soon were pressing Life Science to submit to a voluntary inspection, according to former epidemiologist Jackson. But every time they were ready to visit the plant, Life Science begged off the appointments with such excuses as unexpected production problems and shutdowns.

The state lacked the authority to come in for inspections

unannounced, because its own work-safety plan was not approved by the federal government. Until Virginia's safety program attained approved compliance with federal guidelines, only the admittedly understaffed federal Occupational Safety and Health Administration (OSHA) could go barging into the plant uninvited.

Later OSHA was discovered, however, to have fumbled the ball already with a work-safety complaint by a Life Science production worker.

It happened in September of 1974. Orben R. DuBose, a former dryer-room worker at Life Science, personally visited OSHA's field office in Richmond to complain that Kepone dust had been flying about his face as he attempted to clean some gears. He had refused a supervisor's orders to continue cleaning them, and was fired. By an OSHA spokesman's account, the first statement DuBose made to the compliance officer interviewing him in Richmond that day was: "I wish to complain about the safety conditions at the plant. . . ."

The compliance officer nevertheless decided the worker's complaint should be processed as a discrimination complaint. "We can't process this as a regular safety complaint," he told DuBose, "because you are not an employee there anymore. But we will see what we can do in another area . . . if you were fired because you complained about safety, maybe you have a case of discrimination here." The "catch-22" of a work-safety complaint not being allowed by a nonemployee shortly was followed by another.

To pursue its case, OSHA needed the corroboration of someone who had witnessed the argument preceding DuBose's dismissal. Corroboration was necessary because the burden of proof in any proceeding against Life Science would be upon OSHA. According to testimony before the subcommittee by Lapsley Ewing, head of OSHA's Richmond office, DuBose said that he, Supervisor White and a man named Coy Rory were in the plant at the time of the firing. Although not sure of the third man's last name, DuBose said the man could "back up my story that that is why I was fired." Ewing said DuBose was told that a third-party statement confirming his story would provide a "good case" against his employer.[27] But, according to Benjamin W. Mintz, OSHA's associate solicitor, the agency did not pursue the witness.[28]

The work-safety agency did write Life Science asking for an explanation of the DuBose incident. Life Science eventually responded that adequate work-safety procedures were in force the night of the workman's departure. In its response, the company also criticized DuBose's prior job performance and confirmed that he had been sacked for refusing to follow orders.[29]

So DuBose was told that he had to find his missing witness himself. And OSHA let the case rest. No attempt was made to check the reported working conditions at the pesticide plant in Hopewell.

At the Senate subcommittee hearings, subcommittee member Patrick Leahy, a Democrat from Vermont, reacted sharply to Ewing's story:

> Too often we get carried away . . . [in] the federal govern-
> ment with everything being in the proper form. "If it is not on
> Form 5, we can't consider. If you are found murdered, sorry, it
> has to be Form 6." . . . Let us not lose sight of what the [DuBose]
> complaint said.
> The date received was 9-20-74. Here they have the em-
> ployer's name: Life Science. Kind of business—pesticide. Where
> alleged violation is located—dryer, top of dryer. . . .
> Kind of business—pesticide.
> Complaint—fumes and dust coming up in your face.

Actually, Ewing told the same subcommittee, his staff "did pursue the safety-complaint aspect of it." But it was a mild effort at best.

By Ewing's account, an OSHA staff industrial hygienist who also conferred with the complaining worker "looked up what meager literature he had available to him . . . and determined that Kepone did not have the high toxicity rating that we know it has today." Unfortunately, the hygienist's literature focused on Kepone diluted for application in the field as a pesticide.

"[He] told me that Kepone is known as one of the safest pesticides in the application stage that we have for humans," added Ewing. In addition, he said, his hygienist called friends in Virginia's Bureau of Industrial Hygiene, who didn't have "anything more than he had in his own files."

At one point in the subcommittee hearings, Chairman James Allen asked Ewing: "Didn't you have access to the dozens of articles on the toxicity of Kepone? Dozens and dozens of articles appeared." Ewing informed the panel, "there is no formal procedure for transmitting such information to an area office." And he agreed, "in hindsight," that the best way to check the work-safety complaint would have been to inspect the manufacturing operation at Hopewell.[30]

The fact is, many articles detailing Kepone's toxic impact upon various animal subjects were available then to even fairly determined investigators. Reading the current literature could have raised a red flag not only for OSHA officials but for any of the other government agencies that were aware of problems at the Kepone plant by the end of 1974 and the beginning of 1975. The list of agencies includes Virginia's air and water pollution boards, its health department, the federal EPA and OSHA, plus departments of the city of Hopewell.

Among the published studies any investigator could have consulted was a 1962 Kepone experiment with quail in an Alabama field. Their death rate was "heavy," and "tremors and other symptoms of poisoning implicated Kepone as the cause of death." A 1968 quail study reported "whole-body tremor," enlargement of the liver, and death. A 1964 report on reproductive effects among chickens cited "reduced" production of eggs, and newly hatched chicks that suffered "quivering extremities." Mice studied in 1964 produced less frequent litters after eating Kepone. Meanwhile, researchers interested in reproductive effects among quail had this to say in 1974: "Kepone . . . interferes with the reproduction of birds and mammals and affects various organs of the body."[31]

Allied Chemical itself had been among the earliest to compile data on the compound's effects, most pertinently upon mammals—dogs, rats and rabbits in the laboratory. "The characteristic effect of this compound is the development of DDT-like tremors, the severity of which depends upon the dosage level and duration of exposure," was one conclusion. Among other adverse effects repeatedly noted by Kepone's researchers over the years: depressed growth, the compound's fat-seeking tendency in the body, kidney lesions, atrophy of the testes and other reproductive impairment.[32]

One of the earliest and most ominous findings was abnormality of the liver; specifically, enlargement, congestion and lesions. Said a key 1961 Allied report: "In rats surviving for between one and two years on [the test] diet, two tissues, liver and kidney, presented lesions that were subjected to special study and interpretation." The acknowledged concern in this experiment: "In the liver, the problem concerned a possible carcinomatous nature of the lesions seen in six rats." The question, 15 years before discovery of work conditions at Life Science in Hopewell, was of carcinoma—cancer. But the answer was discouragingly ambivalent.[33]

Three outside experts were asked to rate liver sections from five rats, while Allied's own research pathologist studied samples from all six animals. One of the outsiders rated four of his sections as cancerous and said the fifth had "atypical areas not quite enough to call cancer." A second consulting expert rated two sections negative for cancer, two as "suspect" and one as cancer-affirmative. Allied's own pathologist called five of his six samples "evolving carcinoma" and the sixth, suspect. Only one of the four researchers rejected a diagnosis of cancer altogether. He defined all five of his liver sections as a proliferation of cell growth known as hyperplasia, which can be interpreted as a warning of cancer development or of other problems.[34]

The conclusions drawn in the study? The toxic potential of concentrated Kepone reaching the liver appeared "clear," but "lack of uniformity of interpretation" left the question of Kepone's cancerous potential for the liver "equivocal." Or, as state health official Jackson has said, the study established "a clear probability" that Kepone could induce cancer of the liver "in all animals studied long enough." Others later viewed the study more conclusively.

In his 1978 article, environmental-researcher Samuel Epstein looked exhaustively at the Kepone literature and found:

> The high acute toxicity of Kepone was established in studies contracted by Allied Chemical Company in 1949–50. . . .
>
> Kepone was first demonstrated to be neurotoxic in rats, in studies contracted by Allied Chemical Company in 1949 . . . DDT-like tremors were induced. . . .
>
> Kepone was first reported to induce reproductive impairment in male rats in 1961 in studies contracted by Allied Chemical Company. . . .

And, about Allied's study of cancer:

> Kepone was first demonstrated to be hepatocarcinogenic in male and female albino rats in studies contracted by Allied Chemical Company in 1961. . . .[35]

A WAY OF LIFE WITH US

When 1975 began, marking the second year of Life Science's production history, the Kepone bubble still had not burst upon the unsuspecting public. Ice was being sold in the ice house across the street from Life Science—some of it destined, fortunately, to be transformed into imaginative ice carvings used only as ornaments at nearby Fort Lee's cooks' school. Fish from the James, however, were being eaten—by both wildlife and the human animal. The city's sewage sludge was piling up. Even without emissions from the Life Science production line, breezes stirred the Kepone deposits lying about the plant ground. Some people were consuming "industrial water" that apparently was tainted from time to time, even if only minutely, as state health officials later maintained. Production was continuing: Workers were still becoming sick. As any of them would tell you, coming down with "the Kepone shakes" was a common joke for teasing newcomers to the plant.[36] One might reasonably wonder how so many signals could be ignored for so long—especially by the workers themselves.

As the *Washington Star* later reported:

> A puzzle all right, but some of the pieces seem to be these: Workers making good money. Workers who needed the job. Workers with a certain machismo attitude toward the hazards of their job. Workers with no union and relying upon management —and their impression that nothing could be wrong because "The Government" wouldn't allow it. Government agencies asleep at the switch. Doctors nodding off on their job. Workers whose symptoms, similar to those of an alcoholic or drug addict, made it tough to get another job.[37]

According to Dr. Sidney Houff, a member of the medical team at the Medical College of Virginia that treated the Kepone victims in 1975, "they were a group of men, most of which were at the high-school education level, who believed in their employers and, as one stated to me, believed that the government and state would never allow something like this to occur. They believed then, when their employers told them it would not hurt them. They went back to work."[38]

Even a year after the effects of Kepone on the workers at Life Science came to light, other chemical workers in Hopewell were undismayed. Some even sported bumper stickers reading "Kepone truckin'." If the workers were unable—or unwilling— to move against the dangers they faced, what about local physicians? Former state epidemiologist Robert Jackson recalls the first Kepone worker he examined. The man was "so sick, he literally could not sit up by himself. He had to support himself on an examining table with both his hands, with his head against the wall, and with his bottom sitting on it in order to stay upright."[39] By Jackson's account, the symptoms were not "subtle." Yet the same patient "had been in and out of the doctor's office over the past week without anybody apparently giving any thought to the fact that this was a toxic substance that caused neurological illness."

If that sounds unbelievable, Jackson makes a couple of points in defense of the medical community. "The symptoms of Kepone poisoning, now easily recognizable, begin in a nonspecific pattern, and those who sought medical assistance were misdiagnosed and mistreated because of the lack of suspicion of the possibility this was related to a toxic substance." Then, too, "where there are multiple doctors in town, many times the workers will not all go to the same one, and consequently, should a pattern of unusual illness develop . . . it might not be picked up, because it would, in fact, be an isolated case to the physician who was seeing it." Eventually, though, one physician did conclude that something was unusual—and that man took the first of the steps that led to the shutdown of the Life Science Kepone plant.

Another factor in the community-wide disregard of such signals as the white powder that occasionally spewed from the Kepone plant was Hopewell's own history. Its industrial development dates from 1912, when the DuPont Company established a dynamite plant at Hopewell, population then less than 1,000. By the middle of World War I the town's population had swelled to 45,000 people, the bulk of them an international force of workers occupying a hastily constructed city of tar-paper shacks and wooden sidewalks. They wore wool even in summer; cotton might have sparked a horrendous explosion.

Hopewell then produced 1.5 million pounds of explosives a day for the war. Ironically, Hopewell itself was a casualty of peace, when DuPont closed its plant one week after the war's end. Soon the town's population was back down to less than 2,000. A firm pioneering in rayon development came and, in the aftermath of a strike and riot, left. The Depression soon followed—but in that economically harsh time, Allied Chemical also arrived in Hopewell, a rescuer. Allied's first Hopewell product was nitrate of soda, a fertilizer that sharply improved corn yields and averted disaster for many American farmers.

With Hopewell's population reaching a more stable 26,000 by the mid-1970s, Allied's two large plants together employed more people than any other industry in town. They alone accounted for 3,500 steady jobs. Allied combined with Hopewell's other big industries—Continental Can, the Firestone Company and Hercules Powder—employed 7,000 workers, occupied 1,100 city acres, and annually pumped out $97 million in payroll checks. And hardly anyone seemed to mind the smoke-stacks belching out their familiar odors. "There would be no Hopewell, period, without those chemical plants," Gus Robbins, retired editor of the *Hopewell News,* told the *Washington Star*'s John Sherwood in 1976. "They're our bread and butter. Almost everyone benefits in one way or another from the industry here. It's a way of life with us."

"There would be a lot of starving sons of bitches in this town if them stacks weren't smoking," explained Hugh Brown, an instrument mechanic at Allied. "It's a damn fine town to live in. The economy is good. It may seem like a baddy to some people, but them stacks make money. The plants here pay on Tuesday, Wednesday and Thursday because they can't haul this much money in town on one day."

Another Allied worker—utility man Charles Bell—told Sherwood, "I don't feel the chemicals are any more dangerous than any other stuff we're exposed to. We smoke, we drink, it's all bad for our health. It's a great place to work. We're required to wear safety clothing. There are very rigid safety programs . . . if you have to have industry, you have to put up with certain things."

More explicit was Steve Gorkiewicz, a sulfuric-acid-maker for Allied fresh from a $700 workweek bolstered by overtime. "Why should we bite the hand that feeds us?" he asked. "A bunch of EPA nit-shits that don't know their ass from a hole in the ground come down here and drive us crazy. . . . This environmental stuff is driving me up the wall."

A Hopewell police lieutenant offers a related postscript on local attitudes. One night in July 1975, just before the illnesses in the Life Science plant came to public light, he discovered three or four men in a pickup truck on an empty lot. "I asked them what they were doing," he later told *Washington Star* reporter Robert Pear. "They told me flat-out where they were from. They said they were from Life Science." And? "They were dumping waste water into a pit." The pit drained into Bailey Creek, the same stream that carried effluent from the sewage-treatment plant to the James River. Six or eight dark-looking oil drums sat in the bed of the pickup.

"I had no reason to question them or suspect them," said Lieutenant Richard Anderson. "I know why they were doing it at that hour." Nor, until the Kepone time bomb detonated a few days later, did he feel obliged to report his discovery to anyone. "It wouldn't have made any difference who I reported it to. It wouldn't have made any difference. I don't think anybody would have done anything."

Further, says Jackson, state investigators later discovered that Life Science workers dumped as many as six to eight truckloads of Kepone waste products on the empty lot each night shift—with the owner's permission. This was in the first half of 1975—while Life Science was struggling to meet a June 1 deadline set by Virginia's Water Control Board for installation of new filtering and cleansing facilities at the Kepone plant itself.

Another force at work in Hopewell's simmering disaster was the growing pressure on Life Science to produce more and more Kepone for Allied's overseas market. According to the small firm's co-owner Hundtofte, "we were struggling to make the production, which was increasing even from the outset of the venture."

In West Germany, Spiess and Sohne, makers of Despirol— the pesticide that used Kepone as a key ingredient—had expanded its own plant by mid-1974. It was operating around the clock and selling its product in Spain, Portugal and East Europe. Further, the German firm was dickering with the Soviet Union, which had tested Despirol. At a luncheon meeting with Allied officials in October 1974, Wolfram Spiess said that a major reason for his company's growing Kepone need was the Russians' interest and their large-scale testing. The implication was of potentially large sales to the USSR. By 1974, Spiess had tripled its demands for Kepone since 1971, and had doubled its order in the past year alone. The projected order for 1974 was 1.2 million pounds; Spiess reported he would need at least 2.2 million pounds of the white powder in 1975. And he mentioned the lure of still another untapped market—Red China. His lunch companions from Allied recalled company plans to visit a pending trade fair in Canton and promised to help the German firm find a Chinese contact.[40]

Overall, in Life Science's 16 months of operation, it turned out 1.7 million pounds of Kepone for Allied. To maintain that frantic pace, Life Science often doubled its initial design capacity of 3,000 pounds a day. "We were not getting it produced as rapidly as I think it might have been sold," said co-owner Moore later. And Hundtofte reported, "We were told by Allied that they could take all the product that we could produce."

By Hundtofte's account, the demand for Kepone produced "overwhelming" stress. In his appearance before the Senate subcommittee, Hundtofte blamed on that stress a lack of "opportunity" to give the pesticide's toxic potential real review. "The real tragic thing in this is that we did not know the degree of toxicity that we were really coping with," he asserted.

They began to learn.

On May 30, 1975, the municipal sewer worker collapsed two miles away from the Life Science plant.

As Jackson tells the story, several thousand gallons of Kepone's volatile ingredient HCP poured from a railroad tank car into the sewer system. The worker down the line was overcome by fumes, but later recovered.

Subsequently, a state industrial hygienist exploring the possible dangers remaining in the city sewage-treatment plant traced the routinely reported spill back to Life Science Products. And there, adds Jackson, "he noted some disturbing things about the plant itself." At this juncture, the Health Department's industrial inspectors began pressing Life Science to submit to a voluntary inspection and were stymied by both management's broken appointments and the federal OSHA pre-emption of the state's own no-knock authority.

Meanwhile, in June 1975 a technical representative from Hooker Chemical, Allied's supplier of HCP—and a company with an array of environmental problems of its own—became alarmed by conditions he witnessed in a visit to the Life Science plant. In an internal memo his superiors forwarded to Allied itself, he reported seeing white powder . . . "everywhere."[41] Finally, Moore and Hundtofte themselves warned Allied in a July 7 meeting in Washington of their inability to meet sewer-discharge limits established for their plant. While production continued, Allied personnel visited the plant to evaluate the small firm's proposed plan to reduce its Kepone discharges— Allied had set a precedent by financing other pollution controls for its subcontractor.[42]

By then, shift supervisor Dale Gilbert, who once had laughed at his friend's difficulties in holding a can of beer, was experiencing severe chest pains in addition to Kepone's classic "shakes." By his account, a company doctor "told me he thought it was hypertension." But Gilbert later told his wife, Janice, "that's not my problem."[43] Gilbert then visited Dr. Yi-nan Chou, an internist new in town. Unused to Kepone or the workers producing it, Chou admittedly was puzzled by what he saw. "I couldn't put anything together on the patient's symptoms," he later recalled.[44]

Modestly enough, Chou claims, "I didn't think I was doing anything different from what other doctors do." But he did; he took the one step that no other doctor had. He asked the federal Center for Disease Control (CDC) at Atlanta for a reading on Gilbert's blood contents. And Gilbert's blood sample was loaded with Kepone.

As the first of many repercussions, the CDC alerted state epidemiologist Jackson. Together with a Virginia industrial hygienist, Jackson descended upon the Life Science plant on the midsummer afternoon of July 23, 1975, in a pair of galoshes— a wise precaution, as it turned out. "I was struck by the large amount of the gray, whitish brown material that was literally covering everything at the plant site," Jackson recalls. "There were three to four inches of the material on the ground. In the areas that were enclosed, there was a one- to two-inch layer of dust encrusting everything."

Also prevalent was contaminated waste water, or slurry. As for the dryer room: "The material came down a chute and was placed in barrels by hand, and this chute blew the material out fairly rapidly, filling hundred-kilogram barrels, and the operator had to stand there and check this canvas chute until the barrel was full. Of course, all the time, the dust was erupting out of the barrel. When it reached approximately the fullness that he desired, he would move the barrel or stop the chute and move the chute out of the way, where the dust would go all over him."

What about the respirators? the two visitors asked plant manager H. D. Howard. "He went to a desk, lifted a mound of papers, sort of shook up the dust and came up with three small light plastic dust-protection devices, one of which had a broken strap. It was clear they were not used, and the workers confirmed that they seldom used any kind of protection."

Jackson was shocked, but not entirely surprised. He already had examined 10 of the plant's workers in a borrowed medical suite a few blocks away. Seven of the 10 clearly were sick. The first Jackson examined, described earlier, "was so sick he was unable to stand . . . was suffering severe chest pains, and on physical examination had severe tremor, abnormal eye movements, was disoriented and quite ill." Under Jackson's threat of an emergency closure order by the state Health Department, Life Science's owners agreed to shut down their plant.

In time, about 30 production workers or their dependents were hospitalized one or more times for treatment of Kepone poisoning. Altogether, 76 workers or relatives probably suffered the compound's toxic effects. Another two dozen or more of the plant's transient work force never were located. In addition, 40 of 216 Life Science "neighbors" carried traceable Kepone residues in their bloodstreams, a subsequent State Health Department survey disclosed. At least 20 consistent consumers of James River fish who voluntarily sought medical examination also carried the chemical. "Kepone was found in the blood of all [Life Science] employees at levels from 165 to 26,000 ppb (parts per billion)," wrote Samuel Epstein. "Kepone blood levels in the surrounding community were approximately linear as a direct function of proximity to [Life Science] with a maximum of 50 ppb within a radius of 0.25 miles. . . ."

The ranks of Kepone victims exhibiting medical symptoms, in addition to detectable levels of Kepone in their blood, included several wives and children of the workers, who were exposed to Kepone dust brought home on shoes and laundry. In one case, in the spring of 1975, a couple and their months-old infant moved into a home just vacated by a Kepone worker. By fall 1976, after the child had played and crawled for hours on the carpeting the former owners had left behind, two-year-old Ryan Eller was found to have detectable levels of Kepone in his blood. And his mother, Libby Eller, was left wondering "whether 15 years from now, something will come up."[45]

And more may be affected. "Many thousands of Virginians were exposed to Kepone outside the occupational setting," noted a state medical study proposal two years later. "Many were exposed to low, but measurable levels in the community; many were exposed by consumption of contaminated ice; but by far the largest group was probably the thousands who were regular consumers of James River fish beginning in 1966."

Nineteen sixty-six? That was the year that Allied itself began producing batches of Kepone at its Hopewell Semi-Works. That operation too has been criticized. Ernest Raley worked at the Semi-Works in 1968 and 1969.

"There was no way in the world you could possibly duck it," Raley said in 1976. "I got it on the lips, and your lips get dry and you lick them, you know, you eat it. It had a kind of bitter, hot taste." Raley asserted that Kepone dust was "on the ground and around in the building" during his tenure at the Semi-Works. He called conditions there "just about as filthy as they could be."

A conflicting view was offered the Senate subcommittee investigating the disaster by Jameil Ameen, "area supervisor" at Semi-Works from 1966 to 1969. "I made sure that each employee was familiar with the safety instructions," Ameen said. "My office was about 100 feet from the area of the plant where Kepone was produced, and I observed the area practically every day. I can tell you from my own observations that the Kepone area was kept neat and clean." Ameen also said that future Life Science founder Moore not only was a frequent visitor to the production line but was a harsh judge of sloppy conditions. "Mr. William Moore insisted that we do everything by the book," said Ameen. "He also insisted that the plant be kept clean at all times. He made frequent inspections of the plant and was impatient with sloppiness."[46]

But Raley recalled differently. "The wind blew Kepone, and you get it all over your clothes and all around in your mouth. . . . My clothes got so contaminated with this Kepone that you could pull them off and stand them in the corner." And Raley eventually became ill: "I was getting sick from a sickness I could not understand." A public-health physician working with Robert Jackson in 1975 and 1976 said Raley did have traces of Kepone in his blood. The physician said Raley exhibited "some very mild symptoms that could be consistent with Kepone exposure, but could be something else, too."

Subsequent federal trial testimony disclosed that unfiltered production wastes containing Kepone, THEIC and TAIC were allowed to drain from Allied's Semi-Works into Gravelly Run, another creek that ends in the nearby James River. Former Allied employees already had told investigators that Kepone wastes were thrown down the Semi-Works drainpipe by the shovelful. And Ameen himself had informed the Senate subcommittee that routine cleanups after a Kepone production run each yielded one or several shovelfuls of waste Kepone dust from the floor of his plant. He wasn't asked, however, how the waste was disposed of.

Once Virginia's marine scientists were alerted—not months, but years later—they went back to old, frozen samples taken from the James. They found Kepone residues in the marine "archives" dating back as far as 1967.

THE COSTS OF KEPONE

The final act of Virginia's Kepone disaster has been predictably long-lasting. An EPA survey mounted immediately after the Life Science illnesses came to light disclosed airborne residues of Kepone as far as 16 miles away, soil residues 3,000 yards from Life Science, riverborne traces 15 miles distant, and contaminated shellfish 64 miles downstream in the James. Later, more elaborate studies established that a sediment belt of Kepone extends within the river for 55 miles. Continued high readings of Kepone were found in river "fin," or finned fish, but only minor residues were found in marine specimens taken from the lower Chesapeake Bay—residues below "action levels" established by the federal Food and Drug Administration (FDA) for human consumption.[47]

Late in 1975, Carl G. Hayes, director of the initial EPA survey at Hopewell, said he knew of no pesticide contamination of matching scope.[48]

The federal OSHA, in the meantime, added the weight of a federal stop-work order to the shutdown and hit Moore and Hundtofte with $16,500 in penalties.[49] The EPA turned to the U.S. Justice Department, which convened a grand jury and, in mid-1976, obtained indictments with 1,097 counts against various parties to the Kepone affair—a record for a federal environmental case.[50]

Defendant Allied Chemical reacted vigorously by branding the massive indictments an "extreme reaction" stemming from "official frustration over the failure of the regulatory agencies to coordinate their activities and to perform their duties with respect to events that took place at the Life Science plant, matters apparently not addressed by the indictments."

As U.S. District Court Judge Robert R. Merhige, Jr., sorted through the various charges, the city of Hopewell pleaded no contest to 10 pollution-related counts. It was found guilty of four, fined $10,000 and placed on probation for five years. A city put on probation! Turning government witness, meanwhile, Hundtofte testified that he and others at Allied's middle-level echelon in Hopewell had withheld information from the government on Semi-Works discharges while he was manager of the agricultural division's complex in the small city. He called these omissions in 1971 and 1972 a "compromise." Merhige said, "I call it a lie."[51]

But Merhige already had dismissed a conspiracy count against the giant chemical firm. He now acquitted two Allied officials from Hopewell of an accompanying conspiracy count. Earlier, Hundtofte and two more Allied men had pleaded guilty to lesser misdemeanor counts in that case.

The real shocker, for Allied and industry observers

throughout the United States, was the judge's reaction to Allied's no contest plea to 940 water-pollution charges, one count for each day of violation between mid-1971 and early 1974.

Imposing the maximum fine on each count, on October 5, 1976, Merhige socked Allied with a fine of $13.24 million—a considerable sum, but only a small fraction of the costs resulting from Kepone contamination, and equaling then less than the income of two days of Allied's sales. No officials from Allied went to jail because of the Kepone disaster. Hundtofte and Moore walked away with a $25,000 fine each and five years of probation. And in May 1980 Judge Merhige reduced to $10,000 each the fines against the two businessmen.[52] Still, the fine against Allied was the largest ever obtained by the federal government in a pollution case.[53]

Allied also was slapped with a host of potentially more costly lawsuits—personal-injury claims from Life Science workers, damage claims by James River and Chesapeake Bay watermen, a civil proceeding by the state of Virginia, even a complaint by two of its own stockholders. The legal morass facing the corporate giant included one early class-action suit asking for billions on behalf of an alleged 26,000 watermen from Maryland and Virginia (at the rate of $3.4 million in damages for each plaintiff), but Allied's attorneys gradually whittled down the claims in a series of settlements out of court.

By the time of its 1978 annual report, the company was able to cite settlement of 109 of 111 personal-injury suits at "nominal cost." The two suits remaining were brought by a pair of railroad employees alleging exposure to Kepone.

In another settlement, in 1980, Allied came to unspecified terms with about 230 James River watermen and seafood dealers who had sued Allied and three codefendants for $5.6 million in damages to their livelihoods.

The company also later agreed to a $5.25 million settlement with Virginia that nonetheless allowed future state claims for removal of Kepone from Virginia waters. For the record, Allied steadfastly denied liability in any of the suits, but as late as its 1978 report it still warned stockholders that future liability or loss could be "material." And in 1980 a group of Virginia oyster tongers filed still another suit, for $2.5 million in damages, against Allied, Hooker Chemical, the defunct Life Science firm and the city of Hopewell.

In all, estimated *Fortune* magazine in 1978, "the company has paid a staggering $20 million in fines, settlements, and legal fees to date, and some important suits are yet to be disposed of." *Fortune* also observed:

> The cost to Allied also includes the consequences of a badly tarnished reputation. Two years ago *Smithsonian* magazine, citing the Kepone affair, refused to run an institutional ad submitted by Allied. Top management at the company's Morristown, New Jersey, headquarters has been jarred by the affair, and has turned understandably timid. No one is more shaken than John T. Connor, Allied's chairman, who views the debacle as a stain on a distinguished public and private career now moving toward a close (he was Secretary of Commerce in Lyndon Johnson's Administration). There is cruel irony in the fact that Kepone was a minor product on which Allied's net profit never exceeded $600,000 a year.[54]

In June 1976 the EPA and Allied Chemical came to an agreement that resulted in the cancellation of Kepone's registration and the formal end of its production in the United States. However, manufacturers using Kepone in bug and roach traps were allowed to continue using the stocks on hand. In December 1977 the use of Kepone in any accessible traps—that is, traps that might expose people to the Kepone—was banned. And as of May 1978 the production of inaccessible traps—those that keep the Kepone sealed away—was banned as well. But merchants were allowed, and still are allowed, to sell the inaccessible Kepone traps that were on their shelves or in their storerooms at the time of this ban.

Meanwhile, further news caused even more environmental grief. At State College, Pennsylvania, Nease Chemical had produced batches of Kepone for Allied in 1958, 1959 and 1963. Nease manufactured in all no more than 100,000 pounds, reported Nease's president, Robert H. Wecker, in comparison to the 1.7 million pounds turned out by Life Science alone in Hopewell.[55] Yet, 13 years after Nease halted its Kepone production, residues were found in soils near the Nease Plant and in fish taken from a nearby stream. Next, Pennsylvania's Department of Environmental Resources (DER) reported "very low concentrations" of Kepone in 5 out of 23 private wells surveyed in the area. The DER warned the well owners against use of the water for drinking, bathing or cooking.

Also found near the plant was Mirex, a fire-ant killer more recently produced by Nease on an occasional basis. Chemically similar to Kepone (HCP is their common raw material), the compound is known sometimes to break down into Kepone. Possibly, but improbably, says an EPA spokesman, the Kepone residues in Pennsylvania originated in Mirex wastes. Whatever their origin, Pennsylvania's DER found "significant quantities of Kepone and Mirex in the soils at former lagoon and spray irrigation waste disposal sites and in the sediments in drainage ways under the company's property."[56]

If that development exemplifying Kepone's persistence wasn't discouraging enough for Virginia, the EPA estimated in mid-1978 that "decades" would pass before natural processes could decrease Kepone accumulation in much of the James River's marine life to a point below FDA action levels for human consumption. "Based on current evidence, degradation of Kepone in the natural environment is insignificant," said the EPA study.[57] In May 1980 a circuit court judge overturned the ban on marine harvesting in the James in response to a suit brought by a marine supply firm, but Governor John H. Dalton asserted additional "emergency" authority to reimpose it one day later.[58] Citing decreased Kepone levels, the state subsequently lifted its ban on recreational and commercial fishing, for all fish except striped bass and eel.

The only other good news for the environment in the immediate post-Kepone-production years was evidence that the Chesapeake Bay, one of the nation's richest seafood resources, might escape the fate that closed the James River to most marine harvesting indefinitely. For three or four years, at least, the lower strata of the bay's marine life exhibited only slight Kepone residues, while bottom sediments of the Bay remained free of the pesticide. As the EPA said in 1978, "the data indicate no imminent danger," but "major coastal storms and like events could alter these predictions."

Life in the James River hasn't fared as well.

Laboratory tests and limited data from the field have indicated Kepone's toxic impact upon the biota of the James. Kepone is speculated to be the culprit in reduced populations noted in recent years among the blue crab, the osprey and the American bald eagle. Students of the river region's wildlife trends did report in 1980, however, encouraging signs of a possible resurgence among the eagles and ospreys. Even raccoons, one cursory sampling of 1977 suggested, were accumulating low levels of Kepone residues in their bodies.[59]

Yet proposed wildlife studies ran aground on the shoals of inadequate funding soon after Virginia's environmental crisis came to light. Commented one of the EPA's press officers some time later, "Frankly, we've somewhat lost track of it as well since it's moved off page one."

Still, federal agencies, with some EPA funding, and Virginia's own marine scientists at the Virginia Institute of Marine Sciences have continued to study the pesticide's effects upon fish. And the EPA, beyond its earlier efforts that cost millions, did contribute the 1978 Kepone Mitigation Feasibility Study—admittedly not as any panacea, but as a blueprint for specific steps to offset contamination of the James. "Unusual climatic conditions" in that area had prompted the EPA to warn that the river's stores of Kepone could be blown into the Chesapeake Bay.

More generally, and "as might be expected," wrote Deputy EPA Administrator Barbara Blum to the governors of Maryland and Virginia, "this initial study does not provide recommendations that, if implemented, would bring an end to concern about the Kepone contamination problem. . . . I believe, however, that the results of the . . . study will be very beneficial in charting the direction for future surveillance and mitigation actions relating to the Kepone problem."

In Hopewell, meanwhile, Allied Chemical and city, state and federal authorities pitched in to a costly cleanup campaign at and near the errant Life Science plant. Among their efforts, under state and federal supervision: Allied dismantled machinery and other contaminated parts of the plant and buried them in a plastic-lined pit in a city landfill; efforts were made to contain the sewage sludge in Hopewell's "Kepone Lagoon"; Allied disposed of 200,000 gallons of contaminated water by filtering it and spraying it over a 10-acre Allied-owned site nearby; state funds paid for a scrub-down of about 30 worker homes. And Allied found a "home" for barrel upon barrel of Kepone-laden debris gathered both at Hopewell and in Baltimore, after rebuffed exploration of an empty missile silo in Idaho and an incinerator in Wales: The Kepone will nest in an abandoned salt mine in West Germany.

According to *Fortune*, Allied Chairman Connor insisted upon these and other helpful steps over the objections of company lawyers, "who felt that his generosity would be inevitably misconstrued as an acceptance of liability." By this account, a shocked Connor felt, "whether or not we had legal responsibility, we at least had the moral responsibility to resolve the damages and to help the people who were injured." Allied also provided funds for the search at the Medical College of Virginia in Richmond for effective treatment of the most severely affected Kepone victims, who suffered such symptoms as neurological disorder, enlarged liver or spleen, eye tremor, chest and joint pain—and "the shakes." The elusive objective of the research was some means of ejecting the persistent, repeatedly cycled poison from the body.

Not only were the Kepone victims made physically ill, some to remain disabled for years, but they and in some cases their family members had to endure long hospital stays and unpleasant medical tests, and they were subject to the pervasive uncertainty of what it all could mean to their future health prospects. Some victims also were unusually irritable, even depressed. One worker, before Jackson's visit to Life Science disclosed the problem, threw a hammer through his automobile window. Another, hospitalized in the aftermath of the Jackson visit, tried to jump out a window at MCV.

In early 1978 the medical college's Dr. Philip S. Guzelian finally reported success with the binding agent cholestyramine, which had sped bodily elimination of Kepone to two or three times the natural rate. Some of the victims still were disabled, but two-thirds of Guzelian's 22 Kepone patients, he reported, had Kepone levels in their blood lowered to the point of being "undetectable"—and they now had "minimal" symptoms. This good news was relayed to the 50 additional Kepone victims known to the MCV staff, with the advice that they try the drug as well.[60]

A "cure" for Kepone has not necessarily been found, however. By Jackson's reckoning, cholestyramine hastened the rate of natural body elimination of Kepone by only .7 percent. And although acute symptoms among the most severely affected Kepone workers gradually receded, Jackson explains that the long-term, chronic effects of Kepone remain open to question. "There is no evidence that the cholestyramine has any mitigating effects on cancer, fertility, birth defects, et cetera," he notes. A further complication: Because Kepone tends to accumulate in the liver and in fatty tissue, blood tests alone are incomplete indexes of the body's possible hoard of the poison.

In a survey of 120 of the former Kepone production workers at the Semi-Works in Hopewell, Allied found detectable blood levels in 22—two or more years after the fact. But Virginia's Health Department, incorporating results of that Allied survey with its own findings on the firm's one-time Kepone workers, reports detectable levels of the pesticide in the blood of 62 out of 146 tested. And those 146 actually rounded up for testing comprised fewer than one-half the 339 people known to have worked in Allied's Semi-Works during its Kepone production.[61]

Fifty additional workers, from the firm's large Baltimore plant, once a transfer point for Kepone shipments, apparently underwent medical examination as well. In 1977, a ranking Maryland official acknowledged that his state should have pursued the outcome of those examinations.

"It's sad to say no one followed up on these people," said Harvey Epstein, Maryland's Commissioner of Labor and Industry. "We haven't done a whole hell of a lot."

Baltimore, home of at least 5,000 businesses handling dangerous or potentially dangerous substances, suffers high cancer rates—45 percent higher than the national average for white males, for example. Kepone was only one of the potentially hazardous substances to appear in the city, or even at the Allied plant there.

As Jackson notes, whatever the success of Guzelian's new treatment effort, Kepone's cancerous potential remains unknown. But steps have been taken toward defining the risk factor more concretely. The National Cancer Institute (NCI) and the National Institute of Environmental Health Sciences (NIEHS) have planned a joint effort renewing NCI's earlier study of Kepone's carcinogenic potential. Findings that Kepone is less of a cancer threat than feared naturally would brighten the health prospects of those exposed to Kepone. It also could prompt relaxation of the action levels for sale and consumption of seafood from Kepone-contaminated waters.

Those levels, eased slightly in 1977, had major economic impact upon marine-related industry in the James River and the Chesapeake Bay in the immediate aftermath of the Kepone disaster. Some seafood dealers actually closed down in the Kepone "scare"; many fishermen and charter captains were idled for at least the summer of 1976. Reliable indexes of the overall disruptions are hard to come by. As one indicator, however, U.S. Commerce Department marketing estimates for the James River in 1975 indicate the fin-fish catch alone that year was 3 million pounds—$1.2 million worth of fish. (The stream wasn't closed down officially until mid-December 1975.)

Virginia health officials have planned to supplement the new NCI-NIEHS Kepone study with their own analysis of consistent consumers of James River seafoods. Neurological, sterility and cancer histories would be among the foci of the study planned by Johns Hopkins University and the state. "If we can show that there has been no effect," said Jackson, "you can then make a very meaningful statement relating to humans." As Jackson also had observed some months earlier, "Once we know the answer to some of these questions, we'll know whether we really have a problem. But as long as it's unknown, it's a big problem."[62]

Dredging, a project costing billions if mounted at full scale, appeared an unlikely remedy for the hard-hit James, although spot dredging and diking were seen as containment possibilities. Scientists briefly weighed more exotic ideas as well—one of them introduction of a fungi shown in lab tests to absorb and break down Kepone.

Three years after Kepone's public discovery, the chemical still was a potentially hazardous source of pollution in the Hopewell area. "Small inflows of Kepone continue into the James River," noted the EPA's 1978 report. Even earlier, in 1976, a limited EPA survey indicated Kepone dust was circulating in the air near the defunct Life Science plant. The remedy recommended then was to cover or to remove Kepone-laced soils near the plant. Yet, as the EPA's broader study released in early 1978 stated, "Kepone residuals persist in the Hopewell soil areas," and, "human health effects have not been determined for Kepone dispersion by soil or air transfer."[63]

In October of 1978, at the prodding of Governor John N. Dalton, the city moved more than 15 truckloads of topsoil scrapings from the Life Science plant's vicinity to a pit on Allied property. But other hot spots lingered. One was a quarter-acre marsh adjacent to Bailey Creek that the EPA considered a repository of 3,000 pounds of Kepone. Another, ironically, was the city sewage plant, which that October was routing an average of six grams of Kepone a day to a new regional sewage-treatment facility.

The EPA warned, too, that Kepone Lagoon, containing an estimated 220 pounds of Kepone in its mass of sludge, could be leaking the pesticide into Bailey's Creek. On the average, said the 1978 report, runoff from the Hopewell area contained 3.3 grams of Kepone a day in dry weather and 64 grams a day under storm-flow conditions. Neither state nor federal officials had settled then upon an effective—and environmentally safe —means of disposing of the Lagoon's bulk content. Incineration was studied at great cost and length, but officials eventually settled on a far less expensive, apparently simple answer: encapsulation in sealed concrete. With this accomplished in 1979, says Jackson, Hopewell's irksome Kepone Lagoon "no longer poses a problem."

Despite the human tragedy and the persistent environmental threat, the Kepone incident has stimulated some positive action. Virginia's legislature enacted new toxic-substance controls for the state and revamped its work-safety legislation for submission to the federal government. In addition, Allied's stinging penalty served as a warning bell for industry in general. Further, the binding agent proven helpful to Kepone victims may have more widespread use in other poisoning cases.

As another hard-won Kepone "bonus," Allied's stiff fine was mitigated by a unique compromise worked out in Merhige's courtroom. Presented with a broad hint that Merhige would like to see the money remain in Virginia for the benefit of its people, Allied offered an $8 million gift establishing the Virginia Environmental Endowment. On February 1, 1977, Merhige accepted. The result was the only grant-making organization in the nation devoted exclusively to the quality of the environment. Among the board directors named by Merhige were William B. Cummings, the U.S. attorney who prosecuted Allied, and Cathy Douglas, wife of the late Supreme Court Justice William O. Douglas. And among the Environmental Endowment's initial grants were funds establishing a mediation service for environmental disputes; a number of awards for academic research; and funding for field studies, environmental conferences or further medical study of Kepone's effects upon the human animal.

By the same arrangement, meanwhile, Allied earned itself a welcome tax bonus. After the company donated the money,

Merhige reduced his fine against it by a matching $8 million. This move enabled Allied to take a major tax deduction on the money it had given away, rather than having paid the $8 million to the U.S. Treasury as part of a nondeductible fine.

But what of the Kepone incident's more subjective impact upon Allied and its ranking officers? Allied internally has become, reported *Fortune,* "much more conservative in its attitude toward new ventures." Further, "Allied . . . has moved to tighten its procedures. A senior corporate officer must now approve any tolling contract, and agreements with former employees must now be approved by Connor personally. Another change is a new incentive-compensation program. . . . The plan downgrades profitability as a measure of a manager's performance and gives much greater weight to his regard for social and environmental responsibilities."[64]

Whether the principals of the Kepone disaster learned its lessons, only passing years will reveal. Surely none would dispute one federal official's view that everyone took it on the chin in Virginia's shattering experience with Kepone. "Individuals, industry, local, state, federal government—in this one, everyone's a loser."

But Russell E. Train, the EPA administrator at the time the Kepone incident burst upon the public, warned that regulation alone is not the solution. Calling Virginia's crisis "one of the most serious incidents of environmental contamination that has occurred," Train noted that "even strengthened authority will provide limited protection in cases of gross disregard of regulatory requirements, as apparently occurred in Hopewell.

"The Kepone disaster underlines the fact that the use of toxic materials in our society inevitably carries with it grave risks," Train continued. "It illustrates how dangerous chemical contaminants can be when introduced into the environment without adequate controls."

And, as Senator Leahy of Vermont said at the end of the subcommittee's 1976 Kepone hearings:

Throughout all of it, one thing that comes through very, very clear is that the Government cannot give the answer to everything. The Government cannot cover every single problem. The Government cannot protect us from every possible danger. There is such a thing as corporate responsibility.

It is the personal feeling of this Senator, at least, that the major corporation here, Allied . . . owed a great duty to the employees of Life Science as did the people who were running Life Science owed [sic] a great deal to their employees because it was known to be a dangerous substance; the steps that should have been taken by those companies . . . were not taken.[65]

NOTES

1. Fitzgerald testimony, hearings January 1976 before U.S. Senate Subcommittee on Agricultural Research and General Legislation. All further attribution to Fitzgerald experience is from same testimony, January 23, 1976.

2. Thurman Dykes testimony before subcommittee, January 23, 1976.

3. Gilbert and White conversation over beer; reported in the *Washington Star,* November 30, 1975.

4. Fitzgerald testimony.

5. C. Cueto et al., *National Cancer Institute Bioassay Report on Technical Grade Chlordecone (Kepone),* January 1976.

6. Bender's estimates are from written testimony before a joint hearing, U.S. Senate Subcommittee on Resource Protection and Environmental Pollution, March 28, 1979.

7. *Washington Star,* September 21, 1976.

8. Department of Neurology, Medical College of Virginia, *Kepone Intoxication in Man, I: Clinical Observations* (presented in part before the American Academy of Neurology, April 26–May 1, 1976).

9. G. C. Matthiesen testimony, U.S. Senate Subcommittee on Agricultural Research and General Legislation (94th Congress), January 23, 1976. All subsequent Matthiesen quotes are taken from same testimony.

10. Allied first considered building its own Kepone plant in Europe, but rejected the proposal when such a facility was discovered to cost "close to a million dollars." (Plaintiff reply brief, *Moore v. Allied et al.,* CA #77-0379R, page 5.)

11. Moore testimony, U.S. Senate Subcommittee on Agricultural Research and General Legislation (94th Congress), January 26, 1976. All Moore quotes are from same testimony.

12. Matthiesen testimony.

13. William P. Moore deposition, *Moore v. Allied.* "I think you needed toxicological data. I think you needed all of the information. We needed it all. And

we didn't get it. We didn't get anything. We got the Ameen memo [the 1966 production manual for Kepone by Allied area supervisor Jameil Ameen of the Hopewell Semi-Works] that I had to go look up. And we got a black book that was primarily efficacy data. Yes we needed toxicological information. We needed industrial hygiene data. None of which we had. And Allied had *beaucoups* [sic] of those. Or, at least, toxicological data, I have subsequently found. And they had a toxicologist who was never made available to us and never saw me."

14. Hundtofte testimony, U.S. Senate Subcommittee on Agricultural Research and General Legislation (94th Congress), January 26, 1976.

15. Samuel S. Epstein, "Kepone Hazard Evaluation," *The Science of the Total Environment*, vol. 9, no. 1 (January 1978), p. 15. Elsevier Scientific Publishing Company, Amsterdam, Netherlands.

16. VA Air Board Account, U.S. Senate Subcommittee hearing, January 22, 1976. Dust catcher-EPA references: EPA, *Kepone Levels Found in Environmental Samples From the Hopewell, Virginia, Area*, December 16, 1975.

17. Meyer testimony, January 22, 1976.

18. See the *Washington Star*, September 25, 1976. Also, EPA, Health Effects Research Lab, *Preliminary Report on Kepone Levels Found in Human Blood From General Population of Hopewell, Virginia, Area*, March 3, 1976. Also, personal communication with Dr. Jackson.

19. Hundtofte testimony before Federal District Court for the Eastern District of Virginia, September 28, 1976. *Washington Star*, September 29, 1976.

20. Personal communication with Dr. Jackson, fall 1975.

21. Jensen testimony to Senate subcommittee, January 22, 1976.

22. John Reeves, sanitary engineer for the State Water Control Board, memo dated December 6, 1975.

23. *Washington Star*, December 2, 1976. Based on summary sheets of a Kepone analysis of the Hopewell water supply, Bureau of Sanitary Engineering, Virginia Department of Health, late-1974–mid-1976.

24. Moore testimony to the Senate, January 23, 1976.

25. Joseph Galda testimony to the Senate, January 26, 1976.

26. See the *Washington Star*, September 30, 1976. Dr. Jackson referred to the EPA official visit in August, in personal communication.

27. Ewing testimony, January 27, 1976.

28. Mintz testimony, January 27, 1976.

29. *Appendix*, Miscellaneous Exhibit, Senate hearings, January 22–27, 1976.

30. Lapsley Ewing testimony to the Senate, January 27, 1976.

31. *Washington Star*, September 24, 1976.

32. Ibid.

33. Under contract to Allied Chemical, a two-year rat study by Dr. P. S. Larson, Medical College of Virginia, et al., 1961.

34. Edward Callahan, general manager, Allied Chemical Environmental Services Department, in a statement prepared for submission to EPA hearings, January 1977.

35. Epstein, "Kepone Hazard Evaluation," pp. 60–61.

36. Fitzgerald testimony.

37. *Washington Star,* September 27, 1976.

38. Ibid.

39. Ibid.

40. Reference to Allied-Spiess luncheon and facts about it are from an internal Allied memo of October 28, 1974, by M. S. Meo, titled, "Visit of Dr. W. Spiess, Spiess & Sohne, Kleinkarlback Uber, West Germany." The meeting took place October 25, 1974.

41. Testimony by Joseph A. Stickl of Hooker, in Federal District Court, Eastern District of Virginia, Richmond, September 28, 1976.

42. Trial testimony, September 27–28, 1976, in Federal District Court, Richmond.

43. *Washington Star,* November 30, 1975.

44. *Washington Star,* September 27, 1976.

45. *Washington Star,* October 3, 1976.

46. Ameen testimony to the Senate, January 23, 1976.

47. EPA, *Kepone Levels Found in Environmental Samples from the Hopewell, Virginia, Area.*

48. *Washington Star,* December 17, 1975.

49. The fine was levied against Moore and Hundtofte jointly—for the pair, it totaled only $16,500. It was later appealed, in a plea rejected by the U.S. Fourth Circuit Court of Appeals, February 2, 1979.

50. Indictments were issued May 7, 1976, by the Federal Grand Jury in Richmond, Virginia.

51. Two Allied supervisory personnel were tried on a federal charge of conspiring to cover up company pollution of the James River; they were acquitted in Federal District Court in Alexandria, the Eastern District of Virginia, September 1976.

52. Associated Press, May 6, 7, 1980.

53. The huge fine was levied against Allied on October 5, 1976. Moore and Hundtofte were fined $25,000 each on the same date. Life Science Products, Inc., was by then defunct, but nonetheless was fined $3.8 million.

54. Marvin H. Zim, "Allied Chemical's $20 Million Ordeal With Kepone," *Fortune*, September 11, 1978.

55. Nease President Wecker's report of the no more than 100,000 pounds of Kepone manufactured appeared in the *Richmond Times-Dispatch*, August 15, 1976.

56. Department of Environmental Resources press releases, 1977 and 1978.

57. EPA, *Executive Summary, Mitigation Feasibility for the Kepone-Contaminated Hopewell/James River Areas*, June 9, 1978.

58. Bill McAllister, "Lament For a River Befouled," *Washington Post*, May 24, 1980.

59. C. P. Brylant, R. W. Young and R. L. Kirkpatrick, VPI, "Kepone Residues in Body Tissues of Raccoons Collected Along the James River, East of Hopewell, Virginia" (presented at Virginia Academy of Sciences meeting, spring 1978). The abstract says that while James River coons carried residues several times greater than those of a fairly distant control group, Kepone does not appear to be entering these animals "to any appreciable extent." (Only five river animals were tested; they were compared to only four control raccoons.)

60. Kepone elimination was announced in a press conference at MCV February 1, 1978, by Guzelian. By mid-1980, Guzelian reported that his studies indicate that humans eventually convert Kepone to a form allowing natural elimination.

61. According to Moore's reply brief (pp. 24–25) in *Moore v. Allied et al.*, he was unaware of an insurance company inspection of the Semi-Works in 1972 that "classified it as an 'imminent danger' and one which would cause OSHA to shut the plant area down." Moreover, "blood tests performed after the closing of the Life Science plant on Allied employees formerly engaged in Kepone manufacturing indicate high levels of Kepone in their blood and signs and symptoms of Kepone poisoning. Therefore, presuming Allied's own employees followed the precautions of the Ameen memo, they nevertheless became contaminated with [sic] made ill by Kepone which points to the inadequacy of the warning to Mr. Moore."

62. *Richmond Times-Dispatch*, December 11, 1977; February 25, 1979.

63. EPA, *Executive Summary, Mitigation Feasibility for the Kepone-Contaminated Hopewell/James River Areas*.

64. Zim, "Allied Chemical's $20 Million Ordeal With Kepone."

65. Hearings transcript, January 27, 1976.

Chapter 4

West Valley

JO-ANN E. ARMAO

IT SITS SILENTLY in the rolling farm country of New York State, just 35 miles southeast of Buffalo. Outwardly it looks harmless. The buildings are an innocuous-appearing clump of squarish cement-block structures, neither large nor threatening. No unseemly smoke rises from the blue-green stacks. Only the unusual symbol on the smokestack—a wheel of alternating pie slices—suggests that something sets this complex apart from other commercial developments.

The symbol is that of the nuclear age. The place is West Valley, a sparsely settled hamlet in upstate New York's Cattaraugus County. And the building is the Western New York Nuclear Service Center, the nation's only commercial nuclear reprocessing plant. A venture of Nuclear Fuel Services Inc. (NFS), now a subsidiary of the Getty Oil Company, the plant was built as the final link in the nuclear fuel cycle, intended to receive the spent fuel of the atomic power industry and reprocess it for renewed use.

After six years of operation in which about 625 metric tons of fuel were reprocessed at a loss exceeding $40 million, the plant shut down in 1972 for a supposedly temporary hiatus for expansion and modification.[1] The planned reopening with expanded facilities never came; in 1976 Nuclear Fuel Services announced its withdrawal from the reprocessing business.

A technological and economic disaster, the plant stands today as evidence of the failure to solve the problem of nuclear-waste disposal.

More remains in the meadows and woods of Cattaraugus County than buildings and signs, however. The misadventure at West Valley leaves an awesome legacy—one that could well cost state and federal taxpayers a billion dollars, threaten the health of nearby residents and their descendants, and endanger for centuries the surrounding environment. That legacy—which one New York politician regularly refers to as "that crap" —is a vast amount of highly toxic nuclear waste.

Situated on the 3,300-acre site are 170 tons of spent nuclear fuel rods in storage pools; the reprocessing plant, which should be decommissioned and safely disposed of itself; 140,000 cubic feet of solid waste, basically leftover hardware; 2.4 million cubic feet of buried radioactive trash (originating largely from medical and chemical laboratories, hospitals, equipment manufacturers, nuclear reactor facilities, and nuclear fuel fabrication and reprocessing plants); and—deadliest of all—nearly 600,000 gallons of highly radioactive liquid waste.[2] This so-called high-level waste, leftovers of the reprocessing operations now stored in an underground carbon-steel tank, will be lethal—and accordingly must be kept safely stored—for the next 200,000 or so years.

Under the terms of a contract that made the NFS venture possible, in 1981 responsibility for the care of these nuclear wastes shifts to the state of New York. This arrangement was made in the early 1960s, when the federal Atomic Energy Commission (AEC) refused to license the plant unless a government would pledge to take care of the long-lived wastes. Governor Nelson Rockefeller, eager to bring the nuclear industry to New York, took on the responsibility. The price tag on the clean-up project now facing the state (or the federal government, if New York is successful in shifting the bill) has been estimated at almost $300 million, not including the costs of handling the low-level wastes.

The importance of the cleanup costs pales, however, beside

the dangers that radioactive wastes pose to people and property. A failure of the underground tank would be catastrophic, resulting in permanent contamination of the environment and untold deaths. This tank, a vessel good for only another 25 or so years, is similar in design and construction to tanks that leaked at the federal reprocessing plant in Hanford, Washington.

Already, late in 1978, a small hole was discovered in a catch-pan in which the high-level-waste tank sits. The catch-pan (or saucer pan) is one protective barrier—built to catch and contain any radioactive materials in the event of a leak. The state ordered NFS to repair the hole. However, whether the defect can be corrected is uncertain; one of the original safety systems is feared lost. Karl Abraham of the Nuclear Regulatory Commission (NRC) said of the situation: "It's not a trivial problem. It's possible that they may never be able to restore the integrity of the pan."[3]

Because the pan rests underneath the storage tank, NFS engineers cannot gain access to the hole to assess the extent of the damage and what a repair job would entail. The defect may have been present since construction. "It is conceivable," Charlie Haughney of the NRC explained, "but not certain that this pan may have been defective from the start. I don't know if we can ever determine this."[4]

Because the wastes cannot stay forever in the tank they are in now, officials intend to solidify the wastes through some still-undecided and unproved process. The wastes then would be transported to a yet-to-be-designated federal repository.

Another problem centers on the burial ground used for the low-level wastes. Water has leaked through the burial ground, sending radioactivity into Cattaraugus Creek, a creek that flows into Lake Erie, which in turn provides drinking water for some 400,000 people living in the city of Buffalo. The burial ground is now operated in a shut-down condition: The trash it holds is guarded and monitored, but no more waste is accepted. Periodic pumping and other remedial procedures provide stop-gap relief to the twin problems of erosion and seepage.

The public and its officials, as well as the media, have come to view this situation as some sort of natural disaster. Such a representation holds that for the government to step in and assume rescue responsibility is right and proper. Yet the West Valley complex is the result of a private firm's profit-seeking. NFS entered the reprocessing field expecting to make money by selling recovered uranium and plutonium. Instead, NFS (later owned by Getty Oil) lost money and learned that the technology was too risky and the product too difficult to sell. In short, nuclear reprocessing was a flop. And—well aware of the enormous demands of managing radioactive wastes—private business has dumped the matter into the government's hands. Thus, in a bailout that calls to mind Ralph Nader's notion of "lemon socialism," New York State soon will become owner of a facility that not only has no value but has the potential of causing great harm and draining the public treasury.

The public has been placed in the position of ultimately underwriting the facility by the shortsightedness of the state government under Governor Rockefeller. Rockefeller, anxious for the jobs, taxes and other economic benefits then promised by what seemed the pioneer venture in a profitable new business, was quick to believe the plant would be safe and seemed unwilling either to carefully investigate the potential risks or to share any discomforting information with the public. The state became so committed to the idea of the pioneer business that it failed to develop a real understanding of the nature of this peculiar nuclear-power venture. Consider, for example, the words of one New York State official who talked about the "several hundred years" that the wastes must be isolated; the wastes remain dangerous, of course, for tens of thousand of years.[5]

The government subscribed, too, to the belief that any problems would be answered sometime in the future. As the West Valley plant opened, America had a trust in technology and a faith in the future. But the plant's closing has not been kind to that trust; and shattered with the plans for West Valley is the dream that the high technology of nuclear energy holds all the answers to this country's power needs. The NFS plant was built in a time of unconstrained optimism about atomic power. Nuclear power would provide electricity "too cheap to meter." The reality is embodied at West Valley today: The atomic industry is unable to clean up after itself. That simple fact has dealt a terrible blow to the expectation that nuclear power will satisfy America's energy appetite.

To the West Valley residents, the plant is no symbol—it is a part of life. Here, stories of its effects are well-known: local workers such as Walter Zefers and Haafez Saadeck who have placed the cause of their illnesses at NFS's doorstep; the area physicians who acknowledge that numbers of birth defects "seem" to be higher in the area.[6] But no statistical studies either support or disprove these fears. Incredibly, no studies have been done.

And, many in the West Valley community would say no need exists for any type of health study. The community is a proud one and takes umbrage at any suggestion that its populace may be more susceptible to cancer or its children have a higher than average number of birth defects.

Insight into this community's psyche is provided in a story the district's congressman likes to tell. Representative Stanley Lundine spent a day talking with members of the West Valley community about their concerns over the plant and NFS's imminent pullout. Lundine termed the group a representative cross section.

"I pointed out to the group at one point," Lundine remembered, "that we had talked about tax base and economics and jobs and a whole range of topics, but at no point had we discussed health concerns.

"I told the group," Lundine said, "that I didn't understand this omission. I told them 'it seems to me this would be an overriding concern.'

"One lady then turns to me and says, 'You know, Congressman, we can understand taxes and jobs and all of that. But that other stuff, we can't understand it. That's your responsibility.'

"The point I think the woman was making," said Lundine, "is that if you live there you can't think about the health effects. It would be like living on the edge all the time. So instead you rely, you trust in government—people like me—to be responsible. I felt that that placed an additional burden on me."

If any part of the West Valley story can be called the brighter side, it is the work of citizens' groups that have called attention to the problems at the plant and have demanded solutions. Citizens in the West Valley area, most notably across the Erie County border, in Springville, where the largest number of plant employees lived, started to express some concerns in the early 1970s—a few years after the plant opened, and just as NFS was talking about doubling its capacity. The citizens—predominantly housewives, but also farmers, lawyers and even plant employees—weren't antinuclear, weren't even environmentalists. Many had fully supported the plant's being established in their community. Typical is Holly Nachbar, who remembered that when the plant opened "I found it so progressive. A thing of the future." Her thinking, and that of other residents, slowly changed as rumors of lax safety precautions filtered through the countryside. One result was the Springville Radiation Study Group, a group that eventually was joined in its questioning of the plant's practices by such organizations as the Sierra Club and the New York Public Interest Research Group.

Early on, authorities tended to dismiss these groups as packs of cranks who didn't know what they were talking about. Slowly that thinking, too, changed, and Mrs. Nachbar can look back at her years of involvement with great satisfaction. She would not attribute credit for the plant's decision to shut down solely to citizen action. Yet, she feels, the citizens' groups in West Valley and across the country have planted a seed of doubt about nuclear energy that has grown into today's furious debate on the risks and benefits, the pros and cons of nuclear power.

"THE WAND OF HISTORY"

An early and energetic member of the atomic industry's fan club was New York's governor, Nelson Rockefeller. It was Rockefeller's goal that New York lead the nation into the atomic age. "The atomic age, rich in challenge and opportunity," Rockefeller exhorted the state legislature in 1962, "stretches limitlessly into our future."[7] Rockefeller's interest in making New

York a prime participant in the fledgling nuclear industry coincided with the efforts of the Atomic Energy Commission encouraging private industry to commercialize nuclear-fuel reprocessing.

In 1959, Rockefeller created the Office of Atomic Development (OAD) as an independent agency in the State Executive Department to coordinate the government's atomic regulatory and development functions. The office, under the leadership of Director Oliver Townsend, issued in 1959 its first major report. It was a document that well described the agency's goals.[8] Entitled "An Atomic Plan for the State of New York," the report proposed that New York undertake an aggressive and coordinated effort to attract the nuclear-power industry to its borders. Specifically, the report proposed:

> We believe that the state government should attempt to identify and through appropriate catalytic action help bring into being within the state those projects which can find in New York and [sic] economically sensible home, and which, as time passes, are likely to serve as magnets for further atomic and other industrial development. In this way, both the cause of the state and the overall cause of atomic progress can be most effectively served.[9]

Among the industrial opportunities the OAD forecast for New York were such grandiose schemes as construction of two test reactors and establishment of massive port facilities for the new fleet of nuclear-powered merchant ships that surely would be built. Also forecast were large-scale fuel reprocessing, waste storage and fuel fabrication.[10]

Nuclear-industry officials felt the industry direly needed reprocessing facilities. One factor that had retarded the use of nuclear energy for generating electricity was the high cost of producing usable atomic-fuel elements. Power plants use only a portion of a nuclear-fuel element's potential energy before waste products render the element commercially useless. The essence of reprocessing is the chemical extraction of uranium-235 and plutonium-239 from the radioactive spent fuel rods of power reactors. Reprocessing was seen as the way to stretch the nation's supply of uranium, which like oil or coal is finite. The nuclear-power industry also foresaw reprocessing to be a profitable venture, because a firm such as NFS could, in theory, sell the material it extracted for less than newly mined fuel.

Armed with its atomic-development plan under the aegis of the OAD, New York pursued the new reprocessing industry. The first step was finding land, and the OAD launched a statewide search for a suitable site. State officials claimed the search, conducted by a specially constituted site-selection committee of state officials with the advice of the AEC and independent consultants, included assessments of the safety, geological, hydrological, meteorological and engineering requirements for the storage of radioactive waste products.[11]

In June 1961 Governor Rockefeller announced the selection of 3,331 acres within the Town of Ashford, Cattaraugus County, midway between Springville and the hamlet of West Valley. The governor said these factors were taken into account in the selection of the western New York site:

—the assured protection of the public's health and safety;

—the suitability for construction of a reprocessing plant;

—the low cost of the land;

—the availability of an adequate water supply;

—its accessibility by rail and truck.[12]

The state, eventually using its right of eminent domain and about $400,000, acquired 44 parcels of land in Cattaraugus County, displacing some reluctant farmers from thriving dairy farms.[13]

The OAD then began looking for a private company interested in building and operating a reprocessing plant on the land. The state advertised West Valley as the keystone to the development of a complete commercial nuclear industry in the Northeast. Cattaraugus County, so the sales pitch went, was to be one of the major nuclear-power centers in the nation.

The group selected by the state was the Davison Chemical Company, a Baltimore division of W. R. Grace and Company.

OAD Director Townsend said the state gave the option to the Grace firm because its plans for the plant and storage facilities were the most substantially advanced of any company expressing interest in building and operating the complex. To run the operation, the firm created a subsidiary, Nuclear Fuel Services Incorporated. W. R. Grace owned 78 percent of NFS, and 22 percent was owned by American Machine and Foundry Corporation. NFS began negotiations with the New York State Atomic Research and Development Authority (ARDA), newly created by the state legislature.[14] Negotiations followed involving the state, Nuclear Fuel Services and the AEC; and on June 29, 1962, ARDA gave NFS the official go-ahead to proceed with plans for a reprocessing facility.

No time was wasted in getting the project off the ground. Indeed, plant critics were later to point to the hasty approval as the reason for many of the plant's failings. On July 26, 1962, a mere four months after its own formation, NFS filed a construction permit and license application with the AEC. On October 11, 1962, less than three months after this application was filed, the Advisory Committee on Reactor Safeguards approved the site in a report to the AEC. The facility's design similarly was approved, on December 26, 1962. "There is reasonable assurance," the AEC's Division of Licensing and Regulation said, "that a facility of the type proposed can be constructed and operated at this site without endangering the health and safety of the public."[15]

Public hearings on construction of the facility were held in March 1963 in nearby Olean. The same month, ARDA purchased 14 more acres adjoining the site. And ARDA officially took title to the land. The AEC issued a construction permit on April 30, 1963, and construction began 2 months later—only 15 months after the Nuclear Fuel Services company was formed.

At the ground-breaking ceremony for the $33 million facility on June 13, 1963, Governor Rockefeller summed up all the state's expectations for the plant and all of the age's hopes for the atom:

In short, we are launching a unique operation here today which I regard with pride as a symbol of imagination and foresight on the part of your state government—an operation which will make a major contribution toward transforming the economy of Western New York and, indeed, of the entire state. . . . The radioactive waste products of the plant's operation will be stored in the state-owned facilities at this site. Some of these have considerable potential value as radiation sources in industry and medicine. . . . The Western New York area is already a substantial center of atomic development, and with the coming of the reprocessing industry, holds promise of becoming one of the principal regions of atomic industry activity in the world . . . in short, this state-sponsored project, operating through private enterprise with federal cooperation, places New York in the forefront of the atomic industrial age now dawning—to the benefit of the health, safety and prosperity of this generation and many generations to come.[16]

The same day, OAD Director Oliver Townsend entoned: "Ashford Hollow . . . has now been touched by the wand of history. It is now part of and in phase with the times in which we live, and—I have no doubt—to its future benefit."[17] The doubts didn't come until the plant actually began operating.

Financing for the plant came from several sources: ARDA initially invested $8 million for site improvements and construction; $8 million came from NFS ($6 million from W. R. Grace and $2 million from the American Machine and Foundry Corporation); $2 million was invested by way of a research grant from the Empire State Atomic Development Association (an amalgamation of five New York State power facilities); and W. R. Grace additionally obtained $13.5 million in bank loans, using a state guarantee against default.[18]

Construction was completed in February 1966. The plant's principal contractor was the Bechtel Corporation of San Francisco, and the plans were based on those of the reprocessing plant operated by the Atomic Energy Commission at Hanford, Washington. A provisional operating license was issued on April 18, 1966. NFS was licensed as operator of the facility, and the renamed ARDA, which in 1964 had become the New York Atomic and Space Development Authority (ASDA), was licensed as the owner and lessor. One day after the license was issued, the first commercial reprocessing of spent fuel in the United States began.

Before that license was granted, the state had satisfied federal demands for the caretaking of the highly radioactive wastes that would be produced as a byproduct of reprocessing. Early on, NFS officials had indicated to the AEC that the company did not consider it proper for a private business to assume responsibility for the continued care of nuclear wastes. In March of 1963 NFS wrote to the AEC, "We wish to reiterate our conclusion that the storage of nuclear waste is a government responsibility."

The AEC fully agreed.[19] Robert Lowenstein, director of the AEC's Division of Licensing and Regulation, wrote to Townsend in February 1963 expressing the AEC's concern. The chore of caring for the wastes would span generations, Lowenstein told Townsend, and only the state or federal governments could provide reasonable assurances that such care would be provided.[20] Accordingly, the AEC indicated it would not allow construction to proceed unless the state assured that it would care for the wastes.[21]

The state gave the AEC what it was looking for. It told the federal agency that ARDA would take possession of the West Valley site and hold it in the name of the state as provided by New York law. The arrangement was spelled out in three major agreements executed by NFS and ARDA in the spring of 1963. The first granted NFS a lease on the site for an annual rental payment to the state of New York of $660,000. Under the lease, NFS would construct, own and operate the reprocessing facilities. The ARDA would be a coapplicant with NFS for the licensing of the facility. The lease's term was 17 years—until December 31, 1980—with provisions for renewal. If the lease were not renewed then, New York would assume ownership of all the facilities.[22]

The second agreement was the Facilities Contract, under which NFS was to construct facilities for receiving fuel and storing wastes and also to make related site improvements.[23]

Finally, and most important, the two parties entered the

Waste Storage Agreement that was made a part of the lease. Under the terms of this agreement, ARDA was obliged to assume jurisdiction over the West Valley site in the name of the state. Accordingly, ARDA was to arrange for the establishment of maintenance, surveillance, insurance and replacement funds in amounts deemed by the authority sufficient to provide for the perpetual care of the high- and low-level waste-storage facilities at the site.

The Waste Storage Agreement made NFS responsible for each tank as it was being filled during reprocessing operations and required ARDA to then accept the filled tanks for perpetual care. A fund for the care of the wastes indeed was established, intended to enable New York to replace the waste tanks every 50 years and to maintain the site. NFS was required to set up the account and by March 31, 1980, according to New York energy officials, had deposited $4 million in it. NFS is expected to have contributed another $180,000 by the end of 1980. The agreement also allowed NFS to delay transfer to ARDA if the company wished to mine any valuable materials from the wastes.[24] Although the agreements were executed between NFS and ARDA, they bind the state of New York as well: The state agreed that if the authority ever ceased to exist, the state would "reassume jurisdiction over and hold the site and all improvements thereon and care, manage, use and dispose of the radioactive wastes."[25]

A decade and a half later, state officials viewed the document with a mixture of wonderment and anger. How could the state have agreed to accept all the risks for taxpayers and to allot all the profits to corporate officials?

New York State Assemblyman William Hoyt of Buffalo, a self-labelled critic of the nuclear-power industry, calls the agreement an "awful mistake" and half-seriously says the lawyer who advised the state should be hanged from the rafters of the reprocessing plant. From start to finish Hoyt believes the entire venture "was typically Rockefeller, a classic Rockefeller —he forged ahead in this blind belief that this new industry would be a boon. There was no caution, just action and no one seemed to realize they were playing with fire." In 1977 Rockefeller told the *New York Times Magazine* he had wanted to provide jobs for a state that needed them, and the contracts "may have been the only way we could get the operator [NFS] to come in."[26] Indeed, in the early sixties Rockefeller was forecasting that the plant eventually would result in 2,000 new jobs for western New York. That dream ran aground, too. At the plant's peak in 1968 it employed 264 regular workers, not including supplemental workers hired for brief periods of time, or such contracted jobs as security guards. Employment at the plant began a long-term nose dive from the 1968 high of 264 to 225 in 1969; 164 in 1970; 116 in 1974; 85 in 1975; to the skeleton force in 1979 of some 50 employees.[27]

Another explanation for the generous agreement is offered by Dr. Marvin Resnikoff, a University of Buffalo physicist who has worked actively with the Sierra Club in its critical examination of NFS. "The haste in which this tremendous state commitment was finalized is difficult to imagine," he says. The period between the AEC's broaching the problem of responsibility for radioactive wastes and the state's full contractual commitment was only two months. "The state," says Resnikoff, "was so anxious that it land this reprocessing plant, that it rushed into a binding agreement."

Resnikoff also doubts state officials actually realized what they were getting into. "It seems," Resnikoff says, "that except for the AEC, none of the principals seemed to recognize the nature of the commitment by the state." Resnikoff cites as evidence a March 8, 1963, letter by OAD Director Oliver Townsend in which he speaks of "several hundred years" as the time period for isolating the wastes.[28]

The media was as ignorant of the risks inherent in the project as the state. Both major Buffalo newspapers reported on the plant extensively, from the moment it was rumored to be slated for western New York through each phase of its construction. The news stories had some common themes. First, all accounts prominently mentioned the number of new jobs the facility would create. Second, the stories repeatedly played up reassurances of the plant's absolute safety—never was there a hint of any dangers. Both newspapers also extended hearty and enthusiastic welcomes to the new industry on the Niagara Frontier.

One Buffalo newspaper regularly called the plant an industrial giant. A 1963 editorial in the other Buffalo newspaper was typical, headlined "Nuclear Plant Adds to WNY Potential":

> Approval by the Atomic Energy Commission of a proposed $30 million nuclear-fuel processing plant in the Town of Ashford near the southern boundary of Erie County is the birth of the nuclear industry in Western New York. Construction of the processing plant—the first privately owned and operated of its kind in the nation—is almost certain to attract new industry to Erie, Cattaraugus and Chautauqua Counties, and it will become increasingly important as n-power augments and possibly replaces the nation's dwindling organic fuel supply.
>
> The plant will boost Western New York as a scientific research center and that, too, should enhance our potential as a center for new research and development industries.
>
> There is no apparent limit to the potential which this new plant—added to the existing industrial facilities—gives Western New York. . . .[29]

Neither paper carried any account of the nuclear-waste agreement.

Perhaps the best explanation for the omissions by the state, from Governor Rockefeller on down, is the overall optimism of the day. After all, no one really expected NFS to exercise its option and back out of the reprocessing business. In short, no one imagined that NFS could fail. T. C. Runion, president of NFS, speculated in 1963 that, for example, the volume of business would be such that in just five short years a second plant would be needed.

The enthusiasm was infectious. University of Buffalo Chancellor Clifford C. Furnas hailed the plant as a "great stroke of good fortune for the Niagara Frontier" and a "dramatic step forward for the state of New York in the development of atomic energy for peaceful purposes."[30] Senate Majority Leader Walter J. Mahoney of Buffalo observed: "This pioneering step has a tremendous potential for jobs and new and expanded industry in the Buffalo area. It represents an opportunity for economic growth and increased employment which is rarely presented to an area."[31] Buffalo was eager to claim some of the plant's spin-off benefits, and the city's officials were talking of such projects as a western New York port on Buffalo's waterfront to handle the fueling of atomic vessels and the transfer of radioactive materials.

Nowhere was the excitement more infectious than the immediate area of the plant, in the rolling foothills of the Appalachian Mountains. Sparsely settled, the land is noted for its scenic beauty. Hiking, fishing, white-water canoeing and camping are just a few of the recreational sports offered. An agriculture center with numerous dairy and truck farms, it is the kind of country, as one Buffalo newspaper reporter aptly described it, "where every other car on the road is a pick-up truck."[32]

Residents expected that when the plant was built this all would change, and change soon. They confidently awaited a boom—a population and economic explosion. Springville, a village of about 4,000 people just 2.5 miles from the plant, expected its population to jump to 20,000 within 10 years. The town of Ashford, home of the plant, expected its 1963 population of 1,600 to jump to 5,500 and eventually to 10,000. Such was the confidence that Springville village officials purchased more than 300 acres along the highway bordering the plant and zoned it for industry. The Springville Chamber of Commerce established special committees to provide information on industrial opportunities.[33] West Valley floated a bond issue in anticipation of increased school enrollments.

The boom never came. Springville's population in 1975 was 4,563; in 1970 the town of Ashford recorded a population of 1,577. And, ironically, Cattaraugus County itself experienced a population decline of more than 6 percent between 1960 and 1970.[34]

At the time, though, news of the plant was welcome for seeming to promise new jobs, new industry and new taxes. The area badly needed all three. The early 1960s were, as the U.S.

Department of Energy noted in its assessment of the area and its needs, "in general a period of industrial dormancy, population exodus, chronic unemployment and economic stagnation in the area. Marginally productive farms were being abandoned. . . . In this context, the announcement of plans for the development of the NFS plant stimulated expectations of imminent economic recovery and growth. It also promised to convert dormant farmland into economic assets as the State of New York initiated the land acquisition program. . . ."[35]

Accordingly, the plant was little opposed. Some farmers, especially those reluctant to be forced off their land by the state, were not thrilled about NFS's choice of location. At a public hearing on the plant's licensing held in Olean in March 1963, the only dissenter was a representative of Rochester's photographic industry, who was concerned about the possible effects of airborne or waterborne contamination. Dr. Charles F. Fordyce, a research scientist with the Eastman Kodak Company, said: "We can't prove our operations will be in trouble but we do not believe it can be proven that they won't."[36]

BURNING BODY BANKS

Nuclear Fuel Services occupies just a fraction—250 acres—of the 3,345 acres purchased and set aside by the state. Its closest municipal neighbor, about 5 miles away, is West Valley, an unincorporated hamlet that in 1978 boasted a population of 713 people. The major structure on the NFS grounds, just behind a blacktopped parking lot, is the main reprocessing building, a structure that resembles a small chemical plant. Its most striking feature is the high ventilating stack rising above the ground. Inside the plant are facilities for the reprocessing operation, as well as receiving and storage facilities used to store spent fuel prior to reprocessing.

Outside, north of the plant, are the tanks that store the highly radioactive wastes left over from the years of reprocessing. Three separate vaults made of reinforced concrete are buried beneath the silty till of the plant grounds. One vault contains a carbon-steel tank that holds neutralized wastes. In a second vault is a duplicate tank that stands empty and is maintained as a spare in the event of a leak. The third vault holds two identical stainless-steel tanks; one holds acidic wastes and the other, duplicate tank is another spare.

In one of the carbon-steel tanks sits 561,000 gallons of high-level radioactive liquid wastes, including 120,000 gallons of radioactive sludge. This waste is primarily composed of two sets of isotope pairs—strontium-90–ittrium-90 and cesium-137–barium-137. Of these elements, cesium-137 has the longest half-life—30.2 years. The liquid waste and sludge, however, also include traces of such highly radioactive materials as zirconium-93, half-life 1.5 million years; palladium-107, half-life 6.5 million years; and cesium-135, half-life 3 million years. Also in the tank is about 77 pounds of plutonium.

One of the smaller, stainless-steel tanks contains 12,000 gallons of acidic, high-level waste produced in a single "campaign" from November 13, 1968, through January 19, 1969. In this period, approximately 16 metric tons of thorium-enriched uranium fuel from the Consolidated Edison Indian Point reactor near New York City was processed. The waste in this tank is composed of thorium, uranium and other fission products.[37]

The NFS complex also contains two separate burial grounds, used for the interment of solid radioactive wastes. One is a commercial area licensed by the state for the burial of wastes with relatively low levels of radioactivity. Situated near the middle of the 3,345 acres, this burial area occupies about 22 acres of land and consists of several excavated trenches. Here lie the wastes from NFS reprocessing as well as wastes from hospitals, laboratories, manufacturing plants and others licensed to use atomic products. These wastes, such as dead lab animals used in experiments and hospital gowns exposed to x-rays, were encased in plastic bags, casks or other containers before being buried between November 1963 and March 1975. Then, filling was suspended voluntarily by NFS after leakage from one of the trenches was detected. Remedial construction work has since been performed.

Immediately adjacent to the commercial burial area is the

burial ground licensed by the Nuclear Regulatory Commission (NRC). Occupying 7.2 acres, these grounds have been in operation since 1966. Wastes with higher radioactivity—such as spent-fuel hulls—are buried in deep holes here.

Additional facilities on the NFS grounds include an office building, a warehouse, maintenance shops and a low-level-waste treatment facility with an accompanying system of disposal lagoons.[38]

All these facilities proved, at best, to be of limited value. In NFS's six years of operation, the government was its best customer. The government, committed to the success of reprocessing, had signed a contract guaranteeing 125 days of work each year and, when operation began, had assigned fuels for reprocessing from AEC reactors. More than 60 percent of the 625 metric tons of nuclear fuel reprocessed by NFS in its lifetime came from the government-owned reactor at Hanford, Washington. The remaining 40 percent came from commercial atomic power plants in Michigan, Minnesota, Illinois and Puerto Rico, and a little came from New York State.[39]

The fuel was shipped to the plant, generally by rail or truck, in heavy casks. These were unloaded under water, at the bottom of a pool inside the main building. One by one, the long fuel bundles were transferred to upright storage racks—still under water—to await their turn in the reprocessing line. When that turn came, the bundles were moved individually to a cavernous cell where the walls were more than four feet thick. There a remotely operated shearing machine sliced the bundles into small pieces, which then were carried in steel baskets to a vat to which nitric acid was added. In the vat, a series of chemical extractions separated the dissolved uranium, plutonium and waste materials: The acid dissolved the fuel compound, but left the metal cladding intact. That accomplished, the bits of metal were washed, removed, packaged in drums and then buried on the site's low-level burying grounds. The remaining acid was treated with an organic solution in which uranium and plutonium tend to collect. The vat's contents then separated into a highly pure uranium-plutonium solution and a water solution of the waste fission products. The highly radioactive liquid wastes were stored in the large underground tank. More chemical processing would separate the uranium from the plutonium, each in dilute acid solution. Then the uranium and plutonium were converted into compounds suitable for transfer to enrichment and fuel fabrication facilities respectively.[40] Countless fuel assemblies were run through this process.

Actual operations were rarely as tidy as described, however. The more than 600 tons of fuel processed in the plant's lifetime contained upward of two billion curies of radioactive material. Leaks, unanticipated and undesirable, occurred.

The frequency of such leakage was not widely known during the years the plant was operating. But after the plant shut down in 1972 for its repair and expansion project, a clear picture of the plant's operation began to emerge. As the Department of Energy was dryly to observe about that period in its 1978 review of media coverage of West Valley: "Rather than being portrayed as a potential 'industrial giant,' the NFS plant often was portrayed as a potential hazard to the health and safety of the region, a nuclear 'garbage dump,' and a national liability which had been imposed on the region."[41]

Inspection of AEC records and former employees' accounts reveal that significant problems did exist, and startling incidents occurred regularly. "From the inspection reports," said physicist Marvin Resnikoff, "the plant seemed like a leaking dike—no sooner would one problem be resolved, than another would arise." The *New York Times* reported in April 1977 that its investigation of the plant had turned up at least 400 such problems. Among the cases cited by the paper:

—On June 11, 1968, a venting stack malfunctioned, sucking in a filter, grinding it up and snowing radioactive bits into lobbies and a workers lunchroom and out second- and third-floor windows onto the front lawn. The lunchroom was decontaminated the next day. The lawn was dug up, taken to a radioactive burial site and buried. The *Times* could find no satisfactory explanation for the malfunction.

—On one occasion, an improperly trained worker did not turn on a valve, and highly radioactive water coursed through regular drainage pipes that were designed to be used for only nonradioactive water.

—Two workers showed up for work one night after they had attended a Christmas party. Drunk, the workers slept through their shifts. Said one of the workers to the *New York Times:* "We were not in the best of shape to be around nuclear materials." Another employee admitted working while "stoned" on marijuana.

—During Christmas week of 1969, one worker left the NFS plant and arrived home after running some errands. Upon his subsequent reentry to the plant, he was discovered to be contaminated. Trying to retrace his steps, NFS officials found his home badly contaminated. Among the items confiscated because of contamination were a rug, a baby blanket, a bedsheet, a pair of socks, a pair of pants and some work boots. How long the items had been in the home before the contamination was discovered was not known.

—A worker's hair became contaminated. He was advised by his supervisor to have a haircut "on the outside." His barber was not advised of the problem.

—A government inspection team noted in a July 1966 report that workers had found a way to remove the yellow paint dabbed on company-provided workshoes. The company applied the paint so the employees who wore the shoes wouldn't remove them from the plant—nor track radioactivity through the countryside. According to the government report, the company found out about the practice of removing the paint but did nothing, and "now most personnel freely wear the supplied clothing [shoes] to and from the NFS facility."

—According to some former workers, some employees stole or "borrowed" highly radioactive tools from the plant and either sold them or used them in their own homes.

—On two occasions railroad workers who coupled cars to locomotives on the plant grounds found that their gloves had become contaminated. NFS personnel confiscated the gloves and provided payment of $3 for new gloves. According to federal records, a brakeman asked plant personnel if the contamination could reoccur and was told, in effect, "How should I know?"[42]

Most of the incidents involved the plant's workers, and in this area—labor practices and worker safety—NFS's record was perhaps its worst. Excessive doses of radiation, inadequate—if not nonexistent—training for employees and the excessive use of transient workers, and a poor plant design that posed hazards to workers all marked the years of operation. In fact, Dr. Karl Z. Morgan, considered the father of health physics for his role in establishing the federal nuclear-safety code, believes that the NFS plant—along with the Kerr-McGee Corporation's plutonium plant in Oklahoma City (where Karen Silkwood worked)—ranks as the nuclear facility most lax in worker safety.[43]

According to AEC records, NFS workers received the highest doses of radiation of any chemical workers in the country.[44] New York Attorney General Louis J. Lefkowitz said, in papers to the AEC expressing opposition to the company's planned expansion, "The operational record of Nuclear Fuel Services Inc. . . . raises serious questions about risks to those who work there. Commission records show that numerous employees have been exposed to excessive dosages of radiation. . . ."[45]

NFS's practice was to allow worker exposure to the maximum amount of radiation permitted an individual, making little effort to limit rems received until the maximum was reached. How much radiation the federal guidelines allowed a nuclear worker to receive in a year varied according to previous years' exposure. The guidelines limited exposure to 5 rems a year. But if a worker received less than five rems in one year, he was allowed to receive as many as 12 rems in each succeeding year—until he reached a five-rem-per-year average.

"If a worker could receive five rems a year in his 'body

bank,' " reported one former NFS employee, "he got five rems; if he could get 12 rems a year, he got all 12 rems. The company didn't try to keep the dosages to a minimum."[46]

The AEC examined the problem and reported late in 1971 that the upward trend of radiation exposure at the plant was of "serious concern." The inspection report noted that the worker standards set by the federal government are intended "to establish upper limits based on health and safety considerations; these regulatory standards are not intended to establish normal exposure limits." Contrary to these precepts of radiation safety, the AEC found, "NFS appears to have limited their efforts for the control of radiation exposure to workers to the maximum allowable limits." Such a practice, the AEC ruled, is "to the detriment of providing adequate protection for plant workers."[47]

In essence, Marvin Resnikoff later reported, NFS was "burning out" its workers; that is, the company worked each employee until he reached his dose limit and then put a new worker in his place. In testimony prepared for the Nuclear Regulatory Commission (NRC), a successor to the AEC, Resnikoff pointed out that "the whole body dose to full-time employees increased from 2.74 rems in 1968 to 7.24 rems in 1971." Additionally, he reported that "records for 1968–71 show accumulated whole-body radiation exposures of greater than five rems per year to 66, 73, 117 and 123 individuals in respective years." Such doses were unmatched in the United States in either the military or industrial sector. To place the matter in perspective, Resnikoff pointed out that in the last two full years of its operation, NFS recorded exposure amounts equal to those recorded during 33 years by 28,000 workers at a government plant in Hanford, Washington, where plutonium was produced, primarily for military purposes.

Even while exposing its full-time workers to maximum doses of radiation, NFS still found it necessary to hire temporary workers to do such short-term, high-radiation-level work as burying trash and decontaminating equipment—chores caused by repeated equipment breakdowns and radiation spills. And NFS's need for these workers increased every year of its operation. In 1967 no supplemental workers were employed. But 106 supplemental employees were put on the payroll in 1968, 465 supplemental workers were hired in 1970 and 1971, and 696 were hired in 1972.[48] Many workers came from the Buffalo branch of a temporary-labor company.

They were college students or unemployed laborers or farmhands from nearby, and they were paid exceptionally high wages for short periods of work. They were hired because they were fresh bodies—they could be sent in to perform some particularly dirty mop-up job because they hadn't had previous exposures to radiation.

Use of these temporary workers was the first of NFS's practices to attract Lefkowitz's attention. In his petition to the AEC in 1974, the attorney general wrote: "Temporary workers were hired for short periods of time to do hazardous jobs without adequate instructions or supervision and without being informed of the risks to their health from radiation." He noted he had received complaints from parents of teenagers who were hired for short periods without being told of the risks involved in their otherwise routine jobs.[49]

One complaint came from John and Dorothy Cairns, a couple who live near the plant. In 1967, their eldest son, then 18, took a summer job at the plant. Although Mrs. Cairns had been concerned about his possible exposure to radiation because of a family history of cancer, "my son assured us that his work involved just sweeping hallways and emptying ashtrays and such in the office building and he did not go into other areas of the plant."

However, according to the couple, "Only after it had happened did we learn that he had been asked to work in an area of high contamination when there apparently was a need to clean a radioactive 'spill' quickly. He said that other office personnel were also put to work at such times.

"He was also used to dump contaminated air filter parts into a deep pit on the property. A truck backed up to the pit, and he pushed the material off.

"As an 18-year-old," the Cairns said of their son, "he

thought the work was exciting and a real change from sweeping hallways. Now . . . he recognizes the risks he ran."[50]

Meanwhile, the full-time workers felt their own risks were augmented by the extensive use of these supplemental workers, whose inexperience or ignorance increased the possibility of accidents. The qualifications for temporary employment at the plant were few: The worker had to be 18 years of age or older and physically able to do the job. Only fundamental training was given; supervision often was lacking. Said one former employee: "I can remember a lot of close calls because a worker couldn't remember what to do or did something the wrong way." The AEC shared the permanent staff's dismay. On November 10, 1971, AEC inspectors charged that "some of the employees have not been adequately instructed in the radiation hazards involved in their jobs or their training program has not been effective."[51] Referring to some 20 abnormal incidents between 1968 and 1971, the AEC said such a record "shows continuing, repetitive occurrences related to inadequate training and instruction and/or inadequate procedures and surveys."[52]

Little of the conflict between the AEC and NFS came into public view until after the West Valley plant was closed for renovations. AEC officials increasingly were concerned about the plant's operations, but, mindful of the agency's role to promote the industry, were reluctant to press NFS too hard.

The experience of David R. Whitehead, an elementary school teacher from Boston Spa, New York, who worked one summer, is typical for temporary NFS employees. Whitehead, describing his experience in the October 11, 1974, issue of *Science* magazine, reported he was called to the plant to help decontaminate a crane room. He and several other men were suited up in protective clothing and given instructions about the use of a hose and brush outfit. Whitehead recalled for *Science:*

> I don't recall a lecture about safety procedures as such. Mainly someone told us about the tools we would be using, that we had to remove some particles [from the walls] and they [NFS] didn't want to burn out their technicians on the job.

We worked in a team, rotating one at a time, 10 minutes in the room, half an hour out. You'd be all alone in there. The technician was outside, on the other side of an airlock and around a corner.

Asked if he felt instruction and supervision were adequate, Whitehead replied:

I don't know how much supervision is necessary, but I trusted them. I guess I was too dumb to be frightened. But if I'd known more about what I was getting into I would have been more wary on the job.

Whitehead reached his dose limit within three days, and his summer job at NFS ended.[53]

The use of temporary workers is a common and accepted practice in the nuclear-power world. What was unusual at NFS was the large amount of outside help required. NFS stood alone in its need to hire so large a staff of temporary workers; at times the permanent staff was outnumbered ten to one.[54]

The equipment breakdowns and malfunctions that necessitated the large crew of temporary workers were facts of life at NFS.

David Pyles, a lab supervisor from 1967 to 1972, recalls that many of the plant's air monitors—all-important machines used to detect the presence of radiation—always were on the blink. "Even if they reported a dangerous situation, chances were employees would disregard the warning as just another instance of bad equipment," he said. In fact, Pyles claims that the firm had only one technician to repair equipment, and he was generally six months behind in his work.

Pyles recalled that the company response to employee calls for improved working conditions was simple: If you don't like it, quit. Pyles did just that, telling his bosses in a one-sentence letter of resignation that he was leaving because of increasing safety and health hazards in the plant. Pyles went on to jobs for the Hooker Chemical Company in Niagara Falls and the Environmental Protection Agency in North Carolina before returning to Buffalo to work full time for the Sierra Club and its Radioactive Waste Campaign.

Pyles was not alone in his concern about working conditions. During the winter of 1970, employees of NFS struck the plant over wages, union representation and safety standards. Early in January 1970, University of Buffalo engineering professor David B. Reister had talked to some of the striking workers and relayed their concerns to Herbert Crocker, compliance representative for the AEC.

Reister wrote to Crocker: "I feel that it is imperative that NFS be a model plant. My conversations with the striking employees demonstrate that they do not feel that NFS is a model plant. They feel that their safety is often ignored. Many of them have gotten excessive doses of radiation due to malfunction of detection instruments, inadequate 'standard operating procedures,' inadequate safety surveillance by inexperienced personnel, and inadequate ventilation."[55]

Not all the workers had such worries. The plant offered jobs at a time when jobs were hard to come by, and plant work paid good money—more than the minimum wage. Pyles recalls, for instance, workers who used dual identification cards as a way to beat the restrictions on exposure limits and log more hours. "The feeling was," said Pyles, "you can't smell it, you can't see it . . . so why worry?"

In testimony prepared for an NRC hearing on reprocessing, Resnikoff detailed what he termed a lack of "respect for radiation" on the part of NFS and some of its employees. "The older [instruction] booklets [given to workers] do not even mention radioactivity," he said. "The newer booklets and training program discuss the theory of radioactivity, but not the biological effects of radiation. . . ." The possibly most forthright comment came from an AEC inspector: "We were aware of the fact that radiation exposure was getting to be too much of a way of life for them."[56]

In conversations with NFS workers, one topic recurs: the amount of radiation exposure. For David Pyles, it was 25 rems in five years. He said: "It [the exposure] is something I live with . . . sometimes, sure, you worry about it."

One worker, Daniel G. Pomerhn, can't help but wish he

had worried earlier about radiation and its possible effects. Pomerhn, a 34-year-old father of two, is an electrician who works for a contractor in Buffalo. In the fall of 1971, NFS hired Pomerhn's employer to repair a crane used to transport radioactive materials. Pomerhn remembers the piece of equipment being in a "hot area" of the plant. He worked for two days and then was notified he had reached his maximum dose of radiation.

Pomerhn didn't give the matter another thought until several years later when, after feeling ill, he was diagnosed as having Hodgkin's disease, cancer of the lymph system. "It was chilling," Pomerhn remembers. "My doctor asked me if I had ever worked around radioactive materials." Pomerhn's physician says there is no evidence to link his disease with the NFS experience, although that could be a factor. Pomerhn has no doubt. He is convinced that if he hadn't worked at the plant, he wouldn't today have Hodgkin's disease.

Pomerhn, a resident of the Niagara County town of Pendleton, consulted a lawyer about possible action against NFS. The advice he received was not encouraging. He also has attempted to determine if others who worked at the plant have experienced any problems. And he makes it a point to go to the various meetings and rallies centering on West Valley to tell his story. Mostly, though, he is cautiously optimistic that his cancer, now in remission, will stay that way.

Pomerhn's exposure was within the federal limitations, as was the exposure of the vast majority of NFS employees. But, according to Dr. Irwin Bross, director of biostatics at Buffalo's Roswell Park Memorial Institute, just because the firm complied with federal guidelines does not mean that no health problems occur. "Compliance isn't the same thing as safety," Bross said. "You can kill with impunity as long as you comply." He argues that the federal limitations on worker exposure are at least 10 times what they should be.

At hearings preceding the licensing of South Carolina's Barnwell Facility, Karl Morgan, the health physics specialist, testified:

Every normal living cell of the human body has a nucleus in which are 46 chromosomes (with the exception of germ cells which contain only 23). Each of the chromosomes carries the genes which in combinations correspond to millions of books instructing the cell what to do under a great variety of situations (for example, when to reproduce, when to produce certain essential chemicals, how large an organ should be and so on). When radiation enters this cell it is like a madman entering the library and destroying pages from thousands of books in this 'cell library.'[57]

For years, scientists have known that high levels of radiation can damage the cell "library," causing leukemia and other cancers, birth defects, mental retardation and long-term genetic damage. Now scientists are discovering that much lower levels of radiation also can cause cell damage. The lower levels simply take longer—sometimes as long as from 15 to 30 years —to manifest the damage as cancer or genetic defects. "The scientific evidence linking low-level radiation exposure to serious health hazards is as strong as the evidence linking smoking with cancer," said Bross.

Agreeing with Irwin Bross is his former colleague at Roswell, Dr. Rosalie Bertell, a biostatician and a cancer researcher studying low-level radiation. In an interview with the *Buffalo Courier-Express* on June 25, 1978, Bertell reported: "I have found that exposure to radiation, even at levels now permitted by the government for nuclear plant workers or the general public hastens the aging process and the onset of older age diseases, including leukemia, cancers, heart disease, diabetes, arteriosclerosis, anemia, respiratory problems and cataracts. . . . It can even hasten a person's hair turning gray."[58]

And in Hanford, Washington, where a government reprocessing facility went on line in 1945 and still operates, high rates of breast cancer in women and lung cancer in men have been discovered, according to Bross.[59]

And what of NFS workers? Are they carrying around time bombs that will have destroyed their health in 10 or 15 years? Will their offspring suffer?

The answers to these questions are unavailable, because no study has been conducted on the health of NFS workers and their offspring (who generally are considered good indicators of the effects of radiation on their parents). In 1976, Erie County's Department of Environmental Quality asked NFS officials for the names of people who had worked at the facility, to check on their health. NFS refused that request and other similar requests on the dubious grounds that release of worker names would violate workers' privacy and civil liberties.

Irwin Bross believes that some people have been harmed by their exposure. Unfortunately, the information available is predominantly anecdotal. Take, for instance, the cases of Walter Zefers and Haafez Saadeck, workers in the plant's laundry room, where radioactive clothes were cleaned. The room was poorly ventilated and no standard operating procedure was established there.

On February 9, 1967, Zefers and Saadeck had to leave the laundry area because high radioactivity was detected.[60] A month later, the AEC was informed that the two workers had high plutonium counts in their urine samples.[61] Seventy-year-old Walter Zefers now walks with a cane; he suffers from Paget's disease, an affliction of the skeleton. There is no proof that his work at the plant has any connection to his disease. But, he believes, those years certainly didn't help.

Saadeck died on April 19, 1972, of lung cancer. Saadeck was a heavy cigarette smoker—two packs a day since a young age. His widow, though, will tell you her husband was a healthy man until he went to work at NFS.

Perhaps the best known case of an NFS worker whose health may have been affected at the plant is that of Gerald Brown. The story of Brown and his wife was told in articles that appeared April 10, 1977, in the *New York Times Magazine* and April 24, 1977, in the *Buffalo Courier-Express* Sunday magazine. Gerald Brown was one of the temporary workers at NFS —a boy of 18 who did some dirty clean-up jobs in the summer and fall of 1972. Brown and his wife later had two children, boys a year apart in age. Both children, Kenny and Jerry, have Hurler's syndrome—an incurable and terminal disease characterized by a gradual degenerative process, dwarfism and retardation. Victims of the disease usually die by the age of 10.[62]

The causes of the disease are genetic; Hurler's syndrome can occur when both parents carry the recessive gene. Yet neither Brown nor his wife know of any other occurrence of the syndrome in their families. According to Bross, "The company can't say for sure whether this was caused by their genetic backgrounds or by radiation. Both are possible, and we can't be sure which."[63]

Equipment malfunctions and design deficiencies and faulty supervision not only threatened the NFS labor force, they also posed dangers to the surrounding community and its environment. Not unusual was the incident involving Jim Chowaniac. On November 18, 1969, Chowaniac cleaned an operating aisle. Upon finishing, he found that a radiation detector called the Class Master was dead. Checking with supervisors in the Health and Safety Department, he was told they were too busy to check him out and he should shower and then check out on the hand-and-foot counter. It detected no radiation, and he went home. On November 19, he returned to work and, after a few hours, a routine check disclosed that his right shoe was hot (radioactive). He went to the decontamination room and cleaned it, and the hand-and-foot meter indicated he no longer was hot. After lunch, he decontaminated a truck. When he finished the job, he used the Class Master to examine his body; his shoe was slightly hot, but his foot and the inside of his shoe were very hot. He couldn't figure out how his foot had become radioactive so, while getting dressed, he checked his street clothes—they were as dirty as his work shoes. Plant personnel determined that the inside of his shoe had been contaminated the night before, and that the thickness of his shoe shielded its inside enough to prevent the hand-and-foot monitor from sounding the alarm. Backtracking Chowaniac's movements, NFS personnel determined he had contaminated a rug in his home and a footstool at his grandmother's house.[64]

Other accidents occurred, and the result was contamination slipping past the gates of NFS and into the community. On July 6, 1972, a worker handling solid waste contaminated his head and hair and carried the contamination to his home; a towel and pillow subsequently were removed. In the summer of 1970, a spill in the analytical laboratory caused some contamination. However, detection monitors were on the blink, and two workers later found to be contaminated passed through the gates. And, during Christmas week 1969, a worker badly contaminated his own home.[65]

Even halting the plant's reprocessing operations did not remove all immediate threats to the environment. In March 1975—several years after reprocessing had ended—monitoring by the state showed that some water was leaking into the trenches containing buried radioactive trash, then running out into nearby streams that eventually feed Lake Erie. Following that discovery, NFS voluntarily agreed to suspend its burial of low-level trash and shut down the ground. The state ruled that no immediate hazard existed, so as a temporary measure NFS agreed to annually or semiannually pump out the trenches.

In August 1978, after the U.S. Environmental Protection Agency expressed concern about leakage from the grounds in the event of heavy rains or melting snow, NFS performed remedial construction. It added soil to mounds covering the trenches and compacted the soil to reduce seepage. The U.S. Department of Energy noted in its 1978 report that this action should help, but "it is too soon to determine the effectiveness of these procedures."[66]

THE END OF A DREAM

In the early years of the plant's operation, the community paid little attention to the reprocessing facility. In fact, most people generally were unaware of the plant's existence. Resnikoff recalls that as late as 1970 he had only had a vague notion that some sort of nuclear facility operated in Cattaraugus County, and Congressman Lundine remembers that he first became aware of the plant's existence when he made his first bid for Congress in 1976.

As Mrs. Nachbar, who was instrumental in the founding of the Springville Radiation Study Group, remembers, curiosity about the plant picked up after a few years of its operation. "It was all word of mouth," she recalled, "and it was a slow process

. . . stories were being circulated . . . workers told their friends and families stories about their jobs . . . parents of young boys with summer jobs there heard stories which they first thought was boasting . . . the theft of the tools was reported."

Mrs. Nachbar decided to act after she overheard a luncheon conversation between NFS officials and AEC inspectors. According to Mrs. Nachbar, NFS responded to AEC complaints about the plant by threatening a legal battle to tie up the AEC. Both NFS and AEC officials denied the story, but Mrs. Nachbar remained unconvinced. The result was the Springville Radiation Study Group.

Initially, the group was concerned with checking out the rumors floating through the countryside about the plant. They were able, for instance, to discount the story about a little girl receiving facial burns from water in Buttermilk Creek and the rumor that a plant employee suddenly had become impotent. But the group did find out that some plant tools had been stolen and that some farmers near the plant were reporting high incidences of cows aborting.

"The more we looked, the more we found out—and the more we found out, the more worried we got," said Mrs. Nachbar. Still, the group was decidedly in the minority, and in the beginning comprised only about 10 people.

The first public "controversy" over the plant surfaced in 1968, when a group from Rochester, New York, expressed concern about the levels of radioactivity being discharged into Buttermilk Creek. The Rochester Committee for Scientific Information reported that samples it had taken of outflow from the plant contained 36,000 times more strontium-90 than was permitted by the AEC. Buttermilk Creek runs off the plant grounds and empties into Cattaraugus Creek, a major stream that runs through dairy-farming lands before feeding Lake Erie.

NFS argued that the radioactivity levels were acceptable because the public could not gain access to the creek—it was on the plant grounds and it was fenced off. The AEC allows higher levels of radioactive discharge into waterways that are neither used by the public nor accessible. Residents, however, objected to the discharges into Buttermilk Creek because the fence consisted of only three strands of barbed wire, and it could not effectively keep out children or wildlife. Cows were spotted drinking from the stream. Because animals and people could not be kept away, residents argued, lower discharge limits should be imposed on Buttermilk Creek.

The AEC agreed, and in 1968 the agency told NFS "it appears impractical to restrict public access to the segment of Buttermilk Creek flowing within the NFS boundary. In view of these considerations, significant reduction in the levels of radioactivity discharged to the watershed should be made, particularly in Buttermilk Creek which should be considered to be a public stream."[67]

The public debate on NFS began in earnest when the firm disclosed its modernization and expansion plans. In 1972, NFS stopped all reprocessing so the plant could be decontaminated and the building project begun. Estimated to cost $15 million, the program was slated to take three years and, in the words of NFS officials, was "aimed at better servicing the growing utility load, as well as keeping pace with changing regulatory standards."[68]

The company applied to the AEC for an expansion permit in 1973, but its application was delayed several times. Then in the summer of 1976 the company announced its intention to withdraw its application and to abandon the enterprise altogether. Estimates of the cost of remodeling had soared from $15 million to more than $600 million. NFS, in making its announcement, reported that costs had escalated because of changing regulatory requirements.

NFS President Ralph W. Deuster said the single most overpowering change was a drastic increase in the seismic criteria for the West Valley site, which cast doubt that the plant ever could be licensed for expanded commercial reprocessing operations. Ironically, one of the reasons cited in 1962 by NFS and the state for selection of the West Valley site was its favorable geological conditions. In the studies completed for the plant's initial construction, the nearest earthquake fault located was at a distance of from 35 to 40 miles. But the nearest fault turned out to be only 23 miles from the site. Between 1840 and 1967, 13 significant earthquakes occurred within 100 miles of the NFS plant. Moreover, a 1976 study conducted by the Battelle Pacific Northwest Laboratory concluded that an earthquake of significant tremors could occur once every 750 years.[69] The wastes kept on the site will be dangerous for as many as hundreds of thousands of years.

Resnikoff believes that the discrepancy between the initial seismology data and the newer surveys was caused by the haste that accompanied NFS's birth. NFS studies and the review by the AEC were incomplete and poor. The analysis of seismology done by the AEC consisted of ten sentences.

The plant presented other problems as well. New York State's Department of Environmental Conservation (DEC) regularly monitored the area by collecting air, water, milk and other samples, and these showed a build-up of radiation in the environment while the plant carried out its reprocessing activities. A 1972 DEC report observed that "radioactivity attributed to releases from the Nuclear Fuel Services was detected in many environmental samples."[70] Among the discoveries made through the DEC's sampling:

—Detectable amounts of iodine-129 were found in the milk from farms around the plant. The presence of the radionuclides first was observed in December 1971, and they reached peak amounts in the spring of 1972. Once the plant ceased its operations, the presence of I-129 in milk decreased to undetectable levels.[71]

—Surface water samples collected during the period from 1968 to 1977 have shown a progressive decrease in radionuclide levels since the shutdown of the plant.[72]

—Stream-bed sediment collected from Cattaraugus Creek behind the Springville Dam during 1975 contained above-background levels of radionuclides.[73]

—Fish samples collected from Buttermilk Creek and Cattaraugus Creek during the plant's operation showed a

steady pattern of contamination, with the highest concentrations of radionuclides found in samples collected nearest
the plant.[74]

None of these radioactivity levels ever exceed AEC limits;
the DEC calculated that a person would have to eat more than
564 pounds per year of the fish in Buttermilk or Cattaraugus
Creeks to exceed the allowable limit of strontium-90. Yet, with
exposure to radiation through the food chain, as with worksite
exposure, scientists are unsure about the low-level, long-term
effects.

Doubts about all these problems have been expressed in a
public-opinion and regulatory climate increasingly cool to fuel
reprocessing and to nuclear power in general. In 1974, the
federal government's energy agencies were restructured; the
Atomic Energy Commission was divided into the Nuclear
Regulatory Commission and the Energy Research and Development Administration. The NRC proved to be tougher than
the AEC had been. The state also became more critical. Attorney General Lefkowitz intervened in the licensing hearings—
taking a decidedly antagonistic stance on such issues as worker
exposure and the use of supplemental help. The Erie County
Legislature became a party to the hearings. Moreover, in 1975,
New York's Atomic and Space Development Authority was
abolished and replaced by the New York State Energy Research
and Development Authority, whose mandate was to develop
nonnuclear energy sources.[75]

Another factor in the cooling climate for nuclear power has
been the respectability and credibility built up by consumer
and environmental groups. The Springville Radiation Study
Group and the Sierra Club were most effective in convincing
both the media and area lawmakers to take a closer and more
critical look at the plant. Under that scrutiny, the flaws of past
operations came to light, and concern grew about the proposed
expansion. The aim of the groups, its leaders stressed, was not
to close down the plant; only to ensure its safe operation. Still,
even this effort encountered considerable resentment from a
segment of the West Valley populace concerned about loss of

jobs and tax dollars. These people viewed West Valley as their home and the plant as their concern; they resented the intrusion of "outsiders."

Such a viewpoint was apparent as recently as March 1978, when the federal government came to West Valley to gather some facts and to hear some opinions about the defunct nuclear facility. During the day-and-night-long hearing held in the auditorium of the West Valley High School, Michael Parson, president of the West Valley Volunteer Hose Company, described NFS as a "good neighbor." Parsons, railing against some recent media depictions of his community, maintained: "We, the natives of 'this sleepy little town,' have learned not to fear nuclear energy but to live with it." Daniel G. Salem, president of the union that represents the employees at the plant and a worker there for the past 15 years, said the only catastrophe that could occur would be the plant staying closed forever.

Mrs. Nachbar resents any suggestion that the West Valley plant is the concern of only the 700 people who live closest to its gates. "How dare they think it's just their problem . . . West Valley concerns us all."

But perhaps the most important factor in the death of the plant's commercial operation was the simple fact that economically it was an albatross around the neck of its owner. Getty Oil owns five-sixths and Skelly Oil owns one-sixth of NFS, having purchased the stock in 1968 and 1969. Getty viewed the firm as an investment that would pay off when the nation's need for energy, coupled with declining oil supplies, brought nuclear energy into its own. Instead, NFS lost an average of $6 million for its owners in each of the six years the plant operated commercially. Reprocessing was an economic loser, and private business no longer is interested in the plant or the deadly wastes stored there.

THE END IS JUST THE BEGINNING

Unfortunately, when NFS goes out of business, the state can't merely shut the plant's doors and lock the gate.

Under the terms of the Waste Storage Agreement, New York State becomes in 1981 the owner of nearly 600,000 gallons of highly radioactive nuclear wastes. The wastes are stored in a 750,000-gallon underground tank that, according to a study by the federal General Accounting Office, could develop leaks at any time. The wastes are deadly and will remain so for hundreds of thousands of years. To place that figure in perspective, consider that Jesus taught his lessons less than 2,000 years ago, recorded history began 3,000 years ago, and civilization itself goes back only 8,000 or so years. Neutralizing the wastes and converting them to a solid form is a task of enormous difficulty and expense. The estimated cost hovers at around $1 billion. State officials have insisted that this tab should be picked up by the federal government because, they argue, New York initially got itself into nuclear reprocessing with federal encouragement and support. And only the federal government is generally agreed to have the resources and technology needed for the cleanup job. For example, some 30,000 gallons of radioactive sludge, containing nearly all of the long-lived fission products (such as plutonium) in the wastes, has formed at the bottom of the tank. Removing this sludge will be no easy task; it may require that the entire tank be dug up and dismantled. The state also will become caretaker for the low-level burial sites, and for the plant buildings.

State officials tried throughout 1978 and 1979 to convince the federal government it should assume the costs of the cleanup. In March 1979, state officials appeared to have convinced the U.S. Department of Energy to pay the bill. In exchange for that help, however, the federal government wanted to make West Valley a national nuclear-waste dump. When details of the deal, which had been worked out secretly, became known, an immediate cry of outrage rose from western New Yorkers and government representatives. The reception to the plan resulted in it being scrapped—at least for the moment. On July 12, 1979, Governor Hugh L. Carey signed into law a bill prohibiting the establishment of a permanent nuclear-waste disposal site without the approval of both the state legislature and the governor. (Carey vetoed a bill to ban temporary storage.)

The long state–federal negotiations ended in November

1980, when the Department of Energy and ERDA signed an agreement to implement cleanup legislation passed by Congress two months earlier. Under the agreement, the federal government will pay 90% of the cost of a $285 million, 17-year "demonstration" project to solidify the wastes for disposal. The participants estimate that even selecting a solidification method will take three years. No agreement has yet been reached on what to do with the low-level wastes. New York State had to go to court in the final days of 1980 to keep NFS from renouncing responsibility for the low-level wastes. According to a *New York Times* report, state officials said NFS and Getty "have made it clear that they do not intend to pay a fair share or participate in any meaningful way in cleaning up the mess which they caused."

Once NFS leaves the picture, West Valley will feel another void—right in the pocketbook. NFS is the vicinity's biggest taxpayer, picking up some 20 percent of town, school and county taxes. Once NFS shuts down, $70,000 a year less will be paid in school taxes, and $35,000 less each for town and county taxes. Lundine, who was unsuccessful in his attempts to win some state or federal compensation for the lost taxes, believes that the failing enterprise at West Valley may destroy the economic base of the community.

Other problems will linger: The NFS land will always have some type of radioactive materials, and this condition will make the rolling countryside off-limits to generations.

Such problems, awesome though they be, appear miniscule when compared to the real horror of West Valley: its potential for harm. And no solution to the waste problem is forthcoming during this generation; nor is a solution likely in the next. Perhaps members of the House Government Operations Committee had such thoughts in 1977, when they penned these words:

> This material cannot be left in its present condition indefinitely, as the carbon steel tanks will corrode, the ground over the low-level burial trenches is eroding and the plant has not been fully decontaminated. . . . Furthermore, at the present time, the tech-

nology to store this material permanently has not been demonstrated, despite several decades of power development.[76]

And:

We have no demonstrated final answers on what steps the nation will take to safely guard and store this deadly waste over the many centuries ahead.[77]

Professor Marvin Resnikoff has a recurring nightmare about West Valley. It's the year 3000, or 7000 or 9000. Headlines as urgent as those for the Love Canal debacle tell the media has discovered that a housing and park development has been built on previously buried radioactive wastes. The site is West Valley, and the problem never was solved.

NOTES

1. *Western New York Nuclear Service Center Study, Companion Report,* U.S. Department of Energy, 1978.

2. Ibid.

3. "State Probes Nuclear Storage Defect," *Buffalo Courier-Express,* December 19, 1978.

4. Interview with Charles Haughney, June 1980.

5. Letter from O. Townsend, ARDA, to R. Lowenstein, AEC, March 8, 1963.

6. "Too Hot To Handle," *New York Times Magazine,* April 1977.

7. "State of the State," Governor Nelson Rockefeller, February 5, 1962.

8. *Report of the New York State Energy Research Development Authority With Respect to Federal Acquisition of the West Valley Facility.*

9. Ibid.

10. Ibid.

11. Ibid.

12. Douglas Turner, "Site Near Springville To Be A-Waste Center," *Buffalo Courier-Express,* June 3, 1961.

13. *Western New York Nuclear Service Center Study.*

14. *Report of the New York State Energy Research Development Authority.*

15. *Western New York Nuclear Service Center Study.*

16. Donald Gilligan, "The Time Bomb South of Buffalo," *Empire State Report,* vol. 3, no. 1 (January 1977), pp. 3–11.

17. "WNY Potential Spotlighted at A-Center Groundbreaking," *Buffalo Courier-Express,* June 13, 1963.

18. *Western New York Nuclear Service Center Study.*

19. *Report of the New York State Energy Research Development Authority.*

20. Letter from R. Lowenstein, AEC, to O. Townsend, ARDA, February 13, 1963.

21. *Report of the New York State Energy Research Development Authority.*

22. *Western New York Nuclear Service Center Study.*

23. Ibid.

24. Ibid.

25. Gilligan, "The Time Bomb South of Buffalo."

26. "Too Hot to Handle."

27. *Western New York Nuclear Service Center Study.*

28. Letter from O. Townsend, ARDA, to R. Lowenstein, AEC, March 8, 1963.

29. "Nuclear Plant Adds to WNY Potential," *Buffalo Courier-Express,* May 5, 1963.

30. Turner, "Site Near Springville To Be A-Waste Center."

31. "Coordinate Nuclear Fuel Set-up is Goal," *Buffalo Courier-Express,* July 15, 1962.

32. Rich Scheinin, "Nuclear Plant Publicity Jars West Valley," *Buffalo Courier-Express,* March 25, 1979.

33. Phil Joyce, "Springville Is Expecting Boom," *Buffalo Courier-Express,* May 19, 1963.

34. *Western New York Nuclear Service Center Study.*

35. Ibid.

36. "Opposition Voiced to A-Waste Site," *Buffalo Courier-Express,* March 5, 1963.

37. *Western New York Nuclear Service Center Study,* section 3, pp. 17–18 and pp. 22–27.

38. *Western New York Nuclear Service Center Study.*

39. Ibid.

40. *Nuclear Fuel Reprocessing—The Step That Makes It a Fuel Cycle,* pamphlet by Nuclear Fuel Services, Inc., issued May 1974.

41. *Western New York Nuclear Service Center Study.*

42. "Too Hot to Handle."

43. Howard Kohn, "Justice for Radiation Victim," *Chicago Tribune*, May 27, 1979.

44. Robert Gillette, "Transient Nuclear Workers: A Special Case for Standards," *Science*, October 11, 1974.

45. Petition of the attorney general of the state of New York, Louis Lefkowitz, for intervention, in the matter of Nuclear Fuel Services, docket no. 50-201, dated September 12, 1974.

46. Jo-Ann Armao, "Nuclear Waste: Two Sides," *Buffalo Courier-Express*, October 9, 1974.

47. Ibid.

48. *Western New York Nuclear Service Center Study.*

49. Petition of the attorney general of the state of New York.

50. Letter from John and Dorothy Cairns to Lefkowitz, July 24, 1974.

51. Armao, "Nuclear Waste: Two Sides."

52. Ibid.

53. Gillette, "Transient Nuclear Workers: A Special Case for Standards."

54. Ibid.

55. Letter from D. Reister to H. Crocker, AEC, January 13, 1970.

56. Marvin Resnikoff, Sierra Club testimony related to Section IVE Reprocessing, Final Gesmo I, U.S. Nuclear Regulatory Commission, *Generic Environmental Statement on Mixed Oxide Fuel*, docket no. RM-50-5.

57. Keith Coulbourn, "The Most Hazardous Business," *Atlanta Journal and Constitution Magazine*, February 9, 1975.

58. Gerry Fedell, "Rally Hears Nun Urge N-Plant Worker Study," *Buffalo Courier-Express*, June 25, 1978.

59. Thomas F. Mancuso, Alice Stewart and George Kneale, "Radiation Exposures of Hanford Workers Dying From Cancer and Other Causes," *Health Physics* 33 (November 1977), pp. 369–385.

60. *AEC Inspection Report*, docket no. 50-201, April 17–21, 1967.

61. *Abnormal Occurrence Reports*, Nuclear Fuel Services, docket no. 50-201.

62. Marcia Kelly, "Pretty Little West Valley, NY, Where the Nation's Nuclear Garbage Goes," *Buffalo Courier-Express*, April 24, 1977.

63. "Too Hot to Handle."

64. Armao, "Nuclear Waste: Two Sides."

65. Marvin Resnikoff, Sierra Club testimony.

66. *Western New York Nuclear Service Center Study.*

67. Armao, "Nuclear Waste: Two Sides."

68. *Western New York Nuclear Service Center Study.*

69. "Too Hot to Handle."

70. Armao, "Nuclear Waste: Two Sides."

71. *Western New York Nuclear Service Center Study.*

72. Ibid.

73. Ibid.

74. Ibid.

75. Gilligan, "The Time Bomb South of Buffalo."

76. "West Valley Nuke Site Draws Fire," *Buffalo Courier-Express,* October 8, 1977.

77. Ibid.

Chapter 5

PCBs in the Hudson River

JIM DETJEN

Early in 1975, after years of neglect, years during which New Yorkers had all but turned their backs on the scenic beauty of the Hudson River, environmentalists in the Hudson Valley were optimistic.

The Scenic Hudson Preservation Conference had successfully stymied the Consolidated Edison Company's efforts to build a massive hydroelectric plant on top of Storm King Mountain in the heart of the Hudson Highlands. Although Con Ed had not yet admitted defeat, an *ad hoc* band of conservationists had delayed the utility company's plans to construct the 2,000-megawatt plant for more than 12 years. Through vigorous legal challenges, lawyers for the citizens' group had prevented one of the nation's largest and most powerful utilities from scarring one of the valley's most picturesque regions.

The success of "Scenic Hudson" stimulated renewed interest in the long-neglected Hudson River, and many say the organization spurred the rebirth of the valley's environmental movement as well. Such other environmental groups as the Hudson River Fishermen's Association then were formed, and in 1973 several groups hired the nation's first public guardian of a river—Hudson Riverkeeper Thomas Whyatt, whose duties were to monitor the many environmental controversies brewing up and down the valley.

Perhaps nothing so symbolized the revitalization of the Hudson Valley environmental movement as a 106-foot-long replica of a 19th-century sailing vessel known as the sloop *Clearwater.* In an effort spearheaded by folk singer Pete Seeger and other environmentalists, the 100-ton ship was launched in South Bristol, Maine, in 1969; soon it was spreading the message of a cleaner river down the Hudson to school children, civic groups and citizens from Troy to Manhattan. By 1975, the sloop already had become an institution. With its annual summer folk picnics and October "pumpkin sails," tireless workers educated the public about the river's heritage and value.

For decades the Hudson River had been synonymous with polluted water. Comedians joked about the raw sewage poured into the river by cities and industries throughout the valley, and many New Yorkers assumed that all of the river's fish long since had died. But environmentalists knew that more than 90 varieties of fish called the Hudson home—including an estimated 17 million striped bass[1]—and that a multimillion-dollar fishing industry could be developed if only the river's purity could be restored.

And by 1975 the tide did seem to be turning. Eleven years earlier Governor Nelson Rockefeller had pledged to eliminate all water pollution in the Hudson and other New York waterways by 1970. Although that goal hadn't been met, the evidence everywhere was that progress was being made. In 1965 the state's voters passed by a four-to-one margin a $1 billion Pure Waters Bond Act to construct sewage-treatment plants throughout New York State. When that money proved insufficient, the voters decisively approved another $1.15 billion bond to complete the job.[2]

By 1975 workers had constructed 302 sewage-treatment plants, 159 water-monitoring stations and 300 industrial facilities along the state's waterways, at a cost of $1.4 billion. Mammoth treatment facilities had been completed in Troy and Albany; a Yonkers plant was under construction; and dozens of other facilities along the river had been upgraded.[3]

In 1974, then governor Malcolm Wilson (Rockefeller had

moved to Washington to become vice president) enthusiastically proclaimed the success of the "Pure Waters" program, saying, "our waters are demonstrably cleaner." His environmental
commissioner, James Biggane, released impressive statistics to
support Wilson's claim and announced that "all major polluters,
municipal and industrial, are now under commissioner's orders
or are on a supervised abatement schedule."

Few disputed that the state's Pure Waters program had
reduced the volume of raw sewage flowing into the Hudson.
Tugboat pilots, oil-tanker captains, Coast Guard officers and
amateur divers all agreed: The Hudson looked noticeably
cleaner. Biologists reported that Lafayette, or "spot," fish were
returning to the Hudson after an absence of 30 years; commercial fishermen reported increased numbers of bluefish, striped
bass and blue-craw crabs; and even the Fulton Fish Market in
New York City began selling Hudson River shad again for the
first time in many years.[4] Communities talked enthusiastically
about reopening commercial beaches along the Hudson—
beaches that had been closed decades before because dangerously high levels of disease-carrying bacteria had lived in the
sewage-contaminated water.

But on August 7, 1975, all that optimism, all that excitement, all the hope for a cleaner Hudson River came crashing
down when state officials revealed the results of decades of
pollution by the state's largest industrial employer. Newly appointed Environmental Commissioner Ogden Reid announced
that dangerously high levels of PCBs—a toxic, possibly carcinogenic chemical similar in composition to the banned pesticide
DDT, and which was being used by the General Electric Company in the production of electric equipment—had been found
in Hudson River fish. He warned the public not to eat striped
bass, the most valuable commercial fish in the Hudson, because
studies had determined that unsafe levels of the colorless chemical contaminated the fishes' organs.[5]

Reid's announcement was merely a warning shot in what
was to become a major, years-long battle over PCB pollution in
the Hudson River. Within a month he would order GE to stop
dumping PCBs into the upper Hudson River. In February 1976

Reid ordered many Hudson River fisheries to be closed—the first such ban on commercial fishing in the 350 years since the Dutch settled in the Hudson Valley. The ban, forced by the dangerously high levels of PCBs in Hudson River fish, devastated a $5 million-a-year fishery, and many feared it ultimately would sound the death knell of a fishing industry rich in history and folklore.

The PCB crisis would grow to affect not only workers in the GE plants exposed to the cancer-causing chemical, and the fishermen whose lives were upended by the ban, but more than 100,000 New Yorkers living in communities that drew—and still draw—their water from the Hudson. About 150,000 New Yorkers drink water taken from the Hudson, with Poughkeepsie's 90,000 water consumers composing the largest share.[6] Other communities that take water from the Hudson include Rhinebeck, Highland, Port Ewen, Waterford, Queensberry and Winebrook Hills.

The New York State Department of Health has measured the PCB levels in water filtered through the Poughkeepsie treatment plant at as high as 100 parts per billion. Department officials have maintained consistently that this level is too low to present a problem. But many scientists disagree. Dr. Gilman Veith, of the Environmental Protection Agency's (EPA's) laboratory in Duluth, Minnesota, has noted, "Any drinking water with a PCB concentration greater than one part per trillion is likely to result in a residue in man and animals which could affect the organism's behavior."[7] The concentration of PCBs in Poughkeepsie's drinking water is hundreds of thousands of times greater than that level.

And hundreds, perhaps thousands, of Poughkeepsie residents, such as Jerry Chiumento, have stopped drinking Poughkeepsie water. Chiumento has led a personal crusade to upgrade the city's antiquated water-treatment plant. So far, his petition drives, letter-writing campaigns and repeated meetings with officials have been in vain.

So, twice a week Chiumento loads up the family car with a gaggle of plastic jugs and makes a pilgrimage south to a public spring near Roseton, New York, where he fills the jugs with fresh water and carts the water home for drinking and cooking. "Poughkeepsie officials have been dragging their feet for years trying to pretend that a problem doesn't exist," he said. "Well, I'm not going to jeopardize the health of my children while politicians squabble. That's why thousands of people in Poughkeepsie either buy bottled water or cart their water in from the outside. PCBs could be having an effect on us that even scientists don't fully understand."[8]

THE FLUID OF CHOICE

Scientists do understand some things about PCBs, or polychlorinated biphenyls. They belong to a class of chemicals called chlorinated hydrocarbons. In recent years, many chemicals in this family have been banned—the pesticides DDT, Mirex, dieldrin and aldrin to name just a few—after scientists discovered they caused cancer in laboratory animals. In 1979, Congress banned the production of PCBs in the United States —but considerable environmental damage already had been done.

PCBs first were synthesized in 1881, but not until 1929 did the Monsanto Chemical Company of St. Louis, Missouri, begin producing them commercially.[9] Almost immediately, industrial engineers realized the great commercial value of this man-made substance. Their usefulness had to do with their molecular structure.

A PCB molecule consists of two benzene rings of hydrogen and carbon atoms. These rings are the building blocks of petroleum, gasoline and other fuels, and by themselves are extremely flammable. However, scientists found that substituting chlorine atoms for hydrogen atoms along the benzene rings created a flame-resistant substance. Such molecules with more than one chlorine atom are called polychlorinated biphenyls. PCBs actually are a group of chemicals, not one specific compound. As many as 209 chlorine combinations on benzene rings are possible, but only 50 or 60 of these combinations have been used commercially.

Because PCBs are flame resistant, they soon replaced mineral oils—which had produced many fires—as the fluid of choice in electrical products. "In terms of performance, it was the best material—as perfect as an industrial chemical can be," said William Papageorge, a chemical engineer and a PCB expert for Monsanto, the sole producer in the United States until the chemical was outlawed. "It doesn't burn, it doesn't break down, it doesn't react with other materials. In virtually every case, the substitutes that have been developed have had to sacrifice some characteristics that PCBs contributed."[10]

Initially, Monsanto produced PCBs for use as flame retardants and as electrical insulators in transformers, capacitors and other electrical equipment. Numerous other uses soon were found. PCBs were used in heating coils to heat products in factories where an open flame would have been a hazard; in carbonless carbon paper; in lubricating oils for industrial drills; in caulking compounds for skyscraper windows; and in the electrical motors of refrigerators, air conditioners, typewriters, power saws and a host of other products.

Before long, PCBs seemed to have a use in almost every product. Among the many products that have contained PCBs at one time or another are ironing-board covers, highway striping paints, bread wrappers, toilet soaps, safety glass, brake linings, upholstering materials, cereal boxes, grain silos, varnishes, lacquers, plasticizers, degreasers, waterproofing materials and even baby bottles.

PCBs became an industrial staple, an inexpensive "wonder chemical"—one of the many synthetic organic chemicals upon which the post-World War II society was built. Since 1930, the EPA estimates, 1.4 billion pounds of PCBs have been manufactured in the United States. At least another billion pounds have been manufactured by Great Britain, France, Germany, Italy, Spain, Czechoslovakia, Japan and the Soviet Union.[11]

Long before production reached such tremendous heights, glimmers of the "wonder" chemicals' health and environmental problems were seen. In a paper published in 1936, Drs. Jack W. Jones and Herbert S. Alden of Atlanta, Georgia, reported the case of "O.D.," a 26-year-old black factory worker who began distilling chlorinated diphenyl (biphenyl) in April 1930. Within three years, "O.D." developed a severe skin disease, chloracne

—his body became covered with pustules. By October 1933, 23 of the 24 men working in O.D.'s plant had acne-like eruptions on their faces and bodies. In December 1933, "O.D." complained of lassitude, loss of appetite and loss of libido—now classic symptoms of PCB poisoning. But Jones and Alden were oblivious to this, and less than enlightened in general. They wrote of "O.D.": "On examination he seemed in good general health. His complaint of lassitude was not borne out of anything more than the usual temperament of the Negro towards work."[12]

Few precautions were taken to protect workers from the dangers of PCBs. The industrial demand for this inexpensive and extraordinarily stable chemical was so great that little attention was paid to early health warnings. Not until the mid-1960s, in fact, did some environmental scientists begin to worry that the use of PCBs might be getting out of hand. In 1966, Swedish scientist Dr. Soren Jensen reported finding PCBs building up in animal tissues. After discovering PCBs in an eagle and a fish, he carefully analyzed eagle feathers preserved for many years in a Swedish museum; he found residues of the chemical in eagles as early as 1944—about the time that PCB production was rapidly expanding.[13]

In recent years, other scientists have reported finding widespread PCB contamination in wildlife around the world. The chemicals have been found in seals in Scotland and fish in the Atlantic Ocean; in snow in Antarctica and in the breast milk of nursing mothers across America. According to the U.S. Fish and Wildlife Service, PCBs have been found in animals and fish in the Allegheny, Ohio, Mississippi, Missouri, Kanawha, Cumberland, Kalamazoo, Columbia, Yukon and Rio Grande rivers, in addition to, of course, the Hudson.[14]

Much of the Great Lakes system, the single largest supply of fresh water in the world, is contaminated. Levels of the ubiquitous pesticide DDT have been dropping in Lake Michigan fish in recent years, but the levels of PCBs remain ominously high.[15] Scientists in Duluth, Minnesota, say that all Lake Michigan trout and salmon more than a foot long almost certainly are unsafe to eat.

"PCBs have been found in all organisms analyzed from the North and South Atlantic Oceans, even in animals living under 11,000 feet of water," wrote Dr. George Harvey of the Woods Hole Oceanographic Institution. "Based on all available data it seems safe to conclude that PCBs are present in varying concentrations in every species of wildlife on earth."[16]

That includes humans. EPA scientists say the indiscriminate use of PCBs has been so widespread that virtually everyone is contaminated with low levels of the toxic chemical. The EPA calculates that 91 percent of all Americans have detectable levels of PCBs in their tissues, and that 5 percent have PCBs in their fatty tissues at levels the federal government considers unsafe to eat in fish. Moreover, both the percentage of Americans showing detectable levels and the extent of the contamination have increased in the past few years.[17]

PCBs have caused environmental problems in many cities, including Washington, D.C.; Bridgeport, Connecticut; New Bedford, Massachusetts; Escondido, California; Sellersburg, Indiana; and Winnebago, Illinois.[18] Property owners near Lake Hartwell, South Carolina, have filed a $1 billion class-action suit against the Sangamo Electric Company because PCB discharges have poisoned the lake's fish.[19]

Unlike DDT, which was spread intentionally throughout the environment to kill insects, PCBs have contaminated all corners of the world via industrial sewer pipes, factory smokestacks, the weathering of asphalt and of other substances containing PCBs, and the burning of PCB-laden products in dumps.[20]

This careless handling in the past is a problem that will remain for future generations, because PCBs are extraordinarily persistent, even more so than DDT. They are essentially unalterable by microorganisms or chemical reactions. The only effective way to destroy PCBs is to burn them in special industrial incinerators capable of generating temperatures of at least 2,400 degrees Fahrenheit.

Once PCBs have entered the environment, their concentrations can increase hundreds of thousands of times as they move up the food chain. For example, PCBs discharged from a sewer pipe may be eaten by microorganisms which then are consumed by tiny fish. The PCBs accumulate in such organs of the fish as the liver and are passed on to the next consumer—and the next. Some fish have the ability to bio-accumulate PCBs —to absorb them from waterways and store them in fatty tissues—at concentrations 200,000 times greater than the water in which the fish are swimming.

Health scientists are extremely concerned about these findings because of the toxic nature of PCBs. According to Irving Sax in *Dangerous Properties of Industrial Materials,* exposure to PCBs can produce chloracne, lesions of the liver, vomiting, loss of weight, jaundice, internal swelling and abdominal pain.[21] And the EPA has concluded that the long-term effects of exposure to PCBs could be "insidious and devastating."[22]

One of the most disturbing studies was conducted by Dr. James R. Allen, a pathologist at the University of Wisconsin Medical School. He fed 16 female monkeys PCBs in concentrations similar to those found in Hudson River fish. When the monkeys mated, seven miscarried, two could not conceive at all; and uterine growths were recorded in others. The monkeys developed facial sores and swollen eyelids, and they lost their hair. Their offspring all were undersized, and the infants' bodies had detectable levels of PCBs. When the infant monkeys were breast fed, they all developed the same symptoms as their mothers. Within four months, half of the offspring had died. And two years later—even when the monkeys no longer were being breast fed—they exhibited learning and behavioral difficulties.[23]

The importance of Allen's findings are underlined by EPA studies revealing that virtually all samples of human mothers' milk tested since 1976 contain detectable levels of PCBs. The average level found in the mothers' milk—1.8 parts per million (ppm)—is seven times greater than the amount permitted by the Food and Drug Administration in milk for sale. One nursing mother in Michigan had 10.6 ppm of PCBs in her milk—a dosage level approaching the levels that in Allen's laboratory monkeys caused learning disabilities and hyperactivity.[24]

Scientists at Michigan State University have found that minks had complete reproductive failure when they ate food contaminated with 5 parts per million of PCBs. After 105 days of eating food with 3.6 ppm PCBs, all the minks died. These contamination levels are lower than the concentrations of PCBs found in striped bass and other fish in the Hudson River.

Dr. Ralph Dougherty of Florida State University reported to the American Chemical Society in September 1979 that PCBs had been linked with decreased sperm counts in human males. He found that 23 percent of the college males tested were functionally sterile—their sperm counts were low enough to make fertilization highly unlikely. Such factors as stress may have contributed to the decline; however, Dougherty did find high levels of PCBs in his subjects' semen. Because PCBs are known to interfere with cell division—and sperm production requires prodigious cell division—he thought it reasonable to assume that PCBs contributed to the low sperm counts.[25]

Experiments by Dr. Renate Kimbrough of the Center for Disease Control in Atlanta indicate that PCBs can cause liver cancer in rats. In a study described in the *Journal of the National Cancer Institute,* she fed 200 female rats a mixture of PCBs for 21 months while feeding a control group of 200 other female rats a regular diet. Kimbrough found that 26 of the rats fed PCBs developed liver cancer and that 146 others developed precancerous growths. In the control group, only one rat developed liver cancer, and none experienced liver growths.[26]

Recent studies show the chemical may be having a synergistic affect on animals, and possibly on people. Milton Fried and Daniel O. Trainer reported in *Science* magazine in 1970 that many more PCB-fed mallard ducklings died when exposed to duck hepatitis virus than did ducklings that had not eaten the chemicals.

PCBs have tainted many lives since their introduction. Ron and Sally Nehrig moved to Bloomington, Indiana, to homestead and quietly raise their family away from the pollution of industrialized cities. They were interested in improving their soil, so in November 1975, after being assured by Bloomington officials that the city's sewage sludge was safe to use, they spread 100 tons of it on their farmland.[27]

The Nehrigs soon learned, however, that they had made a terrible mistake. In December 1975 they discovered that the Westinghouse Corporation plant in Bloomington was dumping from three to eight pounds of PCBs into the city's sewers each day. In March 1976 the Nehrigs had their sludge tested; it was contaminated with 300 ppm of PCBs. Moreover, their soil had as many as 50 ppm of PCBs, and the ryegrass they had grown in the soil had 4.1 ppm of the chemical. Each of these levels is unsafe, they were told.

"We were dumbstruck," recalled Ron Nehrig. "But there was more. The state Board of Health tested our cow's milk and found it contaminated with 5 parts per million of PCBs—twice the FDA's maximum limit for cow milk. This was the same milk we'd been drinking at the rate of a half gallon a day for the previous four months."

The Nehrigs scraped the topsoil off their half-acre garden, and Bloomington officials trucked 80 tons of earth and wastes back to the city's sewage-treatment plant at no cost. Despite the scraping, the Nehrigs estimate that their land will remain contaminated for as many as 100 years.

PCBs have poisoned more than farmland. In 1970 more than 146,000 chickens were destroyed after the Campbell Soup Company detected high levels of PCBs in chickens raised in New York State. In July 1971 more than 123,000 pounds of egg products and 88,000 chickens were destroyed after the Monsanto Chemical Company in Wilmington, North Carolina, reported that large amounts of fish-meal chicken feed had become contaminated with PCBs because of a heating system leak. And in 1975, the Food and Drug Administration seized 124,000 cans of Lake Michigan salmon that had unsafe levels of the toxic chemical.[28]

In September 1979 U.S. Department of Agriculture officials seized 399,000 pounds of poultry and 16,000 pounds of fresh pork when 200 gallons of PCBs leaked from a transformer into animal feed at the Pierce Packing Company in Billings,

Montana. Officials say that the PCB-contaminated feed was sent to 17 states, from Oregon to New Jersey.[29]

So far, the most serious outbreak of acute human PCB poisoning has been in February 1968 on the island of Kyushu, Japan. There, 1,291 people became ill after eating rice oil contaminated with 2,000 ppm of the chemical; as many as 15,000 people may have been affected by the rice oil, which was laced with PCBs that leaked from pinholes in factory pipes.[30]

The symptoms of the disease, which became known as "Yusho," or oil disease, included chloracne, darkening of the skin, swollen upper eyelids, nausea, impaired vision, loss of appetite, abnormal menstruation, impotence, jaundice, hearing difficulties, headaches, diarrhea, spasms and fever. In addition, 11 pregnant women contaminated with PCBs gave birth to 10 live born and 2 stillborn children, and 9 of the 10 babies born alive showed some signs of the Yusho disease. Two other children were stillborn.

The children of contaminated parents were nicknamed "cola babies" because of their darkened skins. And through the end of 1977, 51 victims of Yusho had died, according to a June 1978 report by Horomu Koda and two of his colleagues at Kyushu University. Of 31 victims whose cause of death was confirmed, 11 of them, or 35.4 percent, had died of neoplasms, a kind of tumor. Among the dead were a 13-year-old boy and a 25-year-old truck driver. Autopsies disclosed that internal growths similar to chloracne had developed, along with various irregularities in lymph nodes and in glands of the liver.[31]

A MAJOR CONFRONTATION ON THE HUDSON

Eight thousand miles east of Kyushu and 200 miles north of New York City are the industrial communities of Fort Edward and Hudson Falls, New York. Both cities are dominated by the General Electric Company, whose two plants—located within a mile of each other along the banks of the Hudson River —manufacture capacitors for use in such electrical equipment as air-conditioner motors.

General Electric is New York State's largest industrial employer, and no one disputes its importance to either the state or the local economy. Reports prepared by the state's Economic Development Board and Department of Commerce place the gross annual earnings of the GE plants' employees at $14 million, with goods and services purchased locally by the company accounting for $4 million more entering the economy. This money, in turn, generates another $14 million in secondary local expenditures.

At peak production levels, the GE plants' payrolls produce $480,000 in state income-tax revenues. The company pays $318,000 in local property, school and sales taxes, and its operations generate approximately $1.3 million in secondary property and sales-tax revenues.[32]

In addition to revenues, however, both plants produce pollutants—such as the PCBs that leak into waste water, which then is discharged into the Hudson River. The Fort Edward plant had discharged PCBs since 1942, and the Hudson Falls factory had been discharging the chemical since 1951.[33] In each case, the PCBs entered the factory's waste water through a variety of small leaks in equipment during the manufacture of capacitors. Although no one is sure how much PCB has been dumped into the river, records show that, between 1966 and 1972, an average of 30 pounds was discharged each day, amounting to 84,000 pounds during that period. Environmentalists estimate that as many as 500,000 pounds may have been dumped into the river by the two GE facilities.

During the early 1970s, few New Yorkers ever had heard of PCBs; fewer knew of the environmental damage they could cause. Fewer still were aware that the two GE plants were dumping more PCBs than any other industrial facility in the nation.

Yet warnings of the damage being done to the Hudson existed. As early as February 17, 1971, Robert Boyle, a senior writer for *Sports Illustrated,* wrote to Carl Parker, chief of the state's Bureau of Fisheries, to inform him that striped-bass eggs from the Hudson River were contaminated with as many as 11.4 ppm of PCBs, as measured at the Warf Institute in Madison, Wisconsin. "These are grim figures," Boyle wrote. "And I certainly think the state should warn fishermen not to eat striped bass eggs." Rather than acting upon his advice, Boyle recalled, Parker answered his letter with derision.[34]

And Dr. Ward Stone, a wildlife pathologist with New York's Wildlife Research Laboratory in Delmar, first began notifying his superiors of PCB contamination in Hudson River fish in 1970. In that year he advised his department superiors not to do its thinking "along 1945 lines" by waiting until a crisis had occurred before acting. He also began calling for toxicological testing, noting to his superiors in the Department of Environmental Conservation (DEC) that unless something was done soon, Hudson River fish would be unfit to eat. In one blunt memo he wrote, "I hope the department begins to take some of these toxic problems seriously . . . because it is doubtful these problems can be put off. In fact, they have already been put off far too long."[35]

During the 1970s Stone sent his superiors 102 memos warning of PCB contamination in the Hudson River. But his actions drew no response. "It was futile," he recalled later. "No one really cared, and at times I began to wonder if I were crazy and the rest of the department were sane."[36] Ultimately, Stone sent all 102 memos at once to his department superiors, demanding to know why nothing ever had been done. They responded that, since he had not drawn up an exact plan of action, they never were sure what he wanted them to do.

Why was it impossible to get action? Stone's superiors say the language of his alarms was not sufficiently strong to warrant action. "These people [Boyle and Stone] weren't doing handstands," claimed Paul Elston, the department's deputy commissioner. "If you look at the memos, the senders weren't articulating the problems." Another explanation offered by Elston is departmental red tape. "It was a case of simple bureaucratic incompetence. My assumption is that all those memos did not strike a bell with a guy who had a hundred other things on his mind."[37]

Even so, records show that between 1970 and 1975 state officials were well aware the river's fish were contaminated. During that period, the DEC conducted 99 sampling tests; in

52 of them—52.5 percent of the time—PCB levels were greater than the maximum allowable tolerance level of 5 ppm set by the FDA.[38] PCB levels in excess of 5 ppm were found in large-mouth and smallmouth bass, striped bass, northern pike, sturgeon and white perch. The highest concentration was 49.63 ppm—almost 10 times the permissible level.

Still state officials took no action. Prior to Environmental Commissioner Reid's August 1975 warning against eating PCB-contaminated fish, state officials had neither released their findings nor told Hudson Valley residents that a problem might exist. When Lawrence Skinner, an associate aquatic biologist with the department, was asked why alarm bells had not been sounded, he replied that FDA guidelines for PCBs were not issued until 1973. When asked why no warnings were issued between 1973 and 1975, he said, "I don't know. I guess we don't really have an answer for that."

State officials were not alone in their bungling. EPA records show that the federal agency was aware of high levels of PCBs in Hudson River fish at least as early as August 1974—a full year before Reid warned the public. But, like the state's Department of Environmental Conservation, the EPA never informed Hudson Valley residents of the danger.

Under the provisions of the Clean Water Act (formally known as the Federal Water Pollution Control Act Amendments of 1972), on January 18, 1973, GE applied to the EPA for a federal permit to dump 30 pounds of chlorinated hydrocarbons into the Hudson River each day. The application was forwarded to state conservation officials on August 23, 1973; and on September 11 the state recommended that the permit be granted, "since the present discharge complies with water quality standards." Neither agency bothered to check what kind of chlorinated hydrocarbons would be dumped; they could have been relatively harmless or extremely toxic. Records show that officials never asked this crucial question.

The EPA issued GE a draft permit on March 22, 1974; a final permit on December 20, 1974, granted GE the right to dump 30 pounds each day, with a gradual reduction by May 31,

1977, to no more than 3.5 ounces. While GE never specifically applied for the right to dump PCBs, state and federal officials —as well as GE executives—were well aware that the company's waste-water discharges had some PCBs.[39]

In May 1974, quite by accident, Alan W. Eckert of the EPA Office of General Counsel learned through the cross-examination of GE officials at a public hearing on federal toxic-pollutant standards that the company routinely was dumping into the Hudson between 25 and 30 pounds of PCBs each day. This was the largest such discharge into any of the nation's waterways. Shocked by the revelation, he calculated that dumping this amount would produce PCB concentrations of 37.5 ppm in Hudson River fish—levels seven times higher than FDA maximum standards.[40]

Eckert then wrote Meyer Scolnick, director of the enforcement division and counsel for the regional office of the EPA based in New York City, urging careful investigation of the situation. "There is . . . enough here to warrant a careful investigation of these PCB discharges to determine whether or not a health hazard warranting action under section 504 may exist," he wrote. (Section 504 of the Clean Water Act grants the EPA administrator the authority to sue for an immediate restraining order against any party causing pollution that is "presenting an imminent and substantial endangerment to the health of persons.")

The investigation was conducted in August 1974. Dr. Royal J. Nadeau and Robert P. Davis of the regional EPA laboratory reported, based on GE figures, that the Hudson Falls plant was discharging as much as 17.6 pounds of PCBs per day, and the Fort Edward plant was dumping as many as 30 pounds a day. Minnows collected downriver from the GE discharges averaged 78 ppm of PCBs. A rock bass contained 350 ppm, prompting Nadeau and Davis to write, "The PCB level in the rock bass is greater than the maximum level documented for fish taken from any industrial river in the United States. . . . This represents a new record for PCB contamination of freshwater fish."[41] They also noted that "certain areas, particularly downstream from Station 4, are fished primarily by the youngsters of Fort Edward. Ingestion of these fish by the populace would certainly lead to contamination of specific tissues in their bodies."

Despite these findings, the EPA took no action either to halt GE's dumping or to warn Hudson Valley residents about the danger of eating the river's fish. In fact, in March 1975 the EPA's regional office temporarily suspended plans gradually to reduce GE's discharges of PCBs, after the company demanded an adjudicatory hearing to challenge limitations on its right to dump the chemical.[42] A few months later, after Reid ordered GE to halt its PCB dumping completely, EPA officials acknowledged they were considering some sort of legal action against GE. But those plans also were lost in the bureaucratic shuffle. No action ever was taken.

Interestingly, Reid did not learn about the Hudson's PCB-contaminated fish from the extensive memos, lab reports and letters generated by his own Department of Environmental Conservation. He was told about the problem by an EPA official who showed him a survey done in Duluth, Minnesota, on a small number of fish from around the nation. Reid immediately grasped the implications of the report and asked his first deputy, Paul Elston, to read it. Elston has admitted leaving some of this reading undone—"It had a lot of long words," he said with a laugh—but Reid pursued the matter.[43]

Following his August 7, 1975, advisory warning New Yorkers not to eat striped bass or largemouth bass taken from the Hudson, Environmental Commissioner Reid learned all he could about the problem his staff had been ignoring for half a decade. He immediately initiated a statewide fish-sampling program to determine the scope of the PCB contamination. A composite sample of 10 yellow perch caught in the Hudson for the program had a total of 229.3 ppm of PCBs. A single American eel had 559.25 ppm in its flesh—a level more than 100 times higher than the FDA standard. His staff identified GE's two upper-Hudson plants as the major source of PCB pollution; Reid began negotiations with the company to lower its discharges.

On September 7, Reid broke off negotiations with the company and ordered GE to reduce its PCB discharges to two pounds a day by December 31, 1975, and to stop them completely by September 30, 1976. At the time of the order, GE was pouring less than five pounds of the chemical into the river each day—substantially less than the 50 pounds daily discharged into the Hudson only a few years before.

Reid charged that, even though GE had a federal permit to dump PCBs into the Hudson, the company was violating state water-quality standards and was creating grave health problems. He termed the company's past and ongoing discharges "a hazard to human health and the natural resources of New York State." Said Reid, "This is a hazardous condition which requires extraordinary and immediate efforts to solve, particularly in view of the possible irremedial environmental degradation which the company's practices threaten and the widespread adverse social and economic impact upon the river's recreational and commercial fisheries."[44]

In addition, Reid ordered GE to prevent PCB residues situated on the grounds of the two plants from leaking into the Hudson River, and he said GE would be required to pay an undetermined amount of money to clean up the environmental damage it had caused. The environmental commissioner also asked GE to post a $2 million performance bond—an unprecedentedly high amount—which the company would forfeit if it failed to meet the compliance schedule for PCB reduction set forth by the state.

Under the authority of the state Environmental Conservation Law, Reid's orders would become effective only after an administrative examiner found that his order was justified. GE still would have the right to appeal the order in state court. Consequently, Reid set a hearing date for October 6 and appointed Abraham Sofaer, a Columbia University law-school professor, as the hearing examiner.

GE quickly clarified that it would not be able to comply with the order. Officials said they could reduce PCB discharges to three-quarters of a pound a day by December 31, 1975, but that the only way they could comply with Reid's September 30,

1976, deadline would be to shut down the two plants—and thereby throw 1,200 people out of work.

At the same time Reid issued his order against GE, he broadened his advisory about eating Hudson River fish. Further analyses, he warned Hudson Valley residents, indicated they should not eat white perch, white suckers, smallmouth bass or eels caught in the river.[45]

The stage was set for a major confrontation between GE, the state's largest industrial employer, and Ogden Reid, a millionaire who formerly had served as U.S. ambassador to Israel, as editor of the now-defunct *New York Herald Tribune,* and as a six-term Congress member from affluent Westchester County.

General Electric was well aware of the importance of the case. Thirty-seven plants owned by 30 corporations used PCBs, and environmentalists were looking for a victory in New York State to set a precedent for cases elsewhere. It was a tricky case because, although GE appeared to be violating state law, the company had a permit issued by the EPA, which had been approved by the state's Department of Environmental Conservation, to dump 30 pounds of PCBs into the Hudson River each day.

THE HEARINGS DID NOT GO WELL FOR GE

Just as Reid had anticipated, the state's hearings on PCBs received statewide and even national publicity. The department brought in the top experts on PCBs from around the country. Much of the hearings were devoted to establishing the toxicity of PCBs, and to GE's violation of state conservation laws. Other testimony showed how serious a problem PCBs had become in the Hudson Valley; expert after expert detailed the extent of the river's contamination.

The hearings did not go well for GE. The company admitted that at least 65 of its workers had become ill during a 15-year period under conditions that "may have been caused by or aggravated by exposure to PCB." GE officials testified that 49 of the company's 1,800 employees working in areas exposed to PCBs had reported to dispensaries "complaining of allergic der-

matitis," and the officials added that 16 more workers had reported nausea, dizziness, eye irritation, nasal irritation, asthmatic bronchitis and fungus.[46]

Later research would reveal much more about health problems. In the fall of 1976, a year after the hearings, a team of
health researchers from Mt. Sinai Hospital in New York City
tested 326 employees at the two GE plants for problems relating to PCB exposure. The researchers found that 45 percent of
the workers showed skin abnormalities, and 40 percent exhibited eye and ear irritations. Dr. Alf Fishbein of Mt. Sinai said
that these problems normally are found in only 5 percent of the
population. A follow-up study in the fall of 1979 by Mt. Sinai
researchers found some evidence of reduced lung capacity
among GE workers. Dr. William J. Nicholson, associate director
of the hospital's environmental sciences laboratory, said additional studies will determine whether GE workers' nervous and
lymphatic systems have been damaged. And in early 1980 both
the National Institute of Occupational Safety and Health and
the New York State Health Department were examining death
certificates for any unusual patterns of cancer or other illnesses.[47] Of course, this evidence was not available in October
1975.

Perhaps the most dramatic moment of the hearings occurred December 9, when Dr. Gerald Lauer, a GE consultant,
admitted under cross-examination that the data he had presented only the day before had substantial errors and omissions.[48] Originally, Lauer testified that none of the 13 fish he
had tested had PCBs in excess of 5 ppm, even though several
were caught in the vicinity of the plants' discharge pipes. Under
cross-examination, however, he conceded that decimal points
had been misplaced on a laboratory card and that the PCB
levels in several fish were dramatically higher than the FDA
limit—in four samples, 66, 75, 112.1 and 143.2 ppm. As a result
of the confusion this testimony generated, Lauer withdrew his
data, and GE agreed to accept the studies conducted by the
department's scientists.

On February 9, 1976, four months after the testimony

began, Sofaer released a 77-page "interim opinion and order" in which he found GE guilty on two of the three pollution counts brought against the company. He said the contamination was a result "of both corporate abuse and regulatory failure; corporate abuse in that GE caused PCBs to be discharged without exercising sufficient precaution and concern; regulatory failure in that GE informed the responsible federal and state agencies of its activities and they, too, exercised insufficient caution and concern."[49]

Stressing the gravity of the situation, Sofaer said that eating the single eel caught in the Hudson at Stillwater, which contained 559.25 ppm of PCBs in its edible parts, "would contaminate an adult with over 50 percent of the Food and Drug Administration's estimated lifetime limit and a child with 200 percent of its allowable lifetime limit."[50]

Sofaer's decision came in a shifting political climate. Although Governor Hugh L. Carey and his administration supported Reid's early efforts against GE, the governor's views appeared to change in 1976. In his January "state of the state" address, Carey warned that economic considerations henceforth would carry heavy weight when environmental policy was drawn up.[51]

This strategy was part of what Carey called his "austerity" plan. Business in New York was sagging, and the economy badly needed a boost. Businesses were fleeing the state because of high taxes and a generally poor business climate. "We must regulate no more than necessary," Carey said, referring primarily to environmental regulations.[52]

In December 1975, Carey shifted John S. Dyson, his brash, 32-year-old commissioner of agriculture and markets, to the head position in the state's commerce department. Many observers felt the move was part of Carey's new tilt in favor of the economy over the environment.

Dyson, a multimillionaire with widely known political ambitions, lost no time criticizing Reid and the DEC's hearing against GE. In January, he called upon Reid to end the hearing and said that for the state to demand a complete halt to GE's discharges of PCBs was absurd. "If zero discharge means zero jobs and three ounces means 1,200 jobs, I say we go for the three ounces," Dyson said, referring to the EPA's requirement that GE reduce its discharge of PCBs to 3.5 ounces a day after May 31, 1977.[53] Reid replied that Dyson didn't know what he was talking about and said environmental studies had shown that even 3.5 ounces would cause PCBs to build up in the tissues of striped bass.

On February 4, 1976, after Reid and Dyson had clashed twice again, Governor Carey entered the fray. He clearly sided with Dyson, telling a group of waterfront union leaders, "It will do little good if we rescue our environment at the cost of our economy. . . . Anyone who doesn't agree with that principle won't be working in this government."[54]

On February 17, Reid banned most forms of commercial fishing in the Hudson River because of PCB contamination. The ban, which was the first in the state's history, affected striped bass, eels, white perch, catfish and carp—and, because many of the fish caught off the Long Island coast are spawned in the Hudson, the ban also threatened the future of fishing there.

"The implications of this are far-reaching," said William L. Dovel, a marine biologist with the Boyce Thompson Institute in Yonkers. "The Hudson is indisputably a major source of striped bass for the entire East Coast fishery from Massachusetts to Delaware. . . . If these fish are not fit to eat when taken from the Hudson, then they are not fit to eat when taken off Long Island, the New Jersey coast and New England."[55]

Fish lovers weren't the only ones hurt by the ban. The men and women who fished the river for a living, people such as Ivar Anderson, an eel fisherman who lives in Red Hook, New York, suddenly had their livelihood legally outlawed.[56] In 1975 Anderson gave up an $18,000-a-year job as a truck driver to fulfill a long-time dream: to earn a living fishing from the Hudson. Had it not been for GE, he might have succeeded.

During a four-month period in 1975, Anderson earned $11,000, and he estimates he could have earned four times that much in 1976 by placing 120 eel pots a day in a shallow section of the river between Red Hook and Saugerties. In 1975 he caught 300 pounds of eels a day. The eels then were shipped by tank truck to Massachusetts, where they were exported to specialty houses in Italy and Germany.

But in 1976 the state refused to grant Anderson a fishing license, because its studies showed eels to be contaminated with 30 ppm of PCBs—six times the maximum allowable level of 5 ppm set by the FDA.

"It was a terrible blow, a real terrible blow," said Anderson, who, at the age of 46 and with eight children to support, suddenly was out of work. "The eel business was a real good business. . . . And the eels from the Hudson were much in demand because of their tastiness and uniform size. It's a real shame."

Reid estimated that 500 people made their living either part- or full-time by fishing from the Hudson, and he said the closing would cost millions of dollars in lost wages and taxes. Dyson again used the occasion to attack Reid, arguing against closing GE to save a fishing industry that, according to Dyson's records, provided only 300,000 pounds of fish a year at a net economic value of about $100,000.

At a glance, the records indicate that Dyson was correct at least technically; the records show the yearly loss amounts to no more than $100,000. Yet the total loss is considerably greater. This discrepancy exists because many fishermen "sold their catches under assumed names and never declared their earnings," explained David Seymour, president of the Hudson River Fishermen's Association. "If we assigned a dollars and cents value, the IRS would have clobbered us."[57]

Most officials believe the actual annual economic loss to the state because of the fishing ban—considering both commercial and recreational fishing—amounts to about $5 million a year.

Ironically, the Hudson River fishermen's ongoing deception worked against them. David Seymour originally said that his organization planned to file a multimillion-dollar "classic environmental lawsuit" against GE. But when the state's records were examined to establish the fishermen's loss, attorneys for the association realized that the fishermen themselves had perhaps prevented legal proof of their claim. Consequently, a lawsuit never was filed.

Individual fishermen have tried to take legal action. In September 1976 Anderson brought a $50,000 suit against General Electric for destroying his livelihood. However, in late 1979—one legal delay having followed another—he settled out of court for $23,000. "I have no doubt that I would have won on the local level," he said. "But GE's lawyers were prepared to appeal it as high as they could because they didn't want to see a legal precedent set. It would have taken four or five more years to win. A little guy just doesn't have that kind of money. So, my lawyer advised me that it would be best to settle."

During the spring of 1976, Carey met with Reid, with Reginald Jones, chairman of the board of GE, and with John F. Welch, a GE vice president, to discuss the PCB case. Jones reportedly threatened to pull all of GE's plants out of the state if the case was not settled soon. GE was willing to settle for $2 million, provided that the payment was not considered a penalty and that the company would not have to pay to "restore or reclaim" the river. The company also insisted upon a "good faith" or "exoneration clause" that would say the company had "acted in good faith, unintentionally, and in reliance upon its [federal pollution discharge] permit."

Reid refused those terms and said publicly, in April 1976, "I stand ready to negotiate with General Electric in good faith, but I have no intention of selling out to them. . . . It would be impossible for me to suggest to the hearing officer that this could be the basis for a settlement in the public interest."[58]

By then it was becoming apparent, however, that Reid would not be negotiating as environmental commissioner much longer. Reid had reorganized the department's staff, angering some of his aides. Others charged that he was erratic and incompetent as an administrator. And several upstate, antienvironmental Republicans were pressuring Carey to fire him.

The pressure mounted, and the campaign succeeded. On April 29, Reid announced his resignation. Carey appointed Peter A. A. Berle, a highly regarded environmental lawyer, to be the new environmental commissioner, and on September 7, 1976—exactly one year after Reid issued his order against GE —a compromise was reached. Berle had put together an unprecedented $7 million settlement in which the state and GE accepted "joint responsibility" for the pollution of the Hudson with PCBs. The agreement neither blamed nor exonerated GE for its role in dumping PCBs into the river, and company officials emphasized that GE's payments should not be construed as a fine.

GE agreed to pay $3 million for a variety of Hudson River research and cleanup programs and to perform another $1 million worth of PCB-related research at its laboratories, making the results available to the environmental conservation department. By mid-1980, state officials said, all of the money had been spent or was invested in ongoing research. In addition, the state pledged to contribute $3 million to the cleanup—bringing the total commitment of funds to $7 million.[59]

In addition, GE promised to construct pollution-abatement facilities worth $3.5 million at its Hudson Falls and Fort Edward plants and to reduce their average discharge of PCBs to one gram a day by April 1977. The company agreed to completely discontinue the use of all PCBs in its New York state capacitor facilities by July 1, 1977, through the substitution of an environmentally sound chemical.

Sofaer said the agreement was "an effective precedent for dealing with situations of joint culpability."[60] All of the parties seemed satisfied with the settlement. GE officials were relieved that the company no longer would be portrayed almost daily as an irresponsible corporate polluter. Workers seemed pleased that the two plants would continue to operate with substantially the same work force. And environmentalists also were pleased. Fishermen's Association President Seymour said that, had the case resulted in harsher penalties, GE undoubtedly would have appealed to state courts, not known for their support of environmental causes. What's more, GE would have been able to continue dumping the PCBs while the case worked its way slowly through the judicial system, a process that could have taken many years.

REGULATORY PROGRESS AND
ENVIRONMENTAL LIMITS

Within the past few years, some progress has been made in curtailing the contamination of the environment with PCBs. GE met its July 1, 1977, deadline to cease dumping the chemical into the upper Hudson River. And on October 31, 1977, the Monsanto Chemical Company—the sole U.S. producer—stopped manufacturing PCBs.[61]

In addition, federal regulatory bodies have taken more effective steps to slow the continued contamination.

Effective February 1978 the EPA banned all direct discharges of the chemical into the nation's waterways.[62] The Toxic Substances Control Act of 1976 prohibits the manufacturing of PCBs after January 1, 1979, and the processing and distribution of the chemical after June 1, 1979.[63]

And on August 28, 1979, the Food and Drug Administration, which sets standards for the allowable levels of PCBs in foods, lowered its standards for three of the four food groups in which PCBs are known to be found. The new FDA standard for eggs was dropped from .5 to .3 ppm; for milk and dairy products, from 2.5 to 1.5 ppm; and for poultry, from 5 to 3 ppm. If PCBs in foodstuffs exceed the new maximum levels, the FDA can seize interstate shipments of them.[64]

The National Fisheries Institute, a trade association, filed objections to the FDA's proposal to lower PCB standards for a fourth category, fish and shellfish, from 5 to 2 ppm; the FDA then postponed making a final decision until after a hearing was held. Although no one knows for sure what the impact of a lowered standard for fish would be, the FDA has estimated that approximately $6 million worth of fish now routinely eaten by Americans would be regarded as tainted, and would not be permitted in interstate commerce. Since the PCB levels in Hudson River shad have hovered consistently at about 5 ppm, some anglers believe the new FDA standards on fish would end the long tradition of shad fishing in the Hudson.[65]

Although these corporate and regulatory decisions are expected to reduce PCB contamination nationwide, 640,000 pounds of PCBs still coat the Hudson's sediments as a result of GE's dumping during a 35-year period. What progress has been made to restore the Hudson River?

The answer, simply, is not much. Because money is lacking, almost none of the PCB pollution has been removed. Following the $7 million settlement between GE and the state in September 1976, environmental officials hired 10 private consulting firms to determine the best way to remove PCBs from the river. Among the innovative and experimental methods considered were harvesting the Hudson's fish; absorbing PCBs from the sediments with oil-soaked mats; absorbing the chemicals with activated carbon; destroying the PCBs through ultraviolet ozonation and chemical treatment; and even covering the contaminated sediments with ground-up automobile tires to absorb the PCBs.

"We seriously considered the possibility of biologically harvesting the contaminated fish because of their ability to absorb PCBs out of the water and into their fatty tissues," said Dr. Leo J. Hetling, director of the environmental conservation department's Bureau of Water Research. "But we found out that, for every 10 pounds of PCBs removed, you would have to harvest one million pounds of fish. And then you would have to figure out what to do with all of the contaminated fish on your hands."[66]

By 1978, it became apparent that the only practical means of removing the PCBs was to dredge the PCB-laden silt from the river. The Department of Environmental Conservation proposed "hot-spot dredging," or the removal of PCBs from several extremely contaminated sections of the upper-40-mile stretch of the river between Hudson Falls and Troy. Commissioner Peter Berle estimated that removing 313,000 of the 440,000 pounds of PCBs in the upper Hudson would require three years and $25 million. To remove the remaining 127,000 pounds in the upper reaches of the river would cost $179 million more, for a total of $204 million.[67]

Berle realized that obtaining $204 million to dredge the entire upper Hudson would be just as impossible as pulling together funds to dredge the 200,000 pounds of PCBs spread throughout the lower Hudson, from Troy south to New York City. But he was hopeful that the EPA would provide the $25 million for the hot-spot dredging proposal. He soon learned that even $25 million wasn't available.

Both of the most likely sources of funding for the project have proven to be dead ends. Title I of the Clean Water Act provides funding for research and demonstration projects. But only $15 million has been appropriated by Congress for that purpose. Title II, which provides funding for construction projects, has considerably more money to give out, but the EPA has decided the hot-spot dredging proposal is ineligible for this money.

In 1979, Environmental Commissioner Robert Flacke resubmitted the state's application for $30 million from the EPA. (Flacke replaced Berle in 1978, after Carey forced Berle to resign because he was opposing on environmental grounds projects that Carey said were needed.)

In a letter to the EPA, Flacke noted that the EPA has spent about $1 billion on sewage-treatment plants in the Hudson Valley. "Hudson River cleanup expenditures during the past 10 years completely dwarf the $30 million we are seeking to remove the PCBs. Our treatment plants are improving the Hudson's water quality. This additional $30 million would bring us a giant step closer to a fishable, swimmable river."[68]

In addition, Flacke mentioned that from 5,000 to 10,000 pounds of PCBs flow from the upper Hudson into the lower Hudson each year, threatening water supplies, fish and wildlife. "We have seen no real commitment on the part of the Environmental Protection Agency to join with the state of New York in carrying out this project," he wrote.

In October 1979 Representative Hamilton Fish, Jr., a New York Republican, said he would try to line up New York's congressional delegation in support of legislation to free $30 million in federal funds for the dredging of PCBs from the Hudson. Fish's bill would require the EPA to funnel money originally earmarked for the construction of sewage-treatment plants to pay for the dredging project.[69]

In October 1980 the dispute between the EPA and the

DEC was finally ended. During the height of the presidential race, President Jimmy Carter signed into law a measure authorizing $20 million in federal funds to remove PCBs from the river's sediments. Under the law the state is required to come up with an additional $6.7 million which, together with the $20 million in federal funds, would provide $26.7 million for the project. State officials hope additional funding will be provided by future sessions of Congress.

Dredging of the river's sediments is expected to start in 1982. Meanwhile, 150,000 state residents continue to draw their water from a river laced with 640,000 pounds of PCB.

Dr. Robert Harris, a nationally known expert on drinking water who was on the Council on Environmental Quality, said he is extremely concerned about the relatively low levels of PCBs in Hudson River drinking water because of scientific evidence that PCBs can cause cancer in laboratory animals. "One hundred parts per million has got to be clearly unacceptable. The overwhelming evidence shows there is no such thing as a safe level of a carcinogen. If I lived in Poughkeepsie, I'd be very concerned."[70]

Many residents are. Former Dutchess County Health Commissioner Dr. Stephen Redmond has called the presence of PCBs in Poughkeepsie's drinking water "an environmental timebomb." Redmond has urged city officials to install an activated-carbon filtration system to remove such chemical pollutants as PCBs from the city's water. Poughkeepsie officials repeatedly have rejected these requests.

One study, conducted by the New York Health Department but never officially released, raises serious questions. In the early 1970s, Dr. Robert F. Korns of the Health Department compared the cancer rates in nine small cities in New York, including Poughkeepsie. He found that from 1950 to 1970 the incidence of rectal and colon cancer in Poughkeepsie increased at a rate substantially higher than the other cities. While the national rate for these two types of intestinal cancer actually was declining, in Poughkeepsie, depending on how statistics are tabulated, the incidence of rectal cancer in men increased by 5 to 10 times.[71]

Unfortunately, Poughkeepsie residents may never know what is responsible for this startling increase in the two types of cancer. An epidemiological study of cancer rates and the consumption of Hudson River water has been proposed, but has not been funded. And some scientists say that, even if the money had been allocated, resolving the question of a link between cancer and Hudson River water might have been impossible because of the presence of other toxic chemicals in the Hudson.

"The Hudson is more grossly polluted with toxic chemicals than anyone had previously thought," said Walter Hang, who directed a 20-month-long investigation of toxic chemicals in the Hudson River for the Environmental Defense Fund and the New York Public Interest Research Group, two nonprofit organizations. "There are hundreds, possibly thousands of toxic chemicals in the river. And in most cases, neither the state nor the federal government knows what they are, nor what their impact may be on people."[72]

The joint EDF-NYPIRG investigation resulted in a 210-page report, released in September 1977, entitled *Troubled Waters: Toxic Chemicals in the Hudson River.* The report termed the Hudson "one of the worst environmental disasters in the nation."[73] At a press conference, Dr. Joseph Highland, chairman of EDF's toxic-chemicals program, said, "When it comes to toxic chemicals, the state's water pollution efforts have been a failure. Despite the investment of billions of dollars in the Pure Waters program in New York State during the past 12 years, little or no progress has been made with respect to toxic substances in rivers such as the Hudson."

Even while the state's requests for $30 million to clean up the Hudson have been rebuffed, the U.S. Army Corps of Engineers has been seeking more than 100 times that amount in order to add New York City to the list of communities drawing their water from the Hudson. The Corps has proposed a $3.7 billion project to withdraw as much as 950 million gallons of water a day from the Hudson River just north of Poughkeepsie, and to pump the water south to Manhattan, supplying as much as 40 percent of the metropolitan area's drinking water by the 1990s.[74]

The Corps' proposal is slowly churning its way through Congress. If approved, it would increase the number of people consuming Hudson River water some seventyfold—from 150,000 today to more than 10 million by the turn of the century. "Clearly, the Corps' Hudson River project could subject millions of people to an unnecessary cancer risk," Hang said. "Before the project goes forward, the Corps better be sure of what toxic chemicals are in the Hudson and whether the proposed treatment process has the ability to remove them."

The Corps' optimism notwithstanding, PCBs continue to contaminate life in the Hudson. "Our tests show that the levels of PCBs in Hudson River fish are about the same as they were in 1977," said Mary Kadlecek, a member of the DEC's technical staff. "The levels don't seem to be dropping at all."[75]

Former fisherman Ivar Anderson is convinced that he never will see the commercial fishing of eels, striped bass and other species on the Hudson during his lifetime. And environmental experts have become increasingly pessimistic about the prospects, their best guess for renewal of the industry being in 20 to 100 years—and perhaps never.

Not only the fish are contaminated. Scientists have found high levels of PCBs in Hudson Valley ducks, such as the greater scaup and the white-winged scoter. And in June 1979 Dr. Ward Stone—the wildlife pathologist who first warned his environmental conservation department superiors of PCB problems in the Hudson in 1970—announced he had found an average of 3,000 ppm of PCBs in 11 Hudson River turtles he had tested. The highest reading—8,000 ppm—was found in a 34-pound male turtle taken from Vanderburgh Cove in Dutchess County. As a result of his findings, the department issued a warning that people—and particularly pregnant women, nursing mothers and infants—should not eat snappers.[76]

Stone's research also turned up another disturbing trend. He found that although the highest PCB levels in the state are in turtles from the Hudson Valley, unsafe concentrations of PCBs also exist in areas previously thought uncontaminated. "The findings show that the PCB problem is everywhere. It's not just in areas where PCBs have been dumped into the water supply. It's also airborne from the low-temperature burning of tires, electrical components and other items containing PCBs," he said.[77]

In fact, during the next several decades the level of PCB contamination in the environment is expected actually to increase, not to decline. That is because many of the products containing PCBs that now are in use will be disposed of—improperly—in the years to come. The EPA estimates that the amount of PCBs in the United States' ecosystems will increase some three-and-a-half times—from 150 million to 540 million pounds—as PCBs leach out of landfills and continue to contaminate the water, land and air.[78]

"Although banning the production of PCBs will help the problem of toxic contamination, it will not solve it," said Nolan A. Currey, a consultant on hazardous materials for the EPA. "Electrical capacitors will rupture and discharge PCBs. Control of the disposal of electrical units will be difficult. And the task of intercepting and destroying toxics after they are discharged into the environment will be more difficult, if not impossible."

And the immediate PCB problems remain unanswered. The EPA has expressed much concern about PCBs in the environment, but it has not yet put together a national recovery program for the 758 million pounds of PCBs currently in use.[79] In addition, the EPA has taken no steps to curtail air-pollution problems occurring from the use of PCBs, and has set no standards for PCB levels in drinking water.[80]

Much work remains to be done in the Hudson Valley. Approximately 640,000 pounds of the poisons coat the Hudson's sediments, and no money is available yet to correct the situation. Each year between 5,000 and 10,000 pounds of PCBs enter the lower Hudson River, where they contaminate fish and wildlife. PCB levels in river fish remain high; the contamination of turtles seems to be increasing. More than 100,000 New Yorkers continue to drink water containing low levels of PCBs. And no one has any idea what will be the long-term impact of the chemical on the 1,800 GE workers and the hundreds of thousands of Hudson Valley residents who have been exposed to it.

What does Ward Stone—one of the few heroes in the saga of PCB pollution in the Hudson River—think of all this? He is concerned that the problem of toxic-chemical pollution in the Hudson and elsewhere will not be reduced significantly until American consumers fundamentally shift their attitudes about toxic chemicals.

"We live in a society where toxic chemicals are used without considering their long-term impact. Our whole basic thrust seems to be to fight nature," he explained. "We dump herbicides on our lawns which kill the earthworms which in turn causes the songbirds to disappear. Unless we make major changes to our approach to nature and toxic chemicals, we will wind up creating habitats suitable only for cockroaches."[81]

NOTES

1. Robert H. Boyle, *The Hudson River: A Natural and Unnatural History* (New York: W.W. Norton and Company, 1969), p. 24.

2. "The Hudson Is Cleaner," *Poughkeepsie Journal,* July 21, 1974.

3. Ibid.

4. Ibid.

5. "Hudson River Poison, State Agency Warns," *Poughkeepsie Journal* (AP), August 8, 1975.

6. "Has River Made City Water Unsafe to Drink?", *Poughkeepsie Journal,* October 19, 1975.

7. Ibid.

8. "Some Residents Looking for Other Water to Drink," *Poughkeepsie Journal,* September 4, 1977.

9. "PCBs—New Entry in Environmental Controversy," *Poughkeepsie Journal,* September 14, 1975.

10. "PCBs," *Newsday,* July 20, 1977.

11. "PCBs—New Entry in Environmental Controversy."

12. Robert H. Boyle and the Environmental Defense Fund, *Malignant Neglect* (New York: Alfred A. Knopf, 1979), p. 61.

13. "PCBs—New Entry in Environmental Controversy."

14. "Chemical Threat Held Widespread," *New York Times,* November 21, 1975.

15. Boyle, *Malignant Neglect,* p. 75.

16. "PCBs—New Entry in Environmental Controversy."

17. Boyle, *Malignant Neglect,* p. 56.

18. "Buildup of Chemical Spurs Fishing Curb," *New York Times,* September 26, 1976.

19. "PCB Problem Called Urgent," Washington Post Wire Service, October 25, 1975.

20. "PCBs—New Entry in Environmental Controversy."

21. N. Irving Sax, *Dangerous Properties of Industrial Materials,* (New York: Van Nostrand Reinhold Company, 1979), p. 484.

22. Robert P. Davis and Royal J. Nadeau, *Investigation of Polychlorinated Biphenyls in the Hudson River,"* EPA report, August 1974, p. 1.

23. "PCBs," *Newsday.*

24. Boyle, *Malignant Neglect,* p. 79.

25. Dr. Ralph Dougherty et al., "Sperm Density and Toxic Substances: A Potential Key to Identification of Environmental Health Hazards," *Abstracts of Papers, American Chemical Society,* September 1979.

26. Dr. Renate D. Kimbrough et al., "Induction of Liver Tumors in Sherman Strain Female Rats by Polychlorinated Biphenyl Arochlor 1260," *Journal of the National Cancer Institute,* December 1975.

27. "PCBs and Country Life," *Mother Earth News,* September 1976, p. 22.

28. Boyle, *Malignant Neglect,* p. 77.

29. "Suspected Cancer Agent is Found in Food, Animal Feed in 17 States," *Louisville Courier-Journal* (AP), September 29, 1979, p. 1.

30. "Little Known About the Effects PCBs Have on Humans," *Poughkeepsie Journal,* September 14, 1975.

31. Boyle, *Malignant Neglect,* p. 80.

32. "As GE Goes, So Goes Economy of Two Counties," *New York Times,* February 15, 1976.

33. "State Seeks to Stop General Electric From Dumping Chemicals Into Hudson," *Poughkeepsie Journal,* September 8, 1975.

34. "Poisoned Fish, Troubled Waters," *Sports Illustrated,* September 1, 1975, p. 14.

35. Memo written by Ward B. Stone, wildlife pathologist, July 12, 1974.

36. "PCBs: A Tale of Bungling and Ineptness at the DEC," *Empire State Report,* April 1976, p. 94.

37. Ibid.

38. "Bureaucratic Delays Mark PCB Story," *Poughkeepsie Journal,* September 14, 1975.

39. *Interim Order and Opinion, File No. 2833,* New York State Department of Environmental Conservation, Abraham Sofaer, February 9, 1976, p. 34.

40. "Bureaucratic Delays Mark PCB Story."

41. Davis and Nadeau, *Investigation of Polychlorinated Biphenyls in the Hudson River.*

42. "Bureaucratic Delays Mark PCB Story."

43. "PCBs: A Tale of Bungling and Ineptness at the DEC."

44. "State Seeks to Stop General Electric From Dumping Chemicals Into Hudson."

45. Ibid.

46. "Tons of Chemical Seep Into River, Official Claims," *Poughkeepsie Journal,* November 11, 1975.

47. Personal communication with David Brown, epidemiologist with National Institute of Occupational Safety and Health, Cincinnati, Ohio; and with Dr. William J. Nicholson, associate director of the environmental sciences laboratory at Mt. Sinai Hospital, New York City.

48. "GE Admits Pollution Figures Wrong," *Poughkeepsie Journal,* December 18, 1975.

49. "Guilty Verdict Returned," *Poughkeepsie Journal,* February 10, 1976.

50. *Interim Order and Opinion, File No. 2833.*

51. "Carey Tilts to Economy at Expense of Environment," *New York Times,* February 6, 1976.

52. Ibid.

53. "Two State Officials Split in Controversy Over Discharge of PCBs Into Hudson," *New York Times,* January 16, 1976.

54. "Carey Tilts to Economy at Expense of Environment."

55. "Reid to Ban Hudson Fishing," *New York Times,* February 18, 1976.

56. "Fisherman Sues GE Over PCBs Damage," *Poughkeepsie Journal,* September 14, 1976.

57. "PCBs," *Empire State Report,* Spring 1977, p. 12.

58. "$2 Million Offer by GE Reported in Pollution Case," *New York Times,* April 26, 1976.

59. "GE Agrees to Cleanup of Hudson," *Poughkeepsie Journal,* September 8, 1976.

60. "Battle Over PCBs Ends," *Poughkeepsie Journal,* September 9, 1976.

61. "Firm to Halt PCB Production," *Poughkeepsie Journal* (AP), October 6, 1976.

62. "The End of PCBs is Near, But Problems Linger," *Poughkeepsie Journal,* September 3, 1977.

63. Ibid.

64. "Curb on PCB is Stiffened for Interstate Fish Sales," *New York Times.*

65. "PCBs Revisited," *Environment Midwest,* October–November 1979, p. 11.

66. "The End of PCBs is Near, But Problems Linger."

67. *The Hudson River: A Reclamation Plan,* New York State Department of Environmental Conservation, July 1978.

68. "Flacke Wants Federal Commitment to Hudson," *New York State Environment,* July–August 1979.

69. Peter Sleight, "Fish to Sponsor Legislation for PCBs Cleanup," *Poughkeepsie Journal,* October 20, 1979.

70. "Has River Made City Water Unsafe to Drink?", *Poughkeepsie Journal.*

71. "How Safe Is Our Water? Increase of Two Cancer Types Found in City," *Poughkeepsie Journal,* August 28, 1977.

72. Personal communication.

73. Environmental Defense Fund and New York Public Interest Research Group, *Troubled Waters: Toxic Chemicals in the Hudson River,* September 1977.

74. "River Tap Proposal May Be Catalyst for Action," *Poughkeepsie Journal,* September 8, 1977.

75. Personal communication, May 1979.

76. "Turtle Soup Shows PCBs Widespread," *Poughkeepsie Journal* (AP), June 25, 1979.

77. Ibid.

78. "The End of PCBs is Near, But Problems Linger."

79. Boyle, *Malignant Neglect,* p. 81.

80. Ibid.

81. Personal communication.

Unless otherwise noted, all *Poughkeepsie Journal* articles cited were written by Jim Detjen.

Chapter **6**

An Un-Reserved Judgment

ALDEN E. LIND

LAKE SUPERIOR HAS THE LARGEST surface area of any body of fresh water in the world; in volume it is second only to Russia's Lake Baikal. To the Algonquin Indians, Lake Superior was the "big sea water," and to the Ojibwas, "Gitchee Gumee." Generation after generation have depended on it. When in 1968 the Reserve Mining case began and the lake's quality was questioned, no massive fish kills, no bodies in the street warned that something in the lake had changed. But pea-green clouds floated in the blue water, and a fine gray powdery sediment coated the near-shore lake bottom for many miles. And the conviction was growing that other changes in the life of the lake were occurring as well—changes all attributable to the practices of the Reserve Mining Corporation.

By the mid-1960s, Reserve Mining each day was dumping 67,000 tons of waste rock into Lake Superior—more than 24 million tons of rock a year. Reserve mined ore at its Peter Mitchell Mine near Babbitt, Minnesota, then transported the ore 50 miles to the company's processing and shipping facility on the lake at Silver Bay. Two-thirds of this ore was waste—durable, gritty little particles of very hard rock from which Reserve recovered iron. So fine were the particles ground that in still water a great number of them would remain suspended indefinitely.[1]

Of such particles were the drifting clouds of pea-green water constituted. The heavier particles became the obvious sediment. The discovery of these wastes miles from the plant led to the 1968 opening inquiry by a Department of Interior task force. If Reserve was polluting interstate waters, it could be in violation of the federal Water Pollution Control Act.

During the next ten years, the Reserve case was debated in forums ranging from local governments to the U.S. Supreme Court, as citizens fought to switch Reserve's dumping from the lake to a safe place on land, and to end the company's emissions into the air. What began as a seemingly straightforward pollution case in 1968 changed dramatically in 1973 with the disclosure that Reserve's powdery discharge was not simply the "inert sand" the company continually had contended, but was asbestiform fibers eventually held by the federal courts to be similar and often identical to "amosite" asbestos fibers, a known carcinogen.[2] With that disclosure came the realization that more than the crystal waters of Lake Superior were threatened; also potentially in danger were the 150,000 people in Silver Bay, Duluth, Cloquet, Two Harbors, Beaver Bay and other communities that draw their drinking water from the lake serving as Reserve's dump.

THE BEGINNING

I was only eight years old, so I don't really have any early recollections about the location of Reserve and its impact.—*Arlene Lehto*

I was still in grade school or early high school. . . . That was the farthest thing from my mind in those days.—*Arnold Overby*

It wasn't until around 1946 that several people did start to ask questions when we understood a little more clearly what was happening up in the area and that they might be dumping things into Lake Superior. At this time, the United Northern Sportsmen had just been organized, and it was brought up at one of their meetings that probably we should look into what was occurring. We did, and we were a little bit taken aback by the possibility of what could happen to our lake if it was used as a disposal area for something like this. We did investigate a little more thoroughly as to what constituted these tailings, and we were then a little more apprehensive because of the fact that the particulates are so fine. There was the possibility that they would remain suspended in water for a very long time. So we did take action to try and find an alternative method of disposal of these tailings rather than putting them in the lake. We were afraid of what might happen to our water supply, to our fishing resources, everything, even the clarity of the water.—*Milt Pelletier*

I guess I didn't pay too much attention to it . . . I didn't realize how much of an impact this plant was going to have on the area . . . I just didn't feel right about it but I didn't say much about it to begin with because I didn't realize what a terrific impact it would have.—*Milt Mattson*

The Reserve Mining Company originally was formed in 1939 by four steel companies—the Wheeling Steel Corporation, the Cleveland Cliffs Iron Company, the Montreal Mining Company and the American Rolling Mill Company (later renamed Armco).[3] In 1950 and 1951 Armco and Republic Steel each purchased 50 percent of the stock of Reserve, and it since has been a jointly owned "cost" company (that is, its costs are reimbursed by the parent firms, and it makes no profits on its own books). Reserve is the oldest of eight companies currently mining taconite for its magnetite content, in northeastern Minnesota.[4]

Reserve used a new way of processing taconite, but the company was not the first organized effort to find a replacement for Minnesota's "natural" iron ore—easily mined hematite with as much as 65 percent iron content. The supply had been depleted by the country's voracious appetite for iron and steel during the rapid industrialization of the early 20th century and World War II. As early as 1919, the Mesabi Iron Company operated a plant near Reserve's mine site at Babbitt.[5] Mesabi's process was primitive, its estimate of the market was faulty, and it failed. By 1939, however, the many small "puddles" of natural ore clearly were being consumed. After little more than five decades, the apparent bounty of Minnesota's Mesabi, Vermillion and Cayuna "iron ranges" virtually was exhausted. But an unreckoned additional bounty was bound up in the host rock, taconite.

By the late 1930s, the improved process for removing the

iron from taconite was well along in development, thanks to the support of the University of Minnesota's Mines Experiment Station and Edward W. Davis, a professor after whom Reserve would name its plant.[6] The process is called "beneficiation."

Beneficiation involves several steps and a great deal of energy. First the host rock, often very hard, is blasted into chunks ranging from pebbles to small boulders. These are loaded into trucks or rail cars and transported to a "coarse crusher," where they are ground in a machine similar to a mortar and pestle. From there the rock goes to another crusher, then to a "rod mill," where tumbling steel rods in a rotating drum further crush the rock, and finally to a "ball mill," where the crushing is continued with steel balls instead of rods.

The particles then pass over a rotating drum that contains an electromagnet. The iron particles adhere to the drum and are deposited on a conveyer system for "filtration" (drying) and eventual processing into pellets. Water is added to the rest of the rock, forming a slurry. Until 1980, Reserve's slurry was disposed of in the lake.

The pressures of World War II industrialization so accelerated the depletion of high-grade deposits in Minnesota that, by 1946, Reserve's parent companies determined to move ahead on a commercial use of the improved "beneficiation" process. In January 1947 they filed applications with the state of Minnesota and received permission to appropriate 130,000 gallons of water a minute—more than 187 million gallons a day —from Lake Superior. At the same time, they asked permission to dump into the lake 27,500 tons of waste rock each day.[7]

As the years passed Reserve's production goals would increase, and it would request additional water. In 1956, Reserve would receive permission to appropriate 260,000 gallons a minute; in 1960, 502,000 gallons. Production also would increase, reaching in the early 1960s the current level of about 10 million tons of pellets a year, with more than 20 million tons of solids a year discharged into the lake.

In 1947, of course, those staggering discharge levels were far in the future.

The state of Minnesota responded to Reserve's permit requests by scheduling a series of hearings directed by Chester Wilson, commissioner of the Conservation Department, the forerunner of the state's Department of Natural Resources (DNR). (Wilson also acted on behalf of the state Water Pollution Control Commission, forerunner of Minnesota's Pollution Control Agency, or PCA.)

Reserve contended that the inland Babbitt area was not suitable for on-land disposal, that the area had insufficient water, and that using Lake Superior was necessary for cost reduction sufficient to make Reserve's ore competitive with the natural ore.[8] H. S. Taylor, mines manager for Reserve's managing agent, the Oglebay-Norton Company, stated at the hearings that cost was the determining factor. Edward W. Davis was blunt: "It is simply a matter of economics."[9]

Some people simply weren't convinced by Reserve's public reasons for situating a processing plant on the shore of Lake Superior. "I am just telling you why I am opposing this thing," Karl McGath of the United Northern Sportsmen's Club said at the 1947 hearings on Reserve's application. "I just want you to know. You are going to have tons of that that never settles in Lake Superior, in addition to all this stuff that settles in Lake Superior before it goes out to deeper water."[10]

The Erie Mining Company, whose mine was only a few miles from Reserve's, apparently analyzed the economics differently; at the same time Reserve's facilities were constructed, Erie situated its own beneficiating plant next to its mine. Erie Mining expected no shortage of water and did not find conditions unsuited for a disposal site. Nor did the company believe the economics of locating near its mine unfavorable. (Subsequent developments have demonstrated that Erie made the correct decision. Six other companies have situated plants near their mines; none had water shortages. Adequate disposal sites have been constructed.)

At the hearings, Reserve offered a series of witnesses. E. W. Davis, known as the father of the modern taconite industry, assured the commissioner that the tailings would not affect the chemistry of the lake, that a community of 20,000 soon would develop in the Silver Bay area, and that the tailings, which were inert, could even be placed on land were the economics not so unfavorable.[11]

The University of Minnesota's Mines Experiment Station was a prominent participant. Davis, who represented himself as speaking for the station, was joined by Adolph Meyer and Dr. Lorenz Straub. The former, an independent hydraulic engineer, and the latter, director of the St. Anthony Falls Hydraulics Laboratory in Minneapolis, participated in a "demonstration" at the Mines Experiment Station that showed Reserve's tailings would settle to the bottom of Lake Superior's vaunted "great trough." The major test was conducted by pouring tailings into one end of a tank while at the other the water was pushed with a small paddle to simulate waves. The movies of the demonstration shown at the hearings showed, the experimenters explained, that all of the tailings settled to the bottom quickly because of a "heavy density" current. Because the tailings were in a slurry more dense than the lake water, they would go directly to the bottom, drawing the smallest particles with them.[12]

The demonstration was an absurdity. The tank, which had no lateral currents, could in no way be a simulation of Lake Superior. When the experts were asked about this omission by Commissioner Wilson and various participants in the hearings, the experts said that little was known about the currents. And the experimenters paid no attention to the impact of temperature. Indeed, they apparently had a tank with room-temperature water and were pouring colder water into it. In actual operation, the Reserve plant pours warmer water into the very cold lake.

The demonstration was typical of the quality of evidence offered. Other Reserve advocates, such as the Junior Chamber of Commerce, even went so far as to misrepresent the nature of Reserve's support. The Chamber reported that the U.S. Fish and Wildlife Service (FWS) approved of the Reserve proposal, as did the Minnesota Izaak Walton League. A November 24, 1947, memo in the files of the U.S. Environmental Protection

Agency, from the FWS regional superintendent of fish culture, contradicts both claims.[13]

Clearly speaking with grave reservations about Reserve's plans were a handful of commercial fishermen, representatives of the United Northern Sportsmen's Club, and a few individuals. One of the fishermen, Albin Wick of Castle Danger, expressed his fears about Reserve's tailings: "Well, herring will never live in that stuff, and then we might just as well pull in our nets."[14]

Those who testified asked many of the questions that rose again years later. But with no scientists or lawyers, they were unsuccessful in stopping Reserve Mining.

If the fishermen lacked the resources to unearth hazards inherent in the plan, Reserve itself was not willing to publicize the potential dangers. Dr. Samuel Eddy, a University of Minnesota zoologist, was hired by Reserve to study potential effects of tailings on fish. When he reported that dumping the tailings seriously would upset the food balance in an area extending at least 10 to 15 miles from the plant, Reserve simply did not release his report. Nor was Eddy called upon to testify.[15]

In any case, environmental problems were far from the only consideration in the decision. Residents of northeastern Minnesota were, in fact, keenly aware of the imminent depletion of the high-grade iron deposits. The citizens of Two Harbors, a one-industry town, knew that their chief source of livelihood—transferring iron ore from Duluth Missabe and Iron Range Railway ore cars to U.S. Steel Corporation ships—was about to end. Hundreds were threatened with unemployment. A proposal to build an even larger community only 28 miles from Two Harbors could be expected to receive considerable support. It did. The business community, typically, was enthusiastic.

The balance of power clearly favored Reserve. Not surprisingly, Commissioner Wilson granted Reserve its requested permits, on the conditions that the tailings did not harm public water supplies or fish in the lake, nor unlawfully pollute Lake Superior.[16] Reserve had passed its first major hurdle.

With approval secured, Reserve built a mine and a crusher,

some 50 miles of railroad, a power plant at Silver Bay and the complex of beneficiating and shipping facilities, at a total cost of more than $300 million.[17] Despite the visible clouds of green water and other troubling signs—the unusual deaths of trees in the vicinity of the Reserve plant, for example—Reserve was not to be challenged again for 20 years. Those who would be swept up in the Reserve case when it reemerged in the late 1960s were too young in the intervening years—as were Arlene Lehto and Arnold Overby, or not quite vigilant enough—like Milt Mattson, or without resources adequate to back up their skepticism—as were Milt Pelletier, the United Northern Sportsmen and the concerned commercial fishermen.

By the time the issue reemerged, Silver Bay had grown to a community of about 3,500 people. Students were bustling in three local schools, and a small shopping center was thriving. Many families owned homes, with thirty-year mortgages and low payments. Wage levels, governed by a United Steelworkers contract, were high. The *Wall Street Journal*'s impression was that "it was the kind of place where there were eight churches and only one bar, where nearly everyone owns his own home. . . . The only habitual criminals are window-peeping black bears which occasionally tear screens off homes as they search for food."[18]

Other taconite operations had begun in the region. More were expected. The bottom had not fallen out in northeastern Minnesota, as many had feared it would. And, given this reprieve, the communities were determined that it never would.

WAS RESERVE POLLUTING LAKE SUPERIOR?

Twenty years after Reserve Mining opened its plant, increased public concern about the environment was being expressed in tougher laws. President Johnson, under amendments to the federal Water Pollution Control Act, issued Executive Order 11288 in 1966 requiring federal agencies to coordinate the granting of discharge, construction and other water-related permits. The Department of the Interior (DOI) subsequently agreed with the Department of Defense that all existing U.S.

Army Corps of Engineers permits were subject to review by the same standards applied to requests for new Corps permits.[19] So in November 1967 regional DOI coordinator Charles Stoddard was assigned the review of Reserve's permits.

The Stoddard Task Force obtained information from the federal Bureau of Commercial Fisheries, Bureau of Mines, Bureau of Sports Fisheries and Wildlife, and the Federal Water Pollution Control Administration. The Stoddard Report concluded that Reserve was polluting the lake by increasing its turbidity (the concentration of suspended solids) and eutrophication (the aging of the lake), and stated:

> Improvements of the lake environment cannot be expected until the taconite tailings waste can be disposed of elsewhere.
>
> Therefore, the Department of the Interior recommends that the permit of the U.S. Army Corps of Engineers to the Reserve Mining Company be extended conditionally for a period of three (3) years, sufficient to investigate and construct alternate on-land waste disposal facilities, including recycling of used water, in order to comply with Federal-State water quality standards and to restore Lake Superior waters to their original high quality.[20]

Stoddard sent the report and the recommendations to the Corps and to Reserve on December 31, 1968.[21] But it soon became evident that neither Washington nor St. Paul, Minnesota's capital, was ready for his conclusions. In Washington, Assistant Secretary of Interior Max Edwards said the report contained "conclusions . . . which are obviously incorrect."[22]

In May the *New York Times* reported that northeastern Minnesota's "Mr. Water Pollution Control," John Blatnik, longtime member of the U.S. House of Representatives, also was displeased. "Mr. Blatnik was depicted by a number of reliable sources this week as having played a major role in the submergence of the controversial report. . . . Under reported pressure from Congressional quarters, Mr. Udall's Assistant Secretary for Water Quality and Research, Max N. Edwards, in effect repudiated the report. . . . The report was classified as unofficial and kept out of circulation."[23] Blatnik had done an about-face on the Reserve issue. Often identified as the "father" of clean water legislation in Congress, he appeared to have lost his commitment when an important industry in his own district might be affected.[24] Edwards, for his part, soon turned up on Reserve's payroll as its Washington attorney.

With the report about to be buried, by all indications, Stoddard suggested to *Minneapolis Tribune* reporter Ron Way where he could find copies.[25] Way did, and reported on Stoddard's conclusions. Reserve's pollution was back in the news.

COULD THE FEDERAL GOVERNMENT ACT?

Over the years, the federal government had received some limited authority to deal with water pollution, beginning with the Water Pollution Control Act of 1948. By 1969 a series of amendments to that basic law had produced a procedure known as a Federal Enforcement Conference.[26] The Secretary of the Interior was compelled to call such a conference if requested by the governor or pollution control agency of a state. And in the absence of such a request, the secretary also was authorized to call a conference if interstate pollution is suspected. In that case, a conference's first order of business was to determine whether interstate pollution is occurring.

Even after public release of the Stoddard Report, the state of Minnesota clearly would not act. Director of the Minnesota Pollution Control Agency (PCA) John Badalich told reporters that Reserve was not polluting, that the Stoddard Report had no official status and that the report was intended to inflame people. "If the pollution conference is going to be based on the so-called taconite report that was brought forth by the news media I don't think there's much foundation for an enforcement conference," he told the *Duluth News-Tribune.*[27]

Secretary Stewart Udall—as one of his last acts before turning over the Interior Department to Nixon-appointee Walter Hickel—called for a conference on Lake Superior pollution. But because no state had joined the request, the conference first had to determine whether interstate pollution in fact was occurring.

On May 13, 1969, the conference members met in Duluth to do exactly that. Although the Stoddard Report had precipitated the conference, the report was hardly discussed. Indeed,

Stoddard—who by then had left the Interior Department to become a resource consultant—was not permitted to place certain sections of that report into the hearing record.[28] Instead, the Federal Water Pollution Control Agency submitted its "own" report based largely on Stoddard's findings.[29]

In the Water Pollution Control Agency's report, however, Stoddard's conclusions were diluted. The agency's report quibbled, for example, over what proportion of the more than 700,000 pounds a day of such elements as copper, nickel, zinc, lead, chromium, phosphorous, manganese, silica, arsenic and iron went into solution, as opposed to settling out. And, although the agency with its "official" findings softened the impact of the Stoddard Report, the agency did add what was to become a significant comment: Reserve's tailings were found in the public drinking-water supplies of Beaver Bay, Two Harbors and Duluth. Despite this discovery, the agency's report recommended only that surveillance be continued, that six-month reports be made to the body of conferences and that Minnesota "take such regulatory actions as necessary to control the intrastate pollution resulting from these discharges, *if any.*" (Emphasis added.)[30]

The conference met for three days, during which considerable testimony was offered, little of it based on thorough research. Perhaps the most significant event was the attempted suppression of the first hard evidence that Reserve's tailings were present in Wisconsin waters. Staff members of the Water Pollution Control Agency's Duluth National Water Quality Laboratory had taken sediment samples from Wisconsin's Lake Superior waters in a number of locations. They had found considerable cummingtonite, a kind of amphibole mineral that is a major constituent of Reserve's tailings. Although Reserve insisted otherwise, the cummingtonite was not found in detectable quantities except where the waters had been affected by Reserve's discharges. This finding by the laboratory was well-known, but lab director Dr. Donald Mount was ordered by conferee Carl Klein, an Interior assistant secretary, not to present his data at the conference. A representative of one of the participating environmental groups, Grant Merritt of the Minneapolis-St. Paul–based MECCA (the Minnesota Environmental Citizens Control Association), then invoked the Freedom of Information Act. This forced public disclosure of the report by the lab—and stimulated Congressman Blatnik to "persuade" the conference chair to ask that those findings be made part of the record.[31] Finding Reserve's tailings in Wisconsin waters was crucial; it provided the basis for the federal government to continue the conference. Had no interstate pollution been found, the Enforcement Conference would have had no legal basis for further action.

Four and one-half months later, in late September 1969, the conference met again and adopted a resolution that, based on the testimony of staff members of the National Water Quality Laboratory, presumptive evidence existed that Reserve was causing interstate pollution.[32]

The conferees met again in April 1970 and received a staggering report from the Water Quality Laboratory. The lab found that much of Reserve's discharge of various minerals did go into solution, and that tailings were spread through a thousand square miles of the western arm of the lake. Worse, the lab had determined that the tissues of aquatic organisms were absorbing the tailings.[33] When Reserve again disagreed with the lab's findings, the conference recessed to await another report from the company.

This administrative process dragged on until the third meeting of the second session of the conference, in April 1971. Reserve repeatedly was late in submitting reports. Evidence accumulated that Reserve's discharges were harming the lake aesthetically, chemically and biologically. New, more environmentally conscious administrations in Wisconsin and Minnesota, joined by Michigan, formally called for the Enforcement Conference—this allowed the conference to bypass a determination of interstate pollution before proceeding. And on April 23 Commissioner David Dominick finally issued a statement giving Reserve 180 days to submit an acceptable plan to the federal government or to face suit by the U.S. Environmental Protection Agency (EPA) under the Water Pollution Control Act.[34]

The stage was set for the next act in the Reserve case. The government, after two years of delay, had delivered an ultimatum.

A JUDICIAL FORUM

In the Environmental Protection Agency, Reserve had an adversary without a long track record. The agency had been formed only recently, in December 1970. It already had taken occasional steps backward on the case—such as failing to support the eventual unanimous recommendation of the conferees that Reserve be required to dispose of its tailings on land. And the agency was heavily pressed by prominent Republicans—including the presidents of Armco and Republic Steel—to accept Reserve's proposals for continued lake dumping and to stay out of court.[35]

During the six-month negotiating period, Reserve continued to insist on lake dumping, contending that on-land disposal was environmentally unsound. Despite the political pressure, EPA administrator William Ruckelshaus decided to sue Reserve. In February 1972, the EPA filed suit in U.S. district court alleging that Reserve was violating provisions of the federal Water Pollution Control Act, that Reserve's emissions were crossing state lines and endangering human health, that Reserve was violating provisions of the Refuse Act of 1899 and depositing materials into navigable waters without proper authorization, and that Reserve's air and water emissions violated the common law of nuisance.[36] (Polluting fibers became airborne in two stages of the production cycle.) Judge Miles W. Lord was assigned to the case.

Reserve came to this judicial test with a recent victory under its belt. In November 1969, Minnesota's Pollution Control Agency had adopted WPC 15, a water pollution regulation that, among the limits it set, established a standard for suspended solids in effluents. Reserve's effluent had nearly 1,000 times more suspended solids than permitted by law as the effluent left the plant, and had nearly 500 times more than permitted where water passed the edge of the tailings delta and spilled into the lake.

In late December Reserve had sued in what turned out to be, even years later, a very friendly forum—Lake County District Court. (It was to be known for some time as Reserve's "home court.") Judge C. Luther Eckman had acknowledged that he was "completely lacking in personal expertise" in such fields as "ecology and limnology (including chemistry, bacteriology and biology), sociology, economics and cost accounting," yet he concluded that WPC 15 was arbitrary and capricious as applied to Reserve. He ordered the PCA to negotiate a variance for Reserve.[37]

The federal court, however, could be another matter. And Reserve had an additional worry: The case was taking a dramatic turn. What seemed to be a pollution problem was becoming a potential threat to public health. The public-health implications of Reserve's emissions had indeed been festering since, at a December 1972 meeting concerned with the Reserve case, a University of Wisconsin–Superior professor of geology had mentioned in passing that many of the particles in Reserve's emissions resembled asbestos fibers. Hearing that, Arlene Lehto seized on the professor's offer of an article on asbestos fibers in Japanese rice. And using the material in the article, she amplified her public remarks planned for the following day.[38]

"Nobody had considered that [the discharges] might have an impact on human beings—that the people of Duluth might be ingesting cancer-causing particles," she said later.

People at the state and federal levels were listening. Each independently began to examine the asbestos link. Lehto's warning particularly struck Drs. Gary Glass and Phillip Cook, EPA chemists. "I found myself thinking about it each time I turned on the tap," Cook said later.[39] In late spring Glass, Cook and other EPA scientists determined that the set of similar minerals cummingtonite-grunerite, long known to be in Reserve's emissions (and even used for tracing emissions during studies done for the Enforcement Conference), essentially was identical to amosite asbestos—whose carcinogenic qualities were well known.[40]

At first, Judge Lord was skeptical of these findings. Fearing public panic, he decided to keep the state and EPA researchers silent.[41] But Lord soon realized the implications of the studies and released the agencies. On June 15, 1973, both announced that asbestos-like fibers contaminated the drinking water of several north-shore communities. "While there is no conclusive evidence to show that the present drinking water supply is unfit for human consumption," the EPA announced, "prudence dictates that an alternate source of drinking water be found for very young children."[42]

With the warning came a shower of equivocations. The EPA itself suggested in its statement that nothing was conclusive. Reserve responded immediately by calling the announcement a scare tactic without basis in fact. "We know of no evidence and no indication to support the charge that there is any present or future hazard to drinking water supplies due to tailings," said Edward Schmid, an assistant to Reserve's president.[43] Duluth's Mayor Ben Boo echoed Schmid: "There is not enough evidence to warrant any sense of panic," he said.[44] Public health officials, notably the commissioner of the Minnesota Department of Health and the director of the St. Louis and Lake County health departments, declared there was no cause for alarm.[45] (People calling the St. Louis Health Department, however, were advised not to let children under five drink the water).[46]

The announcement also triggered a local boom in bottled water sales. "Water," said one supermarket manager, "is selling to beat hell." Stephen Slotness, manager of the Duluth Heights National Supermarket, told a reporter, "That phone's been ringing all day long. And people don't care about price."[47] Duluth received a $100,000 federal grant to buy bottled water for children in low-income families.[48]

Reactions to the EPA announcement varied widely. EPA chemist Phillip Cook said of the water: "I wouldn't let my wife shampoo the rug with it."[49] Tourists—whose summer pilgrimages help sustain the area's economy—seemed less plentiful. And the ones who arrived were concerned. "We don't seem to be getting the families," said one motel owner. "And everyone asks about the water."[50] "It's scary, that's what it is," said Kathy Burbul, a day-care worker with a seven-year-old daughter.[51] Mrs. Orval Chatfield also was concerned: "This is bad for the tourists, and to think it's polluting what was once the freshest body of water. That Reserve plant—something should be done."[52] Others took the news stoically. "All of my friends have been drinking [the water] for twenty years," said Robert E. Ball, "and they say, 'What am I going to do without water?' A switch to bottled water wouldn't do much good now."[53] Amid the confusion, on July 6 Mayor Boo called for construction of a filtration system for Duluth's water supply: "It is my judgment that the people of Duluth will not want to use water containing these asbestos particles regardless of the outcome of scientific research on the possible health hazards of the fibers."[54] Families lined up outside fire stations for filtered water.

Judge Lord convened the trial on August 1, 1973. By then the struggle over only pollution was little more than a memory. The new question—the one gripping the thousands of area residents—was whether Reserve's emissions were capable of causing cancer. Minnesota's north shore awaited an answer.

For many of those who had campaigned against Reserve's dumping over the years, the opening of the trial was a vindication. One of these people was Verna Mize, who had written letters to every official she could contact, trying to make them aware of the damage to the lake. Mize stood in front of the federal courthouse holding a sign that read, "Lake Superior; Preserve It! Don't 'Reserve' It!" "After all," she told a reporter, "this lake is poetry incarnate. To say Lake Superior is 'just another lake' makes as little sense as to say the Grand Canyon is 'just another ditch.' "[55]

Judge Lord obviously was impressed with the magnitude of the task in front of him. Much of the evidence would be at the frontiers of knowledge, especially that relating to the health effects of ingested fibers. Virtually all the available research was on inhalation in occupational settings; in Minnesota, new questions were being asked. Clearly the answers were critical to the health of tens of thousands.

Lord departed from ordinary practice. He chose "court appointed" witnesses to help him sort through evidence. He commissioned his own studies. And he embarked on a trial that occupied the courtroom 139 days, had more than 100 witnesses, and yielded more than 1,600 exhibits and 18,000 pages of transcript.

The most explosive testimony came in September from Dr. Irving J. Selikoff, the reknowned director of the Environmental Sciences Laboratory at Mount Sinai Hospital and one of the world's preeminent authorities on the hazards of asbestos. Selikoff spent a week on the stand—and the front pages of the local newspapers—outlining in no uncertain terms the magnitude of the health threat posed by Reserve's dumping.

On September 18, Selikoff warned of possible cancer of the larynx from asbestos exposure.[56] On the 19th he reported that, based on his own study, the families of Reserve workers may be exposed to dangerous levels of asbestos in their homes.[57] On September 20, he made the biggest splash of all: He called the water supply "a distinct public health hazard."[58] Selikoff's dramatic courtroom appearance rekindled the Reserve controversy. Duluth Mayor Boo announced that he supported Selikoff's assertions, but Frank Scheuring, mayor of Silver Bay, said, "I don't place much stock in testimony in which a person exaggerates to that degree. Things don't seem that bad to me."[59] After months of such testimony, Lord issued a broad range of conclusions:

> Reserve's fibrous emissions either were identical or similar to amosite asbestos, a commercial name deriving from Asbestos Mines of South Africa.
>
> Cummingtonite, a mineral that constituted about 26 percent of Reserve's raw ore and that overlapped in its mineral composition with amosite, was a valid "tracer" of Reserve's tailings.
>
> Tailings were transported by currents throughout the western end of Lake Superior.
>
> Exposure to asbestos was dangerous to health, and the length of the asbestos fibers was of no consequence. (Reserve's fibers are, on the average, much shorter than fibers used commercially.)

No exposure is risk-free; no threshold level of safe exposure is known to exist. (Lord was especially concerned about asbestos's possible synergistic effects, for example with tobacco. Even if a threshold level for asbestos could be determined, he argued, the threshold for any individual affected might be considerably different.)

Asbestos fiber levels were significant in both air and water. (The matter of fiber counting was probably the least satisfying aspect of the case. Judge Lord had ordered his own air sampling, and even these studies showed such inconsistency that he found determining absolute pollution levels impossible. He could conclude only that levels in the drinking water supplies amount to "millions of asbestos fibers to every quart" at all times, and that measure of asbestos fibers in the ambient air were significant.)[60]

With these conclusions drawn, on April 19 Lord ordered the Army Corps of Engineers to provide emergency water supplies to people on Minnesota's north shore. One day later he ordered Reserve to stop its discharges.[61] He made his feelings about the danger clear. When C. William Verity, chairman of the board of Reserve and Armco, told Lord on April 20 that "it is our judgment the discharges don't constitute a health hazard," Lord snapped back, "I regard your suggestion that I change my opinion . . . as preposterous."[62]

Although the weight of the evidence on the environmental and public health threats undoubtedly was the key factor in Lord's decision, he noted that Reserve's behavior during the trial made deciding otherwise impossible. Reserve repeatedly had been asked for any information it had concerning alternative disposal techniques. The officials had replied each time that Reserve had no contingency plans for on-land disposal. However, late in the trial Reserve was revealed to have commissioned a report about an on-land project, and as early as 1972 an engineering committee of the parent companies had rejected a deep-pipe plan as infeasible. Lord responded bluntly:

> Throughout this opinion the Court has frequently referred to the credibility or lack thereof of particular witnesses. After listening to testimony for over nine months the Court has formed the opinion that the credibility of the defendants collectively in this

case is seriously lacking. They have misrepresented matters to the Court, they have produced studies and reports with obvious built-in bias, they have been particularly evasive when officers and agents were cross examined.[63]

Nonetheless, two days after Lord's decisions Reserve convinced three judges of the U.S. Court of Appeals for the Eighth Circuit, in a meeting in a Springfield, Missouri, motel room, to stay Lord's order.[64] Less than a month later, having heard preliminary arguments, the circuit court declared that parts of Lord's findings were not justified. It suggested that, in the circuit court's judgment, Reserve would prevail on the health issue and the plaintiffs on the pollution issue.[65] The judges appeared to be offering the EPA a deal: If the EPA was willing to drop the health complaints, Reserve still would be ordered to dump its wastes on land.

No clear timetable was established, however, and with the prospect of Reserve winning by default a precedent on the health issue that the evidence did not warrant—the plaintiffs did not accept the offer. The circuit court was forced to make a ruling. In its final decision, issued in March 1975, the court accepted Lord's assessment of the health risk but concluded that the danger was not so imminent as to require that Reserve shut down. "The best that can be said," the judges wrote, "is that the existence of this asbestos contaminant in air and water gives rise to a reasonable medical concern for the public health. The public's exposure to asbestos fibers in air and water creates some health risk. Such a contaminant should be removed." "But," they added, "an immediate injunction cannot be justified in striking a balance between unpredictable health effects and the clearly predictable social and economic consequences that would follow the plant closing. . . ."[66]

Yet the Circuit Court also went further than Lord had in fashioning a standard for Reserve to meet in its emissions into the air. The court had concluded that airborne fibers are known to be hazardous:

Furthermore, Reserve must use such available technology as will reduce the asbestos fiber count in the ambient air at Silver Bay below a medically significant level. According to the record in this case, controls may be deemed adequate which will reduce the fiber count to the level ordinarily found in the ambient air of a control city such as St. Paul.[67]

Although the decision prohibited Lord from immediately stopping Reserve's discharges, it had affirmed the dangers of emissions into the air and water. At the same time, the circuit court's decision called on Lord to gather new evidence and to oversee the provision of clean water—directions that, despite the explicit restrictions, suggested Lord ought to do something.

So, in November 1975, with no official action yet taken by local officials to secure safe water supplies, Lord convened what he termed an "extraordinary session" of his court, an educational session, to which he summoned public officials from shore communities, witnesses on health and other matters, and Reserve officials. Lord cross-examined the witnesses himself, permitted no cross-examination by Reserve, and lectured the officials, especially those responsible for the welfare of children—whom he considered most at risk. Finally he pressed the city of Duluth to file a motion seeking recovery of costs for providing emergency water supplies.[68] For this courageous act, on January 6, 1976, he was removed from the case by the circuit court.

But Lord's "extraordinary session" had provided the impetus for local action. Within months Edward Devitt, chief judge of the Federal District Court, Minnesota District, had assembled a committee to oversee the provision of safe drinking water. Judge Devitt ordered Reserve to pay for bottled water being distributed to all the affected communities. Duluth, using an EPA design, contracted to build a $7 million filtration plant with federal demonstration grant funds. Two Harbors and Silver Bay undertook similar projects. By December 1976, Duluth's plant was operating and after a few months was removing more than 99 percent of the fibers from the city's water. Later, in 1977, Silver Bay and Two Harbors completed their plants. (To this day, neither Beaver Bay nor Cloquet, which take a portion of their water from Lake Superior, has filtered its water.) Three months later, Devitt ordered Reserve to pay filtration expenses of more than $1 million. Reserve's claim that its "discharge does not create a health hazard sufficient to justify removal of the wastes," he wrote, was "fatuous."[69] After five years, the case appeared to be nearing its end.

It wasn't.

BACK TO THE STATE

The circuit court decision gave Reserve and the state one year to negotiate a suitable on-land disposal site. If they couldn't come to terms, the court said, Reserve would have another year to shut down.

After the circuit court decision, Reserve had no choice but to switch to on-land disposal. The question was where. Dumping the tailings onland might take care of the problem of unsafe drinking water, but where Reserve stored its wastes was by no means irrelevant. On-land disposal, too, can present potential dangers. Tailings dams have been known to break: Dumping the wastes where a break would release them into the lake would be risky. And if the ground under the wastes were permeable, fibers would leach into groundwater supplies, and people who draw well water from the aquifer would be exposed. The vast numbers of fibers also could be carried by winds into populated areas.

In November of 1974 Reserve first proposed dumping its tailings at what became known as Mile Post 7 (MP7)—a site just north of that mile post on Reserve's railroad link to its mine at Babbitt. Once again the regulatory process geared up: The state decided to require a full-scale environmental impact statement (EIS) on the proposal and assigned Wayne Olson, a Minneapolis attorney, as hearing officer of combined EIS and permit hearings.

As had happened in earlier debates on Reserve, the lines were clearly drawn between those favoring and those against the site. At hearings in Silver Bay, local officials, business people and residents told Olson that Reserve was critical to the health of northeast Minnesota. While gazing over the lake, Patty Torgeson, a sixteen-year-old waitress, summed up the attitude for an out-of-town reporter one afternoon. "Sure is pretty, isn't it," she said. "I wouldn't want to live anywhere else. But everything in my family depends on the Reserve plant staying open because my dad works there. Everything we talk about at home, including whether we stay here, winds up 'if Dad still has his job.' "[70]

Undoubtedly, many other families in the area had similar conversations around the house. By any definition, Reserve was crucial to the area's economy. The company directly employed nearly 2800 people. It was literally the only reason for Babbitt and Silver Bay to exist. Shutting down Reserve would have a devastating impact on thousands of people. One Silver Bay resident of 23 years, James Cone, put his feelings this way:

> Well, what would you think if you'd worked here for . . . 18, 19 years and all of a sudden they're going to shut you down for something you can't see is hurting anything. I mean, you've got a house about half paid for and you know with the plant down it isn't going to be worth 5 cents if you walk away from it. And, basically you can't see where anybody is worse off in 1974 than they were in 1956. . . .[71]

Reserve used its hold on the local economy as leverage throughout the case. The company had threatened to close if it was ordered to dump on land; when the courts ordered Reserve to do so, it threatened to close if forced to use any site but MP7. As hearing officer, Olson was pressed by others as well. Governor Wendell Anderson already had signaled his preference for MP7. The departure of Grant Merritt, an environmentalist who had vigorously pursued the Reserve case as head of the state Pollution Control Agency, further suggested a swing by Anderson toward Reserve. Yet the weight of the evidence presented at the hearings cast doubt on the wisdom of using the MP7 site. Reserve's plan was to construct dams and "splitter" dikes of coarse tailings. A slurry of the fine tailings would be pumped into cells fashioned by the dams and dikes, within the general basin site. The dam would be one of the largest of its kind in the world: The largest of those proposed would be more than

14,000 feet long and 195 feet high. From the base of the dam the land angled toward the Beaver River, which drops 500 feet in about 2.5 miles, ending at Lake Superior at the town of Beaver Bay.

If such a dam failed, the environmentalists argued, the danger would be staggering. The state shared their concern. It hired three consulting firms to evaluate the design proposed by Reserve. Each testified that the dam would be safe. But one said, "Obviously, if a mining company would say to me, so far as we are concerned you make the choice, it doesn't make any difference, obviously I would lean toward a safer location. . . ."[72]

The vast dry beaches of tailings that would be created under the Reserve plan posed another threat. Reserve argued that watering and vegetation would minimize emissions into the air. Reserve's vegetation consultant promised "we can establish vegetation on those taconite tailings in one growing season."[73] But the state consultants doubted that such efforts would eliminate the airborne-fiber problem.

And despite Reserve's persistent protests, whether the corporation actually could not afford to dump its tailings elsewhere, farther from population centers, remained uncertain. Reserve made *its* position clear. Armco Steel's chairman, C. William Verity, said:

> Earlier this week you heard from the Arthur D. Little representatives [Reserve's consultants] a series of updated figures. . . . What this really means is that only the Mile Post 7 site can be seriously considered. If those of us in this room cannot find a way to use the Mile Post 7 site or some less expensive plan that I am not aware of, such failure will, in effect, shut down Reserve Mining.[74]

But the Arthur D. Little Company representatives' testimony was weakened by their not having access to the financial records of Reserve's corporate parents. Because Reserve is a cost company, it generates no profits; no accurate picture of its financial situation could be pieced together from its own records. (The state concluded, when finally it gained limited access to the records of all three companies—Reserve's on July 11, 1975, Armco's on August 20, and Republic's on August 18—that no reasonable barrier prevented Reserve from developing an alternative site.)

Olson recommended against Reserve, rejecting the applications for MP7 permits.[75] But, as with Lord's decision on water pollution, Olson's decision was rejected a few days later by a second body, in this case a PCA citizen board. Environmental groups immediately requested the board to reconsider.

The PCA staff had good reason to welcome this request. When the agency's citizen board voted against Olson, the prevailing board members were left the task of writing new findings to repudiate Olson's conclusions. With the evidence of the danger so strong, this was not easy to do. And it became harder, after July 1, when Reserve officials admitted under questioning that the company's profits for the previous three years had not been figured into projections of the suitability of any site but MP7. Later that day, Department of Natural Resources (DNR) Commissioner Robert Herbst announced that he agreed with Olson's findings. And, after a ten-hour meeting, the PCA fell into line. While Reserve workers and other businessmen who had cheered the first vote jeered, the PCA voted six to three to reject the MP7 site. Shortly after the final announcements by both the DNR and the PCA, Reserve filed an appeal with state district court, their "home court" in Lake County. The Reserve case was back in the courts.

BEFORE THE DUMPING ENDED

If the land-dumping site ultimately chosen was as crucial an issue to the environmentalists as the lake dumping, for Reserve's allies the new controversy was no more persuasive than the earlier one. "I didn't know, or I didn't feel, that dumping rock in the lake was as dangerous as they said it was, and I'm still not sure it is," said one Silver Bay resident.[76] He was not alone. In Silver Bay, many felt it would have been disloyal to the community to insist otherwise.

Olson and the PCA had concluded that fiber emissions

from a dump at MP7—even with the best control measures—
would exceed safe levels in Beaver Bay and Silver Bay. Both
Olson and the PCA had argued that moving the site an additional 13 miles to MP20 would cut down the fiber levels at these
populated areas. The small number of people living near MP20
then would be affected seriously. Because no safe level of exposure to fibers is known, one state attorney summarized, "less is
better than more." The state had concluded with similar logic
that, in numbers of people to be exposed to the fibers, fewer is
better than more.

In November 1976, the three state court judges took up the
question whether the agencies had decided on the basis of substantial evidence. Once again Reserve disputed Olson's
findings. And, not surprisingly, Reserve found a sympathetic
ear. The court found that the agencies had acted arbitrarily and
capriciously, and it overturned the decision.

The judges said:

> On the basis of the record in its entirety, the Findings, Conclu-
> sions and Recommendations of the hearing officer, and the deci-
> sion of the PCA based thereon to deny permits for Reserve's
> proposed Mile Post 7 on-land tailings disposal facility are unlaw-
> ful, unreasonable and not supported by substantial evidence.[77]

The state and environmental groups promptly appealed to
the Minnesota Supreme Court, but on April 8, 1977, a single day
after having heard oral arguments, the supreme court announced it was sustaining the lower court. Seven weeks later,
the court issued its final decision, awarding Reserve use of the
MP7 site—with a catch.[78] It ruled that the "less is better than
more" argument, which governed the state proposal, was not
justified. The state supreme court declared: "What the application of the 'less is better than more' doctrine overlooks is the
fact that what is 'less' for Silver Bay is 'more' for the users of the
Superior National Forest if Mile Post 20 is selected."[79] Reserve,
then, it ruled, would have to meet the air pollution standards
at *its property line,* not miles away in Beaver Bay or Silver Bay.

The dispute over air quality was not trivial. Reserve promised an upper limit of 13,289 fibers per cubic meter in the air

at Silver Bay. At this concentration, an adult would breath in nearly 270,000 fibers in a twenty-four-hour period. And Reserve's limit may have grossly understated the number of amphibole fibers emitted. Evidence presented indicated that, in the electron microscope analyses, probably two additional amphibole fibers—exceptionally thin fibers—resisted definite identification for each that was positively identified.

The state consultant testified that MP7 emissions most likely would supply Silver Bay 132,000 positively identified amphiboles per cubic meter, and a total per cubic meter of 402,000 fibers.[80] This concentration in the air breathed by an average adult would result in daily inhalation of more than 8 million fibers. The environmental groups found even this estimate low: Their projections for total fibers per cubic meter at Silver Bay ranged from 624,000 to 1,891,500.[81] Exposure at the higher level would be daily exposure to almost 38 million fibers.

Many of Reserve's vocal advocates in Silver Bay and elsewhere accepted the company's projections. In any case, many said they remained unconvinced that the fibers could be harmful. Long-time resident and Reserve employee James Cone relied heavily upon results of x-rays of a group of Reserve workers: "I know from these x-rays . . . that the guys have had who have worked here for a length of time, that they don't seem to be any more prone to get cancer than anyone else." Reserve's own consultants differed slightly on the interpretation of those x-rays. One reported no instance of significant change in lung tissue; another reported changes in about 5 percent of the cases.[82]

Although the state supreme court decision appeared to close the books on the Reserve case, the decision was not to be the end of all state court proceedings: A few months later Reserve returned to the local district court to plead the PCA was imposing permit conditions that the company could not meet and that were not sanctioned by either the federal or the state courts. By July 1977, it had become apparent that Reserve was intent upon slipping out of the assurances it had made to the supreme court. First, Reserve wanted to modify the "control city standard" imposed by the federal court of appeals; Reserve wanted additional permit language that would have forced the state—in each case—to prove that the fibers had harmed health. Second, Reserve wanted to define "fiber" in such a way that virtually anything three times longer than it was wide would qualify—whether or not it even was suspected of presenting a hazard to health. This language would have elevated the "fiber" level in any control city so high that Silver Bay could have met it, or so Reserve believed.

The state district court ruled in late October 1977 that Reserve's demands were legitimate. The decision was appealed to the Minnesota Supreme Court, and this time the supreme court balked. On April 14, 1978, its "last word" was issued. It reversed the lower court, pointing out that the state district court did not have the power to overrule the federal circuit court on the control city standard it had set, and that Reserve's attempt to redefine "fiber" would "grossly distort the process of comparing fiber counts in a control city with those at Silver Bay since it would include a comparison of innocuous fibers with those which were carcinogenic."[83]

Reserve stopped dumping into Lake Superior in March 1980. The MP7 site opened in spring 1980. Determining whether the state of Minnesota and its courts have made a fatal mistake may take twenty years.

WHAT DID IT ALL MEAN?

In dealing with this vast environmental and health threat, the environmental laws of the federal and state government worked—at least to a point. Ten years were required, from the time the Stoddard Task Force reported that Reserve was polluting the lake, to force a final decision on where the tailings should be deposited. Another two years passed before Reserve's lake dumping ended.

During that time, approximately 150,000 people were exposed to cancer-causing fibers in their drinking water or in the air they breathed. Several thousand more people—employees of Reserve—spent years in doubt about their employment futures, and now have reason to doubt their health. Eventually

Duluth received federal funds for a water filtration plant, and the city provided both bottled water and water filtered at fire-halls at many locations. Silver Bay and Two Harbors also were given public money for filtration plants. But Beaver Bay and Cloquet still do not have facilities; the two towns are unlikely ever to have filtration. And if not prodded by the concern of Judge Lord, many more of the local governments probably would not have acted.

Reserve Mining received "due process," to say the least. Reserve is estimated to have spent more than $15 million on the case. The state, which at times characterized itself as "neutral," spent about $2.5 million; the environmental groups, no more than $50,000 through the decade-long case. So in all, Reserve spent at least five times more than its opponents. "As it was, it took us until late 1979 to complete paying off a very reasonable attorney's bill," says Arnold Overby, board chairman of the Save Lake Superior Association. "With such an imbalance, it may be that Reserve got more than due process."

Possessing economic and political clout commensurate with its resources, Reserve also had the benefit of access to information and other resources that environmental groups simply could not match. Overby recalls, "In the early days of the case, for example, Max Edwards, who had been Assistant Secretary for Water Quality and Research in the DOI and who had tried to discredit the Stoddard Report, was hired as a Washington attorney for Reserve. At another point Reserve hired yet another former Assistant Secretary of DOI, Leon Weinberger, to present its case before the Enforcement Conference. We knew that relationships between Reserve and government agencies were pretty good."

When on-land disposal became inevitable, for example, Reserve officials could simply call the local congressman, James Oberstar—within whose district all of Reserve's facilities are located—and have him appear at administrative hearings to extol the virtues of Reserve and the MP7 site. Oberstar's broad support is apparent in a statement he made before the administrative proceedings:

They've got all the engineering work done, studies by the most prestigious nationally known and recognized engineering firm, Arthur D. Little. I have read the study. I am very impressed with it. I think they have looked at virtually every aspect of the scientific and engineering problems presented by this proposal. I think it's a good one. . . . And I shall support on my part on whatever extent is needed the company's justifiable request, the interest in industrial revenue bond financing or whatever their needs may be on the same terms and on the same conditions that other companies throughout the U.S. have applied for and received those benefits.[84]

When legal help was needed, Reserve could draw on the teams of attorneys it retained at two law firms. Each of its parent companies retained its own lawyers, as well.

The imbalance of power and resources was clear to the environmental groups from the beginning. On both scientific and legal questions, they were outnumbered: They simply didn't have the resources to compete. Overby summed it up:

During the last years of the case we were faced with the need to have a clear strategy which could make the most of our limited resources. First, we had to clearly identify the one or two most important issues and concentrate on them. It turned out that air quality was our central concern. Second, we had to depend heavily upon finding the flaws of omission and commission in the work of the state and Reserve. For example, we found in Reserve's own exhibits the evidence that the chemicals they proposed to use to suppress dust were not as effective as they claimed and that the state's consultant had not taken into account the dust emissions from compacting the surfaces of the dams. Third, we had to read everything offered by each of the other parties to find inconsistencies. For example, the PCA at one point literally contradicted its own expert witness on fiber counting. As it was, this effort was to play an important role in allowing the state courts to favor Reserve but it could have been even worse had we not spotted the inconsistency. And, finally, of course, we had to have a top-notch attorney who could bring these matters out on the floor. We did.

Environmental groups weren't the only ones short on resources. The citizens of Silver Bay, too, could have used independent technical expertise. They were caught between trust of their employer or of those who appeared to be threatening their jobs. With no way to evaluate the volumes of conflicting evidence, Reserve's contentions were easier to accept than the paradox that their own jobs should end to preserve their health.

As it is, the Reserve case may live on. MP7's contributions to fiber levels in the ambient air outside the boundaries of the site are not yet known. Within two to three years they will be. If the state's or the environmental intervenors' projections are correct, the entire matter is likely again to be before the courts. Furthermore, research remains to be done and the results issued on the health effects of Reserve's current emissions. Although lake dumping ended as of March 1980, the fiber level's rate of decline in drinking water is not known, and neither are the effects of ingestion and inhalation of fibers at past levels. In the Reserve Mining Case, the most fearful lessons may remain to be learned.

NOTES

1. U.S. Department of the Interior, *Summary Report on Environmental Impacts of Taconite Waste Disposal in Lake Superior,* 1968, Part II, p. 18, Table 7. Otherwise known as the "Stoddard Report."

2. Testimony before Judge Lord indicated that Reserve had known of the presence of "amphibole asbestos" in its ore no later than 1960. It had submitted a sample to Dr. James Gunderson, who, on July 1, 1960, had reported its composition as amphibole asbestos. See Judge Miles W. Lord, U.S. District Court (Minn. 5th Div.) *Supplemental Memorandum,* No. 5–72 Civil 14, May 11, 1974, p. 25. This was not publicly known until spring 1973.

3. E. W. Davis, *Pioneering with Taconite* (St. Paul, Minn.: Minnesota Historical Society, 1964).

4. Ibid.

5. Ibid.

6. Ibid.

7. Stanley Ulrich, Timothy J. Berg and Deborah Hedlund, *Superior Polluter* (Duluth, Minn.: Save Lake Superior Association and Northern Environmental Council, 1972), ch. 2.

8. Reduction of cost was cited as the principal reason by Reserve witness H. S. Taylor, mines manager, in the 1947 hearings. See transcript, *Second Public Hearing on Applications of Reserve Mining Company,* June 17, 1943, St. Paul,

Minn., p. 35. E. W. Davis likewise cites cost as primary. See Davis, *Pioneering with Taconite*. But the comments of Reserve attorney Edward Fride mention only an alleged absence of sufficient water and suitable disposal site. See *Conference Proceedings, Third Meeting of the Second Session (Reconvened)*, Duluth, Minn., April 22–23, 1971, pp. 70–71.

9. Transcript, *Public Hearing*, Davis, June 17, 1947, p. 47; Taylor, June 5, 1947.

10. Transcript, *Public Hearing*, June 17, 1947, p. 105.

11. Transcript, *Initial Public Hearing on Applications of Reserve Mining Company*, June 5, 1947, Two Harbors, Minn.

12. Meyer's testimony is found in transcript, *Sixth Public Hearing*, September 4, 1947, St. Paul, Minn. Straub's is in transcript, *Seventh Public Hearing*, September 30, 1947, St. Paul, Minn.

13. Ulrich, Berg and Hedlund, *Superior Polluter*, p. 12.

14. Transcript, *Seventh Public Hearing*, September 30, 1947, p. 228.

15. Ulrich, Berg and Hedlund, *Superior Polluter*, p. 11.

16. Ibid., pp. 12–13, in summary form. It is found in full in *Proceedings of a Conference on Pollution of Lake Superior and its Tributary Basin, Minnesota-Wisconsin-Michigan*, May 13–15, 1969, Duluth, Minn., pp. 1200–a–d.

17. Davis, *Pioneering with Taconite*.

18. "New Environment: Furor Over Plant on Lake Superior is Warning to Industry: Challenge to the Dumping Of Iron-Ore Waste Shows How Rules Can Change: A Shadow Over Silver Bay," *Wall Street Journal*, August 26, 1974.

19. This process is nicely summarized in Ulrich, Berg and Hedlund, *Superior Polluter*, chap. 4

20. Stoddard Report.

21. Ulrich, Berg and Hedlund, *Superior Polluter*, p. 40.

22. *Duluth News Tribune*, January 24, 1969.

23. "Politics and Pollution," *New York Times*, May 11, 1969.

24. Blatnik's role is described in Wade Green, "Life Versus Livelihood—Lake Superior Illustrates the Epic Struggle Between Environmental and Economic Values," *New York Times Magazine*, November 24, 1974.

25. Interview with Charles Stoddard.

26. The Federal Water Pollution Control Act of 1948 as amended. It was section 10(c) (5) that provided for the abatement conference process.

27. "LeVander Backs Parley on Pollution," *Duluth News-Tribune*, January 17, 1969, and "Official Says Pressure Applied," *Minneapolis Star*, January 23, 1969.

28. Ulrich, Berg and Hedlund, *Superior Polluter*, p. 77.

29. Federal Water Pollution Control Agency, *Appraisal of Water Pollution in the Lake Superior Basin,* April 1969.

30. Ibid., p. 48.

31. Ulrich, Berg and Hedlund, *Superior Polluter,* pp. 76–77 and fn. 50, p. 93.

32. Ibid., p. 86.

33. U.S. Department of the Interior, Federal Water Pollution Control Agency, *Effects of Taconite on Lake Superior,* April 1970.

34. *Proceedings of the Conference,* April 23, 1971, pp. 88–93.

35. The political pressures are described in various articles. See *Duluth Herald,* January 20, 1972; *Duluth News-Tribune,* January 23, 1972; and John G. Mitchell, "Corporate Responsibility in Silver Bay," *Audubon* 77 (March 1975).

36. Judge Miles W. Lord, U.S. District Court (Minn. 5th Div.), *Supplemental Memorandum,* No. 5–72 Civil 14, May 11, 1974.

37. *Opinion,* Judge C. Luther Eckman, Minnesota District Court, Lake County, December 15, 1970.

38. The article was R. R. Merliss, "Talc-Treated Rice and Japanese Stomach Cancer," *Science* 173 (1971), 1141. Subsequent analysis has cast some doubt on the study's conclusions. See G. N. Stemmermann and L. N. Kolonel, "Talc-Coated Rice as a Risk Factor for Stomach Cancer," *Am. J. Clin. Nutr.* 31 (1978), pp. 2017–2019.

39. "Each Glass is Another Moment of Truth," *Today's Health,* October 1973, p. 46.

40. P. M. Cook, G. E. Glass and J. H. Tucker, "Asbestos Amphibole Minerals: Detection and Measurement of High Concentrations in Municipal Water Supplies," *Science* 185 (1974), pp. 853–855; S. Burrell, *Amphibole in Taconite From the Peter Mitchell Mine, Reserve Mining Company, Babbitt, Minnesota,* a report submitted to the Minnesota Pollution Control Agency on June 12, 1973.

41. Judge Lord's handling of this matter is described in Robert V. Bartlett, *The Reserve Mining Controversy: A Case Study of Science, Technology, and Values* (Bloomington, Ind.: Indiana University, Advanced Studies in Science, Technology, and Public Policy, 1979), pp. 161–162.

42. "Report Says Asbestos Fibers Found in Duluth Drinking Water," *Minneapolis Tribune,* June 16, 1973.

43. Ibid.

44. Ibid.

45. *Minneapolis Star,* July 13, 1973.

46. "Bottled Water is Selling Fast in Duluth Stores," *Minneapolis Tribune,* June 19, 1973.

47. Ibid.

48. "Duluth Gets Grant to Buy Bottled Water for Poor," *Minneapolis Tribune*, June 30, 1973.

49. "Each Glass is Another Moment of Truth."

50. Ibid.

51. "Bottled Water is Selling Fast in Duluth Stores."

52. "Duluth Stoically Awaits Tests for Cancer Risk in Its Water," *New York Times*, June 24, 1973.

53. Ibid.

54. "Duluth Mayor Proposes Water-Filtration System," *Minneapolis Tribune*, July 7, 1973.

55. "Lake Lover is Happy Reserve is in Court," *Minneapolis Tribune*, August 2, 1973.

56. "Dr. Selikoff Takes Stand, Testifies of Fibers' Effect," *Minneapolis Tribune*, September 19, 1973.

57. "Witness: Fibers Can Hurt Workers' Families," *Minneapolis Tribune*, September 20, 1973.

58. "Dr. Selikoff Calls Lake Superior Drinking Water a Hazard to Health," *Minneapolis Tribune*, September 21, 1973.

59. Ibid.

60. *Memorandum and Order*, No. 5–72 Civil 14, April 20, 1974, Judge Miles W. Lord, U.S. District Court (Minn. 5th Div.).

61. Ibid.

62. "Reserve's Minnesota Taconite Plant Shut as Judge Rules Asbestos Wastes Harmful," *Wall Street Journal*, April 22, 1974.

63. *Memorandum and Order*, No 5–72 Civil 14, April 20, 1974.

64. *Reserve Mining Co. v. United States*, 498 f, 2nd 1073 (8th Cir., 1974).

65. U.S. Court of Appeals (8th Cir.), *Reserve Mining Co. v. United States*, June 4, 1974.

66. *Reserve Mining Co. v. United States*, 514 f. 2nd 492, 1539 (8th Cir. 1975).

67. Ibid., p. 103.

68. Transcript, *United States v. Reserve Mining Co.*, U.S. District Court (Minn. 5th Div.), No. 5–72 Civil 19, November 14–15, 1975, Miles W. Lord, Judge.

69. *U.S. v. Reserve Mining Co., Order*, 5–72 Civil 19, U.S. District Court (Minn.) February 21, 1976.

70. "New Environment: Furor Over Plant on Lake Superior is Warning to Industry."

71. Interview with James W. Cone.

72. Transcript of the *Environmental Impact Statement Hearings,* Sept. 17, 1975, p. 4484.

73. Transcript of the *Environmental Impact Statement Hearings,* November 21, 1975, p. 6513.

74. Transcript of the *Environmental Impact Statement Hearings,* July 11, 1975, p. 3041.

75. *Findings, Conclusions and Recommendations* of Hearing Officer Wayne Olson, June 25, 1976.

76. The resident wishes to remain anonymous.

77. *Order,* Minnesota District Court, Lake County, Judges Donald Odden, C. Luther Eckman and Nicholas Chanak, January 28, 1976.

78. *Opinion,* Minnesota Supreme Court, *Reserve Mining Co. v. Robert Herbst et al.,* May 27, 1977.

79. Ibid., p. 50.

80. "Brief of Respondent Minnesota Pollution Control Agency," to Minnesota District Court, Lake County, December 24, 1976.

81. "Brief of Intervenors Save Lake Superior Association and Sierra Club," to Minnesota District Court, Lake County, December 24, 1976.

82. Transcript, U.S. District Court, Judge Miles W. Lord, *United States v. Reserve.* See testimony of Bristol, p. 7201, and Morga pp. 10656–10663.

83. *Opinion,* Minnesota Supreme Court, *Reserve Mining Co. v. MPCA,* April 14, 1978, p. 8.

84. Transcript of the Environmental Impact Statement Hearings, July 11, 1975, pp. 3019–3020.

Chapter 7

The Politics of Poison

JOHN DAVID RABINOVITCH

THE HATHENBROOK FARM has become a kind of twilight zone. No more birds appear in the sky. The polliwogs and salamanders have disappeared from Calvin Hathenbrook's stream, and a strange white residue continually reappears on the drain pipe opening. No one can understand what has happened to his barnyard animals. The cat gave birth to a litter of deformed kittens, and the hens stopped laying eggs—until Hathenbrook replaced the rooster. He himself has recurring dizzy spells. His hands and feet sometimes go numb. Nobody can tell why.

"I just can't get anybody to listen to me," says farmer Hathenbrook. "I been down to the county health office, they don't wanna see me. The county agriculture officer, they're supposed to investigate these things, can't get them to come up here."

Since serving in the Korean war, Calvin Hathenbrook has been farming and working in the remote forests of Humboldt County, California, one of America's great timber-producing areas. He's seen the freeway cut through the redwood forests, shouldering up to his clapboard house.

Calvin Hathenbrook is an unlikely protester, but he has enlisted—he has joined ranks with the millions of Americans fighting the herbicide wars. The enemy is 2,4,5-T, a powerful phenoxy herbicide contaminated with dioxin, generally considered the deadliest substance ever created by chemists. The story of 2,4,5-T symbolizes many environmental issues, pitting a powerful corporation against a grassroots movement unaided by the government agencies designed to protect the environment and the public health.

One question lies at the heart of the controversy. Why—after 30 years of study, after thousands of testimonials on human, livestock and property damage, after 35,000 laboratory studies had been conducted[1]—why did the government permit the use of herbicides containing dioxin to continue while evidence of their danger had prompted review of the registration of those materials?

Each year more than 40 million pounds of phenoxy herbicides are used to kill unwanted leafy vegetation in forests, on rangeland, in rice fields and along highways and power lines across America. The phenoxies are selective killers, affecting leafy vegetation but leaving coniferous plants unscathed. They are the poisons you can buy at your corner store. They are sold under 424 trade names—among them, 2,4,5-T; Silvex; Kuron; Weed-b-gone. Your local golf course uses Silvex to kill dandelions. For nearly 20 years, the manufacturers' assurances that these herbicides are safe went unchallenged. The safety data on file with the Pesticide Regulatory Division of the U.S. Department of Agriculture, supplied in the late 1940s, was not even reviewed until the mid-1960s.

Then, frightening abnormalities began to appear in test animals and people exposed to 2,4,5-T.

In Vietnam a mixture of the herbicides 2,4,5-T and 2,4-D, called Agent Orange, was used by the U.S. Air Force to destroy North Vietnamese crops and to expose Viet Cong supply trails. The incidence of miscarriages and severely deformed babies in Vietnamese areas sprayed appeared to increase. Secret tests on mice and rats done under government contract suggested that the herbicides were responsible.

Concern further increased in 1969 with a report from

2,4,5-T's principal manufacturer, the Dow Chemical Company. (Other manufacturers of 2,4,5-T have included Hercules; Diamond-Shamrock; Monsanto; and Thomson-Hayward, a subsidiary of North American Philips.) Dow acknowledged that 2,4,5-T contains tiny amounts of another chemical, an unwanted contaminant called 2,3,7,8-tetrachlorodibenzo-p-dioxin, often abbreviated TCDD or simply called dioxin. Dioxin is a fetus-deforming agent 100,000 times more powerful than thalidomide. Dioxin is also more insidious. Small, undetectable amounts of it build up in animal fat over long periods of time, the body's chemical reaction continuing after exposure. According to Senate testimony by a Dow vice president, the company had been aware of dioxin in 2,4,5-T since 1964.[2]

Dr. Matthew Meselson, a biochemist at Harvard University, pioneered in the analysis of dioxin. The Harvard laboratory developed a sophisticated process involving a device called a mass spectrometer to detect dioxin in levels as low as the parts-per-trillion (ppt) range. Minute amounts of it may be measured, yet, according to Meselson, no safe level of exposure for human beings has been determined. Many unknowns remain; in fact, he says, "the cause of death from dioxin poisoning is not known. One suspicion has been that dioxin acts by stopping cell division."

The phenoxy herbicides cause plants to enlarge and distort, growing themselves to a twisted, tortured death. As the herbicide moves through a plant's arteries, the plant's hormones seem to go berserk, causing leaves and buds to curl and die, and stems to twist grotesquely. A heavy dose to vegetation can cause almost instant death. In Vietnam, some heavily defoliated areas may not regain their former condition for almost a century.[3]

The "miracle" of the phenoxy herbicides is that they are selective; they kill or maim not every plant they contact, but only the broad-leaved varieties. Foresters use the herbicides to kill off deciduous trees, encouraging the growth of the more commercially valuable softwoods, such as redwood and Douglas fir. The plants receiving doses of herbicide pose no danger to society; the work of the sprays could in fact be accomplished by forestry workers. The benefits of the phenoxies, then, are solely economic. And even the economic benefits are disputed as an argument for herbicide use rather than other means of clearing.

The timber industry claims that "three-fifths of the commercial timberland is producing forest products at less than two-thirds capacity due primarily to competing undesired vegetation,"[4] whereas a study by the California Economic Development Department states that alternatives to use of the phenoxy herbicides can be developed, "such as new herbicides . . . or improved site-preparation techniques that would eliminate the need for any type of conifer release."[5]

However, the argument over economic benefits surely must be secondary to the basic scientific question: Can a plant hormone killer also affect hormones in people, causing changes in physical, mental and emotional behavior?

Tests on laboratory animals using 2,4,5-T with the lowest possible levels of dioxin contaminant have produced cancer, abortions and impairment of the body's immune system. "Even a hundredth of a part per trillion of dioxin in the human diet should be regarded as dangerous," says Meselson.

Even much larger quantities are imperceptible by unaided human senses; this "invisible" quality of dioxin confuses the issues at stake. Many people find it hard to accept that their illnesses could be caused by a poison they cannot see, smell or taste. Calvin Hathenbrook is one who became convinced that herbicides were the cause of his troubles. "I was out on the job, about seven weeks or so after they sprayed this hill up behind my place. Anyways, my knees got real weak and wobbly, and I went down when I was opening the shed. So, I figure, the spray kind of sneaks up on you."

"Chemical McCarthyism" is what Cleve Goring, Dow Chemical director of agricultural products research, calls complaints like Hathenbrook's. "I see it as a situation where chemicals are attacked indiscriminately, basically their reputation is ruined ·without having to resort to facts. A lot of misguided, cynical, and self-serving people are getting in our way. The voices of chaos are a mixed bag and much too noisy. Who are these people? What are they like?

"There are the fearful, the ignorant and the superstitious

who see demons in the form of pesticides around every corner; the antitechnologists who promote the fear of pesticides to hasten their demise; the scientist who promotes the fear of pesticides in hopes of gaining funds for support of his research; and the politician who promotes the fear of pesticides for political gain and power."

Dow promotes pesticides for its own reasons. 2,4,5-T brings in about $20 million, which is less than one percent of Dow's total annual sales. But though the federal review of 2,4,5-T use is the immediate focus of the controversy, far more is at stake than the registration of 2,4,5-T alone. The U.S. market for all pesticides in 1978 was $3.04 billion and is expected to climb to $3.3 billion by 1984.[6] Eight hundred seventy-seven million pounds of pesticides were produced in the U.S. in 1965; the 1.4 billion pounds produced in 1978 nearly doubled that.[7] In March 1979, 2,4,5-T was removed from this market by the Environmental Protection Agency (EPA), which issued an emergency suspension of its most common applications.

"We've got to fight to have a set of values operating here," said former New Jersey Congressman Andrew McGuire, "which are, briefly, that life and health is the first principle. If we don't have life and health, we don't have much of anything. In that context, you have to look very closely at the question of whose [are the] benefits and whose [the] cost."

"ECONOMIC POISONS"

The phenoxy herbicides, which include 2,4,5-T and 2,4-D, were developed during World War II at Fort Detrick, Maryland, as instruments of chemical warfare. For peacetime use, they are considered to be "economic poisons," and as such they are subject to regulation by the EPA, the successor to the old Pesticide Regulatory Division of the U.S. Department of Agriculture (USDA). The pesticide 2,4,5-T has occupied much of the EPA's attention since the agency's inception in 1970.[8]

In 1974, under legal pressure from the Environmental Defense Fund (EDF), a public-interest law firm, the EPA announced that it would hold cancellation hearings for 2,4,5-T.

Then on the eve of the hearings EPA withdrew, announcing that it needed more time to collect scientific evidence.

In withdrawing its cancellation suit, the agency announced the creation of a special group called the Dioxin Implementation Plan (DIP) to study low-level effects of dioxin. The members of the DIP are the Dow Chemical Company; the EPA; a group of university laboratories called "the collaborators," all of whom are in line for research contracts from EPA; the USDA and the U.S. Forest Service, which have promoted the use of 2,4,5-T; and one representative from the Environmental Defense Fund. From 1974 through 1979, action on the regulation of substances containing dioxin was stalled in this group.

William Butler, general counsel for the EDF, which has persisted with court actions against the regulatory agency, feels that the "EPA has really not regulated, very heavily, any herbicides. 2,4,5-T, like DDT for an insecticide, has been viewed as the test case. But our feeling is that the burden of proof is up to Dow to show beyond a reasonable doubt that their product is safe before it is used . . . and not [to] wait for disasters to develop in the environment, before taking it off the market."

The industries that might feel the financial pinch of regulatory action by the EPA are busy lobbying for 2,4,5-T through such trade organizations as the National Agricultural Chemicals Association and the American Forest Institute, and through such front groups as the Council for Agricultural Science and Technology.[9] The resources pouring into the legislative lobbying and propaganda campaigns are soaring.

Dow Chemical alone spent $286 million in 1977 complying with what it calls "excessive government regulation." Dow has even argued that dioxin is produced spontaneously in nature. Dow made this claim in 1978 after the Michigan Public Health Office warned residents living near Dow's world headquarters in Midland, Michigan, that fish in the local Tittabawassee River were contaminated with dioxin. As dioxin is produced only during the manufacture of a chemical called trichlorophenol, used in the production of 2,4,5-T, the contamination of the

Tittabawassee River was assumed to have come from the Dow plant.

In response to the Public Health Office announcement, Dow produced a study that exonerated the company of any responsibility for contaminating the Tittabawassee River. The dioxin, said Dow, came from local cooling towers and incinerators, from internal-combustion engines, and from cigarette ends. Dioxin, the company claimed, is not produced only by the process of creating trichlorophenol; dioxin is ubiquitous. No responsible scientific journal has accepted these radical pronouncements for publication.

"We think 2,4,5-T is a very important symbol. If we were to lose on this issue, it would mean that the American public has been taken back a couple of hundred years to an era of witch hunting, only this time the witches are chemicals, not people," says Cleve Goring of Dow. "So that is the importance of the issue, it certainly isn't the size of the product to the Dow Chemical Company."

Sales of 2,4,5-T and the other phenoxy herbicides peaked in the 1960s when the Pentagon ordered them for use as Agent Orange in Vietnam. The pilots who flew the defoliation missions —the "Ranch Hands"—had a motto: "Only we can prevent forests." Between 1962 and 1970, 50 million pounds of Agent Orange, containing as many as 360 pounds of dioxin, were sprayed over five million acres of Vietnam.[10] Until 1979 an area greater than that sprayed in Vietnam during the entire war was sprayed each year in the continental United States.[11]

With the increased production of 2,4,5-T for the war effort, workers at a Dow Chemical plant in Michigan suffered an epidemic of chloracne, a severe skin disease. Other symptoms noted were fatigue, depression, nervous disorders and loss of memory.

Similar ailments were developing in the American troops in Vietnam. Army veteran Richard Almdale, who now lives in Humboldt County, California, recalls that "we would see helicopters going across in the distance from where we were, and there would be clouds coming out of them. We knew that they were defoliating, and at the same time we were told nothing about it. After my first patrol I started to develop blisters all over my hands, slowly [spreading] upwards to about my elbows. I wore typical Army fatigues and usually rolled them up because of the heat . . . all the blisters broke, and I thought I had leprosy. I would never have associated it with the spray; we were told it was a fungus."

In the summer of 1969 Saigon newspapers published reports of deformed babies born to women exposed to herbicides. An abnormal number of children with severe birth defects—Down's syndrome, spina bifida, cleft palate, twisted limbs—were born to Vietnamese women who appeared to have one thing in common: Each claimed to have been exposed to phenoxy herbicides.

Links between 2,4,5-T and birth defects had been observed before—but not publicly. In 1965, a study by the Bionetics Research Laboratory under United States government contract concluded that 2,4,5-T caused birth defects, including cleft palates and defective kidneys, in laboratory animals. That study was suppressed for four years. It finally was released in 1969 after a student from a Ralph Nader–sponsored group investigating pesticide problems, who had obtained a copy, showed the study to Harvard scientist Matthew Meselson. Meselson's personal influence finally brought the issue to the attention of White House staff, and this extraordinary series of events touched off another.

In an unprecedented tridepartmental announcement representing the combined authority of the Departments of Defense, of Agriculture and of Health, Education and Welfare, on April 15, 1970, the Air Force was ordered to stop using Agent Orange. It was considered so deadly that the Air Force was unable to obtain permission to return its stockpiles to America. They were not disposed of for another seven years. In 1977 two million gallons of Agent Orange were incinerated in the far reaches of the South Pacific aboard a specially built ship, the *Vulcanus.*

Not until nine years after the suspension of military use of Agent Orange did the EPA issue its suspension order against some uses of 2,4,5-T in the United States. For nine years, the government permitted the use of "the population at large as Dow's guinea pigs, and the environment at large as their laboratory," according to William Butler of the EDF. "With 2,4,5-T ... [there is] involuntary exposure to the range of people around that may be hit by drift or [may] ultimately eat animals contaminated with it, or drink water which has dioxin—those people don't know what they're doing, would not do it if they did know about it, but the choice is being made for them. It's being made by the manufacturers, and by the users, and ultimately by the government in permitting this material to be used while the studies as to its safety are going on."

THE OPPOSITION UNITES

Humboldt County, in northern California's redwood forests, has been divided by the controversy over phenoxy herbicides. New alliances are forming and old antagonisms being exacerbated. Groups of farmers, fishermen, Indians, Vietnam veterans and even the sisters of a nunnery—some of these groups traditionally opposed to each other—are united in their opposition to herbicides. There is talk of violence, and violent talk. "Spray Watch" committees have been formed, alert for helicopters, linked by an informal Citizens Band radio network.

Humboldt County Agriculture Commissioner John Hart has enraged herbicide opponents. Under federal law, the EPA delegates to the states enforcement responsibility for pesticides such as 2,4,5-T; under California law, this authority is further delegated to the county agriculture commissioner—in this case, Hart. Hart drew the wrath of the opponents of 2,4,5-T spraying by continuing to issue spray permits for 2,4,5-T right up until the suspension order, despite the wealth of information appearing on the herbicide's potential environmental and public-health hazards. Ted Eriksen, agriculture commissioner of neighboring Mendocino County—another low-income timber area—used his discretionary authority to cancel or withhold spray permits. (In June, 1979, Mendocino became the first county in the nation to use the ballot-initiative process to ban aerial spraying of herbicides.) Hart, however, maintains that "my job is merely to issue permits when an herbicide is registered with EPA."

Hart's position is in concert with that of the county's powerful timber industry. Humboldt County produces a billion board feet of lumber annually, and behind its "Redwood Curtain" the lumber corporations—Simpson, Barnum, Arcata Redwood, Louisiana Pacific—control the local economy. They employ more than a quarter of the county's population. Of equal significance, another 20 percent of the county's population are unemployed. So the timber industry's tremendous influence within the county surprises no one. And the industry backs herbicide use 100 percent.

The Simpson Timber Company's chief forester, Jim Reydalius, is one who believes in herbicides. A forestry graduate of Humboldt State University, Reydalius blames the controversy on the publicity that surrounded Agent Orange and Vietnam. "There just aren't any proven risks from these herbicides," Reydalius has argued. "We don't want to hurt anybody, but if we want a well-managed forest, then we've got to have them." Other observers are less confident that herbicide use guarantees a healthy forest. "Years of poor logging practices have left the timber industry in bad shape," said Jim deMulling, a forester for nearly all of his sixty years. "In Humboldt County, the industry has applications to spray about ten thousand acres a year with 2,4,5-T and 2,4-D. This would kill off the unwanted hardwoods, which shade the growth of the more valuable redwoods and Douglas firs."

No one has ever determined whether the phenoxy herbicides have a stunting effect on conifers themselves—the very trees whose growth the users are trying to promote. In June 1979 Oregon Congressman James Weaver announced that the House Agriculture Committee's Forest Subcommittee, of which he is chairman, would hold hearings on the effects of herbicides on conifers and Douglas firs. "I was shocked," Weaver told a congressional subcommittee, "to find out that we are spraying millions of acres of forest land in this country with these killer chemicals to kill the broad-leaved plants without one single research study on the effect on [the] conifer itself of these herbicides. I was so flabbergasted I could not believe this."[12]

Even more important, the evidence on 2,4,5-T raises deep doubts about its effects on the health of the *people* living in or near the forest land. "These are killer chemicals," said Weaver, "They are designed to attack the chromosomes, the genetic structure of all living organisms—our own as well as plants. . . . It was from my area, in a place called Alsea, Oregon, that a woman named Bonnie Lee, who had miscarriages, decided there might be a connection between the spraying of these chemicals and her miscarriage. . . . This is an area of rather pristine purity. This is way up in the forests where normal pollution, cars, and so on, do not come."

A study of the incidence of miscarriages in Alsea helped to prompt the EPA's partial emergency suspension order against 2,4,5-T on March 1, 1979.

A few hundred miles down the coast from Alsea is Denny, California, a tiny hamlet just across the Humboldt County line, in Trinity County. Nineteen winding miles of mountain road from the nearest highway, Denny is surrounded by national forest land—land that has been sprayed repeatedly with herbicides by the U.S. Forest Service. Denny residents, like Linda van Atta, feel like the guinea pigs William Butler described. "People have no freedom of choice," said van Atta. "I made a decision to come out here so I could raise my own food and so I could raise my own livestock without chemicals and now all of a sudden I have to take them whether I want them or not."

Linda van Atta became concerned about possible chemical contamination following her third miscarriage. "I myself have had three miscarriages, my daughter-in-law had a miscarriage, and a friend of mine had a miscarriage and had cancer, and another friend just had a baby born with a harelip. I think this is very unusual. I've never lived in a place before where so many women all in one small area had so many problems."

Mrs. van Atta contacted doctors at the Humboldt Medical Center in the Indian village of Hoopa, some 35 miles away.

They could not determine any significance in the incidence of cancer, ovarian cysts and menstrual irregularity. But Dr. Scott Sattler wrote to the director of the County Health Department, "I am quite bothered by what appears to me to be documentation of seven miscarriages in such a small community during such a short time. . . . I'm concerned with the baby born with the harelip. The information that I have does say that miscarriages and congenital deformities are related to these herbicides."

More than half the women of Denny claim they may have been affected by herbicides. Denny resident Katherine Spohn, the local postmistress, said she thinks "it's happening to an awful lot of communities wherever you have the national forests. I think people are really getting tired of it because people are getting sick, children are being born with birth defects, to normal, healthy young women."

In May 1979, following the broadcast of the television documentary "Politics of Poison," which featured the Denny situation, van Atta and another woman filed a $1.5 million claim against the U.S. Forest Service charging they had suffered miscarriages and, in van Atta's case, cancer, because of herbicide spraying. The women also brought suit against the Dow Chemical Company, the major supplier of 2,4,5-T and 2,4-D, and the Evergreen Helicopter Company, which sprayed the herbicides in the New River watershed for the Forest Service. If this case is a typical herbicide suit, years will pass before it is resolved.

In addition to filing the lawsuits, the citizens' movement in Humboldt County has fought herbicides in several other arenas. One group took its case to the North Coast Regional Water Quality Board, asking that no 2,4,5-T be permitted in the water supply.

"We felt someone in California should assume the responsibility for regulating [2,4,5-T]," said attorney John Corbett. "The regional water quality control boards have a concurrent legal jurisdiction, and though it has not been exercised in the past, it is there on the books and we felt this was an issue and this was the time to use it."

By a four-to-three vote at an emotionally charged meeting, the Water Quality Board did adopt a motion that 2,4,5-T not be permitted in the water supply. The commissioners cautioned that their decision would be reconsidered following the EPA's current review of 2,4,5-T. Nevertheless, the board's decision was a rare legal victory for the citizens of Humboldt County.

Corbett commented, on the opposition of citizens to major industries, that "the people we have are ordinary people; they're people with limited resources, and it is not unheard of to have the chemical industry spend a hundred thousand dollars on a single case, a single administrative hearing. We're dealing with highly technical matters. Consequently, it makes it very difficult to be effective."

Dr. Irving Tessler, who works in a rural medical collective in Redway, California, became frustrated similarly with the paid experts from such organizations as CAST (the Council for Agricultural Science and Technology) who appeared at herbicide hearings. "Everywhere I go," said Tessler, "the same people get flown in, the same experts that are flown in by these various companies come to testify and say this stuff is perfectly safe and nobody ever gets sick from it. I get up and say, 'I have a whole list of people that got sick, at the time of the sprays.'

"I have seen the people," Tessler continued. "They are my patients. I have been responsible for their care. I have seen the harm done by the sprays."

Tessler first became concerned about the impact of the herbicide after spraying by lumber companies in the spring of 1977. People began to come to his rural clinic complaining of sore throats, colds and the flu, illnesses that were out of season. Others experienced gastrointestinal problems, vomiting, diarrhea, uterine and urinary tract infections, and inexplicable skin rashes.

In an effort to unravel the medical mystery, Tessler prepared a rough study that compared cases during six-week periods prior to and following the spraying. "I could see some of the illnesses increased four or five fold, and I didn't know why," Tessler recalled. "When I tried to culture some of these infections in the laboratory to find a virus, nothing grew out." Tessler said he was amazed at the increase in illnesses in the period following the spraying.

And the evidence of damage kept coming in. Take the case of Ernest Freeman. An exemplary salt of the earth, born in Arcata, California, in 1904, Freeman worked in a timber company office before starting his own insurance agency in Eureka; it has become the town's largest agency. He now prefers to spend his time on his farm near Maple Creek, in Humboldt County. The farm's orchard is what he really loves. But the land is dead; the trees are burned; the fruit has developed mutant and deformed.

In 1970 Freeman's neighbor three miles down the road hired a pilot to spray some brush with 2,4,5-T and 2,4-D. There was a noxious odor in the air that day. Fall seemed to come to the orchard a month early that year, Freeman recalls.

The explanation for the early fall was obvious the following year when the apples failed to mature. Freeman sued his neighbor and the spray operator. After five years of legal maneuvering, in 1976 the suit finally came to trial. The trial took three weeks; the transcript runs eleven hundred pages. Freeman spent thousands of dollars preparing his case: commissioning aerial photographs, water samples, laboratory tests, slides of damage and more. "It was the principle I cared about," Freeman says.

When Freeman walked into the Humboldt County Court, he faced representatives of eight timber companies and nine chemical companies. Neither the neighboring landowner nor the county agriculture commissioner could furnish a copy of a permit to spray, which state law requires. The pilot, when asked if he had measured the wind's speed and direction to prevent drift, replied that he had dropped toilet paper out the window of the plane and watched it fall to the ground.

Freeman introduced aerial photographs that clearly showed burns on his land caused by drifting herbicide spray. Despite the overwhelming weight of testimony, Freeman lost the case. "There's no point in going to appeal," he said, "because there's no justice in Humboldt County. With all of the timber companies' influence, you just can't afford to go to court."

Freeman locked the transcript of the trial in his vault and then set about replanting his orchard. At seventy-six he is determined that trees will grow on his land, even if he never sees their fruit.

The McGaughey family owns a ranch next to Ernest Freeman's orchard. Theirs is an isolated place, homesteaded by Marvin McGaughey's grandfather in the 1880s. When the McGaugheys first moved to the ranch, they had no water supply —so they took their water from Ernest Freeman's spring. Their son Jeffrey was born with a rare birth defect. Marvin McGaughey describes it: "His food pipe came down into a big ball and that was it, it didn't go to his stomach. They operated on him on the third day, and he made it."

The McGaugheys had their genetic histories traced. They found no incidence of birth defects in either parent's family. Marvin McGaughey reasons, "We don't smoke. We don't take aspirins or any type of drugs, so that was completely out. What was the cause of Jeffrey's birth defects? The only thing that I could think about later was that it had to be the spray."

Verna McGaughey's concern has led her to study environmental and public-health issues in some detail. She is outraged: "How many children have been deformed by chemicals, and their parents weren't even aware they had been contaminated? In the past two years there have been five pregnancies at the Simpson Tree Nursery in Korbel, and two have terminated because of miscarriages. The connection wouldn't necessarily have been made, except . . . pellets of 2,4-D were negligently stored in an employee work area."

Silas Biggins' family used to live on a ranch adjoining the McGaugheys'. Silas is the same age as Jeffrey McGaughey. Silas was born with a cleft palate, as well as other severe birth defects.

"Silas doesn't smile much," says his mother, Sally Biggins. "He kind of has this special personality, because of all the pain he's been through. I never knew what a cleft palate was until my son was born with a cleft palate. Then, all of a sudden, ten kids would show up with cleft palates at our clinic in Eureka [the county seat]. With some children, the hard-palate cleft will affect the bone structure all the way up to the lip; then there will be a cleft lip involved."

The Bigginses took their case to a geneticist. He put them on the defensive, looking for parental neglect during Sally's pregnancy. "Now it just strikes me that I think they were asking the wrong questions," says John Biggins. "They should have asked, where were you living, what were you eating, things like that, what kind of work do you do, to search for an exposure link. They never did that."

The pieces of Humboldt County's herbicide puzzle fit together more clearly in the isolated Klamath River town of Orleans. Silas Biggins attends the Orleans Child Care Center where his father, John, is a teacher. In all, 3 of the 15 children at the center have cleft palates. The normal incidence of cleft palate is one in a thousand.

Orleans, population six hundred, is nestled in a valley surrounded by forest hillsides. The Forest Service sprayed 2,4,5-T and 2,4-D on those hillsides repeatedly throughout the 1970s. Mavis McCovy, an Orleans resident all her life and a community health worker, recalls: "They've been spraying with that herbicide around here since 1975. They sprayed in 1975 and 1976 and in Somes Bar area in 1977.

"Once, I was on the phone [with the Forest Service district office in Eureka] and I was watching them on the hillside fly over top of this water. I told them they were going over the water as I could see it. He [a Forest Service official] made some remark that I probably couldn't see that far, and his last statement was that the Forest Service never goes over water. That was it."

The statistics are appalling. In the spring and early summer of 1976 seven pregnant women lived in Orleans. Of those seven, one woman was medically aborted; one had a spontaneous miscarriage for no apparent reason in the fifth month of pregnancy; and one suffered a mole pregnancy, an unusual condition in which the fetus turns into a grape-like cluster of fetal matter. Estimates of the normal incidence of mole pregnancy vary between one in 3,000 pregnancies and one in 10,000.

Debbie Johnson, a healthy young woman then 21, recalls that when her pregnancy of several months terminated, "it wasn't even a normal miscarriage. I was proven pregnant by doctors and then there just wasn't nothing there afterwards. There was nothing that looked like a baby at all by the time it was over with."

Four children were born that summer of 1976: one with a cleft palate; one with displaced hip positions; one with an eye deformity; and one apparently healthy, normal baby.

From August 1977 to June 1978, of 23 pregnancies in Orleans two more were mole pregnancies; eight ended in spontaneous miscarriages; two children were born with congenital hip deformities and one with a cleft palate; one child died, the cause recorded as "failure to thrive." In two years, fewer than 50 percent of the pregnant women in Orleans gave birth to normal, healthy children. Community health workers became alarmed. Genetic histories were traced; the Department of Health tested the water supply for bacterial content (but not for dioxin). No cause was found for the abnormalities.

The EPA has yet to respond to the Orleans situation. Following the telecast in 1979 of "Politics of Poison," the National Institute of Environmental Health Sciences conducted a limited epidemiological study in Orleans. Preliminary results of the study did not indicate an above-average rate of miscarriage. But a close examination of the institute's unpublished study reveals that its statistical base was expanded to include more than 80 pregnancies, including those from villages as far away as 30 miles. The team conducted interviews with only a dozen women. (Among these women's children, the researchers found a forest ranger's young son born with a penis having the opening at the wrong end. The boy's mother felt that her husband's work with herbicides could have been the cause of the deformity, but she was afraid to allow her name to be used in the study out of concern for her husband's employment.) The possibility of dioxin contamination by other than direct exposure during spraying was discounted, and the records of community health workers most familiar with the cases were ignored.

This experience was not the first disillusionment with federal agencies for the families in Humboldt County. With reports of injuries caused by spraying coming in from forest communities up and down the Pacific Northwest, the EPA—in an effort to verify human exposure to 2,4,5-T and its dioxin contaminant —launched in fall 1977 a study of the milk from nursing mothers in those areas. Because dioxin dissolves in body fats, breast milk is the likely place to locate human contamination. In November 1977, the EPA took 105 samples from mothers in sprayed and nonsprayed (control) areas. The agency released its conclusions more than two years later, saying the tests "found no detectable residues of the chemical dioxin" in any of the milk at levels higher than between one and four parts per trillion, which is the lowest level that can be measured currently. "It is not known whether any dioxin is present below the limit of detection," the agency said.[13]

Even as the situation in Orleans drew national attention, and after the EPA had suspended use of 2,4,5-T on forests, in the fall of 1979 Orleans again was targeted by the U.S. Forest Service as an area to be sprayed with 2,4-D. Residents complained of receiving little or no notice of when spraying would occur. One family and their pregnant visitor were drinking coffee made with water from a creek when a forest ranger arrived to tell them that the hills above them had been sprayed that morning.

And as the spraying season for the fall of 1979 rolled around, the conflict in Denny continued. Seasonal workers, including women, employed by the Forest Service were ordered to participate in spraying operations, and they did or were fired. No big-city media were interested in covering this remote labor dispute with its far-reaching implications for occupational safety. Environmental bulletins by local groups reported that the Forest Service brought in armed security men to patrol the tracts to be sprayed and to protect helicopters. In one protest, two women and their children tried to sit on one of the helicopters, and loaded rifles were pointed at them.

Humboldt County Supervisor Eric Hedlund has joined the Hoopa and Yurok Indian tribes in filing an appeal with the Forest Service against spraying. Said Hedlund, "No possible benefit, no money, no increased yield of timber can justify any injury to a human being. Whether or not the reputation of 2,4-D for causing birth defects and miscarriages is true, the people of the Orleans community are concerned that it might be—and their concern is justified by the high incidences of such abnormal pregnancies in their area."

The dead and deformed children of Orleans and Denny are the innocent victims of the herbicide wars, casualties of the struggle to determine our values in this chemical age.

THE HERBICIDE WARS

Dioxin is teratogenic, embryotoxic, fetogenic, mutagenic and carcinogenic even at doses so low they are measured in parts per trillion. In laboratory studies where dioxin was administered, resulting deformities were cleft palates, kidney abnormalities, umbilical hernias, clubfeet, retracted tongues and congenital hip deformities. Exposure to dioxin induces lethal and sublethal chronic health effects.[14]

Dr. Irving Selikoff, director of the Environmental Sciences Laboratory at the Mount Sinai School of Medicine in New York, is one of the country's foremost authorities on environmental medicine. His group recently has completed a survey of workers in the Nitro, West Virginia, plant of the Monsanto Company, which manufactured 2,4,5-T during the late 1940s; and currently Selikoff's group is planning a field survey of the health status of workers involved in the waste-product disposal of a 2,4,5-T operation. Selikoff also has studied workers exposed to trichlorophenol, the chemical precursor of 2,4,5-T.

"I don't know any safe level for dioxin," Selikoff says. "I don't think anyone knows any safe level for dioxin. I don't think that materials that contain dioxin should be broadcast—used as weedkiller. There are a lot of other weedkillers. In fact, if the only way to get rid of every last weed is to use something that contains dioxin, I'd say let's have a few weeds."

Scientists have been unable to determine a "threshold" limit for dioxin in living creatures, below which it does no harm. A threshold of injury continues to elude scientists, while improvements in detection have permitted dioxin to be discerned in decreasing quantities—from parts per million to parts per billion to parts per trillion. The lack of a known critical threshold raises serious questions about, for example, trace amounts of dioxin present in some cattle. Even Dow Chemical's own scientists have found evidence of dioxin entering the food chain. "They collected samples of cattle that had grazed on treated land, and analyzed the fat, and," according to Dr. Louis Shadoff, a Dow senior research chemist, "in a portion of those samples we did find TCDD. [Some animals studied were] range-fed beef, which does go to market and so, yes, it is possible that some of this beef has very, very small amounts of TCDD in it."

New Jersey Congressman Andrew McGuire has a more dramatic view of the situation. "Right now, nobody can tell you if you're a housewife or somebody going into a store to buy, that the material you are buying is, in fact, safe for you and your family and your children. That's an intolerable state of affairs."

McGuire should know. As a key member of the Oversight and Investigation Subcommittee of the House Interstate and Foreign Commerce Committee, McGuire participated in a series of congressional hearings on chemical issues. In December 1978 the subcommittee published "Cancer Causing Chemicals in Food," which concluded:

> American consumers cannot be sure that the meat, poultry, fruits and vegetables they buy are not tainted with potentially dangerous pesticide residues. . . . Our examination leads us to believe that we cannot rely on the Federal government to protect us. . . . The Environmental Protection Agency's system for setting tolerances (safe, legal limits of chemical residues that may be found in specific foods) is outdated, ineffectual, and showing few signs of im-

provement. EPA's Office of Pesticide Programs is veering away from the health-oriented language of the Federal Food, Drug and Cosmetic Act, which administers the tolerance-setting program, toward the "risk-benefit" balancing language of the Federal Insecticide, Fungicide, and Rodenticide Act (FIFRA), under which pesticides are registered for use. In doing so, EPA is putting the public at greater risk. Many tolerances remain in effect for pesticides that are known to be suspect carcinogens. Scores of other tolerances are for chemicals that have never been tested for carcinogenicity and/or other equally serious effects.[15]

A recent Government Accounting Office report substantiated the subcommittee's charges. The GAO estimated that 14 percent of all meat and poultry samples tested over a two-year period contained illegal and potentially harmful residues of pesticides and animal drugs. The GAO report also charged the USDA and the Food and Drug Administration with laxity in their inspection procedures. "They cannot locate or remove the residue-containing meat and poultry because the animals are sold and often consumed before the sample analysis is computed," the GAO concluded.

In the Environmental Protection Agency, the 2,4,5-T issue is tangled in conflicts of interest and bureaucracy. Another Oversight Subcommittee report, on "Financial Conflicts of Interest in Regulatory Agencies" (February 1978), presents the case of the head of the Quality Assurance Laboratory in the EPA's Office of Pesticide Programs. This man owns shares worth approximately $11,900 in several corporations that manufacture pesticides. His job is to review chemical data for registration and to submit recommendations for the evaluation of problems concerning human health and the environment.

The story of Dr. Ralph Ross represents another kind of conflict. Dr. Ross was the first chairman of the EPA's Dioxin Implementation Plan, a supposedly impartial position. He held that office for a year and a half from the DIP's creation in 1974. Then Dr. Ross appeared at the DIP representing the Department of Agriculture, which supports the continued use of 2,4,5-T. His own position is hardly impartial: "I act as a resource agent to the Department of Agriculture in preparing the benefit studies to give EPA with reference to the Rebuttable Presumption Against Registration of 2,4,5-T. Right now, number one, we do not have an alternative [to the herbicide] which is cheaper; secondly, we do not have substantial data to tell us that this compound is being misused. So I cannot say that we are pro– 2,4,5-T, I say that we are interested in providing adequate food and fiber for this country."

If there is a pesticide "conspiracy," as the eminent entomologist Dr. Robert van den Bosch has charged,[16] then certainly it is a conspiracy supported by an "old boys" network of people like Dr. Ross, who move from one job to another in government bodies and regulatory agencies that are supposed to protect the public health.

"The Environmental Protection Agency is not doing its job," charges Dr. Melvin Reuber, one of the country's foremost pathologists, at the National Cancer Institute's Frederick Cancer Research Center.

Reuber used to work for the EPA. His last assignment there was to review safety data on 23 registered pesticides, including 2,4-D, to determine whether they cause cancer. The data on file were intended to prove the safety of the chemicals, but he found them largely worthless and so did further research of his own. That research led Reuber to believe that most of these pesticides, including 2,4-D, are carcinogens.

However, the officials to whom Reuber reported his findings did nothing about his report; and the 23 pesticides still are registered and available for use. Reuber therefore resigned from the EPA. He despairs about the quality of science there: "Members of the Cancer Assessment Group were not qualified —and the work that they were turning out was unsatisfactory. Toxicologists would do the pathology, anybody would do the epidemiology, and there were actually students—high school and college students working part time—who even prepared reports for the CAG."

Erik Olson was one of those students. "I didn't have any background in toxicology or anything. I did have some college courses in biology and chemistry. That's it." Olson was assigned to do a preliminary review of Silvex, another form of 2,4,5-T. The existence of Olson's report, which advocated suspension of Silvex, has been denied by EPA.

2,4,5-T is one of more than 40,000 pesticides that are up for reregistration. The safety data for many of those pesticides were submitted by manufacturers as long as 30 years ago. The files, minus some misplaced by various bureaucratic and physical moves, are now stored in the basement of the Waterside Mall in Washington, D.C.

"Over a seven or eight year period they were supposed to have achieved a review of all of the pesticides or 1,500 active ingredients in those pesticides," says Representative Andrew McGuire. "The fact of the matter is that they didn't get the job done and, as a result, we have serious public-health problems.

The EPA acknowledges that it will need 10 to 20 years to complete a full review of these chemicals. Steven Jellinek, assistant administrator for toxic substances, explains: "It's the lawyers. They say we can't proceed to ban a chemical until we have scientific evidence that will stand up in court. So then it's the scientists—they want to keep lowering the levels at which they can measure the effects of dioxin—from parts per million to parts per billion to parts per trillion. So we have to wait for the answers before we can recommend a suspension to the [EPA] administrator."

It is a bureaucratic formula rivaling "catch-22."

The cost in human terms of industry's promotion of herbicides cannot yet be reckoned. The Veterans Administration (VA) has been as unresponsive in dealing with servicemen exposed to Agent Orange as the EPA has been with domestic civilian cases. Robert Muller of the Council of Vietnam Veterans told a congressional subcommittee, "When we were in Vietnam there was no problem in acting aggressively. There was little hesitation about using these defoliants in the first place. It is an outrage that when the war . . . [is] over that same sense of urgency and aggressiveness seems to be lacking. . . . I am deeply fearful that many veterans may have died in Vietnam and not known it. I am deeply fearful that the body count may not be over."[17]

Veterans exposed to the chemicals have claimed injuries ranging from cancer, skin diseases and nervous disorders to birth defects in their children. By early 1980 more than 1,200 veterans had filed claims with the Veterans Administration; only two had been directly compensated. The VA continues to assert that "there is currently no medical basis upon which adverse health effects of late-post-exposure onset can be reasonably tied to Agent Orange."[18] In summer 1980, though, scientists on President Carter's interagency task force studying Agent Orange said that recent European studies "show a correlation" between herbicide exposure and cancer.[19] And in June 1980 the National Cancer Institute released two new studies that found links between dioxin and cancer in laboratory animals.[20]

In fall 1979 a U.S. district court judge ruled that suits over health effects on Vietnam war veterans would be tried in federal court. Victor Yannacone, attorney for 362 Agent Orange victims, said that theirs could become the largest class-action suit in history, with as much as $40 billion in damages claimed. As many as 46,000 veterans throughout the nation may have been exposed. Material is being gathered, too, for a second class-action suit, involving more than 200 veterans from Texas to California. (Exposed veterans should contact Swords To Ploughshares in San Francisco, Citizen Soldier in New York City, or the Vietnam Veterans of America in Washington, D.C., for further information and advice.)

After nine years of study, on March 1, 1979, the EPA declared its emergency suspension of 2,4,5-T and Silvex use on forests and along highway rights of way. The emergency was based on "imminent hazards" to pregnant women. The agency has continued to permit the use of these chemicals hazardous to pregnant women, on cattle grazing land and rice paddies. Eleven chemical companies and industry associations have appealed the suspension.

The EPA admits that its cancellation proceedings against

2,4,5-T may not be resolved for more than two years; the EPA administrator's final decision on 2,4,5-T, whatever it will be, is expected to be challenged in the courts. And although 2,4,5-T has gained more public attention, the closely related chemical 2,4-D also has come into question. The EPA announced on April 20, 1978, that 2,4-D had been selected for an intensive pre-RPAR (Rebuttable Presumption Against Registration) review because of tests indicating that its "risk criteria" was met or exceeded for cancer, birth defects and effects on nontarget organisms. (An RPAR functions as public notice that the registration of a particular chemical is up for review.) Two years later, on April 19, 1980, the agency issued the requirement that manufacturers of 2,4-D provide more information on the chemical's health effects, charging that "significant information gaps exist on the effects of 2,4-D."[21]

2,4-D and 2,4,5-T are nearly identical, differing chemically in that 2,4,5-T has one carbon atom where 2,4-D has a chlorine atom. The two herbicides have had extremely similar effects on test animals and in toxicological studies.[22] But 2,4-D is still at the beginning of the regulatory marathon that has been unable to deal with 2,4,5-T effectively in a decade.

The politics of poison are perpetuated; the issue is shuffled from the bureaucracy of the regulatory agencies to the inadequacy of legislative hearings to the inaction of the people's elected representatives.

As the spraying season of 1980 approached, the northern California herbicide wars were continuing. A dozen people—nearly half the population of a hamlet called Forks of Salmon, 20 miles upriver from Orleans—traveled to Forest Service offices in San Francisco for a confrontation with Chief Ranger Zane Grey Smith. "They're going to spray 408 acres of national forest land with 2,4-D, Atrazine and Dalapon [all herbicides]—and they'll be spraying within fifteen hundred feet of our homes," said group spokesman Fred Mindlin.

"We'd like to see more than just an end to aerial spraying," according to Mindlin. "What we'd really like to see is a cooperative task force with citizen participation to design an 'integrated pest-management' program for both plant and insect pests. A lot of people in our area do not regard these native plants as pests."

The timber companies apparently do consider some native plants pests. And they have sternly resisted any move away from the use of the herbicides. "There just aren't any real alternatives," claims Jim Reydalius, of Simpson Timber. "The one most often mentioned is manual labor. That could be done, but at very, very high cost."

Yet the California Economic Development Department has determined that hiring people to do the work of the sprays would increase the production cost of lumber by less than 2 percent.[23] And throughout the north coast forests, unemployed forest workers already have formed cooperatives to exploit hardwood wastes from the redwood forests. Near Redway, in Humboldt County, FLAPCO (Forest Lands and Products Cooperative) has 75 members operating a portable eight-foot mill to clean up the material that big corporations leave behind. Then the mill, called a Mighty Mite, is trucked to a new location. "With wood returning to importance in the energy-short economy of the 1980s, FLAPCO's objective is an efficient use of forest waste," says forester Jim deMulling, who is FLAPCO's chairman.

The pilot project of another forestry collective, GOATS (Group for Organized Alternatives to Toxic Sprays), and the Forest Service also has indicated that manual brush-clearing is an effective alternative to herbicides, in addition to creating jobs. Forest Service Ranger Zane Grey Smith used the results of a GOATS experimental program in the Six Rivers National Forest in reaching this assessment: "We found," says Smith, "that people can perform several tasks in addition to conifer release, including stream clearance and erosion control, making the entire operation more cost-efficient than the use of chemicals."

Not to mention that using manual labor is far less hazardous, for both the workers and the people living in the forests. Many people who live there consider the real costs of herbicide use to be vastly greater than the financial requirements of chemical companies and helicopter firms. "I don't know," says farmer Calvin Hathenbrook. "Just take a look at that white stuff on my drain pipe. Just seems that nothing will grow there any more."

NOTES

1. Council for Agricultural Science and Technology, *The Phenoxy Herbicides*, 1975.

2. Dr. Samuel Epstein testified on July 22, 1980, that Dr. Julius Johnson, a former Dow Chemical Company vice president, told a Senate panel in 1970 that Dow had known of the contaminant in 1964. See "House Hearing Is Told Dow Knew In 1964 That Defoliant Was Toxic," *New York Times*, July 23, 1980.

3. Thomas Whiteside, *The Pendulum and the Toxic Cloud* (Yale University Press, 1979), p. 5.

4. *The Phenoxy Herbicides.*

5. Employment Development Department, State of California, Health and Welfare Agency, *The Employment Effects of SB 1357*, May 30, 1978.

6. United States Department of Agriculture, *Pesticide Review*, 1978, p. 5.

7. Ibid., p. 3.

8. For a detailed account of the tangled regulatory history of 2,4,5-T in the years 1970–1974, see Whiteside, *The Pendulum and the Toxic Cloud.*

9. "CAST-Industry Tie Raises Credibility Concerns," *Bioscience*, vol. 29, no. 1 (January 1979).

10. National Research Council, Committee on the Effects of Herbicides in Vietnam, Assembly of Life Sciences, *The Effects of Herbicides in South Vietnam* (NAS, 1974).

11. Whiteside, *The Pendulum and the Toxic Cloud*, p. 3.

12. *Involuntary Exposure to Agent Orange and other Toxic Spraying.* Hearings before the Subcommittee on Oversight and Investigations of the House Interstate and Foreign Commerce Committee, June 26, 27, 1979, p. 134.

13. Environmental Protection Agency, "Dioxin Not Detected In Mother's Milk" (press release), January 14, 1980.

14. "Toxic and Teratogenic Effects of 2,4,5-T and 2,3,7,8-TCDD," statement by Dr. Theodor Sterling to Wisconsin State Assembly Committee on Natural Resources, March 19, 1975. Dr. Sterling served on the National Academy of Sciences' Advisory Committee on 2,4,5-T to the Administrator of the EPA during 1970 and 1971. The group also conducted field research in Vietnam.

15. Oversight and Investigations Subcommittee, House Interstate and Foreign Commerce Committee, *Cancer-Causing Chemicals in Food* (Washington, 1978), p. 39.

16. Robert Van den Bosch, *The Pesticide Conspiracy* (Doubleday, 1978).

17. *Involuntary Exposure,* p. 21.

18. Testimony of Max Cleland, Veterans Administration, before Subcommittee on Medical Facilities and Benefits of the House Veterans Affairs Committee, February 25, 1980.

19. "Link Between Agent Orange and Cancer Found in Europe Study, U.S. Panel Says," *Wall Street Journal,* August 4, 1980.

20. "Two Studies for National Institute Link Herbicide to Cancer in Animals," *New York Times,* June 27, 1980.

21. "EPA Asking Producers to Submit More Data on Versatile Herbicide," *Wall Street Journal,* April 30, 1980.

22. E. A. Woolson et al., "Survey of Polychlorodibenzo-p-dioxin Content in Selected Pesticides," *Agri. Food Chem* 20 (1972), pp. 351–354. One of the 28 samples of 2,4-D contained 10 ppm of hexachlorodibenzo-p-dioxin (HCDD), but levels below .5 ppm were considered nondetectable.

23. *The Employment Effects of SB1357.* Also see cover letter from Martin R. Glick, Director of EDD, to State Senator Peter H. Behr.

Chapter 8

Love Canal

RUSSELL MOKHIBER
LEONARD SHEN

In 1966, PATRICIA and Peter Bulka moved their family to the LaSalle district of Niagara Falls, New York. They were moving to a community filled with growing families and young children; the local elementary school was only one block from their home. The realtor who sold the Bulkas their house promised that a park would be built in a vacant field adjoining their backyard. To Mrs. Bulka, LaSalle looked like a good place to raise a family.

The park never was built, though the vacant field was used as a playground—on rainy days a muddy one—by John and Joey Bulka and the other neighborhood children. In the spring of 1966, while playing in the field, Joey fell into a muddy ditch and John went in to pull him out. The boys came home "covered with this oily gook," says Patricia Bulka. "I threw their clothes away and scrubbed them down good, but the smell didn't go away for two or three weeks."[1]

Alarmed by the persistent odor, the Bulkas called the Niagara County Health Department and reported the unusual effects of the accident. Health Department employees arrived at the field, took samples, and told the Bulkas that "nothing was wrong." Although partly relieved by this judgment, Patricia Bulka incurred wrath and ridicule from her neighbors. "Our neighbors were mad at us because we called the Health Department," she said. "They wouldn't talk to us for the longest time "[2]

Twelve years later the world learned that the field Joey and John and countless other children had used as a playground was the top portion of a dumping ground in which a chemical company had buried hundreds of 55-gallon metal drums containing nearly 22,000 tons of chemical refuse. The waste material consisted of 82 chemical compounds, including some of the most deadly substances known.[3] Today Joey Bulka suffers from chronic ear problems that began after he fell into the ditch. His brother, John, suffers from chronic respiratory problems. Other area residents are plagued with a wide variety of medical problems that include miscarriages, birth defects, epilepsy, liver abnormalities, sores, rectal bleeding and headaches. For the Bulkas, and for the hundreds of other afflicted families of the "Love Canal" area of LaSalle, the County Health Department's assurance that nothing was wrong has been terribly costly. But that error was only one small link in the thirty-year-long chain of events that made possible this social catastrophe.

THE WITCH'S END OF FAIRYLAND

To travelers everywhere, Niagara Falls is known as the honeymoon capital of the world. The city is built on the banks of the Niagara River and around one of the most spectacular waterfalls on earth.

Every minute at Niagara Falls, hundreds of thousands of tons of water plunge hundreds of feet into a gorge filled with huge boulders, creating a mist that covers the local landscape, cleanses the air, and attracts thousands of tourists each year to view what has been called one of the seven wonders of the world.

For the residents of the city of Niagara Falls, however, tourism always has taken a back seat to the heavy industry that dominates economic, social and political life. Even the tourists who flock to the falls through the southeastern corridor along Buffalo Avenue can't escape the gritty scene—the industrial plants lined up side by side, emitting long puffs of smoke from tall, sooty smokestacks. Passing them on a "nasal sight-seeing tour" of the city,[4] young children roll up car windows and cover their noses with their hands and clothes. Their parents, too, roll up car windows, but the adults make no effort to cover their noses. The adults accept the noxious smells of the city as part of their lives, understanding a basic fact of life in Niagara Falls: The companies who pollute their air—the Olin Corporation, Union Carbide Corporation, DuPont, Hooker Chemical and Plastics Corporation—are the same companies that sign the residents' weekly paychecks. They believe—or did believe—that they have no choice but to roll up the windows and drive on through what one writer has called "The Witch's End of Fairyland."[5]

Less than a mile from this heavily industrialized section of Buffalo Avenue lies the 16-acre residential area that surrounds the field known as "Love Canal." The canal was named after William Love, a nineteenth-century entrepreneur who had planned to construct a navigable power canal between the upper and lower portions of the Niagara River. Love envisioned a model city built around a massive industrial complex with access to inexpensive hydroelectric power and the major economic markets of the Northeast. He began digging his canal in 1894, but as the country swung into a period of full-scale economic depression, Love's financial backers pulled out of the deal, and the model-city project came to a halt. The partially completed canal was abandoned and eventually became known to city residents as the "Love Canal."[6]

Over the years, rains filled the canal with water, and children in the area used it as a swimming hole in the summertime and as a skating rink in the winter. To the local residents, the canal became a recreational asset where people could swim, skate and visit with neighbors and friends. From across Buffalo Avenue, however, the Hooker Chemical and Plastics Corporation was eyeing the canal as a potential dumpsite for its chemical waste products. In 1942, Hooker put an end to the swimming and skating by negotiating an agreement with the county power company, which owned the land, to dispose of wastes in the canal. Five years after dumping began there, Hooker bought the disposal site and surrounding land.[7] At the time, organized citizen protests against attacks on the environment rarely were contemplated. Nineteen forty-seven was 15 years before Rachel Carson exposed those who had "silenced the voices of spring."[8] Not for 29 years was a major piece of federal legislation designed expressly to govern the dumping of hazardous wastes. Besides, the purchase was not immediately seen as an attack on the environment. Residents were annoyed at the loss of their recreation area to a dumpsite, but they expressed little antagonism to public officials or to Hooker executives, and the fact that the waste products came from a chemical manufacturing plant was of little, if any, added significance to them.

Hooker drained Love Canal, lined it with a clay casing, and began transporting chemical waste products to it from the company's main Niagara Falls production facility at Buffalo Avenue. The chemical refuse was transported in 55-gallon metal drums that were placed in the canal and covered with a clay casing and dirt. Sometimes liquid wastes were drained from their drums directly into the canal.[9] Ultimately, grass and weeds grew atop the covered canal, creating a field that gave no indication of the grave of substances beneath the surface.

What lay beneath the surface was 43.6 million pounds of 82 different chemical substances: oils, solvents and other manufacturing residues. The mixture included benzene, a chemical known to cause leukemia and anemia; chloroform, a carcinogen that affects the nervous, respiratory and gastrointestinal systems; lindane, which causes convulsions and extra production of white blood cells; trichloroethylene, a carcinogen that also attacks the nervous system, the genes and the liver; and methylene chloride, whose effects include chronic respiratory distress and death.[10] The list of chemicals buried in the Love Canal seems endless, and the accompanying list of their acute and chronic effects on human beings reads like an encyclopedia of medical illness and abnormality.

Of the 82 chemicals dumped at the canal, though, one evokes more fear and anxiety among scientists and doctors than all the others: trichlorophenol. The 200 tons of trichlorophenol wastes dumped at the canal contained an estimated 130 pounds of a chemical called dioxin, or TCDD (2,3,7,8-tetrachlorodiben-zo-para-dioxin); 3 ounces of dioxin can kill more than a million people.[11] The compound is a contaminant created during the manufacture of certain herbicides and disinfectants, including the now infamous hexachlorophene. Today scientists warn dioxin has many harmful effects on the human body. "Dioxin is the most poisonous small molecule known to man. It is also one of the most powerful carcinogens known," says Matthew Meselson, professor of biochemistry at Harvard. "We have not yet found any dosage at which it is safe, at which it has no observable effect . . . it is possible that dioxin is cumulative in our bodies. It is quite stable and is soluble in fat, but not water, and will build up in body fat."[12] But in the 1940s, when the Hooker wastes were buried in the canal, warnings about dioxin were little known. Yet some evidence of the danger did exist. Dr. Robert Mobbs, a Boston physician active in research on pesticide control, published evidence in 1948 that lindane, one of the chemicals dumped at the canal site, was "a possible cancer-causing agent." Mobbs would later dispute Hooker's claim that the company was ignorant of this danger.

Twenty years later the world learned about the potent effects of dioxin when the United States used 2,4,5-T—an herbicide inevitably contaminated with dioxin—in Agent Orange to defoliate the Vietnamese countryside. Rural Vietnamese reported shocking birth defects, and thousands of servicemen exposed to Agent Orange now are afflicted with serious health problems that they and many scientists attribute to dioxin poisoning. In July 1977 the attention of the entire world was riveted on the dangers of dioxin; an ICMESA Corporation plant in Seveso, Italy, producing trichlorophenol exploded, sending a "toxic cloud" over the countryside. Animals literally died in the streets, people developed severe skin lesions, and hundreds of Seveso residents were forced from their homes.[13]

Until 1978 Vietnam and Seveso were the two sites where scientists could study the effects of dioxin on non-industrial human populations. Then a third was added to the list: Niagara Falls, New York.

LIKE WAVING A RED FLAG IN FRONT OF A BULL

"Upon my arrival at the Hooker dump," wrote Niagara Falls City Fire Chief Edwin S. Foster to City Manager Percy Weaver, "the wind was blowing from a westerly direction and the area was permeated by the odor of chemicals and fumes emitting from a pile of chemical wastes at the dump." The letter was dated November 2, 1964. Foster addressed his comments to the chief executive of the city instead of an executive at Hooker because a decade earlier Niagara Falls' Board of Education had bought the dumpsite from Hooker. Foster was alarmed by what he witnessed on that fall day in 1964. He wrote that he had observed a person "using a high lift to cover this fuming substance with earth" and warned that "this unknown substance was an irritant to breath and obnoxious to smell. . . ." His opinion was that the noxious material "could be a detriment to the health and well-being of residents in this area," and he recommended that the "proper authorities be notified and remedial action be taken."[14]

Foster's recommendation went unheeded by city officials. It was not the first warning to be ignored. As early as June 1958 the City Air Pollution Control Department notified Hooker that several children had been burned by wastes surfacing at the canal. Hooker sent two men to investigate. They found that wastes had surfaced on both the north and south sides of the canal, and that benzene hexachloride, a carcinogen that can poison the nervous system and cause convulsions, was exposed. The investigators also learned, as a memo from a supervisor put it a few days later, "that the entire area is being used by children as a playground even though it is not officially designated for that purpose." After discussing the problems, Hooker officials decided not to take any action beyond notifying the school board of the incident.[15] Testifying before Congress many years later, Jerome Wilkenfeld, the Hooker official who wrote the June 1958 memo, said the company failed to warn residents of the dangers because "we did not feel that we could do this without incurring substantial liabilities for implying that the current owners of the property were [taking] . . . inadequate care [of] . . . the property."[16]

The Board of Education had owned the property since May 1953, when its nine members had agreed to purchase a piece of land the board knew to be filled with tons of chemical wastes. At the time, the board, like most other school boards throughout the country, was experiencing the massive post-World War II baby boom. The board members, aware of the need for more grade schools to accommodate the thousands of new baby-boom children, began an ambitious land-acquisition program with an eye toward building new school facilities throughout the city. In 1953, as part of this program, the board began consideration of a parcel of land in the LaSalle section of Niagara Falls. At the time, LaSalle was a growing residential area that urgently needed a new elementary school. Area parents were pushing for construction of a new facility closer to their homes, and the grass-covered field appeared to the board to be an ideal location.

The location was ideal on all counts but one: Underneath the grassy field lay the 55-gallon metal drums containing a witches' brew of hazardous chemical wastes dumped by the previous owner, the Hooker Chemical and Plastics Corporation.

At the meeting of the school board on a spring evening of 1953, each member was presented with a proposed copy of the transfer papers drawn up by the Hooker lawyers. Hooker's deed advised that the land in question had "been filled, in whole or in part, to the present ground level . . . with waste products resulting from the manufacturing of chemicals by . . . [Hooker] at its plant in the City of Niagara Falls, New York," and that "the [Board of Education] . . . assumes all risks and liability incident to the use thereof."[17] With the insertion of these words into the deed, Hooker sought to free itself from any potential liability for damage by the chemicals to the neighboring environment, people or property. Although two of the board members were attorneys, no legal training was necessary to pick up the meaning behind the language of the deed, in light of the circumstances of the proposed sale.

The board was in a vulnerable position. With a limited budget, the board desperately needed to purchase land, so that construction of new elementary schools could begin. Without a series of quick, inexpensive purchases, some school children might not have schools in the upcoming years. Hooker, on the other hand, owned a piece of property in an up-and-coming residential area of the city beneath which the company had buried a chemical garbage dump.

Hooker offered to sell this land to the board for one dollar and the majority of the school board members took this to mean that Hooker, as a concerned corporate citizen, was offering its land as a gift to the city of Niagara Falls. Geraldine Mason, former director of elementary education, reported that "talk about parents wanting more schools and about the generosity of Hooker for donating the land" dominated the school board's conversations that day.[18]

One of the few city officials who saw through Hooker's "gift" was Ralph Boniello, the attorney who represented the Board of Education during the negotiations for the land. Both prior to and during the board's May 7 meeting, Boniello urged that the members hire a chemical engineer to study the Love Canal site before they accepted the land from Hooker. Boniello also warned the board of the "risk and possible liability" in accepting the land on Hooker's terms. He pointed to a second clause in the deed that made clear what Hooker expected in return for the single dollar: "As a part of the consideration for this conveyance . . . no claim, suit, action or demand of any nature whatsoever shall ever be made by the [Board] . . . for injury to a person or persons, including death resulting therefrom, or loss of or damage to property caused by reason of the presence of said industrial wastes."[19]

Boniello felt obliged to warn the board about the risks the city would assume if the deed were accepted, but the members failed to listen, or they ignored their attorney's warnings. "It was self-evident that there were chemicals buried," Boniello said, "but nobody on the board or the administration questioned the acquisition, as far as I know. I warned them because the release clause was like waving a red flag in front of a bull."[20]

The 99th Street School was unlike other elementary schools in Niagara Falls. Built atop the old Love Canal, it had no basement and no swimming pool. Any digging at the canal site had the potential of rupturing the containment drums and allowing the chemical wastes to escape.[21] Even the daily task of reaching the school from one of the neighborhood houses was delicate for many of the 400-odd students. On some days, at seven o'clock in the morning, terrible odors would fill the neighborhood, forcing the children walking to school to cover their noses until the odors had vanished. The Love Canal children, already exposed to a wide variety of similar odors throughout the city, gradually grew accustomed to the adulterated air and suffered quietly.

Through the fifties and sixties, the baby-boom students came and left the 99th Street School, attending classes, playing in the ballpark and adjacent field and eventually moving on to junior high schools in other parts of the city. For many of the school's graduates, however, leaving the school did not necessarily mean leaving the canal, because their homes were situated adjacent to the old dumpsite. The students who lived in these homes, no matter what schools they attended, always returned to the canal in the late afternoon—or, if they attended college, on weekends or vacations. For these students, and for their parents, the canal was home.

As time passed, unusual events besides the occasional early-morning odors signaled that something was rotten in the Love Canal neighborhood. For instance, children were attracted to a neighboring field by unusual rocks that, when thrown against a wall or concrete, would explode spectacularly. "We used to go over and pick up these things called firerocks," explains Terence McCartney, a long-time resident. "They were red and like pumice stone. You'd throw them on a street and they'd spark off and catch on fire. I wasn't supposed to play in there because one kid had some in his pocket one time and the friction set them off and he was burned pretty bad. But, you know, we played there anyway." McCartney went on to work in the chemical industry, where he learned what the "firerocks" were that he'd played with as a child. "I worked for Hooker for about eight years when I grew up," he says, "and that's how I found out that the things were chunks of phosphorous."[22] Hooker's infirmary regularly received calls for information from parents whose children had been injured by chemicals while playing in the area.[23]

Sometimes the residents noticed that the odors were stronger than usual, as though they were coming from the basements of people's own houses. For Alice Warner, the onslaught took on an added dimension whenever a noxious white cloud hovered over her home, causing its paint eventually to blacken, and causing a burning sensation in her eyes. Down the block from the Warner house, at the baseball field adjacent to the schoolyard, large crater-like holes appeared in the outfield, requiring that maintenance crews fill them in with dirt and smooth out the field. One year, the area around third base was sucked into a large depression in the ground.

Despite these frightening events, the residents of Love Canal were reluctant to seek advice or official help. As Mrs. Bulka discovered, neighbors often ridiculed anyone who posed questions about the air or land or water quality in the city. Hooker was, after all, an industrial giant in Niagara Falls—the company most important to the city's economy, employing 3,200 people, including many residents of Love Canal. For these people, it was better to be quietly grateful to the company that paid the bills than to question company or city executives about the effects of the chemicals in the dump.

This attitude, which prevailed throughout the city from the mid-fifties to the mid-seventies, allowed the steady evolution of a disaster to go unheeded. Firerocks, strong odors, children playing in oily substances, noxious clouds, burning eyes, a school without a basement, a fire chief's warning, a deed with a "red flag," potholes in a baseball diamond, and medical problems caused by "something in the environment"—all came and went with no organized response from the victims and with no action from government officials or the corporate executives whose company had dumped the wastes.

OILY GOOK AND SUMP-PUMPS

In the spring of 1976, as one of the heaviest snowfalls in the city's history melted away, Love Canal–area residents began talking among themselves about the unusual persistence of the horrible smells and noxious odors filling the neighborhood. These new odors were even stronger than those of previous years, and residents began searching for the source. Many found that the smells were coming from the basements of their own homes. In the summer of 1976, Patricia Bulka discovered that a black, oily substance was oozing through the drainage holes and into her basement. Alarmed, the Bulkas obtained a sump-pump and began pumping the gook out of their homes and into the city sewers. "The stuff coming into the basement made the air stink," complained a neighbor.[24] He, too, began using a sump-pump to rid his basement of the substance. Soon, many of the residents whose homes bordered the canal were occupied with the black, oily substance, and sump-pumps were in great demand.

One resident, apparently disturbed by this new development at the canal, wrote a letter to the *Niagara Gazette*, the city's major newspaper, expressing concern for the residents of the area and especially for the children who attended the 99th Street School. The *Gazette* assigned reporter David Pollak to the story, and on October 3, 1976, his article, "Hooker Dump Troubles Neighbors in LaSalle," appeared, with the following lead sentence: "Civilization has crept to the doorstep of a former Hooker waste deposit site, and the combination contains the elements of an unnatural horror story."[25]

For the first time in the almost thirty years since Hooker began dumping its chemical wastes at the Love Canal, the residents of Niagara County and western New York State began to learn about fellow New Yorkers who were living with a decades-old threat to their health. Chemicals were seeping up through the several feet of permeable soil that covered the bathtub-shaped, clay-lined canal; the compounds were moving into the air, water and soil of the Love Canal neighborhood.

Two days after the *Gazette* ran the article, Pollak returned to the Bulka home to take samples of the oily substance in their basement. He brought the samples to Chem-Trol Pollution Services, a company that had been the subject of several uncomplimentary articles in the *Gazette*. Chem-Trol did a big business in western New York in the transportation and dumping of chemical wastes, and one of its chief customers was the Hooker Chemical and Plastics Company.

Chem-Trol agreed to analyze the sample. The initial analysis indicated that the chemicals found in the samples taken from the Bulka home indeed were products of Hooker's chemical operation.[26] Because the chemicals were wastes from one of Chem-Trol's largest clients, company officials agreed to have further analysis done for the *Gazette* only on the condition that the newspaper would not identify the lab as its source.

The Chem-Trol analysis produced startling results. The black, oily substance leaking out of the dump and into the Bulka home was a horrendous brew of 15 organic chemicals, including three chlorinated hydrocarbons that are toxic by inhalation, ingestion and skin absorption. In its article reporting these findings, the *Gazette* quoted a "private chemist" describing the chemical combination as "certainly a health hazard" and an "environmental concern." The private chemist (Chem-Trol) suggested that the chemicals should be "removed from the ground if they are not entirely isolated from human exposure."[27]

Getting residents out of the canal area and away from the chemicals was the last thing on the minds of Hooker executives or government officials in the fall of 1976. Hooker executives refused to comment on the early *Gazette* articles, and the first official action taken by Niagara County Health Department officials was to threaten legal action against the Love Canal residents—for removing the foreign chemicals from the basements of their homes into the city's sewer system. Department officials, claiming that the chemicals homeowners were pumping into the city sewer system were poisonous to the fish and algae of the Niagara River, into which the sewer system fed, termed the sump-pump operations "illegal." The department threatened to seek $25 fines against the residents for each violation. The county also refused to clean up the chemicals: "It is far better that the material be isolated at the places people live in," reasoned George Amery, a senior county health official, "rather than to be pumped directly into the river."[28]

In mid-November 1976 it appeared the state would rescue Love Canal residents from the incompetence and insensitivity of the county officials—the New York State Department of Environmental Conservation (NYDEC) announced that it had completed a water survey near the canal site, and the results were expected in several weeks. But not until April of the next year were NYDEC results made public. For the six-month interim, canal residents still were unaware of exactly what dangers they had been exposed to. (The NYDEC also urged the city of Niagara Falls to investigate citizen complaints. The city hired consultants in January 1977 and again in February 1978 to conduct a hydrogeological study of the area and to make recommendations—but the city failed to take remedial action until the state stepped in during August 1978.)

Over the winter of 1976–77, Love Canal faded out of the public eye. But when the winter receded, the odors, the black, oily substances and the sump-pumps returned to the Love Canal neighborhood. When they appeared, so did George Amery, the official from the Niagara County Health Department who had threatened the residents with fines for dumping the sludge entering their houses. Amery assured residents no evidence existed that toxic residues seeping from the waste landfill posed an imminent health threat to the families along the perimeter of the canal. "The materials can be quite odorous and very discomforting," he said, "but we hope that the condition will be corrected before any health hazard occurs." Amery went on to advise parents that the black, oily substance was "potentially dangerous," and that "the kids should be warned by their parents to stay away from it by all means."[29]

Area residents listening to the county health officials had ample opportunities to become confused. First, the homeowners were told to stop pumping the gook into the sewers. Next, they were told to leave it alone until corrective actions could be taken. Finally, they were advised to keep their kids away from the basements where the substance was accumulating. Regardless of the difficulty of drawing workable conclusions from the county's advice, it was worthless simply because the families could not live in houses where the noxious chemicals were allowed to build up and taint the air. Parents were receiving conflicting reports on the health effects of the chemicals, too. Did the chemicals pose a "health hazard," as the *Gazette* had reported the year before, or were county officials to be believed when they said the families encountered "no imminent health threat"?

The County Health Department's hope that the condition would be corrected before any hazard occurred rested upon a $400,000 project planned by the city, aimed at halting the spread of toxic chemicals buried at the canal. After spending $20,195 on the research and investigation, however, the city rejected the plan as being too expensive. A year later, the estimated cleanup costs had reached $50 million, or more than 100 times the estimated cost of the rejected project.

The winter of 1977–78, too, passed with the Love Canal residents still in their homes, fighting off the effects of the chemicals—fighting alone with no help from local politicians or Hooker executives.

RUSTED DRUMS AND LEUKEMIA

Though state and city officials were reluctant to confront the problems at Love Canal, they could not be ignored indefinitely. In fact, as 1978 wore on and the situation became clearer, it was worse even than had been feared. Surveys begun by the New York State Department of Health (DOH) in the spring found that 95 percent of the homes in the first ring of those constructed around the canal were contaminated by chemicals. The EPA determined in May that the toxic vapors in the basements presented "a serious health threat."[30] What's more, people living near the former dumpsite were experiencing as many as 3.5 times the expected number of miscarriages, as well as a disproportionate number of birth defects and spontaneous abortions. The state found that the women who suffered miscarriages had lived at the canal an average of about 18.5 years—7 years longer than the average for women who didn't miscarry.[31] Residents, their memories jogged by the newly released reports, began recalling medical problems they now believed were caused by the chemicals at the dumpsite. Mrs. Timothy Schroeder, a canal-area resident, suffered from burning eyes and skin ailments. Her daughter, Sheri, was born with a cleft palate, a double row of bottom teeth, a deformed ear, eardrums that disintegrated, bone blockage in her left nasal passage, a hole in her heart, and slight retardation. In 1978, Sheri began to lose her hair in large clumps. Donald Donoughe, who lived at the northern end of the canal, had a cardiac arrest after swimming in an above-ground pool installed at a home close to the site. He had five children, one of whom was born and raised next to Love Canal. The other four were in generally good health, but the "canal child" suffered with a heart murmur.[32] One woman living in the area had three successive miscarriages before giving birth to a child. The baby was born with three ears. Her second child also was born with deformed ears.[33]

For Love Canal residents, doctors only confirmed the obvious when they suggested that the chemicals "no doubt" had affected residents' health. Indeed, the toxic effects of the chemicals found at the dumpsite coincided with the medical complaints by neighboring residents.[34] Drowsiness and depression in children coincided with the known toxic effects of benzene, methylene chloride, and carbon tetrachloride, all dumped at the canal. Similarly, liver disorders that had been reported can be caused by several canal chemicals, including chloroform, toluene and tetrachloroethylene.[35]

These new reports of high rates of medical illnesses and diseases forced Hooker to abandon its "no comment" posture and to put forth its best defense. Hooker executives claimed that the chemicals were enclosed in 55-gallon metal drums and that the drums in turn were buried in a sealed vault at the canal site. This was considered by Hooker at the time to be a responsible waste-dumping practice. Hooker blamed the escape of the chemicals on excavations which occured at the canal after the land was deeded over to the city. According to Hooker, in building the homes at Love Canal, the housing contractors may have scraped some of the clay off the vault, thus allowing rainwater and melting snow to fill the ditch and to raise the chemicals to the surface.[36] Hooker disowned any liability for damages or injury that might arise. Company officials claimed that by accepting the deed of land the Board of Education absolved Hooker of any responsibility.

Hooker Vice President John Riordan invoked this defense when questioned by reporters on NBC television's "Today Show." Responding to questions about Hooker's dumping practices at the canal, Riordan claimed that "years ago, many companies weren't aware of the hazards of the wastes. We [Hooker] were not aware of them at the time." One of the viewers of the "Today" program that day was the same Dr. Robert Mobbs who had conducted the research into lindane 30 years ago. Mobbs was furious over Riordan's comments and charged that Hooker "damn well knew" that the compounds it deposited in the canal were extremely dangerous to human beings. As evidence to support his claim, Mobbs cited his study of the chemical lindane, which later had been found at the canal site: "I presented evidence that it was a possible cancer-causing agent in 1948." Mobbs' findings had been published in the December 1948 issue of the *Journal of the American Medical Association,* and had been publicized further by Washington columnist Drew Pearson. "Did Hooker come looking for the evidence?", asked Mobbs. "Like hell they did. They ignored, minimized and suppressed the facts. . . . If I found it [the danger] out, why couldn't they?"[37]

And even if Hooker was unaware of the clinical evidence of danger, the company had received the phone calls by worried parents to its infirmary after children came home burned or otherwise hurt by surfacing wastes. The Love Canal dumpsite wasn't the only one causing such problems for local children. At Hooker's 102nd Street dumpsite (which had been used by the Olin Corporation as well), situated only a few miles from Love Canal, children also were being burned by exposed wastes. In July 1967 Richard Sirianni and Michael Gigliotti, two local teenagers, wandered into the 102nd Street dump. The pressure of their steps created sharp popping sounds around them. When they began to run, the popping increased and chemical wastes kicked up from the ground, hitting Gigliotti in the chest, burning his shirt and wrapping him in smoke. Investigators from Hooker concluded a few days later that the explosions were caused by exposed chlorates and phosphorous.[38] Several years later Hooker considered selling the land to the city for a park or residential development.[39]

As the extent of the injuries inflicted on the Love Canal residents drew international news coverage, the authorities were pressed to move in. The local government officials had made an initial policy decision that trying to contain the leaching chemicals and isolate them was cheaper and easier than to evacuate the residents. The local governments could not agree, however, who would pay for the cleanup project. Love Canal residents looked for action, but in the summer of 1978 the only action was bureaucratic finger-pointing. New York State ordered Niagara County to clean up Love Canal. The county in turn ordered the city of Niagara Falls to clean up the canal, but the city refused to act on the grounds that the cleanup was within the jurisdiction of the county. The city resented the county orders to do the job, and the city's bond counsel warned that the city would not be able to borrow money for a cleanup and would not have the legal right to spend tax dollars on any remedy for the canal problem. Meanwhile the county legislature, fearing that it would be hit with the costs of cleaning up the canal, refused to investigate charges that its health commissioner was negligent in not acting sooner upon complaints received as early as 1970 from canal residents. Instead, the legislators chose to place the blame at the feet of the federal government. "During World War II," recalled one county legislator, "all the chemical companies were here and Niagara Falls was made a damn cesspool with what was dumped and buried. If this is to be cleaned up across the city, let's get the Feds to come in here and do it. They're responsible for this mess in the first place."[40]

On August 2, 1978, with national press and television crews descending on the city, State Health Commissioner Robert Whalen finally intervened—two years after the dangers at the dump had been made public. Whalen declared the Love Canal situation "an official emergency" and urged that young children and pregnant women move away from the area immediately. He also urged the Board of Education to delay the September opening of the 99th Street School to minimize the exposure of more than 400 school-age children to waste chemicals.

As the pace of events quickened, residents organized to coordinate their efforts in seeking relief. Getting the government to pay for a multimillion-dollar evacuation and relocation of the hundreds of families living on the periphery of the canal was a monumental task for the newly created Love Canal Homeowners Association, which represented 90 percent of all area residents. The task was made no easier by the county health commissioner, who—despite all the evidence indicating the chemicals posed a serious health threat to children and adults alike—told residents that "most of the chemicals are not a problem as far as adverse effects," adding that "the stuff you smell isn't necessarily anything to worry about."[41]

But new information available to the governor's office showed that air samples taken from many of the Love Canal–area homes were contaminated by organic chemical compounds, some of which were carcinogenic. The governor's office estimated that as many as 300 families would have to be evacuated from their homes and relocated in other parts of the city. At first, however, the state ordered the evacuation of only 100 families. As these first families gathered their belongings for the move, Lois Gibbs, president of the Homeowners Association, a woman whose son's health had been destroyed in the year he attended the 99th Street School, sent a telegram to President Jimmy Carter seeking federal funding for the evacuation of the remaining Love Canal families. The money promised by the state would not be enough to relocate all of the affected families. "The people are desperate," she wrote Carter. "They have no place to go. They are just dying."[42]

After studying the situation, Carter flew to New York City to meet with New York Governor Hugh Carey. Immediately following the meeting there, the president issued an order declaring a national emergency at Love Canal. The declaration freed funds from the Federal Disaster Assistance Administration for use at Love Canal; they were the first funds provided for a human-made disaster.[43]

The painful process of evacuation and relocation began with the first families being moved into the local U.S. Air Force base until more permanent homes could be found for them. "It was boring there," said Ed Voorhees, one of the first to move. "But that wasn't the worst of it. It was military and a lot of the Air Force people didn't want anything to do with us. 'Contaminated civilians' was the scuttlebutt term they used." Others found it difficult to pick up and leave the old neighborhood so quickly. "It was very hard to leave my home," recalls Bonnie Snyder. "A lot of firsts happened there. My doctor said it was like I was mourning for my house. When I got the last furniture out, I felt like I'd buried someone."[44]

As the last residents moved out of a neighborhood that more and more was beginning to look like a disaster area, with its boarded up homes, eight-foot fences and shrill warning signs, they talked about the chemicals and the effects on their children and their children's children. "I don't let her eat sugar," said Bonnie Snyder about her 22-month-old adopted daughter, Bethany. "I open my bread drawer and I see 'no preservatives' and I laugh. She's been breathing chemicals all this time."[45] After Bonnie Snyder and the remaining residents were moved away from the canal, some suggested that the area be put off-limits. "The Love Canal is like Sodom and Gomorrah," said one professor of public health. "It should be walled off and human habitation shouldn't be allowed . . . it will probably be uninhabitable for decades to come."[46] But a little more than a year later it became clear that the Love Canal would not be walled off from human habitation; that, in fact, the state planned to "revitalize" the area and move families back into all but the first ring of homes surrounding the dump. With the declaration of a federal emergency, the story of Love Canal had only begun. As a first-of-a-kind chemical disaster, it became a case study in government failure, corporate irresponsibility and community anger and fear.

THE LONG WAIT AT LOVE CANAL

Even as the first families moved away from the canal and remedial construction began, the Love Canal Homeowner's Association was gathering evidence that the residents remaining might be subject to the same kinds of illnesses that prompted the evacuation of the first-ring families. The residents contacted Dr. Beverly Paigen, a cancer research scientist at the Roswell Park Memorial Institute in Buffalo, to help investigate unusual clusters of illness in certain areas of the neighborhood.

Working under Paigen's direction, the homeowners polled the neighborhood families about their health. By pouring over old aerial photographs and geological-survey maps they found a pattern to the health complaints: The illnesses concentrated in families who lived above old stream-beds or dried up ponds, the so-called wet areas of Love Canal. Women living in wet areas reported three times as many miscarriages as they had had before moving to the canal area. These miscarriages constituted 25 percent of all pregnancies in wet-area women. The survey determined that nine of the sixteen children—56 percent of the children—born to women living at wet areas of the canal from 1974 to 1978 had birth defects. The survey also found increased risks of nervous-system problems, respiratory disorders and urinary illness for families living in the wet-area homes. Also indicated, with less firm evidence, were increases in cancer, skin diseases and interference with the body's immune system.[47]

Paigen and the residents then developed the swale theory, hypothesizing that the chemicals were migrating through these previously wet areas of the canal. In October, Paigen called the Department of Health in Albany to report her findings. Department officials were cool to her suggestion. "I could not seem to get through to the health department," she said later. "I could not seem to get them to look at my information."[48] On November 1 Paigen and another of the homeowners' consultants met with state officials in Albany. "When I got there, they said they had checked the swale theory and it was wrong, and they had checked the increased miscarriages and birth defects and it was wrong."[49]

The dispute between Paigen and the DOH was of more than academic interest. If Paigen's theory was accurate, the state would have to evacuate several hundred additional families at great expense. And according to the theory, residents waiting for a federal decision about further evacuation continued to be exposed to dangerous chemicals.

State health officials said they were reluctant to accept the Paigen theory because the health data had been gathered by the residents themselves, not skilled epidemiologists. Dr. David Axelrod, the state commissioner of health, said later that the DOH was unable to verify many of the residents' accounts of illnesses. In February 1979 the DOH released its own follow-up study. Although the department had disparaged the wet-area theory earlier, the department's study confirmed that some families living above the wet spots were subject to an increased number of miscarriages, birth defects and low weights for newborns.[50]

Axelrod came to Niagara Falls to report on the findings and to meet with residents. At a jammed public-school auditorium filled with protestors and protest signs, he told the homeowners that the state would temporarily evacuate pregnant women and families with children less than two years of age. Throughout Axelrod's speech, cries of protest resounded; residents demanded full evacuation; young children carried signs reading "Don't Make Me Live Here, I Don't Want To Die."[51]

When the shouting was over, the waiting—and the controversy—continued. The Love Canal Homeowners became a powerful political force. Headed by Lois Gibbs, the group became adept at using the media, at pressuring politicians and at keeping public attention on their plight. It was a remarkable performance by a group primarily of housewives with no prior public experience. They protested before county officials, state officials and the federal government. Through their efforts, Love Canal remained in the public eye. Gibbs wrote stinging letters to local newspapers, the *New York Times* and the White House. As the *Times* put it later, "Protesting, picketing, being jailed have become a way of life for Lois Gibbs. Two years ago she could barely pronounce the names of the chemicals detected in her basement. Today she tours the country warning of their effects before audiences large and small. Recently she was invited to speak at Harvard."[52]

Residents reserved their bitterest feelings for the New York State Department of Health. "I think they're trying to minimize the harm [to us] because they're trying to minimize the expenditures and avoid setting a precedent," said Gibbs. Relations between the residents and Axelrod's department became so strained that an EPA/Health Education and Welfare panel headed by Dr. David Rall, Director of the National Institute of Environmental Health Sciences, was convened at the request of the local congressman, John LaFalce, to mediate between the state and Paigen. The panel came down, in large part, on the side of the residents—but in language so guarded that it offered no mandate for action. "Although the data may be incomplete and contain potential biases," the committee wrote in its July 1979 report, "the concerns and questions raised by Dr. Paigen are important and merit attention."[53] When this furor, too, had died down, the residents continued to wait.

By this time, the Love Canal no longer was the only threatening dumpsite in Niagara Falls. In December 1978 three larger dumps were found in the city—at 102nd Street, at Hyde

Park Avenue and at the "S Area" of the Hooker plant—all of them containing Hooker wastes. The Hyde Park site, which Hooker began using after Love Canal was filled to the brim, is packed with 80,400 tons of materials, including 3,300 tons of dioxin-bearing trichlorophenol waste[54] and thousands of tons of the banned pesticides Mirex, Kepone and C-56. The 102nd Street dump, where children have played for years, holds 89,000 tons of such wastes as explosive phosphorous, lindane and a variety of other chemicals.[55]

Worst of all, more than 70,000 tons of chemicals had been dumped at the S Area—adjacent to the city drinking-water plant.[56] An estimated 200 tons of trichlorophenol waste and more than 17,000 tons of pure C-56 were among the compounds deposited in the S Area, a landfill built in the 1930s and 1940s on land then below the level of the Niagara River.

With all these chemicals sitting on a porous landfill only four feet above the river level, state officials suspect the migration of toxics into the river, a scant 200 yards away. Chemical odors originating from the nearby dump frequently have permeated the city drinking-water treatment plant. C-56 and Mirex were found in a well within the water plant itself and, according to the chief chemist of Niagara County, chemicals still may be leaking directly into the water intake.[57] Tested water supposedly treated by the plant contained 22 different chemicals; the state has established permissible limits for only eight of these. (Yet the city's director of utilities has reassured Congress that "the water in Niagara Falls is completely safe.")[58]

Workers in the area hardly were surprised at the state's discovery that these sites were "potentially" dangerous. One union official testified that as far back as 1952 workers at the National Lead Factory watched exposed drums in the Hyde Park dumpsite explode in the rain, emitting fumes that irritated their skin, throats and eyes, and that made a freshly painted wall "look like it had been burned." In the early 1970s union officials at National Lead also began to notice that "there seemed to be too many ailments" among employees, especially cancer and heart disease. Later they found that other factory workers in the area were suffering even worse problems.[59]

One such factory is the Greif Brothers Corporation. Bloody Run Creek, so named because of its peculiar reddish color, runs through the Greif Brothers factory—after it absorbs the runoff from rain on the wet and swampy ground beneath the Hyde Park dump. Among other sources of contamination, Hooker has admitted dumping Mirex directly into Bloody Run Creek. Dioxin has been discovered in Bloody Run at levels billions of times greater than the level estimated by the EPA to cause an additional cancer death in a population of one million people.[60] Until the company covered a manhole in the factory with a 16-gauge steel cap, the hole over the creek emitted noxious fumes into the heart of the plant. Surveys of the workers there reveal high incidence of cancer, respiratory problems, rashes, cysts and eye disease as well as headaches and a general lack of stamina.[61]

These illnesses also have appeared in employees throughout a third factory near the Hyde Park landfill—the Niagara Steel Finishing Company. One after another, workers there have become afflicted with severe skin rashes and inflammation, which appear and disappear for no apparent medical reason. One worker's baby was born with a rash over his entire body, which doctors were unable to diagnose.[62]

Even as these new dangers were discovered, the suffering at Love Canal continued. Throughout 1979, the actions taken by the state confused and often outraged the remaining residents. Although in 1979 the state agreed to temporarily relocate any woman who discovered she was pregnant, residents noted that the aid could be too late to prevent injury to her fetus. By the time the pregnancy was confirmed, as long as six or eight weeks after conception, the fetus's nervous system could be irreparably damaged. "Instead of waiting several weeks," said Gibbs, "we would have liked the state to relocate women who have filed 'intent to conceive' forms, who can be moved out *before* the fetus begins to grow." (Gibbs's emphasis.)

According to Lois Gibbs, many residents failed to qualify for relocation in 1979 under the extremely stringent relocation standards set up by the state. "The burden of proof has been thrown onto us, not the state," explained Gibbs. "We have to show that we're sick specifically because of the chemicals coming out of Love Canal. But how can we prove that? There are so many chemicals around here, in our air and water, that we can't single out one source, or even one combination of chemicals. Besides, scientists don't even know how most of these chemicals affect you." One resident sums up the citizens' frustration with the state: "We the people of the Love Canal are worried, sick and very disappointed with our government who is supposed to be there working for the people and not against us."

From the state's point of view, the cleanup of the canal had become a vast financial burden, blurring the personal tragedies. The cleanup was especially burdensome because the state has more than its share of environmental problems, from Mirex in Lake Ontario and PCBs in the Hudson to poisoned groundwater on Long Island and three other leaking Hooker dumps in Niagara Falls alone. "We are having intrusions from chemicals all around the state," says Marvin G. Nailor, Axelrod's executive assistant. "We don't have enough scientists and resources to do the job."

With New York's own resources insufficient for what was shaping up as a monumental problem, state officials pressed Washington for help. But they ran into the same kind of bureaucratic logjams that frustrated the Love Canal homeowners in Albany. Although the president had declared a federal emergency, the declaration covered only a narrow band of homes; the Federal Emergency Management Administration refused to pay any expenses incurred outside the narrow boundary set. The agency also refused to buy homes or to pick up the cost of maintaining a fleet of buses for possible evacuation of residents during the 13 months of remedial construction. Federal disaster officials told the state that providing extended assistance would be "outside the constraints intended for this program."[63]

The federal provision for crises like the Love Canal area's is the emergency-response fund of the Water Pollution Control Act. But the Office of Management and Budget objected to use of that fund to help the Love Canal residents—because it could open the door to applications by a wide number of municipalities with environmental problems of their own. (Through 1979, the OMB had successfully kept any money from this fund from being spent.) Instead, Congress appropriated $4 million, on a matching basis with state funds, to pay for the remedial work as a one-time demonstration project. In all, the federal government has chipped in about $21 million for cleaning up Love Canal, according to the New York Department of Transportation; by the end of 1980, the total cost of the cleanup had climbed to almost $70 million.

When the first plans for a cleanup were developed, Hooker offered to pay one-third of the originally estimated cost of repairing the south end of the canal. But Hooker has not paid for any of the actual work. According to William Hennessy, New York commissioner of transportation and chairman of the Governor's Love Canal Task Force, Hooker has turned down overtures from the state to buy some area homes and thereby speed the evacuation process. After first denying that the state had made such a request, Hooker's Executive Vice President Bruce Davis told us, "We have indicated that we were not interested in purchasing homes out there. We did not think it would contribute to the revitalization of the Love Canal area."

Instead, with Hooker's environmental problems being revealed at sites as far-flung as Florida and California, the company decided in September 1979 to place ads in 23 newspapers and major financial magazines. Hooker was disputing articles in the *New York Times* and *Business Week* that accused the company of being "careless" with dangerous substances: "Where helpful," the newspaper ads promised, "[Hooker will] in the spirit of a good neighbor . . . go beyond the requirements of the law."[64] Hooker's Niagara Falls plant also ran a series of advertisements in local newspapers—as Davis puts it, "to set the facts straight." For the residents, pushing and protesting to be removed from their homes, the ads were the ultimate insult: Instead of helping to move the residents out, Hooker was spending its money to convince people the problem wasn't all

that bad in the first place. "They really make me angry," said
Gibbs. "It was like a brainwashing technique."

Though Hooker officials argued the danger at Love Canal
was minimal—Armand Hammer, chairman of the board of
Hooker's parent company, Occidental Petroleum Corporation,
told a national audience on "Meet The Press" that "the thing
has been blown up out of context"[65]—many uncertainties remained in the fall of 1979. The dispute pitting the Paigen
findings against the state's was not resolved. The performance
of the elaborate, tiled drainage system completed in November
still was problematic. The system is designed both to prevent
the future migration of chemicals and to bring back those already dissolved in the soils. How completely the system is ac-
complishing the former is unclear. And Dr. Stephen Kim, the
state's chief toxicologist at Love Canal, is one who doubts the
latter is possible. "It's hard to say [whether migration is being
stopped]," he said. "At first we thought, well, that it was doing
something like that, but, you know, these things don't move like
a river so it's hard to tell. We really don't have any information
right now." Kim explained, "I don't know to what degree
. . . [bringing back chemicals] will be done because the drawing
force of the original migration was a very large gradient; a
concentration to bring it back is a very small gradient." John
Beecher, a chemical engineer with the state, adds, "It may take
some time for the concentrations of chemicals in soil samples to
show a significant reduction." But the greatest uncertainty was
on the most basic question: Were the chemicals still harming
the remaining residents of Love Canal?

REPEATING HISTORY

In this climate of uncertainty in November 1979, the state
announced it would buy the homes of any remaining Love
Canal residents who wished to leave. At the same time, the
governor announced plans to "revitalize" Love Canal by moving new families into the homes of those who had left.

To buy Love Canal homes, on November 1, 1979, the New
York State Senate and Assembly had in a special session ap-

proved a bill sent to them by Governor Carey. It provided an initial $5 million—more might ultimately be needed—to purchase the home of any Love Canal resident who wanted to leave. After more than a year of bitter conflicts, the bill's passage was a victory for the Love Canal Homeowners Association. "We are committed to giving everyone who wants to leave the area an equal opportunity," said State Senator John B. Daly, the area's representative. The vote came only two weeks after the federal House Oversight and Investigations Subcommittee released its report on hazardous wastes, following several months of hearings held around the country. The report devoted large sections to New York's handling of the Love Canal —and was extremely critical. "The New York State Health Department has failed to assure residents of the Love Canal that the public health is being adequately protected," the subcommittee wrote. "The State Health Department has not provided residents of the area nor this Subcommittee with a credible refutation of the Paigen study."[66] After accumulating the evidence, the subcommittee suggested that residents living in wet areas be evacuated until the Paigen theory could be disproved. State health officials rejected that proposal. Yet few people doubted that the outside pressure had forced the state government to act.

For the homeowners, victory was tempered, however, by the specifics of the rescue—particularly the plan to move families back to the Love Canal area and once again to build up an entire neighborhood. The legislation established a stabilization and revitalization task force composed of state and local officials responsible for developing "a program . . . to arrest the blight in the area of the Love Canal."[67] As one reporter observed, "Housing blight seems to be the least of the problems that has beset this area,"[68] but the governor apparently was unable to convince the DOH to back the evacuation on health grounds. "Under what authority do we evacuate everyone?" Axelrod said, a few weeks before Carey announced his plans. "Do we evacuate all of Harlem because it has an infant mortality rate four times the state average?"[69] Even months after the bill had passed, health department officials remained cool to the plans. "That [legislation]," said Marvin Nailor, Axelrod's press aide, "was not based on our ability to establish a causal relationship [between the chemicals and the remaining health problems]." Lacking the support of the state's Department of Health, the legislature had approved the program anyway, "to arrest . . . blight."

Love Canal residents huddled for their fourth winter since the official investigations began, but it seemed likely to be their last there. Appraisals were underway; applications were being prepared for federal urban-renewal and beautification funds. Local officials were talking about parks and "making the community whole again." Hooker's Bruce Davis said that the area "could be made kind of a showplace area of Niagara Falls."

Despite the local optimism, some federal officials had their doubts about the wisdom of the plans. "If the price is right, people may be willing to bargain their health for their pocketbook," said David M. Huber, an EPA environmental engineer who supervised the federal action at Love Canal. "My own feeling is that I'd hate to move back myself." Said National Institute of Environmental Health Sciences Director David Rall, in late 1979: "At the moment I would be quite negative [about moving people back]." And, said Rall, "we simply don't know enough about how the chemicals are migrating out."

A few weeks after the legislature approved the plan, the Homeowners Association released a survey of pregnancies begun at Love Canal in 1979. The result was hardly a good omen for the new decade there. Only one of the 15 pregnancies ended in the birth of a healthy baby, according to the survey. Four ended in miscarriages. Two babies were stillborn. Nine others, including a pair of twins, were born deformed.[70]

The state has approached the resettlement guardedly. According to Niagara Falls Mayor Michael O'Laughlin, who heads the task force, New York will likely insert a clause into the deed of any Love Canal home that it resells holding the state harmless against any future claims for injury or disease. Hooker inserted such a clause in its deed when in 1953 the company sold that land to the Niagara Falls Board of Education.

Lois Gibbs isn't a scientist or a lawyer, but she does have a ground-level view of life at Love Canal. "To 'revitalize' it, to move families back in," she says, "is to repeat history."

Six months after the bill was passed—before any homes were purchased—those revitalization plans blew up. On May 17, 1980, the EPA released a study of Love Canal residents by the Biogenics Corporation of Houston, Texas, under the direction of genetic toxicologist Dante Picciano. The study concluded that 11 of 36 Love Canal residents tested had suffered chromosomal damage—which could be a harbinger of future cancer, birth defects and other health problems.[71]

Almost immediately, the study came under attack. Hooker officials said the preliminary results were "not definitive."[72] State Health Commissioner Axelrod had a similar reaction, saying that to base decisions on such a small study was "a major injustice to science."[73] Other federal scientists were concerned about the lack of a control group in the Picciano study.

While waiting for a federal panel to review the Picciano study, the EPA refrained from further action at the site. Residents, their long-standing fears apparently confirmed by the latest indications of chromosome damage, demanded to be relocated. To dramatize their point, the Homeowners Association temporarily held two local EPA officials hostage on May 19 and demanded of federal officials in Washington an immediate evacuation.[74]

Two days later, the stalemate brought on by the Picciano study broke. Another study was released indicating nerve damage among the remaining residents.[75] This study, following on the heels of the Picciano study—disputed though it was—and the accumulating evidence of the previous year prompted the federal government to act.

That afternoon President Carter declared his second federal emergency at Love Canal, permitting as many as 710 families to be temporarily relocated with federal funds. "This action is being taken in recognition of the cumulative evidence of exposure by the Love Canal residents to toxic wastes from Hooker Chemical Company and mounting evidence of resulting health effects," said Barbara Blum of the EPA. "Health effects studies performed by others so far are preliminary. Taken together, they suggest significant health risks."[76]

The Picciano study remains controversial. A federal panel that reviewed photocopies of Picciano's microscope slides rejected his findings in June. Two other prominent geneticists, however, later affirmed the results, one in a letter to the influential *Science* magazine, which also had questioned the study.[77] But then another report to the New York government in fall 1980 criticized the Picciano study. Since the study of chromosomal damage itself is controversial, no consensus is likely ever to be reached.

While the medical dispute continued, so did the acrimony between the state and federal governments. State officials had reacted to the EPA actions with some perturbation, telling the press the state had had no plans, before the Picciano study was released, to move out any more residents.[78] In response to a July 1980 request from state officials, the federal government agreed to loan and grant New York $15 million to purchase Love Canal homes, thus allowing permanent relocation of all residents who wished to leave. State officials, though, complained about the terms of the loan, and negotiations continued.[79] The bitterness between state and federal officials perhaps was symbolized best by an incident on June 5. After months of exasperation, federal prosecutors resorted to suing Axelrod's Department of Health to obtain health-survey information the state had refused to make available for a federal suit against Hooker Chemical. The DOH had ignored a previously issued subpeona.[80]

Meanwhile, the revitalization and stabilization plans ran aground. In May the Niagara County legislature had voted against participating in the project. State officials still were putting together a board of directors in fall 1980—almost one year after the revitalization legislation was approved. Despite the second federal emergency, state and local officials still intended to move families back into the homes of Love Canal.

Coincidentally, Occidental Petroleum, Hooker's parent firm, held its annual meeting on the same day that President

Carter announced the second Love Canal emergency. The company considered among other items a shareholder resolution "to establish policies and procedures to safeguard our company from future environmental contamination and public health hazards that affect our company's profitability and viability."[81] After listening to a Love Canal resident describe the death of her son from a rare kidney disease, Armand Hammer, the company's chairman, said the company "sympathize[s] greatly with your predicament, but I would think what you should be doing is addressing your complaint to the city of Niagara Falls. . . ."[82] When supporters of the resolution continued to speak, their floor mikes were turned off.[83] Sister Joan Malone of Lewiston, New York, then asked Hammer, "Are you refusing to hear?" Hammer replied, "Yes, I am refusing. Go back to Buffalo."[84]

The company rejected the resolution.[85]

"THE PROVERBIAL TIP OF THE ICEBERG"

"Such tragic cases as the Love Canal in New York," noted Congressman James Florio, a New Jersey Democrat, "are, unfortunately, only the proverbial tip of the iceberg."[86] Florio, cosponsor of a "Superfund" bill to fund cleanup of hazardous-waste sites, has testified that Love Canal, far from being unique, has awakened the country to one of the most widespread environmental threats it ever has faced. More than 125 billion pounds of chemical wastes are produced each year; a consultant for the EPA suggests that more than 90 percent of this is disposed of improperly.[87] Between 32,000 and 51,000 hazardous-waste sites may exist in the country; the EPA's preliminary estimate of the cost to permanently clean up these sites is a full $44 billion. And according to one EPA official, simply cleaning up the sites that are "acute problems . . . [requiring] immediate government response" may cost more than $3 billion.[88]

This staggering cleanup figure can be only a crude estimate. "The one thing that has yet to be done," explained Lester Brown, special assistant to the House Commerce Oversight Subcommittee, "is . . . a proper study of sites across the country." Brown suggests, based on a survey of chemical companies completed in the fall of 1979, that the EPA may have grossly underestimated the problem. Precisely how big the problem may be, no one really knows.

Hooker—and Occidental Petroleum—alone are responsible for many more dumps than the four in Niagara Falls. Estimates for the cost of cleaning up only three of Hooker's sites run as high as $150 million.[89]

The federal Justice Department and the state of California have brought suit against Hooker for contaminating the groundwater near the company's plant in Lathrop, California. Although officials of the California Water Quality Control Board were kept in the dark about the discharges until 1979, memos to corporate headquarters in Houston candidly discussed the problems as early as July 1975. "Should the water quality control regulatory agencies become aware of the fact that we percolate our pesticide wastes, they could justifiably close down our entire Ag Chem plant operation."[90] Earlier interoffice memos discussed the fears neighbors had raised—justifiably—about the quality of their drinking water.

Among the wastes Hooker was discharging were DBCP (dibromochloropropane), a carcinogen that also causes sterility in males; DDT; chlordane and heptachlor.[91] Groundwater may have been contaminated at a Hooker dump in Columbia, Tennessee; groundwater and rain water may be entering a Hooker PCB and asbestos dump in Taft, Louisiana;[92] trichloroethylene and vinyl chloride lagoons literally were pumped into the surroundings of Hooker's Hicksville, Long Island, plant;[93] and two Hooker plants in Tennessee have violated governmental standards for pH levels in water discharges more than a hundred times.[94]

In October of 1979 Hooker agreed to give $15 million to the state of Michigan to clean up massive C-56 pollution of water supplies and a scenic lake near its dumpsite in Montague.[95] A Hooker memo dated November 4, 1955, began with the assertion, "The disposal of plant residues at the Montague plant is a major problem. . . ."[96] And in August 1979 the *New*

York Times reported that Hooker internal memos indicate Hooker's top management may have authorized violations of pollution laws at the White Springs, Florida, plant and failed to report several other environmental problems.[97] In July 1980 the Securities and Exchange Commission charged Hooker's parent, Occidental Petroleum, with failing to disclose hundreds of millions of dollars of potential liabilities from environmental pollution. The commission ordered Occidental to establish a companywide environmental-monitoring system.[98] One Love Canal resident summed up Hooker's performance—she fumed, "Industry has been getting away with too much, for too long. We can no longer as citizens afford to pay the price of their doing business."[99]

The federal government, long overwhelmed by the vastness of the problem, is beginning to offer solutions. A "Superfund" for emergency cleanup of oil and chemical spills and of hazardous waste sites was signed into law in December, 1980. Of the $1.6 billion total, $1.38 billion will be paid by oil refiners and chemical manufacturers, with the rest coming from taxpayers. Such a fund, although hardly enough to foot what could be a $44 billion bill for cleaning up this national problem, is a first step toward making industry pay for its negligent disposal of wastes. (For more on the Superfund, see the next chapter.)

Merely cleaning up existing dumpsites will not close the books on toxic waste, however. Former Senator John Culver observes, "There is no magical 'quick fix' to the chemical waste problem. . . . We must take preventive action to assure that these situations do not occur again." To safely dispose of the chemicals at Love Canal would have cost no more than $4 million, in 1979 dollars. Already, the emergency action taken merely to temporarily stave off the "imminent hazard"[100] has cost almost $70 million.

The centerpiece of the government's preventive actions is the Resource Conservation and Recovery Act (RCRA), which was signed into law in October 1976. The RCRA was passed with the understanding that previous laws designed to clean up the air and water had increased the likelihood wastes would be disposed of on land—often improperly. Like other pollution laws, the RCRA was to be managed by the individual states, working under minimum national guidelines set by the EPA.

But the states have been hamstrung because the EPA was more than 20 months late in promulgating the RCRA regulations. The bulk of the regulations were not issued until spring 1980. New York State Health Commissioner Axelrod has attributed many of New York's hazardous-waste problems to this extended delay. "We have had difficulty moving ahead because of the absence of federal regulations which would apply uniformly to the entire country," Axelrod has said. Without EPA guidelines, the state is in "continuous conflict with industry in New York because New York is enforcing regulations that go well beyond what Federal regulations currently require."[101] Other state officials have given Congress the same message.

In March 1979 hearings before his House Oversight Subcommittee, Congressman Andrew Maguire, a New Jersey Democrat, probed for the reasons the EPA has delayed: "There is pressure inside EPA as a result of the fight against inflation from the President's economic advisors not to take on more than they can handle."[102] While the EPA battles uphill for more funding, though, the need for regulations increases. States need EPA technical guidelines on permissible chemical limits and procedures for cleanup before they can write regulations. In many states the regulations that now have been drafted won't become final until several months after the EPA rules come out, supposedly so that state agencies will have time to revise their draft regulations before industry begins to comply with them. Even if one state does enact tough controls on waste disposal, without uniform EPA standards companies can simply dump their wastes in neighboring states with weaker laws—increasing the dangers associated with hazardous-waste transportation as well. And, waste generators are inclined simply to move away from states with tougher laws; without the equalizing effect of federal regulations, such a company has a competitive advantage.

As long as the EPA rules remain unfinished, industry is reluctant to set up new disposal sites, which may have to be revamped when the regulations do appear.[103] This reluctance has exacerbated the severe shortage of legal dumpsites. In part, this shortage stems from people's reluctance to see new sites set up in their backyards. One state official describes the difficulty: "I might be able to go out and condemn a site [for a new dump], together with a huge buffer zone around it, and override the local zoning board and people carrying placards, and newspaper publicity. But I would have to do it with a contingent of troops."[104]

So while the amount of hazardous waste generated continues to increase (based on EPA estimates), the numbers of sites, incinerators and other repositories have not grown commensurately—according to some estimates, they have declined in the past decade. The information in this crucial area, too, is indefinite. No one knows exactly how much waste is being generated or how many sites are able to safely handle it; the EPA expects these figures to be shored up once the final RCRA regulations are promulgated.

The need for preventive action is underscored by the ever-accelerating rate at which hazardous wastes are produced. Luckily, most of these wastes don't have to be buried: High-temperature kilns are capable of incinerating most chemicals safely—although the kilns can cost as much as $45 million apiece, and few communities are willing to host new incinerators. Other wastes can be purified or even reclaimed through elaborate chemical processing. Some 75 companies "subscribe" to the Calgon Corporation's activated-carbon filter system, for instance, which Calgon claims can recover 98 percent of the valuable solvent of many wastes, while almost completely removing such chemicals as trichlorophenol and Mirex. (Because of the versatility of the activated-carbon filter, Calgon has been hired to purify contaminated run-off at Love Canal.) Valuable metals in waste streams can be recycled. (See the conclusion.) Finally, acidic or basic wastes already in the ground can be neutralized with ordinary sewage sludge, reducing the effects of chemical dumping. (In 1978, 81 acres of strip-mined, highly acidic land near Harrisburg, Illinois, were ploughed and infused with 51 million gallons of liquid sludge from nearby

Chicago. The land has since been test-planted successfully with trees and grass.)

These means of disposal are worthless, however, unless industry is convinced that it must use these safer—and costlier —methods. Lester Brown observes that "industry basically knew even in the 1950s of other means of disposal, but without regulations, either state or federal, there was no incentive for them to use them." At the Lathrop, California, plant, for example, an internal Hooker memo stated that "No outsiders actually know what we do, and there has been no government pressure on us, so we have held back trying to find out what to do" to clean up the plant's leaking dump.[105] The government's role, Brown believes, is to "lean on enforcement, be really tough, and put a lot of information from hearings about industry violations into the public record. Then individual citizens can sue— and it's the threat of those kinds of enormous suits that will whip industry into line." Love Canal residents have filed lawsuits worth more than $9 billion against the city, the state and Hooker. The federal Justice Department has formed an aggressive hazardous-waste unit that in December 1979 sued Hooker for more than $124 million to cleanup its four Niagara Falls sites. That suit was filed only two days after the Lathrop suit, which could cost Hooker another $62 million.

Industry has another incentive to follow regulations besides the threat of lawsuits. One California state official remarks, "The California Manufacturers Association does not want any Love Canals. . . . They want equitable enforcement so that they are not subject to unfair competition." Recently, the CMA supported an increase in its "pollution charge" tax, allowing the state to increase its enforcement staff so that, says one official, California manufacturers "did not get a few black eyes from the unscrupulous, giving all California industry a bad name."[106]

Until the long-delayed EPA regulations go into effect, until the states produce—and police—their own sets of regulations, little identification and cleaning up of other "Love Canals" is likely. Although companies may be pleased when the state catches their competitors red-handed, few companies are willing to call state attention to contamination caused by their own negligence, or to expend stockholder money on cleanup that won't generate any revenue. With the precedent of New York's Love Canal other states now can guide their own cleanup operations. New York has received about $21 million from the federal government to deal with the Love Canal disaster, but most of it came years after the hazard was discovered. The EPA's oil-spill contingency fund is so slim that it nearly has been consumed by cleanup of the Love Canal and of a second dumpsite in Kentucky. And the EPA has found that only 15 or 16 states have contingency funds to clean up hazardous substances—14 of which have allotted $100,000 or less and are "reluctant to spend more than a few thousand on each cleanup." For the next several years, then, an unknown number of sites will continue to contaminate water supplies, chemicals will continue to enter the food chain—and people near these sites will continue to sicken and die.

Even if the Superfund is strengthened, tough governmental standards appear, and industry begins to police itself, the problems never will be eliminated. It's not just that hazardous wastes always will be produced, or that nobody ever will want hazardous wastes dumped in the back yard. It's the human cost that will go on and on—a cost that no Superfund or lawsuit will pay for—because Love Canal doesn't end with this generation's cancer or even with the next generation's birth defects. For many residents, the damage is permanent in their genes and their children's. The mutated genes will affect all of their descendants, one generation after another.

Sandra Pelfrey was born and raised near Love Canal. She remembers playing on "Canal Hill." At age 19 she married and moved to Ohio. At 21 she had her first child, Linda. Linda was born blind. At age 23 Mrs. Pelfrey gave birth to James. James also was born blind. Her doctor recommended that she not bear any more children. At age 25 Sandra had her kidney removed. That operation was followed by a tubal ligation.[107] For Sandra Pelfrey, the nightmare never will end.

For her children, it has just begun.

NOTES

1. "Ooze After Rain Was Part of Life," *Niagara Falls Gazette* (hereafter, the *Gazette*), August 6, 1978.

2. Ibid.

3. ABC, "The Killing Ground," transcript, p. 5, March 17, 1979.

4. "Reporters Notebook; Niagara Olfactory Impact," *New York Times*, August 9, 1978.

5. Ibid.

6. State of New York, Department of Health, *Love Canal: Public Health Time Bomb: A Special Report to the Governor and Legislature*, September, 1978.

7. *United States of America v. Hooker Chemical and Plastic Corporation et al.*, filed December 30, 1979 (U.S. District Court for the Western District of New York), p. 10.

8. Rachel Carson, *Silent Spring* (Fawcett Crest Books, 1962), p. 15.

9. *United States of America v. Hooker*, p. 12.

10. State of New York, *Love Canal: Public Health Time Bomb,"* p. 12.

11. Thomas Whiteside, *The Pendulum and the Toxic Cloud*, (Yale University Press, 1979), p. 141.

12. Personal communication, January 1981.

13. Whiteside, *The Pendulum and the Toxic Cloud*, pp. 31–65.

14. "Foster Memo Cited Chemical Odors in '64," *Gazette*, August 12, 1978.

15. Memo from Jerome Wilkenfeld, assistant technical superintendent, to R. F. Schultz, works manager, "Exposed Residue at the Love Canal," May 18, 1958. Cited in *Hazardous Waste Disposal: Hearings Before the Subcommittee on Oversight and Investigations of the Committee on Interstate and Foreign Commerce*, House of Representatives (Government Printing Office, 1979), p. 651.

16. *Hazardous Waste Disposal*, p. 665.

17. Quit claim deed, as read over the telephone by a reporter from the *Gazette*, November 9, 1978.

18. "School Lawyer's Canal Site Advice Unheeded," *Gazette*, November 9, 1978.

19. Quit claim deed.

20. "School Lawyer's Canal Site Advice Unheeded."

21. Personal communication with Barbara Quimby, Love Canal Homeowners Association.

22. "Several Families Are Sent Away from NF Landfill," *New York Times*, August 7, 1978.

23. *Hazardous Waste Disposal*, p. 665. Wilkenfeld testified to this.

24. "We Watched Them Dump the Barrels," *Gazette*, August 3, 1978.

25. Joe Swan, "Uncovering Love Canal," *Columbia Journalism Review*, January/February 1979, p. 46.

26. Ibid.

27. "Dangerous Chemicals Found Leaking From Hooker Dump," *Gazette*, November 2, 1976.

28. "Dump Site Toxic Chemicals Carried in Storm Sewers," *Gazette*, November 4, 1976.

29. "No Evidence On Toxic Residues—NCHD," *Gazette*, May 3, 1977.

30. State of New York, "Love Canal: Public Health Time Bomb," p. 23.

31. Ibid., p. 14.

32. "Wider Range of Illnesses Suspected," *Gazette*, August 4, 1978.

33. *Hazardous Waste Disposal*, p. 63. Dr. Beverly Paigen testified to this.

34. "Medical Complaints Coincide With Toxic Effects," *Gazette*, August 17, 1978.

35. *United States of America v. Hooker*, pp. 13–20.

36. *Hazardous Waste Disposal*, pp. 500–501, 504. Bruce Davis's testimony.

37. "Hooker Hit as Irresponsible," *Gazette*, June 22, 1978.

38. *Hazardous Waste Disposal*, pp. 616–620. The accident is described in a July 27, 1967, memo from G. F. Brierley of Hooker to J. D. Sweeney, entitled "Injuries to Two Youths Alleged to Have Occurred at 102nd St. Hooker Dump Area." The determination of what caused the explosion is described in a Hooker memo dated August 8, 1967, from W. J. Thompson to N. Hinckley.

39. *Hazardous Waste Disposal*, p. 630. The plans are discussed in a Hooker memo dated October 11, 1972, from John W. Judy to B. J. Carreno.

40. "Clifford Probe Defeated," *Gazette*, August 9, 1978.

41. "Wider Range of Illnesses Suspected."

42. "Senate to Consider $4 Million—State Will Match," *Gazette*, August 7, 1978.

43. Congressional Research Service, *Compensation for Victims of Water Pollution* (Government Printing Office, 1979), p. 205.

44. "Emptied Niagara Neighborhood Now Looks Like a Disaster Area," *New York Times*, November 22, 1978.

45. "Health Chief Calls Waste Site a Peril," *New York Times*, August 3, 1978.

46. ABC, "The Killing Ground," p. 9.

47. *Hazardous Waste Disposal*, pp. 60–87. This is from Dr. Paigen's testimony.

48. *Hazardous Waste Disposal*, p. 80. Paigen testimony.

49. Ibid.

50. "100 Love Canal Families Are Urged to Leave Area," *New York Times*, February 10, 1979.

51. "More Families to Be Moved at Love Canal," *Buffalo Evening News*, February 9, 1979.

52. "Love Canal Families Are Left With a Legacy of Pain and Anger," *New York Times*, May 16, 1980.

53. Dr. David Rall (committee chairman and director of the National Institute of Environmental Health Sciences), "Report of Meetings Between Scientists From HEW and EPA, and Dr. Beverly Paigen and Scientists of the State of New York Department of Health Concerning Love Canal." This is contained in a July 26, 1979, HEW press release, untitled.

54. *United States of America v. Hooker*, pp. 9–10.

55. Ibid., p. 10.

56. Ibid., p. 9.

57. *Hazardous Waste Disposal*, pp. 199–208. Testimony of Elliot J. Lynch, former operator and chief chemist of Niagara County.

58. *Hazardous Waste Disposal* p. 239. Testimony of Robert R. Matthews, director of utilities, Niagara Falls.

59. *Hazardous Waste Disposal*, pp. 32–59. Three union officials testified about the conditions in the area: Dennis Virtuoso, president of local 12256 of the United Steelworkers of America; Clifton Van Epps, vice president, local 8–778 of the Oil, Chemical and Atomic Workers; and Carl Sabey, president, local 12230 of the United Steelworkers.

60. *United States of America v. Hooker Chemical and Plastics Corporation et al.* (Hyde Park suit), p. 11.

61. *Hazardous Waste Disposal*, pp. 33–34. Virtuoso testified to this.

62. *Hazardous Waste Disposal*, pp. 35–38. Van Epps testified to this.

63. Ibid., p. 154. New York Commissioner of Transportation William C. Hennessy testified to this.

64. Advertisement quoted from the *Washington Post*, October 5, 1979.

65. "Meet the Press," transcript, October 14, 1979, p. 6.

66. *Hazardous Waste Disposal: Report by the Subcommittee on Oversight and Investigations of the Committee on Interstate and Foreign Commerce, House of Representatives* (Government Printing Office, September 1979), pp. 5, 16.

67. New York State Senate, S. 18; New York State Assembly, A-18.

68. "The Poisoned Earth: Long Silences Above the Love Canal," *Washington Post*, November 4, 1979.

69. "Home Purchases by State Sought Near Love Canal," *New York Times*, September 10, 1979.

70. Love Canal Homeowners Association, "Pregnancy Outcome Study."

71. EPA press release, "EPA Finds Chromosome Damage at Love Canal," May 17, 1980.

72. Hooker Chemical news release, May 17, 1980.

73. "Love Canal Residents Say the State Has Failed Them," *New York Times*, May 25, 1980.

74. "Homeowners at Love Canal Hold Two Federal Environmental Officials," *New York Times,* May 20, 1980.

75. "President Orders Emergency Help for Love Canal," *New York Times*, May 22, 1980.

76. EPA press release, "EPA, New York State Announce Temporary Relocation of Love Canal Residents," May 21, 1980.

77. "Love Canal's Emotional Roller Coaster," *Washington Post*, July 26, 1980.

78. "A Tangle of Science and Politics Lies Behind Study at Love Canal," *New York Times,* May 27, 1980.

79. "State Seeks Better U.S. Offer in Love Canal Resettlements," *New York Times,* August 6, 1980. Ultimately, the state and federal governments agreed on a $7.5 million federal grant and a $7.5 million loan at 8.25% interest.

80. "U.S. Sues State to Obtain Love Canal Health Data," *New York Times*, June 6, 1980.

81. Text of shareholder proposal.

82. Occidental Petroleum Corporation, *Annual Shareholders' Meeting,* p. 10. The subsequent exchange between Hammer and supporters of the resolution does not appear in the transcript.

83. "Occidental Increases Dividend," *Los Angeles Times,* May 22, 1980.

84. "Hammer Tells Nun to Go Back to Buffalo," *Buffalo Courier-Express,* May 22, 1980.

85. Ibid.

86. *Hazardous Waste Disposal,* p. 2.

87. EPA Office of Solid Waste, "Everybody's Problem: Hazardous Waste," pp. 1, 15.

88. *Hazardous Waste Disposal,* p. 1629. Testimony of Thomas Jorling, assistant administrator for water and hazardous materials, EPA.

89. Congressional Research Service, *Compensation for Victims of Water Pollution,* p. 212.

90. *Hazardous Waste Disposal,* p. 1597. Letter from M. A. Stanek of OxyChem Lathrop to W. A. Meyers, assistant controller, Occidental Chemical Corporation, July 16, 1975.

91. *United States of America v. Hooker Chemical,* pp. 18–22.

92. *Hazardous Waste Disposal,* pp. 546–606, for Taft (exchange between Representative Bob Eckhardt of Texas and Bruce Davis, executive vice president of Hooker); Columbia is discussed on pp. 696–697. See also p. 1716 for Hooker's response.

93. *Hazardous Waste Disposal,* p. 531.

94. *Hazardous Waste Disposal,* p. 698. According to Eckhardt, Hooker's facilities were out of compliance a total of 122 times.

95. "Chemical Dump Cleanup to Cost Firm $15 Million," *Washington Post,* October 25, 1979.

96. *Hazardous Waste Disposal,* p. 608.

97. "Hooker Corp. Papers Indicate Management Sanctioned Polluting," *New York Times,* August 5, 1979.

98. "S.E.C. Says Occidental Hid Potential Liabilities," *New York Times,* July 3, 1980.

99. Marie Pozniak, statement before the Senate Committee on Environment and Public Works, Subcommittee on Resources Protection, *Hearings,* July 19, 1979, p. 147.

100. Ibid.

101. *Hazardous Waste Disposal,* p. 300.

102. Ibid., p. 18.

103. See, for example, the report of the Subcommittee on Oversight of Government Management of the Senate Committee on Governmental Affairs, March 1980 (Government Printing Office).

104. *Hazardous Waste Disposal,* p. 1663. The remark was made by Eugene F. Mooney, the secretary of Kentucky's Department for Natural Resources and Environmental Protection.

105. *Hazardous Waste Disposal,* p. 1587. The remark was from a Hooker memo dated June 25, 1976, from R. Edson to A. Osborn.

106. *Hazardous Waste Disposal,* p. 1600. Dr. Harvey Collins, acting chief, hazardous materials management, California State Department of Health.

107. "Ohio Mother Blaming Canal for Kids' Defects," *Gazette,* August 8, 1978.

NOTE: This chapter was written with the research assistance of Ronald Brownstein.

Chapter **9**

Conclusion:
We Are Not Helpless

RALPH NADER

$\mathbf{W}$E ARE NOT HELPLESS IN the environmental crisis. The spread of cancer—the plague of the 20th century—and of other diseases that spring from hazards induced in the environment can be controlled. Alternatives are available to the pollution of our air, land, water and food. The proper functioning of our economic system does not require the sacrifice of the residents of Love Canal, or of the waters of Lake Superior and the James River.

To protect the environment sensible, practical choices are available in both personal and political spheres. Public awareness and concern, symbolized by Earth Day in 1970, sparked a remarkable, decade-long congressional outpouring of environmental legislation that the *New York Times* has observed was "reminiscent of the codification of civil rights in the 1960s and economic rights in the 1930s."[1]

Now the industries that have been compelled by law to reduce their discharges into the air, water and land have launched a vocal and concerted counterattack in Congress. Both the Environmental Protection Agency (EPA) and the Occupational Safety and Health Administration (OSHA) have been given a difficult time lately in oversight hearings (not to mention in conferences with the Office of Management and Budget). The pressure is not likely to ease up soon. On the eve of Earth Day 1980, Richard L. Lesher, president of the Chamber of Commerce of the United States, had this to say about the environmental imperatives of the upcoming decade: "As I look ahead, what we have to do is balance environmental needs with energy needs, inflation and other national priorities. We have to go back and clean up the laws—get the extremes out of them."[2]

None of these countermeasures is surprising; a uniquely consistent pattern characterizes the response strategy of companies once they decide that they cannot totally defeat the reform drive. Where regulations or standards are issued by an agency for health and safety, a deliberate process of delay, attrition and political influence is initiated. That is why statutes read more promising than the corresponding regulations, and the regulations read more promising than the reality in the marketplace, workplace and environment. Compare the bold call of the Occupational Safety and Health Act of 1970 to "assure safe and healthful working conditions for working men and women"[3] with OSHA's ability to promulgate only 22 exposure standards—and the government's estimate that 9 out of 10 American industrial workers are still "not adequately protected from exposure to at least one of the 163 most common hazardous industrial chemicals."[4]

Whenever the political government is empowered to protect the interest of labor, consumers and other constituencies, the corporate government increases its financing of political elections. As often as the law requires a redirection of investment to reduce the costs of pollution or consumer injury, companies find ways to transfer these costs to the victims themselves, through tax preferences or administered pricing. And because of the inordinate secrecy permitted these multinational companies, their officials can wildly exaggerate the costs of compliance to prod public resistance to health and safety standards, while at the same time keeping secret the evidence of hazards.

Given the historical affinity of Congress for the viewpoints of those with the resources to fund reelection campaigns, only a few fortifications stand between the corporate government and the laws of the land as they are drawn on Capitol Hill. One of these fortifications, fortunately, is the facts. The facts can intrude occasionally on even the most concerted lobbying campaign. While the chemical industry, for example, was assailing Congress last spring against the creation of a Superfund to pay for the cleanup of hazardous dumpsites, a round of studies, though disputed, revealed evidence of unusual nerve and chromosome damage in residents at the Love Canal. Those people still were living at Love Canal—almost two years after a limited emergency was first declared—in large part because no accessible federal mechanism existed to fund their departure.

Facts alone rarely are enough to produce legislative results, however. Even the Love Canal tragedy, and the dangerous potential of tens of thousands of other dumpsites around the country, were unable to produce strict Superfund legislation. The threatened rollback of environmental-protection legislation is occurring—while polls show "that public support for environmental protection remains strong and broadly based," as one recent compilation of public-opinion samplings concluded.[5] This may indicate a new "silent majority." Unless elected officials believe their votes on environmental issues are being monitored and gauged by the voters back home, their commitment to the environment is likely to be sorely tested—and not infrequently broken—by the inducements of industry's campaign funding. "It will be tough," says Brock Evans, the Sierra Club's Associate Executive Director. "Corporate America is using its resources to counterattack. But we will just have to keep slugging away. Things never were easy."[6]

Environmentalists' goals, though never easily attained, have not been unreachable, either. Which brings us back to our first point: We are not helpless in the environmental crisis. There are alternatives.

PESTICIDES AND THEIR ALTERNATIVES

Synthetic insecticides are so heavily used in modern agriculture, it is easy to forget that the human race managed to feed itself for thousands of years without them. Now, even with the use of chemicals, the human race is having trouble feeding itself. This is primarily because world population continues to increase at the breakneck speed of 70 million per year. That means 192,000 new mouths to feed every day.[7]

Many of these mouths are not being fed. An unconscionable number of those receiving food are not getting enough. Around the world, an estimated 462 million people are starving. Another 1.3 billion are chronically undernourished.[8] This problem has many dimensions. Vast quantities of grain that could fill the empty bellies is diverted in America—and increasingly in western Europe and Japan—to fatten cattle. Farmland, too, is being diverted. In America alone, 2.7 million acres of valuable agricultural land is lost annually to urbanization and other development. (Only about half that much tillable acreage is added through irrigation.)[9] Heightening the problem is inadequate attention to soil erosion, and excessive demands on the land that remains in use. Worldwide, according to a United Nations study, one-fifth of the world's cropland is losing topsoil or otherwise being degraded.[10]

Most of the starving people in the world are in the underdeveloped countries. In these areas, the hunger problem has been exacerbated greatly by a skewed model of agricultural development that serves the needs of the multinational food corporations and local elites much more than the host country itself. Pressed by the exigencies of massive foreign debt, and by the requirements for concentration inherent in high-technology agriculture, food staples in many areas have been pushed off the land by "cash crops" grown for export—such commodities as cocoa, coffee and bananas. Some of the poorest countries in the world now devote more land to export crops than to food for their own people.[11] As Richard Barnet notes, "Rich and generally well-fed countries are now importing more and more of their food from countries with a high rate of malnutrition."[12] Poor farmers and peasants in these countries often simply lack the funds to buy the staples—wheat, corn and rice —that subsequently are imported into their countries.

The *Global 2000 Report* by the State Department and the Council on Environmental Quality relates the futility of trying to solve the problem of hunger solely by producing more food. The report projects a 90 percent increase in food production by the year 2000. But because of rapid population growth the increase per capita will be only 15 percent.[13] Moreover, much of that increase will be confined to the already well-fed areas of the world: the United States, western Europe, Japan, the Soviet Union. In the less developed countries (LDCs), the study reports, "rising food output will barely keep ahead of population growth."[14]

Even those meager gains in the LDCs will not be felt by all. In some areas—such as sub-Saharan African LDCs—per-capita consumption will decline by the year 2000. "In . . . South, East and Southeast Asia, poor areas of North Africa and the Middle East, and especially Central Africa, where a calamitous drop in food per capita is projected—the quantity of food available to the poorest groups of people will simply be insufficient to permit children to reach normal body weight and intelligence and to permit normal activity and good health in adults," the report says.[15]

So clearly the course of world hunger is generated by more forces than shortfalls in production. Our environment undoubtedly would be cleaner if no pesticides were used. Our food doubtless would be safer. But to call for a complete and immediate elimination of all pesticides would be senseless in a world where millions of people already are starving, millions more children are born every year, and little additional arable land is available. The relentless pressure of uncontrolled population growth makes compelling the case for limited and carefully controlled pesticide use in some areas when absolutely needed, until a new agronomy replaces chemical applications. Now, the questions about pesticides are: How much should be produced and applied, and when are they absolutely needed?

It is sobering to consider that this country's losses to crop pests have remained constant over the past 30 years—despite a tenfold increase in the use of chemical pesticides.[16] Pesticides and fertilizers have increased yields, of course, but insects, weeds and disease have kept pace. Heavy chemical use also has masked—and thereby promoted—the steady degradation of the soil, which has been called "likely . . . the most serious agricultural environmental problem of the future."[17] Farmers are investing increasing amounts of money in pesticides ($1.9 billion in 1976 alone)[18] merely to stay even with the pests.

Paying more to stay even was not the promise of the new age of chemical insecticides. The ease and spectacular results of early pesticide use upended in a matter of years farming practices that had stood in some cases for millennia. The age-old practices of exploiting the natural enemies of crop pests, adjusting crop-planting times to minimize dangers, and rotating crops —each of which also had been the subject of sophisticated research in the early part of this century—were cast aside.

Chemical pesticides and fertilizers redrew the face of agriculture. They helped make management of sprawling agribusinesses successful, thereby allowing the displacement of the family farm; the chemicals advanced the use of miracle high-yield seeds (often "at the price of lowered resistance to pests and diseases"[19]); and the compounds provided the technological support for the subsequent shift to monocultural (one-crop) planting. With the initial successes of chemical control, it appeared that, like space, the atom, and the sound barrier, nature would be conquered by American technology.

That has not been the case. Worldwide, hundreds of insects have developed resistance to chemical insecticides; some pests are resistant to more than one class of pesticide.[20] Malaria has become a renewed threat in many areas largely because malaria mosquitos have developed resistance to chemical insecticides.[21] The pesticide treadmill is a familiar phenomenon now. And, as noted, crop losses in the United States have remained constant in the past 30 years, despite soaring use of pesticides, with costly side-effects.

Now, a growing number of agricultural experts and entomologists—including, as an official policy at least, the United States Department of Agriculture (USDA)—have realized that chemical pesticides cannot conquer nature. Reviving the scientific disciplines discarded with the advent of pesticides, researchers around the country are developing pest-control plans known as Integrated Pest Management (IPM). These procedures greatly reduce pesticide use as well as the costs of growing crops.

IPM is defined as "a variety of biological, physical, and chemical methods integrated into a cohesive scheme designed to provide long-term protection. First consideration is given to use of naturally occurring mortality elements of the pest environment, including weather, diseases, predators, and parasites. Artificial control measures [pesticides], employed only as required to reduce and maintain the pests at tolerable levels, are based on criteria developed to identify when and where control is justified."[22] In sum, under IPM the entire ecosystem—not just a particular bug—is viewed as the unit to be managed. Insecticides are only one of many tools available (natural predators and parasites, resistant strains, and growing-schedule alterations are others) and are used only as the last resort in limited quantities. A six-year joint study by the EPA, the USDA and the National Science Foundation determined that IPM use on cotton, citrus fruits, deciduous fruits, soybeans and alfalfa (to which are applied 70 percent of the insecticides used on United States cropland) could cut pesticide use 70 to 80 percent in ten years—with no decrease in yield.[23]

IPM programs already have been successful on crops in several states. Soybean farmers in Florida using IPM in 1976 enjoyed profits $35 an acre greater than farmers using only pesticides. In 1977, 60 percent of the fields in the IPM program were not sprayed at all; no field was sprayed more than twice.[24] Using careful management techniques and "short-season" cotton, IPM farmers in the Trans Pecos region of Texas produced higher yields of cotton per acre than conventional growers—without spraying any pesticides at all. The twelve applications of pesticides required under the conventional system drove up growers' costs considerably. "Per acre costs of production were $302 for the IPM system and $445 conventional," says Dr. Ronald D. Lacewell of the Department of Agricultural Economics at Texas A&M University. "Farmer profit for the IPM system was $161 compared to $33 using the conventional system."[25]

The key steps in IPM are perhaps the first ones: assessing the economic threshold at which a pest is a serious hazard to the crop and at that point applying only selective pesticides in judicious amounts. "I still need chemicals," says Dan Pustejovsky, a cotton farmer in Texas who uses IPM. "But I don't spray anymore to kill every last insect—I live with a lot more bugs than I used to."[26] IPM, as one commentator observed, "rejects the notion that the presence of a pest species necessarily justifies action for control."[27] Instead, an IPM operator uses natural enemies, bacterial viruses, the development of resistant crops and a number of other ingenious methods to keep the population of pests below the economic-threshold level.

IPM research has proven an excellent investment in purely financial terms. From biological-control programs, which introduce natural enemies of pests to infested crop areas, economic returns typically are $30 for each dollar invested.[28] The development merely of crop strains resistant variously to the Hessian fly, the wheat-stem sawfly, the European corn borer and the spotted alfalfa aphid have returned approximately $300 in crop losses avoided for every research dollar invested.[29] In addition, by reducing the broadcast of toxic, often carcinogenic or mutagenic, pesticides, IPM can help the nation minimize an untold health burden.

IPM makes even more sense with other vegetation on which insecticides are used, particularly forests. As the chapter on "The Politics of Poison" makes clear, evidence is in that the herbicides sprayed over vast stands of forest have ruined many lives. Herbicides generally are applied to create a monoculture (to eliminate all competing vegetation) that is particularly valuable to the landowner. Besides requiring herbicide use, however, monocultures are exceedingly susceptible to insects and disease, and so eventually need heavy insecticide spraying as well. In Maine, for instance, for the past 25 years millions of acres have been coated annually with a bewildering array of pesticides in a futile, multimillion-dollar effort to eliminate (and lately merely to control) a tiny moth called the spruce bud-worm, which has prospered on the spruce-fir monoculture created by decades of mismanagement. Heavy pesticide use has enabled the paper companies to keep the trees alive from year to year and to maintain the size of the harvests. But the pesticides have hastened the degradation of the forest. "Obviously with the use of chemicals the [infestation] cycle has been prolonged," says M. Rupert Cutler, the USDA's former assistant secretary for conservation, research and education. "I think it's true that they've gotten hooked on a massive annual fix of pesticides to delay the eventual demise of a large portion of the forest."

This "annual fix" of pesticides in Maine has cost more than $17 million in state and federal aid since 1972.[30] Only in 1980 did the U.S. Forest Service decide no longer to fund the spraying of pesticides in Maine and to push the state toward adopting a balanced IPM program. By then, literally millions of acres of forest—to the consternation of the communities scattered within them—had been coated with carbaryl, a pesticide that has been under EPA review as a potential carcinogen, teratogen and, most recently, as a viral enhancer with the ability to promote disease. In 1980, no federal money supported carbaryl use; state and paper-company funds paid for spraying the pesticide again.

The Maine situation illustrates the strength of the impediments to acceptance of IPM. Primarily, the impediments are the pull of tradition and the push of the largest pesticide suppliers. As protest over the use of carbaryl heated up in 1980, Union Carbide—the nation's fourth largest chemical company, with sales about 10 times larger than Maine's state budget—opened an office in Augusta and launched an ad campaign to promote the pesticide's use. "Good news for your strawberries," Union Carbide intoned, "is bad news for the spruce budworm."[31] When Governor Joseph Brennan—who has supported the continued use of pesticides—bowed to growing pressure and offered legislation merely to tighten the state's pesticide laws, the bill confronted well-organized opposition from pesticide users and never got off the ground.

The pesticide industry is strong down on the farm as well. As numerous studies have documented, farmers rely heavily on chemical-industry sales representatives for pest-control information. This practice is somewhat analogous to children relying on the cereal companies for dental advice. Chemical producers have not been interested in developing the narrow-targeted pesticides required for true IPM. Instead, chemical companies market broad-based killers with the potential for many uses and for larger sales. Much less has the industry offered instructions on importing natural enemies, or on crop rotation. Similarly, the land-grant colleges and agriculture schools that rely on the industry for grants historically have been more eager to develop new insecticides than techniques to minimize their use.

Overcoming such obstacles will require spirited research, outreach and political action. But only those who tell us life itself would be impossible without chemicals proclaim pesticide use has no alternatives. We need not remain on the pesticide treadmill. Alternatives do exist.

A similar kind of despair surrounds the spread of cancer. "We've all heard the cocktail party refrain that 'everything causes cancer,' " says Douglas Costle, the former EPA administrator.[32] As one Illinois housewife told a reporter: "I'm sick of hearing that things cause cancer. If you believed it all, you'd be afraid to go out in the air, eat, swim or do anything."[33] To some extent, this reaction is natural. In the early 1970s, a series of research studies came to fruition indicating that several industrial chemicals, pesticides, food additives and other products were cancer-causing agents. After decades of assurances that these substances were safe, the news was unsettling, to say the least. Compounding the confusion have been industry representatives assailing the tests used to determine carcinogenicity. To ridicule tests that pour the equivalent of 800 bottles of diet soda into rats every day has become somewhat fashionable. Who drinks that much? the suppliers ask. From suppliers' claims springs the belief that everything—if forced into a test animal at some astronomical dosage—produces cancer.

"These unfortunate impressions irresponsibly have led people to think that nothing can be done about this tragic disease," says Costle. "That's wrong. We're not helpless in the face of cancer-causing substances."[34]

We're not helpless because, first of all, not everything causes cancer. This is demonstrated by, for example, a National Cancer Institute (NCI) study. One hundred and twenty substances judged potentially carcinogenic by their structural similarity to known carcinogens were tested: Only 10 percent proved to be carcinogenic.[35] Of another 250 chemicals tested under the NCI's bioassay program as suspected carcinogens, only half produced carcinogenic results.[36] Most of the compounds that are carcinogenic belong to certain subclasses of chemicals used heavily by industry.[37]

"So the number of compounds we need to protect ourselves against is not infinite," continues Costle. "The rules and prohibitions issued by Federal agencies to minimize people's exposure to carcinogens can make a difference."[38]

By and large, carcinogens are regulated on the basis of animal tests. Both the federal Regulatory Council and the president's Toxic Substances Strategy Committee—the former an agglomeration of 35 cabinet departments and agencies, the latter composed of 18 such groups—have determined "that animal tests are a valid method for determining whether a substance will cause cancer in people."[39] Getting that many federal officials to agree on anything is something of a miracle, but in this case the determination is solidly backed by science. All chemicals so far identified as human carcinogens (except for arsenic) have been carcinogenic in appropriately tested animals.[40] And high doses are administered in the tests for valid reasons.

High doses of a noncarcinogen cannot produce cancer, scientists agree. In the words of the Regulatory Council, "A non-carcinogen can be toxic when administered in high doses, but it will not directly cause cancer *at any dose level.*"[41] [Emphasis added.]

But high doses of a carcinogen can stimulate carcinogenicity that would not appear at low doses in the small number of animals used in the tests. The Council on Environmental Quality described the statistical and scientific basis for using high doses this way:

> Picture two groups of 100 animals apiece, one a control group, and one treated with a suspected carcinogen. If there were no tumors in the control group, the lowest incidence in the group of treated animals that we could consider statistically valid with 95 percent confidence is 3 percent. An incidence of 3 percent would be enormous in the U.S. population—66,000 out of 220 million people. Any substance that induced that much cancer would probably be rejected outright, even if there were substantial benefits to its use. Even 0.3 percent is a very high risk for a large population. Yet to detect an incidence as low as 0.3 percent, at the 95 percent confidence level, would require test groups of 1,000 animals. To detect incidence levels of 0.03 percent or lower—which are closer to the lifetime risks of the more common human cancers—would require tests of hundreds of thousands of animals. This is not practical. What is practical is in essence to make one animal stand in for a thousand—by increasing the dosage. Increasing the dosage means that cancers will occur more frequently, so that they can be detected in a group of 100 animals.[42]

If animal tests are in error, it is likely to be toward understating the risk of cancer to humans; laboratory animal tests cannot consider synergistic effects or the impact of malnutrition, improper diet or ill health on vulnerability. A more serious drawback to animal tests is that they take time—from two to five years—and are expensive, costing from $200,000 to $400,000. Epidemiological studies, too, yield extremely valuable evidence—the hazards of cigarettes were flushed out in this manner, of course—but these tests too take time and money. Moreover, epidemiological studies, by definition, come after the fact. Given the latency period of cancer, decades may pass before a substance's carcinogenicity is reflected in epidemiological studies—that is, if anyone takes a notion to look for it at all. "Even then," the Regulatory Council noted, "it may be very difficult to associate the occurrence of cancer with exposure to specific chemicals many years previously."[43] For these reasons the council determined: "Because it is unacceptable to allow exposure to potential carcinogens to continue until human cancer actually occurs, regulatory agencies should not wait for epidemiological evidence before taking action to limit human exposure to chemicals considered to be carcinogenic."[44]

To the wait for epidemiological testing, again, there are alternatives. The best known is the "Ames test" developed by Dr. Bruce Ames and Dr. Joyce McCann at the University of California at Berkeley. In it, a chemical is tested for inducing mutations in a population of bacteria; damage to an organism's genetic material is believed essential to the cancer process. The test is quick and inexpensive. Though limits to its reliability have been observed, the test provides a valuable first piece of information about a chemical.

Another quick indicator of potential trouble is contamination of human sperm. As discussed in the opening chapter, Dr. Ralph Dougherty has found that a decline in male fertility correlated with the presence of chlorinated hydrocarbons, such as PCB, and pesticides, in sperm. As Dougherty pointed out, the production of sperm requires prodigious cell division, and "substances that inhibit cell division are very often mutagenic, carcinogenic or both."[45] So eliminating from the environment substances that are reducing male fertility could prevent cancer or birth defects that may not develop for many years.

The science of studying chromosome aberrations, known as cytogenics, can provide regulators with quick, important information, too. Chromosome damage is believed to be a precursor of cancer, birth defects and other problems. Tests to determine chromosomal damage are quick and relatively inexpensive. Chromosomal tests have been conducted on workers exposed to nine different confirmed human carcinogens. In each case, "investigators have been able to detect an increase in the amount of chromosomal damage present in the exposed individuals."[46]

These tests provided part of the evidence for ordering the second evacuation at Love Canal, and they have been used routinely by the Dow Chemical Company at its Freeport, Texas, vinyl chloride plant. The tests could be put to wider use, however, and could indicate a need for emergency action by federal officials more quickly. At present, animal tests provide the most-accepted information on the carcinogenicity of chemicals. But with the new tools available, there is no reason to wait for the results of animal tests before taking precautionary action to limit human exposure to potentially dangerous substances. The consequences of delay, as we have seen with the Love Canal residents, can be tragedy.

WE HAVE PERSONAL CHOICES

We are not helpless—in a more personal sense as well. Changes in lifestyle can reduce exposure to some carcinogens, particularly those in consumer goods. Remember, however, that not "everything" is carcinogenic; that popular refrain is no excuse for inaction. Some substances clearly are carcinogenic, or promote other disease. And these should be avoided.

That cigarette smoking greatly increases the risk of contracting cancer is obvious now—not only cancer of the lung, but of the mouth, the larynx, and other bodily sites. If you are smoking, the advice is simple: Stop. If you are not smoking, the advice is equally straightforward: Don't start. Many programs have sprung up to help people quit smoking, and many millions of smokers have been able to stop on their own.[47] Whatever road is chosen, it should be followed to the end; switching to low-tar cigarettes is no substitute for quitting. Smokers of any sort of cigarette face greater cancer risks than nonsmokers.[48]

As apparent as the risk of smoking is, young people may have neither access to nor the proper appreciation for the risk data on tobacco that has been compiled voluminously since the 1950s. Still-tighter curbs are needed on the advertisers who portray cigarette smoking as sophisticated, adult and, above all, attractive to the opposite sex. As any doctor will tell you, lung cancer is neither attractive nor sophisticated. Yet Congress, at the prompting of the tobacco industry and its most dedicated promoter, Kentucky Democratic Senator Wendell Ford, restricted attempts to limit advertising that depend on such portrayals. Congress has barred the Federal Trade Commission

(FTC) for three years from regulating as "unfair" cigarette advertising aimed at young people.

The same advertising strategy propels the sale of alcohol in this country. One need not stand with the Temperance Union to acknowledge that heavy drinking, especially in tandem with cigarette smoking, can significantly increase the risk of cancer of the mouth and esophagus. Alcohol itself is not believed to be carcinogenic, but it does appear to work synergistically with carcinogens.[49]

Not surprisingly, diet also is important. "A considerable amount of epidemiological evidence suggests that diet plays a prominent role in the causation of certain types of cancer," says Dr. Arthur C. Upton, director of the National Cancer Institute. "Such evidence is found in correlations between cancer incidence and dietary habits in numerous studies of migrant populations and special population groups."[50] The most obvious step in weeding out dangerous substances from the diet is to reduce consumption of highly processed, additive-laden "junk" foods. Many individual additives and food dyes have been identified as carcinogens. The broader dietary picture, too, indicates healthful practices. For example, reducing fat intake is worthwhile. "Both animal studies as well as studies of human populations suggest that a high fat-intake may be associated with an increased risk of cancer," says Upton. "Both saturated and unsaturated fats have been incriminated."[51]

Other sensible steps, too, can mitigate exposure to carcinogens. Avoid home use of pesticides. Avoid unnecessary x-rays, and when you go in for those that are necessary ask for shielding of the rest of your body. Check carefully cleaning products you use in your home, and avoid those with known carcinogenic components, such as carbon tetrachloride. For a more extensive review of the carcinogenicity of specific products and goods, see both *Malignant Neglect*, by the Environmental Defense Fund, and *The Politics of Cancer*, by Samuel S. Epstein, M.D.

Clearly, consumer choices that minimize exposure to hazards in the environment are limited. Looking at a fish in the supermarket, a consumer cannot determine whether its flesh contains PCBs or other potentially harmful residues. We cannot choose not to breathe the air in our neighborhoods. Similarly, residents of Toone, Tennessee, did not choose to have their groundwater poisoned by pesticide wastes from nearby chemical companies. The Toone residents were—we are—involuntary consumers of a host of pollutants.

Reducing this exposure requires more than personal choice. It requires an active involvement in the issues. This can begin on the local level.

For example, even the smallest of communities can reduce the amount of municipal wastes requiring disposal. Nationally, the generation of such wastes continues to mushroom: In 1978, the United States' total was 154 million tons, or approximately 1,400 pounds per person.[52] Such vast quantities of garbage tax our natural disposal systems and present tremendous problems. Only about six percent of that waste is being recycled; another one percent is being converted into energy.[53] "The current wasteful materials policy," the Worldwatch Institute observed in a report on recycling, "could only have evolved in an era of cheap, abundant energy."[54]

The policies allowing the creation of so much refuse are beginning to change. As recently as 1968 Madison, Wisconsin, was the only municipality in the country with a citywide program for separating out recyclables in trash—what is known as source separation. By 1974, 118 communities had such programs, and by 1978, 218 had them.[55] These exist primarily because local citizens pushed for them. Source separation also makes good economic sense; programs can be established with minimal capital expenditure, and they reduce disposal costs significantly by cutting total waste generation. A program in Marblehead, Massachusetts, saved the city $3,000 per month during its first nine months and reduced waste generation by 23 to 33 percent.[56]

Source separation entails merely removing recyclable wastes—such as paper, glass and metal—from other garbage, and subsequently selling them to dealers or manufacturers. Successful programs typically make recycling not only integral, but mandatory, to guarantee participation. Besides reducing the amount of wastes, recycling can save considerable amounts of energy. Processing recycled aluminum requires 96 percent less energy than processing virgin ore; processing recycled copper, 88 to 95 percent less; and steel, 47 percent less energy.[57]

The potential for recycling, with its attendant benefits for energy conservation and the environment, is immense. Two-thirds as much paper and glass is discarded in municipal wastes each year as is consumed across the country. The amount of aluminum in wastes equals 20 percent of that consumed.[58] And more than two-thirds of all metal is used only once.[59] Denis Hayes, now director of the Solar Energy Research Institute, has commented that, in a society based on recycling and reuse, "Both ends of the material chain—the mine and the dump—would fade in importance. . . ."[60]

Mineral losses in industrial waste are vast. According to a General Accounting Office analysis of seven industries (which produce less than one-fourth of the annual national total of solid waste), more than 10 million tons of such minerals as iron, copper and aluminum are lost in wastes annually.[61] To the GAO, the advantages of recycling in both reducing pollution and reducing dependence on foreign sources of minerals are overwhelming. The report observed:

> The importance of extending mineral supplies through recovery from wastestreams is most obvious for those minerals on which the country is import dependent. For example, this Nation depends on large imports of chromium and nickel. We found the wastestreams of four of the seven industries we reviewed contain large amounts of chromium and two contained a substantial amount of nickel. . . . However, only one company we visited has recognized the potential for extending chromium and nickel supplies and is building a recovery plant.[62]

Reusing the minerals also would reduce pollution. The report continued: "An assessment of industrial hazardous waste practices in the metal smelting and refining industries, performed for EPA in 1977, concluded that adequate health and environmental protection from nine different wastestreams in the copper, lead, zinc, iron and aluminum industries could be obtained through resource recovery."[63]

Using a variety of innovative means, other nations are far ahead of the United States in promoting recycling, the GAO found. While "The U.S. steel industry does only a fair job of recovering minerals from its wastestreams," the GAO reported, "Japanese steel companies using technology considered uneconomical in the United States recover mineral values from most of their industrial dusts."[64] Domestic companies have been pleading for import protection against Japanese steel companies. They might do better emulating the Japanese firms' admirable recovery of wastes.

Electroplating, which produces extremely hazardous wastes, is another area of sharp divergence between American and Japanese policies. Recovery of electroplating wastes is extremely limited here; an independent lab has estimated that more than $40 million worth of metals are left in the industry's wastestreams annually. The wastes, instead of being recovered, are diluted and simply dumped into waterways, sewers and deep wells, posing significant pollution problems. In Tokyo, by contrast, financial aid has been provided to relocate 11 electroplaters in an industrial park that "provides a means to recover minerals that the individual firms were not recovering by themselves," according to the GAO. Now more than 600 kilograms of copper and other materials are recovered monthly.[65]

Why has resource recovery lagged in the United States? The depletion allowance on virgin ores—without similar tax encouragement for recycling—has encouraged use of raw materials. Industry has been slow to recognize the potential of recycling. And the federal government has done little to prod industry toward it. As the GAO observed, "Few resource-recovery programs or alternative strategies for the urban wastestream have been proposed, evaluated or implemented, and even fewer for industrial wastes."[66]

The federal government also has done little to promote energy conservation, another way to reduce pollution. Although President Carter called conservation the "cornerstone" of his energy program, the GAO, congressional investigators and the Office of Technology Assessment all agree that the

Department of Energy is doing little to promote more judicious and efficient use of fuel. In the latest of a long series of critical reports, the GAO wrote in September 1980 that the "DOE still has not set overall national conservation goals which articulate conservation's contribution—in the near, mid and long term— to meeting domestic energy needs. . . . In addition, the Department has yet to develop a comprehensive plan which details how the Nation can be moved to greater energy efficiency."[67]

An internal planning document in the DOE's Office of Conservation and Solar Energy expressed a similar opinion: "In spite of the large potential of conservation, its critical role in reducing oil imports during the 1980s, its short lead time relative to supply options, as well as other favorable characteristics, the Department of Energy's program priorities and funding are inconsistent with conservation and supply benefit and cost comparisons."[68]

But conservation can play a great role in the nation's energy program, not only by reducing the energy bill, but by eliminating hazardous pollutants, such as sulfur emitted from coal-fired power plants. President Carter currently is pushing through Congress a costly—and environmentally dangerous— plan to convert 38 power plants from oil to coal use. If all 38 plants are converted, acid rain is expected to increase by 16 percent.[69]

This proposal is typical of Carter's overall energy plan: Maintain the current high levels of consumption by switching fuels, or by developing new sources of energy—such as synthetic fuels. Reducing consumption is given priority in speeches, but at budget time, production clearly comes out ahead. Many an analyst considers this a serious imbalance. Dr. Robert Stobaugh, director of the Harvard Business School's highly respected energy project, recently told Congress, "in terms of expenditures, instead of spending $88 billion on synthetic fuels and $2 billion on conservation, we believe that perhaps $50 billion of Federal funds could be spent cost-effectively for conservation and some solar."[70] An extensive study by the Environmental Defense Fund found that if the money required to open a new coal-fired plant was used instead to support conservation, more energy could be saved at less cost.[71]

COMMUNITIES THAT HAVE FOUGHT BACK

Recycling and conservation are prospective actions—they are designed to minimize problems in the future. To fight on the local level powerful industrial firms that already are established is undeniably difficult, yet some communities have successfully opposed ongoing hazards. One of these communities is Burlington, New Jersey, a heavily industrialized township of 17,000 just east of the Delaware River. The river, says one local reporter, "is the kind you can walk on." Burlington is home to, among other industries, plants run by the Hooker Chemical Company and by Tenneco Chemical, Incorporated, the nation's twentieth largest chemical company.

Tenneco has been in Burlington since 1962. Its plant there produces polyvinyl chloride (PVC) from the raw material of vinyl chloride. Vinyl chloride is a known carcinogen capable of inducing angiosarcoma, a fatal form of liver cancer; symptoms of exposure include dizziness, headaches and drowsiness. The Food and Drug Administration (FDA) has banned the use of PVC containers on food products and beverages, but still allows PVC wrapping on food. PVC also is used in records, floor tiles, vinyl car-seat covers, purses, suitcases and surgical tubing.

Polyvinyl chloride emissions have been a problem in Burlington for years. People living south and west of the plant have found a fine white powder coating their cars or floating in their swimming pools. During 1978 the plant sent out a chemist to check 35 such complaints. Each time he came back with the same message: It was PVC.[72]

In January 1979 Tenneco bid on the grounds of a vacant school adjacent to the company's property, saying the land would be used for administrative offices. A group of residents became concerned that Tenneco intended to use the grounds for an extension of its physical plant. Edward Amato, a steamfitter, and several other people asked the Burlington Town Council to purchase the school instead. The council told them to prove that the community did not want Tenneco to own the school.

So Amato and about 25 others formed an organization called Burlington Township Concerned Citizens, and they collected 1,600 signatures on a petition asking that the sale be put to a public vote.[73]

The school board—which under law did not need public approval—ignored the petitions and sold the site to Tenneco for $900,000.[74]

The Concerned Citizens stayed together, however, hired a local attorney named Steve Warm, and continued to meet with Tenneco and the town council about its concerns. On July 17 Tenneco gave them something else to be concerned about: A safety valve failed on a storage tank and released 300 gallons of vinyl chloride in liquid and vapor form.[75]

With all this as a backdrop, Tenneco formally applied to the town planning board in September to "modernize" its plant—to increase production of PVC from 155 million to 178 million pounds annually. At the first hearing on the proposal, Tenneco brought in Dr. Harry Demopoulos of the New York University Medical Center, who said there was no cause for concern. "There is no way that under either normal or abnormal circumstances, considering the worst possible conditions, that any harm can come to workers at Tenneco or to area residents from inhaling VCM [vinyl chloride monomer]."[76]

Warm contacted cancer researcher Samuel Epstein, who agreed to testify at a later hearing. Two more hearings were held, at which Tenneco continued to press for approval. A fourth hearing, at which Epstein and Dr. Joseph Waggoner, an epidemiologist famous for his work with uranium miners, were scheduled to testify, was set for December 5.[77]

A few days before their scheduled appearance, Tenneco shocked the community by withdrawing its application. Amato, Warm and other local observers believe that Tenneco pulled out because its officials feared the testimony of Epstein and Waggoner. Tenneco officials told us, "The costs became prohibitive and cost forecasts became somewhat illusive." In either case, despite Tenneco's decision, the fourth hearing was held as scheduled. Both Epstein and Waggoner challenged the Tenneco assertions of safety. "It's very clear the facts presented by Tenneco do not reflect reality," Epstein told the board. "They have brought in consultants who are apparently remarkably misinformed." Expanding the plant and maintaining a safe environment, he said, was "absolutely out of the question."[78]

As we write, Tenneco says it has no plans for further expansion in Burlington. It does, however, say the situation might change. Residents are convinced that the giant chemical company is merely marshalling its resources for another try. But the Concerned Citizens are not finished, either; they are investigating legal avenues to shut down the plant—completely and permanently. "As one of the world's largest chemical companies, Tenneco looked unbeatable, particularly with only a small group of people opposing it," says Amato, looking back.

That is probably the way residents of Mendocino and Humboldt counties in California felt when they began drives to ban aerial spraying of herbicides, through the initiative process. In both counties, residents were going up against giant lumber and chemical companies strongly committed to the use of the chemicals. But in both cases, the local groups were successful. "It's not just a matter of rich people in San Francisco wanting to keep their views; it's a matter of survival," says Francia Welker, a Mendocino County attorney. "When you realize that the stuff is coming down from the sky and getting into the water supply, you want to do something."[79]

Likewise, in Maine, residents of Washington County, the state's poorest, have fought a bitter, years-long battle with the state government and the powerful paper companies to end the 25-year-old spray program against the spruce budworm. The residents brought suit against the spraying, marched on the state capitol in Augusta, and occupied a compound when a helicopter loaded with pesticides was about to take off. After years of work they are beginning to make headway. In response to a lawsuit brought by the residents in 1979, the USDA announced it no longer would fund insecticide spraying of the budworm; despite pressure from state officials and Maine's congressional delegation, the department upheld that pledge in 1980, marking a landmark break with the years of federal support.

Perhaps the best example of dedicated, well-informed and effective local environmental activists are the Love Canal homeowners, who protested, conducted health surveys and lobbied in Washington and Albany until federal and state officials finally recognized the hazards the residents faced and agreed to relocate them.

A FRAMEWORK TO ALLOW LOCAL ACTION

Beyond insensitivity, and the fear of setting a precedent for the handling of future hazardous-waste dumps, one reason the Love Canal residents remained there so long was that no federal mechanism existed to pay for their evacuation. If Superfund legislation had been in force, the residents would likely not have had to wait almost two years to be removed. Their case crystallizes the need to tie in local efforts with national action. Effective national law provides the framework for local challenges to polluters, and the basis for seeking compensation for injuries. Without national standards, polluters can simply flee environmentally-conscious states for others with less stringent regulations.

The environmental legislation of the past decade has focused on individual symptoms of the problem—polluted lakes, filthy air, unsafe dumpsites. Further initiatives are needed in this area. We need stronger Superfund legislation to seal up the leaking hazardous-waste dumpsites around the country. The fund should be financed by the industries responsible for the dumps, not by the taxpayers suffering from them. If this financing increases the costs of certain products, it will simply provide consumers with a more accurate picture of those products' true cost.

An effective Superfund should assign joint, several and strict liability to the manufacturers, transporters and disposers of the waste. As one environmental lobbyist observed, this doctrine "assigns liability to anyone who has handled or will handle the substances, thus ending the legal buckpassing that invariably confounds dump-related litigation." Drafts of the Superfund in the Senate contained important provisions making it easier for victims of hazardous pollutants to be compensated for their injuries. Superfund supporters pushed for the inclusion of these sections because persons harmed by hazardous substances often have found it nearly impossible to tie their injuries to a particular pollutant and so win damages in court. For the same reason, the chemical industry lobbied hard—and successfully—against the provisions. As will be discussed further, our compensation system's inability to deal with toxic chemicals has enabled polluters to escape responsibility.

We also need more reliable data about the tens of thousands of chemicals and pesticides used every day. Currently, the manufacturers themselves provide the basic scientific information on which government decisions are based. Samuel Epstein says, "If you ask [an] industry that clearly wants to market a particular product or process, and you say to [its officials] . . . supply us with the information on the basis of which we are going to regulate this product or process, there is an inevitable conflict of interest. And as a result of that, decisions will flow appropriately."[80]

As Epstein and other experts have pointed out, a buffer is needed between those who wish to manufacture a chemical and those who test its safety. To ensure objectivity and reliability, the optimal situation is a "double blind" test, where the manufacturer does not know who is testing the chemical, and the lab does not know who wishes to market the chemical it is testing. This could be arranged by using a governmental or quasi-governmental scientific body as a "buffer" to solicit open bids from labs whenever a chemical requires testing. With this procedure, industry would face the same costs, but commercial labs would be free of their current dependency on private industry for contracts—a situation that strains objectivity. Double-blind testing also would free the government from decisions made with tainted, or at least questionable, data. If some testing must remain in the hands of industry, spot checks and heavy fines should be used to discourage falsification.

Moreover, the Toxic Substances Control Act (TSCA) should be toughened to require the premarket testing of all chemicals, not just those chosen for such treatment by the EPA. During the first few months the TSCA regulations were in effect, virtually none of the chemicals submitted to the EPA had any health data from testing. "It seems to me the system creates a disincentive to test," Jacqueline Warren of the Environmental Defense Fund told a congressional subcommittee in spring 1980. "If I were a manufacturer, I don't know whether I would want to do much testing because my PMN [premanufacture notice] coming in with a lot of testing would stand out in a crowd which has no testing."[81] This is hardly what industry promised when it opposed the bill. Steven Jellinek, the EPA's assistant administrator for toxic substances, told the same subcommittee: "There is no doubt that this general lack of adequate risk related information is contrary to congressional intent in passing . . . TSCA and that it also contradicts industry's oft-expressed view of how it conducts testing of new chemicals."[82]

Remedial testing of the chemicals already in commerce must be speeded. To select high-risk chemicals for priority testing, the TSCA set up an Interagency Testing Committee. Rules to govern the testing are only now being established, however. The tests themselves will take from two to four years more to complete, and promulgating rules based on the tests will require an additional two years—or more, if litigation is brought against the agency's decision. "We will be into the late 1980s before we even get significant testing information about these [chemicals]" says Louis Slesin, a former Natural Resources Defense Council researcher who painted the above scenario. "If some of them should prove to be hazardous, we are talking about the 1990s before EPA will gear up in terms of regulating those hazards."[83]

The limitations of dealing with the symptoms of the environmental problem are well exemplified by the testing dilemma. Government is always trying to catch up with industry.

A chemical company issues a new chemical; the government tries to determine whether it is safe. A paper company decides to spray its lands with herbicides; the government tries to determine whether they pose a health hazard. For the public, this is a no-win situation. The government can hope only to catch the more egregious dangers already existing. Under the current legislative framework, the government and the public do not have time to consider the long-term implications of such private decisions as the introduction of new technologies. We are running too hard to keep up.

What is needed are reforms that treat the primary cause of environmental degradation—the cause that is, as we have seen in eight chapters, the power of large corporations, unaccountable to the workers and communities they make unwilling absorbers of their pollution. Environmental law has stopped at the board room doors. To prevent more Love Canals, more Dennys and Hopewells, the law must move inside the corporate board room. Otherwise, we will continue to be left picking up the pieces of broken neighborhoods and lives.

FEDERAL CHARTERING TO ESTABLISH ACCOUNTABILITY

The reforms recommended here have two basic objectives: to make corporations accountable during the decision-making process, and to make them responsible for the effects of the decisions made. This will not require the construction of any elaborate new regulatory structure. Rather, the largest industrial corporations should be brought up to minimum federal standards of behavior through the process of federal chartering.

Currently, corporations are chartered by individual states. Led by New Jersey in the 1890s, and then by Delaware throughout this century, the states have competed in what aptly has been called a "race to the bottom." Eager to attract incorporation fees, the states have adopted corporate codes that cede away stockholder, worker and public rights. "In short," wrote one professor, "state law has abdicated its responsibility."[84] This has led to the ludicrous if unsurprising spectacle of tiny Delaware serving as the official home of nearly half the Fortune 500, including the Exxon Corporation, which has annual sales larger than many nations.

James Madison proposed federal chartering almost 200 years ago. William Jennings Bryan backed it at the turn of this century.[85] In their time, both men understood the dangers of brute economic power not accountable to the populace. The power to pollute, which threatens future generations as well as our own, makes the case for federal chartering more compelling than ever. Let us consider some of the reforms a federal chartering law would include.

How can we open up corporate decision-making, to prevent future environmental disasters? The institution designed to review and check the decisions of a corporation's management is its board of directors. The board should be the corporation's internal auditor—the sober voice constraining management from ethical or legal violations. The board should take the longer view—which means considering such questions as the possible long-term hazards of new products—and should balance the excesses of management.

It sounds good in theory. In practice, however, the board, like any messenger in the mail room, serves at management's pleasure. Consider these figures from a recent report on federal chartering:

—of the 6,744 corporations required to report to the Securities and Exchange Commission on board elections, incumbent management retained control in 99.9 percent, or 6,734 companies;

—in 10 of the 18 years from 1956 to 1973, management equaled that 99.9 percent record;[86]

—in 1973, 99.7 of the board of directors elections in the largest corporations were uncontested.

Action is needed to end this stranglehold and to subject the decisions of management to serious scrutiny. The majority of a board's members should be independent directors—people with neither family nor business or financial ties to the corporation. To give these directors a reasonable chance to perform their functions, they should have a support staff—responsible to the board, not to management.

To hone and carefully delineate oversight responsibilities, as many as nine board members should be given the responsibility, in addition to their traditional fiduciary obligation, specifically to oversee particular areas of the corporation's environmental and social performance. "Because these concerns become everybody's general interest," supporters of federal chartering have noted, "they become nobody's particular interest—and often go unattended."[87] This division of responsiblity also will enable individual board members to develop the expertise needed to contest management on such complex issues as the safety of a pesticide or an industrial process.

An additional reform will further empower a board to prevent lawbreaking and cover-ups of hazards. Boards should be required to instruct all lawyers and auditors working for the corporation to notify them of any significant action they consider "to be illegal or probably illegal."

All of these reforms, of course, are likely to be greatly muted in effect if future board members come from the same limited social pool as current ones—essentially, balance-sheet–oriented white males not dissimilar to management officials. To diversify the boards, a reasonable number of shareholders should have the right to nominate directors; all candidates should be given equal funds and access to the proxy machinery to make their cases.

Accountability during the decision-making process also can be enhanced by expanding the flow of information to the public. While the chemical industry, for example, has been pouring millions of dollars into glossy ads and slick television spots, it has resisted vigorously the disclosure of even the most basic information about its products and their potential hazards. "In a recent southern California incident, day care children were exposed to a toxic cloud from a nearby company," Peter H. Weiner, a special assistant to California Governor Jerry Brown, told Congress in spring 1980. "The children and teachers suffered liver damage. For weeks the company refused to supply treating physicians with the identity of the substances involved, claiming trade secret protection."[88]

Employees themselves usually are the first to know of potential hazards posed by a corporation's activities. But they also are usually among the last to speak out. This is in part, no doubt, because they have seen "whistle-blowers" who call attention to unsafe products or practices harassed or dismissed.

The code of ethics for most professions, and for federal employees, states explicit that the responsibility of the individual to the public interest, "to the highest moral principles,"[89] supercedes responsibility to the organization. The basic status of a citizen in a democracy underscores the expectation that individuals will not quietly go along with company or government policy if it is illegal, negligent or unjust. At the Nuremberg trials after World War II, of course, the defense of "just following orders" was rejected.

Yet corporations are allowed, under law, to dismiss employees who refuse to acquiesce in illegal activity or to remain silent about dangers. Federal chartering should include constitutional rights for employees, guaranteeing that they cannot be fired except for "just cause." Needless to say, altering society to a festering public-health problem would not be considered just cause for dismissal. By encouraging employees to speak out after reasonable internal channels have been exhausted, and by protecting them when they do go public, we can promote early detection.

Generally, basic information on a company's pollution performance is scattered and difficult to collect. To enable stockholders and other members of the public to assess environmental performance, companies should be required to disclose on a plant-by-plant basis their emissions into the air and water, the level of emissions allowed by federal law, and any environmental legal actions outstanding against them. Companies should make public the details of their solid-waste disposal practices. And companies also should disclose annually the nature and total number of occupational injuries and illnesses suffered by employees, as well as—on request from employees or stock-holders—the dangerous chemical constituents of any substance used in any of its plants. These accounts should be reported in clear language and be on record at local libraries.

This information about a company's operation will be valu-able for more than environmental reasons. Research by the Council on Economic Priorities in New York (and by other groups) has determined clearly that companies with effective pollution-control programs tend to perform more profitably than heavy polluters. Pollution often is a sign of mismanage-ment. Hooker Chemical, polluting communities from coast to coast, plainly has been a company off its bearings. From Hooker, though, comes the most arresting explanation of why we need increased disclosure. It was written in a memo by an engineer at Hooker's Lathrop, California, plant, where pesticide wastes were allowed over a period of years to leach into neighboring wells. Though the engineer warned plant management about the problem—and top corporate officials in Houston were notified—Hooker withheld the information from both the farm-ers who took water from those wells and the state. The memo tells why:

> Most other organizations involved in pesticide handling have spent millions to solve their problems. No outsiders actually know what we do and there has been no government pressure on us, so we have held back trying to find out what to do within funds we have available.[90]

No more eloquent testimonial could expose the need for an open, accountable decision-making process. Discouraging the deceit exemplified by Hooker's strategy will require tough pen-alties for corporate cover-ups.

That criminals must "pay for their crimes" is axiomatic. Every year, a new wave of political candidates calls for a return to respect for the letter of the law, for tough penalties to deter misdeeds by tough criminals. This addresses well-ingrained fears and usually is warmly received by the voters. The political speeches inevitably devote much time and rhetorical fire to muggers, pickpockets and the like but are unlikely to mention chemical criminals. That is not surprising, for chemical crime is a relatively new field of lawbreaking. And it is difficult to see the well-dressed, well-educated officials behind the disasters in this book as criminals. Corporate officials hardly fit the usual mental picture. But their actions can endanger many more people by far than even the most enterprising pickpocket or mugger. "They are polluting our air," says Dennis Virtuoso, a union official in Niagara Falls. "They are ruining our environment. They are killing our people. If that is not a crime, I do not know what is."[91]

COMPENSATION DENIED

No one pays for most environmental crimes but the victims. In the literal sense, despite the increasing awareness of the hazards of radiation and toxic chemicals and the growing realization that exposure to toxic substances is the root of many diseases, victims of environmental pollution usually do not receive compensation for their illnesses. This has been true both for people injured by government actions and for those harmed by private corporations. Consider:

—Only from 2 to 5 percent of the victims of occupational disease receive worker's compensation.[92]

—More than 60 percent of occupational-disease worker's compensation claims are contested, compared to fewer than 10 percent of accident claims;[93] 60 percent of all occupational disease awards initially were denied;[94] and workers disabled by occupational illness wait, on the average, one full year before actually receiving any benefits. Workers injured in job-related accidents usually wait about two months.[95]

—In 1980 the Veterans Administration still was denying a link between Agent Orange exposure and medical problems. Only two of more than 1,200 veterans applying had been granted compensation on the basis of Agent Orange exposure—in both cases, compensation was for treatment of chloracne, a severe skin disease that appears as an acute symptom of dioxin poisoning. Virtually all veterans exposed to radiation during nuclear tests have had their claims denied as well.[96]

—If victims take their cases to court they are likely to find, as the Congressional Research Service concluded, "the burdens of proof are difficult, the outcomes uncertain, and immediate relief impossible."[97]

The two major barriers to compensation are proving causality—isolating a single pollutant from a single source as the cause of injury—and the long latency period of environmentally induced diseases. In some states, the statute of limitations can knock off many claims by itself. In other states, the difficulties of establishing causality and of coping with the legal muscle purchased by corporate defendants can be insurmountable.

"The problem is that the evidence in most cases is not simply overwhelming," says Dr. David Rall, the director of the National Institute of Environmental Health Sciences. "So that allows other emotions to take over. If you are compassionate toward the victim you tend to think, 'Well, there is some evidence and they obviously ought to be compensated.' If you're concerned about setting a precedent and costing oodles of money you say, 'Oh my, there may be a cause, but I don't really think they ought to be compensated.' "

Representative John J. LaFalce, a Democrat from New York whose district includes the Love Canal area, says that "We are talking about an area where the law has not developed adequate legal mechanisms." As LaFalce says, "Now we can . . . let this evolve through our judicial system, which I predict as an attorney who has had some experience in this area, will take perhaps 20 years. . . ."[98]

Or we can do something about it. Congress is considering the problem in a piecemeal manner. Drawing on the black lung disease compensation precedent, bills have been introduced to compensate uranium miners, victims of fallout from nuclear tests in the 1950s and 1960s, brown-lung victims and others. Senator Harrison Williams, a New Jersey Democrat, has been proposing an overhaul of the state worker's compensation system for years, without much success. Bills to establish administrative bodies to investigate and provide compensation for environmentally induced illnesses also have been introduced without any success.

Rall considers these maneuvers "a necessary preliminary to developing some overall compensation system." At the least, Congress should give direction to the courts in establishing the use of toxic materials as an ultrahazardous activity, subject to strict liability. Under strict liability, claimants need not prove negligence to recover damages. As one Senate legal aide put it:

> The question is one of on whom should you place adequate knowledge or having incentive to find out what [danger] is there. . . . Obviously the person who's injured, there's no way they can do anything about it. It's even different than a strict liability situation in product liability where you can say when the person goes into the store and buys the cheap toaster there's a reason the toaster is cheaper. And they have maybe as much chance to tinker with it, or try it out or make an assessment on the basis of price or other things that there might be some greater danger involved. Therefore, maybe they should balance that responsiblity off a little bit more. But there isn't [that option] here. There's nothing in the world they can do.[99]

While an overhaul of the state worker's compensation system—indeed the overall compensation system as administered by the executive branch and the courts as well—is long overdue, the bottom line remains the standard of proof. On whom should the burden of proof lie? Should chemicals be presumed innocent until proven guilty, so that injured people are assumed mistaken until they can tie down the medical questions with incontrovertible evidence? With present scientific knowledge, it is doubtful whether such links can be proved beyond the shadow of a doubt—especially among small groups of people such as those living near a dumpsite.

Joan Z. Bernstein, the general counsel of HEW and head of President Carter's interagency work group on Agent Orange, laid out the problems for a congressional subcommittee:

> "Because of the controversy [over Agent Orange compensation], many may have come to believe that once an optimal research agenda is established and carried out, the research results will provide definitive, incontrovertible scientific information about the health effects of phenoxy herbicides and their contaminants. *I believe this is an unfortunate view because even the best effort of which our scientists are capable may not produce such conclusive results.* In short, we may be left, after the research is done, with many of the same social policy issues we face today."[100] [Emphasis added.]

Bernstein's assessment is sound. Understanding that compensation is as much a political as a scientific problem is essential to developing an effective, humane response to environmental disease, for both those already victimized and those who may face danger in the future. The exaggerated demands from industry in regulatory proceedings and court cases for a scientific "smoking gun" are another tactic to tie up decision-makers and to prevent the banning of hazardous substances. We need to humanize the debate by devoting more attention to the rights of the people than to the presumed prerogatives of chemicals. In its best function, compensation can not only ease the pain of those already harmed, but can be "a hedge against abusing people by technology," in the words of Bob Alvarez of the Environmental Policy Center. In its worst use—which is not far from where we are now—an unresponsive compensation system can be a reverse deterrent—a license to destroy human health.

CRIMINAL PENALTIES FOR CORPORATE CRIMINALS

Each of the environmental disasters in this book, as noted in the opening chapter, was accelerated and expanded through the cover-up of hazards. Yet no one from, for example, the Hooker Chemical Company has gone to jail in connection with the Love Canal. Nor are any jail sentences likely.

The penalties can be different for future chemical criminals. Important legislation has been introduced by Representative George Miller, a California Democrat, to impose jail terms and stiff fines on individual corporate managers who cover up impending hazards, or whose reckless failure to supervise subordinates contributes to a cover-up. "Too often," Miller said when introducing the bill, "offending companies have been fined nominal amounts; in some cases they have been awarded tax benefits allowing them to write off liability losses. This situation cannot continue. When someone makes a decision to conceal information about a product or an industrial process, knowing full well that the product or process jeopardizes someone's life, health or safety, I believe a criminal act has occurred."[101]

So do many others, including more than 40 congressional cosponsors of the bill, the Justice Department and many responsible members of the business community. Like the other corporate reforms suggested here, this bill—and the criminal penalty provisions contained in the Senate review of the Criminal Code—are not regulatory. Rather they seek, through deterrence, to cut off the environmental and occupational dangers before the regulatory system must deal with them. Observed the *Harvard Law Review*, "Individual criminal sanctions also deter corporate crime by strengthening employees' incentives to resist corporate pressures to violate the law in the pursuit of increased profits." Said the *Review*, "The threat of a jail sentence in particular induces employees to forego even substantial corporate profits rather than risk individual criminal liability."[102]

This legislation is a valuable first step. If behavioral sanctions were tacked on, it might be even more effective. For instance, if the Allied Chemical executives had been sent to jail for the Kepone disaster (which they were not), the officials could have been forced to spend a few years cleaning up the James River, along with the other workers on the job. This would do two things. First, it would tell society that the law does not differentiate between rich and poor, because the rich, too, end up in jail after due process. Second, it would engage those at fault in rehabilitation. After watching their fellows try to clean up the James River, many managers in the chemical industry might be less willing to poison our rivers.

As it stands, high-level executives found guilty of serious offenses often remain in their jobs. That hardly encourages rehabilitation, or a respect for the law in others seeking advancement on the corporate ladder. Judges sentencing corporate criminals should be given the authority to disqualify executives found guilty from holding, for a specified period of time, a post similar to the one in which they broke the law. This would not be applicable in all cases, of course. But society justifiably could think twice about handing over responsiblity for a chemical plant to an individual who has been convicted of covering up dangers at a similar facility. Already, the Landrum-Griffin Act of 1959 bars convicted felons from union office for five years. Lawyers and brokers can lose their license for crimes.[103] Holding to the same standard individuals who poison entire neighborhoods or priceless natural resources does not seem unreasonable.

For society to question the internal structure of a corporation that habitually violates the law is equally reasonable. The behavior of such corporate recidivists as the Velsicol and Hooker Chemical companies suggests more than a few unscrupulous managers at individual plants. When a court determines that a convicted corporation's structure inclines it to continue violating the law, the court should be able to place the company on probation. It has been said that a corporation cannot visit a probation officer. But a probation officer can visit a corporation.[104] And with wide access to information mandated by the court, such an officer could monitor a corporation's activities to prevent future offenses.

Generally, fines have been the harshest measure used to deal with corporate crimes. The fines generally have been trifling, the financial equivalent of a mosquito stinging an elephant. Against other kinds of organized crimes, sterner measures have been used. In 1970, Congress passed the Organized Crime Control Act to deal with a pattern of crime that was of great national concern. Under Title IX of the law, the Racketeer Influenced and Corrupt Organizations—or RICO—statute, federal prosecutors can seek stiff jail terms (up to 20 years), fines of as much as $25,000, and complete forfeiture of ill-gotten gains for such crimes as cigarette bootlegging, gambling, counterfeiting and bribing athletes. Under the civil penalties specified by the law, the courts could seek to "prevent and restrain violations" by such measures as ordering an individual to divest his or her holdings in a company, prohibiting an individual from pursuing a particular kind of activity, "or ordering dissolution or reorganization of any enterprise."[105]

Congress passed the RICO statute to take the profit out of organized crime. Chemical crime remains profitable today. Forfeiture provisions in this area would, for example, put an end to the sick spectacle of chemical companies' legal maneuvers dragging out administrative decisions on pesticides, to squeeze out a few more years of sales. If a complete return of all such revenue were to follow all legal maneuvers, the incentive for delay would be sharply diminished. If managers considering the marketing of a hazardous product knew that disclosure of the danger would incur not only jail terms and stiff fines (both personally and as applicable to the corporation), but also the complete return of all revenue derived from the product, the incentive for those actions, too, would be diminished sharply.

The reforms presented here, taken together, represent an integrated, systemic approach to corporate crime and corporate power. Both need to be addressed. Many actions that are not criminal—the decision to increase replacement of natural substances with synthetics, for example—also can have vast and long-lasting effects on society. Opening up the corporate board room will air these questions in the larger forums they deserve.

Because, as the preceding chapters aptly have demonstrated, federal agencies are not always equal to their watchdog responsibilities, the proposed federal chartering law would allow any individual to commence a federal civil action against any person in violation of the act, or against the government for failing to enforce it. Until spray planes begin dusting the Washington Mall with insecticides, or hazardous wastes are discovered beneath the EPA headquarters, the government is not likely to feel the same urgency as those whose neighborhoods have been polluted. The victims must be allowed to defend themselves.

THE CHOICES ARE OURS

We are entering an era of environmental choice. Many of the so-called "easy" moves—combatting the most visible forms of pollution—have been started. The pollutants remaining are stubborn and subtle dangers whose hazards are measured in magnitudes as small as parts per trillion. And the upcoming decisions will be made against a background of tightening resource supplies: The remaining raw materials that are essential to industry, oil the most visible among them, are more difficult to get at than those already extracted and refined. Again, the easy moves have been made. Without basic social commitments to renewable resources and recycling, those resources left in the ground increasingly will be exploited regardless of the difficulty, requiring more blasting, digging, and diversion of water —in short, requiring more disruption of the environment and greater production of dangerous wastes.

Against this background of diminishing resources, the latitude for error, too, is diminished. The increasing population's stress on the world's carrying capacity will mean there is less air, less land, less water to squander.[106] Water rights in the western United States already are a source of serious contention; spot energy shortages have split both the Northeast and the sun-belt states. Similar shortages have produced far more international tensions, which are sure to increase as demands on water, food, energy and mineral resources intensify.

Political lifespans being what they are, elected officials inexorably are pressed to find quick cures for discomforts. The popular wisdom holds that asking voters to make sacrifices in any period but war time is political suicide. Thus we have the seemingly annual calls for a "new Manhattan project"—for some massive investment by the wealthiest nation to accomplish what never has been done—to cure cancer, provide enough energy, achieve material independence, or end poverty.

As the synfuels program, rushed through Congress in 1979, shows, these calls can be difficult to defer, or even to subject to critical analysis. If we are to remain a great and powerful nation, the thinking goes, we have no choice—we must push farther along the paths we are on.

Lately, the chemical industry, too, has adopted this position. For many years, the industry ridiculed the suggestion that synthetics might pose health hazards. Rachel Carson was viewed as a Cassandra. Critics were romantic bird lovers without scientific back-up. The overwhelming evidence of the past decade has made this position untenable. So the argument has shifted. The companies now assert chemicals may be dangerous, but they are indispensible. If hazards exist, we are stuck with them. We can do nothing. "Without chemicals," runs the Monsanto ad, "life itself would be impossible."

Are we really wed to dangerous chemicals? Some uses are frivolous; more than 10 million tons of plastic are used each year merely for packaging.[107] IPM, as we have seen, can reduce pesticide use drastically. The industrial chemicals that are carcinogens, which are limited in number, can be rigidly controlled and, as a new OSHA policy directs, can be replaced when substitutes are available.[108] Moreover, the increased personal and corporate penalties discussed earlier could make the introduction of new dangerous chemicals considerably less likely. We return to our first point: There are alternatives.

In light of these alternatives, the end of the fossil-fuel era presents great opportunities for abandoning the industry attitudes that have been overtaken by events. We can continue down the path established by the oil companies. We can increase exploitation of fossil fuels and maintain consumption at any cost. This policy may shorten Saturday-morning gas lines by a few minutes, enable Detroit to continue building inefficient cars for a few more years, and allow the oil companies to continue posting record profits. But at some point not enough fossil fuels will be left to support continued travel on that path. When that time comes, will we be so committed to industrial and social structures, and to their dependence on fossil fuels, that we cannot adapt?

Another question: What more does clinging to this out-moded model of energy usage entail? It entails the development of synthetic fuels and the creation of toxic wastes and potentially carcinogenic auto emissions. Through the diversion of billions and billions into the technology of that outmoded model, it entails the loss of money and talent from the development of such renewable sources as solar energy and conservation measures. And through the weakening of coal-emission standards, it entails accelerating the greenhouse effect and risking ultimate climatic devastation.

Alternately, we can move now, carefully but assuredly, to reduce our energy consumption and to develop renewable sources of power. We can control our transition into the future, instead of watching it rush by us while we cling to the techniques used in the past. Polls show the public is ahead of its leaders. A 1980 Harris survey, for example, found that 87 percent of the public believes the federal government "should take much tougher measures to conserve energy here at home."[109]

No person, no country is condemned to repeat mistakes. We have learned from the chemical industry that new technologies have strings attached. Applying new technologies induces a range of developments—many difficult even to perceive without careful scrutiny. We have learned from the oil industry that mercantile decisions—such as moving the exploration for oil abroad in search of greater profits—can cause social earthquakes.

Avoiding the application of these lessons appears to be a general government policy. Using the money earmarked for synfuels on conservation could save more energy than we can hope to produce. While the rising national health bill is of great concern, and new schemes are devised annually to cap it, health-and-safety or environmental regulations that would reduce exposure to disease-inducing agents are rejected as inflationary. Only 4 percent of the federal health budget is spent for prevention.[110]

Even regulation enters a game already in progress. As we have argued here, the most effective, inexpensive and efficient way to reduce environmental health hazards is to keep them from being unleashed in the first place. Regulation, as it stands, cannot hope to do better than to save potential victims from harm. The first victims, or more accurately the first several dozen or hundred or even thousands, are likely to be sacrificed in the name of scientific proof and the rights of chemicals to a lengthy trial period.

Within the constricting borders of population growth and resource scarcity, picking up the wreckage left by new technology becomes an unrealistic option. Our focus must be on preventive actions, on assessing long-term implications before we are so locked into a path of development that change is not possible without serious dislocations. We need to inject the rights of society—of consumers and communities—into the front end of corporate decisions. We must question whether the "consume your way to happiness" philosophy propounded by the corporate government is either equitable in a world of scarcity or is in our own interest, in a country characterized by hazardous wastes, soiled rivers and ever-increasing casualties of environmental disease.

Business interests have appropriated the concept of cost-benefit and retooled it to their purposes. They ask: Are the benefits of protecting a resource (the air, the water, the workers) greater than the costs a company will incur to protect them? If the benefits are not greater, they argue, it is uneconomical to offer protection. But this private-sector formulation obscures the public cost-benefit question appropriate to new technology. That is: Are the benefits of a new technology or product greater than what it will cost society? In other words, do we need the thing—the chemical, the synfuels, a new brand of plastic swizzle stick—at all? Will it help us—not just its manufacturer—more than it will hurt us?

For the true picture, we need to consider more than whether a new product might make life a little less disagreeable for just us, or even for the next generation. Such problems as the depletion of the ozone, the buildup of atmospheric carbon dioxide, and the growing piles of nuclear waste show the necessity of a longer view. At the heart of the notion of accountability is stewardship, responsibility to those who follow. More than 20 years ago, Fred L. Polak of the Rotterdam College of Economics put forth this proposition:

> [R]esponsibility for the *future* (especially for the far-away, but also for the near future) forms the central core, is the crystallized essence of *all* responsibility of any kind, always and everywhere.[111] [Polak's emphasis.]

This responsibility, though, is not assumed by the dominant institution of the modern political economy, the multinational corporation. The view through the corporate structure is too short, the multinationals' purposes too narrow to include broad responsibility. Managers who assert that their accountability ends at the balance sheet hardly can be expected to cherish the rights of future generations.

We must cherish these rights, by making the companies with the power to create Love Canals both accountable and responsible. It will be a good investment. In safeguarding the future, people will also be saving themselves.

NOTES

1. "The Ground is Shifting Under Earth Day," *New York Times,* April 21, 1980.

2. "Thousands to Hail Earth Day '80 Tomorrow and Map Battles for a New Decade," *New York Times,* April 21, 1980.

3. From the preamble to the Occupational Safety and Health Act.

4. U.S. Public Health Service, *Healthy People: The Surgeon General's Report on Health Promotion and Disease Prevention,* July 1979, p. 107.

5. Stephen L. Klineberg, "The Social Acceptability of Satellite Power Systems (SPS): A Preliminary Exploration," unpublished paper. Klineberg teaches at Rice University.

6. "Thousands to Hail Earth Day '80 Tomorrow and Map Battles for a New Decade."

7. Lester R. Brown, "Resource Trends and Population Policy: A Time for Reassessment," (Worldwatch Institute, May 1979), p. 5.

8. Richard J. Barnet, *The Lean Years* (Simon and Schuster, 1980), p. 152.

9. Congressional Research Service, *Agricultural and Environmental Relationships: Issues and Priorities,* June 1979, p. 25.

10. Brown, "Resource Trends and Population Policy," p. 12.

11. See Barnet, *The Lean Years*, pp. 162–172.

12. Ibid., p. 172.

13. CEQ and the State Department, *The Global 2000 Report to the President* (CEQ, 1980), vol. 1, p. 17.

14. Ibid.

15. Ibid.

16. Dale R. Bottrell, *Integrated Pest Management* (CEQ: December 1979) p. 47.

17. Congressional Research Service, *Agricultural and Environmental Relationships*, p. 38.

18. Bottrell, *Integrated Pest Managment*, p. 8.

19. Paul Ehrlich and Dennis C. Pirages, *Ark II* (W. H. Freeman, 1974), p. 6.

20. Bottrell, *Integrated Pest Management*, p. 9.

21. Ibid., p. 82.

22. Ibid., p. 19.

23. Ibid., p. 50.

24. Congressional Research Service, *Agricultural and Environmental Relationships*, pp. 566–567.

25. Ibid., p. 569.

26. "The Pesticide Dilemma," *National Geographic*, February 1980, pp. 156–157.

27. Bottrell, *Integrated Pest Management*, p. 19.

28. Ibid., p. 29.

29. Ibid., p. 34.

30. USDA, "Proposed Cooperative Spruce Budworm Suppression Project, Maine 1980," *Draft Environmental Impact Statement*, table 1.

31. Union Carbide took out this advertisement in several Maine newspapers.

32. Statement by Douglas M. Costle, Friday, September 28, 1979, p. 2.

33. "War on Cancer is Hurt by Animal-Test Fight Moves to Ban Products," *Wall Street Journal*, October 26, 1978.

34. Costle statement, p. 2.

35. Environmental Defense Fund and Robert Boyle, *Malignant Neglect* (Alfred A. Knopf, 1979) p. 42.

36. *Environmental Quality: The Tenth Annual Report of the Council on Environmental Quality*, p. 198.

37. Samuel S. Epstein, "Cancer, Inflation, and the Failure to Regulate," *Technology Review,* January 1980, p. 45.

38. Costle statement, p. 3.

39. Regulatory Council, "Regulatory Council Issues First Government-Wide Cancer Policy" (press release), September 28, 1979, p. 2.

40. Boyle, *Malignant Neglect,* p. 48.

41. Regulatory Council, *Regulation of Chemical Carcinogens,* September 28, 1979, p. 6.

42. *Environmental Quality,* p. 202.

43. Regulatory Council, *Regulation of Chemical Carcinogens,* p. 5.

44. Ibid.

45. Dougherty et al., "Sperm Density and Toxic Substances: A Potential Key to Environmental Health Hazards."

46. Biogenics Corporation, *Pilot Cytogenetic Study of the Residents of Love Canal, New York,* p. 13.

47. See Boyle, *Malignant Neglect,* p. 214.

48. Samuel Epstein, *The Politics of Cancer,* (Sierra Club: 1978) p. 214.

49. See Boyle, *Malignant Neglect,* and Epstein, *The Politics of Cancer.*

50. Statement by Dr. Arthur C. Upton before the Subcommittee on Nutrition, Senate Committee on Agriculture, Nutrition and Forestry, October 2, 1979.

51. Ibid.

52. *Environmental Quality,* p. 256.

53. EPA, *Solid Waste Facts, A Statistical Handbook,* p. 13.

54. Denis Hayes, *Repairs, Reuse, Recycling—First Steps Toward a Sustainable Society,* (Worldwatch Institute: September 1978), p. 17.

55. See EPA, *A National Survey of Separate Collection Programs,* July 1979.

56. *Environmental Quality,* p. 268.

57. Hayes, *Repairs, Reuse, Recycling—First Steps Toward a Sustainable Society,* p. 17.

58. *Environmental Quality,* p. 261.

59. Hayes, *Repairs, Reuse, Recycling—First Steps Toward a Sustainable Society,* p. 5.

60. Ibid., p. 38.

61. General Accounting Office, *Industrial Wastes: An Unexplored Source of Valuable Minerals,* May 15, 1980, p. 11.

62. Ibid., p. 16.

63. Ibid., p. 17.

64. Ibid., p. 22.

65. Ibid., p. 25.

66. Ibid., p. 39.

67. General Accounting Office, *Energy Conservation: An Expanding Program Needing More Direction,* July 24, 1980, p. 1.

68. Internal planning memo prepared by the DOE Office of Conservation and Solar Energy.

69. Interview with a staff aide to Senator Paul Tsongas, July 1980.

70. Statement by Stobaugh before the Senate Committee on Energy and Natural Resources, Subcommittee on Energy Conservation and Supply, July 27, 1979.

71. Personal communication with EDF, August 1980.

72. Interview with Ronald Neugold, Tenneco plant manager, February 1980.

73. Interview with Amoto, January 1980.

74. "Board Sells Schools for $900,000," *Burlington County Times,* April 12, 1979.

75. "Tenneco Says Spill 'Minor,'" *Burlington County Times,* July 31, 1979.

76. "Vinyl Chloride Testimony Challenged," *Burlington County Times,* October 12, 1979.

77. "Group To Offer Experts Against Tenneco," *Burlington County Times,* December 5, 1979.

78. "PVC Plant Expansion Unsafe, Experts Testify," *Burlington County Times,* December 6, 1979.

79. "California Conservationists Finding Conservative Support," *Washington Post,* August 29, 1979.

80. Testimony of Samuel Epstein before the House Judiciary Committee, Subcommittee on Crime, December 13, 1979.

81. Testimony of Jacqueline Warren before the House Interstate and Foreign Commerce Committee, Subcommittee on Consumer Protection, May 22, 1980.

82. Testimony of Steven Jellinek before the Consumer Protection Subcommittee, May 12, 1980.

83. Testimony of Louis Slesin before the Consumer Protection Subcommittee, April 15, 1980.

84. Ralph Nader, Mark Green and Joel Seligman, *Taming The Giant Corporation* (W.W. Norton, 1976), p. 61. The discussion of chartering also draws heavily

on "The Case for a Corporate Democracy Act of 1980" (see note 86). Each treats federal chartering in detail.

85. Ibid., pp. 66–67.

86. Congress Watch, Council on Economic Priorities, Building and Construction Trades Department, AFL-CIO, *The Case For a Corporate Democracy Act of 1980*, pp. 31–32.

87. Ibid., p. 36.

88. Testimony of Peter H. Weiner, special assistant to the governor for toxic substances, before the House Judiciary Committee, Subcommittee on Crime, March 24, 1980.

89. Ralph Nader, Peter Petkas and Kate Blackwell (eds.), *Whistle Blowing* (Grossman, 1972), pp. 5–6.

90. See *Hazardous Waste Disposal: Hearings Before the Subcommittee on Oversight and Investigations of the House Interstate and Foreign Commerce Committee*, vol. II, p. 1587.

91. Ibid., p. 35.

92. Department of Labor, *An Interim Report to the Congress on Occupational Disease*, chap. II.

93. Ibid., p. 69.

94. Ibid., p. 3.

95. Ibid.

96. Personal communication with the Veterans Administration, February 1980.

97. Congressional Research Service, *Compensation for Victims of Water Pollution*, May 1979.

98. Testimony of Representative LaFalce, April 22.

99. Personal communication.

100. Testimony of Bernstein before the Senate Committee on Veterans' Affairs, February 21, 1980.

101. Statement by Miller, July 27, 1979.

102. "Corporate Crime: Regulating Corporate Behavior Through Criminal Sanctions," *Harvard Law Review*, vol. 92, no. 6 (April 1979), p. 1245.

103. "The Case for a Corporate Democracy Act," p. 117.

104. Ibid., p. 118.

105. See Public Law 91—452.

106. For a thorough discussion of these impending problems see the CEO's *Global 2000* report.

107. Christopher Flavin, *The Future of Synthetic Materials: The Petroleum Connection* (Worldwatch Institute, April 1980), p. 43.

108. See *United States Department of Labor News,* January 28, 1980.

109. Klineberg, "The Social Acceptability of Satellite Power Systems: A Preliminary Exploration," p. 36.

110. *Healthy People,* p. 9.

111. Quoted in Morton Mintz and Jerry S. Cohen, *Power Inc.* (Bantam, June 1977), p. xxvi.

NOTE: This chapter was written with the research assistance of Ronald Brownstein.

A Selected Bibliography

BOOKS, NEWSPAPERS AND MAGAZINES

Several valuable works treat occupational safety and health. The major case study is Paul Brodeur's *Expendable Americans* (New York: Viking Press, 1974). Also useful are Rachel Scott's *Muscle & Blood* (New York: E. P. Dutton, 1974), Daniel M. Berman's *Death On The Job* (New York: Monthly Review Press, 1978), and *Bitter Wages,* the Ralph Nader Study Group report on disease and injury on the job (New York: Grossman Publishers, 1973).

The classic work on pesticides remains, of course, *Silent Spring,* by Rachel Carson (Greenwich, Conn.: Fawcett-Crest, 1962). Still useful for a review of federal regulation of pesticides is Harrison Wellford's *Sowing the Wind* (New York: Grossman Publishers, 1972). Thomas Whitesides's *The Pendulum and the Toxic Cloud* (New Haven: Yale University Press, 1979) eloquently reports both the dangers of 2,4,5-T and the disaster at Seveso. The late Robert Van den Bosch criticized the pesticide establishment with *The Pesticide Conspiracy* (Garden City: Doubleday & Co., 1978), an indictment of the academic-industrial-governmental axis of chemical proponents. Transcripts of John David Rabinovitch's shattering documentary "The Politics of Poison" are available from the Documentary Department, KRON-TV, P.O. Box 3412, San Francisco, California 94119. Sixteen-millimeter films, and three-quarter-inch and two-inch videotapes, also are available.

Michael Brown, a dogged reporter who uncovered much of the Love Canal tragedy, completed *Laying Waste* (New York: Pantheon Books, Inc., 1980), the first major work on hazardous dumpsites, in spring 1980. Two books on the PBB disaster have appeared. *PBB: An*

American Tragedy (Englewood Cliffs, NJ: Prentice-Hall, Inc., 1979), by Edwin Chen, a former Detroit newspaper reporter, is a journalistic chronicle of the events; the other book, *The Poisoning of Michigan* (New York: W.W. Norton & Co., 1980), by Joyce Egginton, is much more gripping and comprehensive. The tragedy of the mercury poisoning of a fishing village in southern Japan is examined in *Minamata*, with words and photographs by W. Eugene Smith and Eileen Smith (New York: Holt, Rinehart & Winston, 1975).

The best general work on the corporate roots behind the cancer increase is Samuel Epstein's *The Politics of Cancer* (San Francisco: Sierra Club Books, 1978). The Environmental Defense Fund's *Malignant Neglect* (New York: Alfred A. Knopf, Inc., 1979) provides an overview of the ubiquity of carcinogens; Christopher Norwood's *At Highest Risk* (New York: McGraw-Hill Book Co., 1980) scans the impact of toxics on young children and the unborn, though it is light on analysis. A good look at the overall pollution problem is Barry Commoner's *The Closing Circle* (New York: Bantam Books, 1972).

Much of the best work on toxics has been published in newspaper and magazine articles. Richard Severo of the *New York Times* has done extremely valuable pieces on such issues as genetic screening, PCBs in the Hudson, and groundwater contamination. Magazines such as *The Progressive, The Nation, Amicus, Environmental Action* and *Science* regularly have looked at the dark side of the chemical age. The industry trade journals—*Chemical Week* and *Chemical & Engineering News*—are useful for keeping up with current developments that rarely make it into the newspapers. *Critical Mass Energy Journal*, published by Ralph Nader's Critical Mass Energy Project, covers the nuclear industry (P.O. Box 1538, Washington, D.C. 20013).

GOVERNMENT REPORTS AND HEARING TRANSCRIPTS

Most of the best information on toxics still is in government studies, reports and congressional hearings. Indispensable are the annual reports of the Council on Environmental Quality, called simply *Environmental Quality*. The Council's recent report, *Toxic Chemicals and Public Protection*, also provides a thorough overview of the problem, of federal efforts and, in somewhat less depth, the weaknesses of those protection efforts. The CEQ's *Global 2000 Report* takes a look at the trends for the future availability of resources, energy and food—all important factors in the environmental equation. Write the CEQ at 722 Jackson Place NW, Washington, D.C. 20006.

Much more has been written and said by the federal government than done about hazardous wastes. Five especially good studies are: *Hazardous Waste Disposal,* a report by the Subcommittee on Oversight and Investigation of the House Interstate and Foreign Commerce Committee (September 1979); *Report On Hazardous Waste Management and the Implementation of the Resource Conservation And Recovery Act*, a report by the Subcommittee on Oversight of Government Management of the Senate Committee on Governmental Affairs (March 1980); *Health Effects of Toxic Pollution: A Report From the Surgeon General*, available from the Senate Committee on Environment and Public Works (August 1980); *Six Case Studies of Compensation for Toxic Substances Pollution* (June 1980), available from the same committee; and *Compensation for Victims of Water Pollution*, a report by the Congressional Research Service (May 1979), available from the House Committee on Public Works and Transportation. Though voluminous, the transcripts of hearings that led to the *Hazardous Waste Disposal* report contain numerous internal Hooker Chemical Corporation documents and merit study. They are available from the Oversight and Investigations Subcommittee (serial no. 96-48). The committee also prepared the broadest survey yet released of actual hazardous-waste sites, the *Waste Disposal Site Survey* (October 1979). Write the individual committees in Washington for these reports.

For wide-ranging data on pesticide production, see *The Pesticide Review*, published annually by the Agricultural Stabilization and Conservation Service of the Department of Agriculture. The problem of banned pesticides leaving residues on imported crops is addressed in a General Accounting Office report, *Better Regulation of Pesticide Exports and Pesticide Residues in Imported Foods is Essential* (June 22, 1979). Two good government reports look at the overall infiltration of pesticides in the food chain: *Cancer-Causing Chemicals In Food*, a report of the Subcommittee on Oversight and Investigations of the House Interstate and Foreign Commerce Committee (December 1978), and *Environmental Contaminants In Food*, by the Office of Technology Assessment (December 1979). For an overall look at the environmental problems posed by current agricultural practices, see the Congressional Research Service's *Agricultural and Environmental Relationships: Issues and Priorities* (June 1979). A way to get off the pesticide treadmill is offered in Dale Bottrell's *Integrated Pest Management* (CEQ, December 1979).

Two useful government reports on occupational disease are the Department of Labor's *An Interim Report to the Congress on Occupational Disease* (December 1979), which focuses on weaknesses in the compensation system; and the controversial report by the National Institute of Occupational Safety and Health and the National Cancer Institute, *Estimates of the Fraction of Cancer Incidence in the United*

States Attributable to Environmental Factors (September 1978). For further clarification of these findings, see *Toxic Chemicals and Public Protection.*

More general reviews of the health problems engendered by toxic chemicals appear in the annual reports of the Task Force on Environmental Cancer and Heart and Lung Disease and in the Surgeon General's 1979 report, *Healthy People.*

REPORTS FROM OTHER SOURCES

Many of the reports issued by the Worldwatch Institute in Washington concern the interaction between resource utilization, pollution and government policy. The institute's mailing address is 1776 Massachusetts Avenue, NW, Washington, D.C. 20036.

Ralph Nader organizations continue to issue numerous reports on corporate malfeasance; for a publication list, write to P.O. Box 19367, Washington, D.C. 20036. Of recent interest is *Business War on the Law,* a report by the Corporate Accountability Research Group analyzing and responding to attacks by the business community on environmental and health-and-safety regulation.

OTHER SEMINAL WORKS ON THE ENVIRONMENT

Berry, Wendell. *The Unsettling of America.* San Francisco: Sierra Club Books, 1977.

Dubos, Rene. *A God Within—Theology of Earth.* New York: Scribner's, 1977.

Dubos, Rene. *So Human an Animal.* New York: Scribner's, 1968.

Eckholm, Erik p. *Losing Ground.* New York: W. W. Norton & Co., 1976.

Worster, David. *Nature's Economy: The Roots of Ecology.* San Francisco: Sierra Club Books, 1977.

Zwick, David. *Water Wasteland.* New York: Grossman, 1971.

Index